THE IDEA BROKERS

THE
IDEA BROKERS

*Think Tanks and the Rise of
the New Policy Elite*

James Allen Smith

THE FREE PRESS
A Division of Macmillan, Inc.
NEW YORK

Collier Macmillan Canada
TORONTO

Maxwell Macmillan International
NEW YORK   OXFORD   SINGAPORE   SYDNEY

The Free Press
A Division of Macmillan, Inc.
866 Third Avenue, New York, N.Y. 10022

Collier Macmillan Canada, Inc.
1200 Eglinton Avenue East
Suite 200
Don Mills, Ontario M3C 3N1

Printed in the United States of America

printing number
2 3 4 5 6 7 8 9 10

Library of Congress Cataloging-in-Publication Data

Smith, James A.
    The idea brokers: think tanks and the rise of the new policy
elite/James A. Smith.
        p.   cm.
    Includes bibliographical rerferences and index.
    ISBN 0-02-929551-3
    1. Government consultants—United States.   2. Policy scientists
—United States.   3. Research institutes—United States.   I. Title.
JK468.C7S65   1991
353.09′3—dc20   90-39735
                                                            CIP

For A.A.S. and J.W.S.

Contents

Acknowledgments

I began my research for this book while I was on the staff of the Twentieth Century Fund, one of the nation's oldest policy research foundations. From the time I arrived there in 1979, I was curious about the fund's beginnings in the Progressive Era and its role during the New Deal; and as new institutions sprouted in Washington in the early 1980s, the phenomenon of the American "think tank" seemed worth further study. The fund's late director, M. J. Rossant, gave initial encouragement and support. Presidents, directors, and staff members of another two dozen research institutions and philanthropic foundations sat for interviews, speaking with me on and off the record. In all, I have interviewed some 150 people—too lengthy a list to record here—although many of their names appear in the end notes. Their collective insights have proved invaluable.

My research has also been aided by librarians and archivists in a number of organizations. Archives of foundations are one of the best repositories for information about the early history of policy research institutions, as well as about more general developments in the social and policy sciences. For helping me to gain access to primary documents, I am grateful to Ann C. Newhall, formerly the Ford Foundation's archivist; Sara L. Engelhardt, formerly corporate secretary of the Carnegie Corporation; Joseph W. Ernst, Darwin Stapleton, and my friends and former associates on the staff of the Rockefeller Archive Center, where I served as resident scholar in 1988–89 while completing the manuscript; Susan A. McGrath of the Brookings Institution Archives; Camille Motta of the Urban Institute;

and Nettie Gerduk, librarian and unofficial archivist and oral historian of the Twentieth Century Fund.

I would also like to express my gratitude to a number of people who have supplied me with publications and current documents, answered my questions, and arranged interviews with their colleagues. I want especially to thank Herb Berkowitz of the Heritage Foundation; David Abshire and Thomas Bleha of the Center for Strategic and International Studies; David Boaz of the Cato Institute; Patrick Ford of the American Enterprise Institute; Robert Faherty and Margaret Rhoades of the Brookings Institution; Julie Jordan and Gloria Walker of the Hoover Institution; Carol Kahn of the Hudson Institute; Ernest Lefever of the Ethics and Public Policy Center; John Howard and Michael Warder of the Rockford Institute; and Paul Weeks of the RAND Corporation. Lorna Adler and her able associates at the Larchmont Library have also been extraordinarily helpful, handling my many requests for interlibrary loans. I am also grateful to Gareth Esersky and Carol Mann, literary agents, who placed the book with The Free Press and offered considerable encouragement along the way.

And there are those who have read the successive drafts of the manuscript and listened as my ideas took shape. Former colleagues at the Twentieth Century Fund have been especially helpful: Masha Zager and Robert T. Fancher have provided painstaking critiques of various drafts, while early conversations with Carol Barker, John E. Booth, and Ron Chernow proved enlightening. Several friends, historians all, have read drafts of individual chapters or the whole and made useful comments, among them, W. Andrew Achenbaum, Edward Berkowitz, Stanley Katz, Ellen Lagemann, Kathleen D. McCarthy, and James B. Pyle. Adam Bellow, my editor at The Free Press, has shared his astute insights into the history of political advising. He has served as trusted editor, collaborator, and my most expert counselor in a study of think tanks that became a much more expansive exploration of policy expertise and politics under his direction. Wendy Almeleh provided meticulous copy editing of the final manuscript. By way of a disclaimer, I must confess that I have not always acted on the advice offered.

The advice of those experts aside, I have depended throughout on more private, privileged counsel from my wife, Valerie, as well as support from my parents, to whom the book is dedicated.

Prologue

Gulliver thought the professors were out of their senses when he visited the Grand Academy of Lagado on the Isle of Balnibarbi. He was bemused by their many improbable schemes—extracting sunbeams from cucumbers, constructing houses from the roof down, and training pigs to plow with their snouts. Yet however bold and inventive the various projects and their "projectors" (as he termed the scientists) were, there remained something troubling about his visit to the academy, something fundamentally deficient about the experts and their ideas.

Gulliver grew especially melancholy in the company of the political experts:

> These unhappy people [so they seemed to Gulliver] were proposing schemes for persuading monarchs to choose favourites upon the score of their wisdom, capacity and virtue; of teaching Ministers to consult the public good; of rewarding merit, great abilities, and eminent services; of instructing Princes to know their true interest by placing it on the same foundation with that of their people; of choosing for employments persons qualified to exercise them; and with many other wild impossible chimeras, that never entered before into the heart of man to conceive, and confirmed in me the old observation, that there is nothing so extravagant and irrational which some philosophers have not maintained for truth.[1]

Debunking the more fantastic schemes propounded by Lagado's scientists was easy work, but Jonathan Swift's Gulliver never quite accounted for the sadness he felt, especially among the political experts whose ideas were not, after all, completely incredible. Was his melancholy brought on because the professors' reform schemes—both the silly and the sound—were hopelessly unrealistic? Or was he driven to despair because society was intractable and governments apparently immune to improvement by rational, scientific means? Were the experts and their ideas deficient? Or were political leaders incapable of putting moral truth and scientific knowledge into practice? For Jonathan Swift—the pamphleteer of proposals, modest and otherwise, and a cleric who served both Whigs and Tories—the question of how to link knowledge and power was a matter both of theory and of practical political ambition.

Intellectuals and their diverse academies have been the subject of utopian speculation since antiquity, and the relationships of learned advisers to rulers have remained central themes in political histories, biographies, and books of practical statecraft. Yet modern policy experts and their research institutes—no longer fanciful inventions but a fundamental feature of modern political life—have attracted far less attention. And their role in American politics is no less ambiguous than that of Lagado's Grand Academy.[2]

On occasion, the schemes and visions that emanate from contemporary policy research institutes may seem impractical, politically unrealistic, or arcane—although not as comic as Lagado's. More often, the research is diligently pursued, and practically oriented recommendations ensue. Nevertheless, one can visit contemporary policy centers and institutes and feel an even deeper disappointment than Gulliver's. A certain melancholy (an archaic word but apt in this connection) still arises from our all-too-familiar recognition of the gulf that he observed, so long ago, between knowledge and politics. It is compounded by a growing awareness that the financial and intellectual resources that are committed—and have been committed over the past century—to organized social science research and to the invention of expert advisory institutions have not made our politics appreciably more rational, political debates more intelligent, or policies more certain of success.

This is not a book about the relatively small and exceptional group of intellectuals and experts, a Woodrow Wilson, a Paul Douglas, or a Daniel Patrick Moynihan, who have run for office and become political actors. Nor is it about intellectuals of primarily literary, philosophical, or theoretical inclinations. Rather, it concerns a group that now encompasses tens of thousands of experts, operating within or on the margins of government, who advise, consult, serve in various official capacities, and comment tirelessly on public issues. The group includes a Henry Kissinger, Zbigniew Brzezinski, and Jeane Kirkpatrick among its more famous foreign policy specialists and an Alice Rivlin, Charles Schultze, Herbert Stein, and Michael Boskin among its prominent economists. It is an amorphous but influential class of people—first discernible around the turn of the century—who serve in government and whose ideas sometimes shape policy choices or are incorporated into governmental programs and whose reports and studies—their impact often magnified by the mass media—define the boundaries of our policy debates.

The history of policy experts and their role in American life is comprised of three intertwined threads. The longest continuous strand is the attempt, beginning in the mid-nineteenth century, to create a "social" science and to justify it both as a method of scholarly investigation and as a practical tool of social improvement. It concerns the professional training and career paths of those who have used their academic expertise to gain political influence. The second is the ongoing effort to press the experts' knowledge and analytic techniques into public service through a variety of institutional mechanisms, including ad hoc commissions, executive and congressional advisory staffs, and governmental research agencies. It is the story of government and quasi-governmental organizations—Herbert Hoover's research commissions, the Council of Economic Advisers, the Congressional Budget Office, and many others—that have either brought experts into routine contact with political decision makers or made experts responsible for policy decisions. The third, and the central concern of this book, is the emergence of those quintessentially American planning and advisory institutions known as *think tanks*—the private, nonprofit research groups that operate on the margins of this nation's formal political processes. Situated between academic social science and higher education, on the one hand, and government and partisan politics, on the other hand, think tanks provide a concrete focus for exploring the changing role of the policy expert in American life.

The colloquial term *think tank* itself conveys something of the ambivalence that our democratic society feels about experts. Borrowed from World War II military jargon for a secure room where plans and strategies could be discussed, the term was first used in the 1950s to describe the contract research organizations, such as the RAND Corporation, that had been set up by the military after the war. By the 1960s, "think tank" had entered the popular lexicon, but it is an imprecise term that refers to all sorts of private research groups. It is a curious phrase, suggesting both the rarified isolation of those who think about policy, as well as their prominent public display, like some rare species of fish or reptile confined behind the glass of an aquarium or zoo.[3]

Despite their generic label, policy research institutions in the United States are a varied lot. They differ in their sources of financial support, the constituencies they choose to serve, the balance they strike between research and advocacy, the breadth of the policy questions they address, the academic eminence and practical political experience of their staffs, and their ideological orientations. Almost all, including such mainstays of the Washington policy community as the Brookings Institution and American Enterprise Institute (AEI), owe their continuing survival to philanthropic contributions from foundations and corporations, and their fortunes can vary drastically as relations with the philanthropic sector change. Although Brookings, one of the few to have accumulated a significant endowment (some $90 million), has enjoyed close relations with foundations, it has weathered several financial crises during its seventy-five-year history. AEI, with few financial assets, was the beneficiary of energetic philanthropic efforts by conservatives in the 1970s, but saw its contributions, with its staff and budget, shrink dramatically during the early 1980s before rebounding under new leadership. Other institutions, including the RAND Corporation and the Urban Institute, were spawned and are largely sustained by government research contracts and have devoted most of their energies to problems defined by their clients in governmental agencies. Still others, such as the Hoover Institution on War, Revolution, and Peace at Stanford University or the Institute for Research on Poverty at the University of Wisconsin, have operated within a university orbit, albeit with considerable autonomy, relying to some extent on outside funds from foundations, corporations, or individual donors. Yet another cluster, which includes the Heritage Foundation and the Institute for Policy Studies, has been created by partisan or ideological activists. Supported by committed individuals and sympathetic foundations, their research serves ends that are more explicitly activist than academic.

More than one thousand private, not-for-profit think tanks now operate in the United States, approximately one hundred of them in and around Washington, D.C.[4] Brookings, Heritage, RAND, and perhaps a dozen more are reasonably familiar to the public. But despite the grandiose titles they give themselves, most think tanks are tiny and often ephemeral operations—the entrepreneurial venture of a scholar-activist, a Washington-based foundation research project, or a political candidate's short-lived campaign research unit. *Think tank* may conjure up images of elegant town houses or ultramodern offices in which scores of intellectuals with distinguished academic degrees dreamily contemplate the future. The more mundane reality is a warren of rented offices in which a handful of researchers monitor the latest political developments, pursue short-term research projects, organize seminars and conferences, publish occasional books or reports, field telephone calls from reporters, and work hard to obtain foundation grants or corporate support to keep their enterprises afloat.

Think tanks proliferated in the 1970s and 1980s, but they are not a new invention, nor are they necessarily more influential than they were earlier in this century (indeed, their sheer number and clamoring for attention have probably diffused their impact). Yet they are one of the most distinctive ways in which Americans have sought to link knowledge and power. And their existence is a reflection of such elemental political realities as the constitutional separation of powers; a party system historically grounded in electoral political ambitions, rather than ideology; and a civil service tradition that gives leeway to numerous political appointees. They are also shaped by the philanthropic habits of individuals and foundations, intellectual currents in the social sciences, the changeable structures of graduate and professional education, and the efforts of energetic intellectual entrepreneurs.

The first generation of policy research institutions was founded around 1910, an outgrowth of Progressive Era reform and the "scientific management" movement. Established and sustained by private philanthropy, they operated in an era when the government had few intellectual resources at its command, and they were a welcome adjunct to the then much-smaller public sector, often prodding the government to assume new social responsibilities. A second generation—the first to bear the label *think tank*—was created in the twenty years or so after World War II, when the government sought to marshal sophisticated technical expertise for both the Cold War national security enterprise and the short-lived domestic war against poverty. Their services were provided to the government on a contractual basis. A third generation, more numerous but generally with smaller budgets and staffs, was founded in the 1970s and 1980s; these think tanks were outgrowths of the ideological combat and policy confusion of the past two decades. Many of them are geared toward political activism and propaganda, rather than toward scholarship.   /

Think tanks are largely twentieth-century inventions, but the expert adviser and the intellectual working in the shadows of power have had a role in political life for more than two millenia. Political advising in the West began with the famous teachers who tutored young princes and prepared them for leadership. The list is distinguished: Aristotle tutored the young Alexander; Seneca taught Nero; Gerbert of Aurillac instructed both a future German emperor, Otto III, and a king of France, Robert Capet; Thomas Hobbes saw to the education of the young Prince of Wales who would become Charles II; and Cardinal Mazarin took time from other duties to see to the training of Louis XIV. Enduring advisory relationships between intellectuals and rulers often had their beginnings in such youthful associations.

Policy experts continue to serve as teachers even in the late twentieth century. Rexford G. Tugwell thought he and his fellow members of the Brains Trust (as it was originally called) had transformed a simplistic-thinking Franklin D. Roosevelt into a formidable, well-informed candidate. Walter Heller acknowledged using his post on the Council of Economic Advisers to tutor John F. Kennedy in Keynesian economics. And in preparing for the 1964 tax cut, Kermit Gordon, Lyndon B. Johnson's budget director, attended to the president's advanced training in fiscal policy. Now, Straussian-trained political theorists William Kristol and Carnes Lord, who are on Vice President J. Danforth Quayle's staff, are reportedly supervising his education, supplying their pupil with works of history and the biographies of great men.

Some leaders have taught themselves, turning to books for solitary counsel. Long before cost-benefit analyses, terse decision memorandums, or wordy reports from national commissions, political advice came in more artful literary forms. Abraham Lincoln studied *Aesop's Fables*, for example, finding useful political wisdom in the tales. He described the author not as a teller of children's stories but as a "great fabulist and philosopher"—a sign not only of Lincoln's wide-ranging intellect but of his almost reflexive recourse to historical and literary sources for political guidance. In his own day, Aesop, though his life is clouded by myth, was reputedly much sought after as a political counselor. Among presidents who came of political age in the twentieth century, only Harry S Truman seems to have sought counsel in books, reading widely in historical works.[5]

But experts and intellectuals have been more than private tutors to a willing prince or president. As ancient and medieval governments grew more complex, such basic skills as writing and calculating gave intellectuals a set of tools that helped shape the emergence of an expert class within nascent governmental bureaucracies. Experts worked as scribes, record keepers, and officials of the chancery and exchequer, serving in rudimentary advisory institutions and commanding the information that rulers needed to make intelligent decisions. Such practical experience often gave them a vantage point from which to reflect on the nature of knowledge and power.

Niccoló Machiavelli and Francesco Guicciardini, for example, drew on their experiences in the Florentine government to craft books that have served as practical manuals for many generations of aspiring politicians. Indeed, much early writing about statecraft—with frequent injunctions to seek wise counsel (no doubt many authors wrote with their own qualifications in mind)—is to be found in the so-called Mirrors of Princes, which provided exemplary images against which a ruler might be judged. Yet *The Prince*, the most famous (and notorious) example of the genre, was also designed to advance Machiavelli's career by attracting the attention of a potential new patron. Although his courting of Lorenzo de Medici was unsuccessful, Machiavelli's brief tract on virtue and necessity revolutionized political theory and practice. It also permanently stained the reputation of the political adviser, making it all too obvious that knowledge was eager and willing to serve power, rather than higher moral ends (indeed, Machiavelli denied that there were any higher moral ends). Such books, apparently intended to educate or instruct, have long been intertwined with the ambitions of their authors.[6] Proximity to power or ambition for power still inspires the writing of books—and the public's suspicion of some who write them.

There has always been something worrisome about the wise man who seeks to advise the king. Knowledge and expertise are inherently suspect when they become a basis for claims of political influence. Often the expert's power is rooted in arcane skills. Sometimes it is a form of power that challenges traditional authority. And usually it is a kind of power that seems to undermine popular democratic choice. Clinging to a visceral anti-intellectualism, many Americans freely indulge their native suspicion of experts, especially those who aspire to advise the powerful.

In democracies, such suspicion easily shades into ridicule. Socrates, perhaps the first to inspire a think tank, was comically depicted by Aristophanes as descending from the heavens in an observational basket; the playwright satirized the Athenian philosopher and his "Thoughtery" or "Studio of Wise Souls" in a comedy, *The Clouds*. In reality, of course, Socrates' life and death exemplify as tragedy the persistent tensions between speculative thought and political action. Even in the Athenian democracy, where free inquiry was held in high esteem, the intellectual was feared, as well as respected. Plato's portrayal of Socrates poses the dilemma starkly: Either intellectuals and experts can operate on the margins, challenging received opinion and political authority (and suffering the consequences) or they can attempt to serve the powerful, bolstering and justifying a particular regime.

Truth speaks to power in many different tones of voice. The philosopher and cloistered intellectual, free of the ambition to serve a leader directly, can speak with an authority that does not need to bend the truth to justify pressing political ends or personal ambitions. To the philosopher or scientist, the search for truth is central; political power is merely incidental. The policy expert and adviser, however, if they aspire to be of use, must speak to power in a political and bureaucratic context; and they must speak a useful truth. Their claims to speak the truth must always be viewed in light of their relationship with power. Although the insights of some scholars have been seized upon by those in power and have inadvertently drawn the scholars into political controversy, the policy elite comprises those who address policies in explicit terms and who intend to use their knowledge in the policy arena.

Some four hundred years ago, Francis Bacon, a philosopher with political aspirations, took note of the "inseparable conjunction of counsel with kings." An archetype of later experts, he was one of the first to envision a modern research institute, the so-called Salomon's House described in his unfinished treatise, *New Atlantis*. Molded in the arts of statecraft at Cambridge University and Gray's Inn, Bacon, like many who now toil in Washington's think tanks, knew the enduring frustrations of the man of superior intellect who must court the high and mighty to win office. Relegated to the margins of power during the reign of Queen Elizabeth, he was appointed lord chancellor in 1618 by James I, only to be indicted three years later for accepting bribes. In his essay "Of Counsel," one of the shrewdest accounts of the advisory relationship, he concluded—intellectually chastened by the knowledge of his half-spoken truths to power and bitter at his steep fall from grace—that the best advisers are the dead, for books "speak plain when counsellors blanch."[7]

The books that Bacon had in mind—histories, fables, proverbs, and utopias by long-deceased counselors—are certainly not the first recourse of contemporary decision makers. Modern advising is no longer rooted in early education, nor is it based on sweeping historical reflection, moral admonition, or broad principles of statecraft. Advising is now the province of cadres of specialists, and it involves helping officials to frame policy choices, to make particular decisions, and to articulate the reasons for their choices. Indeed, it is now a fully institutionalized function, both within the government and in the research organizations that operate outside it. The advisory institutions—not merely the fanciful inventions of utopian literature but a real and bustling universe of activity—have grown for good reason. The decisions that elected officials make—as well as the choices that citizens make when voting—demand more knowledge than ever. And the ways a society organizes knowledge and puts it into public service are of vital political concern.

Contemporary advisory relationships suggest not only a different kind of adviser, proffering more specialized advice, but a different kind of political leader, one who is considerably more dependent on specialists. The experts set policy goals, chart directions, monitor results, and (having first measured public sentiments) craft the words that will move the electorate. Even though modern presidents are literate (ancient and medieval kings generally were not), they still depend on experts to draft the words they speak and to study and outline the policy choices they confront. Medieval kings who were dependent on their counselors were sometimes dismissed as "feeble creatures." But modern presidents—and other political officials—are arguably feebler still, since government has grown vastly more complex, with leaders becoming far more dependent not only on their immediate counselors but on experts who are scattered throughout the bureaucracy.

Nelson Rockefeller, who served briefly in the 1950s as a special assistant for foreign policy to President Dwight D. Eisenhower, once convened a group of academics to discuss the country's long-range international objectives. Among the experts who assisted him in this and later policy reviews was Henry A. Kissinger, then a young professor at Harvard University. In the initial volume of his memoirs, *The White House Years*, Kissinger described the first encounter between the eager advisers and the buoyant Rockefeller, slapping backs and greeting each scholar amiably by name.

Rockefeller sat stoically through the session as each professor offered his shrewdest practical advice on bureaucratic maneuvers, political manipulations, and tricky interpersonal relations. Having been summoned to Washington, they assumed that the occasion called for tough-minded advice. After taking it all in, Rockefeller said, "I did not bring you gentlemen down here to tell me how to maneuver in Washington. That is my job. Your job is to tell me what is right." Indeed, Kissinger, who dedicated his volume to Rockefeller—a gesture reminiscent of those Renaissance advisers who had dedicated their (much slimmer) political tracts to patrons and princes—concluded, "Of all the public figures I have known he retained the most absolute, almost touching, faith in the power of ideas."[8]

Ideas are indeed powerful political instruments. Masses can be moved, misled, or immobilized by them. Political leaders can seize upon ideas to uplift, to misinform, or to serve personal ambitions. Expert advisers, courtiers, and bureaucrats can use them to challenge authority, to curry favor, or to improve our understanding of politics and human affairs. The story of both ancient intellectuals and modern experts is often one of knowledge coupled with ambition. Few intellectuals and experts are so free of Faustian pride that they do not secretly believe they are better qualified to execute policy than are the elected or appointed officials they advise. Thus, it is not surprising that the relationship between the expert and the leader has often been problematic, raising questions about who is really ruling whom. As Swift once angrily wrote of the earl of Oxford, whom he advised, "If we let these great ministers pretend too much, there will be no governing them."[9] The relationship between the expert and the body of citizens who rule in a democracy is no less ambiguous, and in our time, one must ask whether the experts as a class have used mystifying jargon and an array of bewildering models and specialized tools to interpose themselves between the citizenry and their elected leaders.

Any survey of the ways in which knowledge and politics have been linked in the United States—a nation in which unparalleled resources have been channeled into social science research and into the creation of a huge infrastructure of private advisory institutions—can be only tentative. It can be a voyage no more final or definitive than Gulliver's; a solitary traveler cannot visit every island in the sea or stay for long on any one of them.[10] In exploring some of the nation's think tanks, I have not attempted to recount their histories in detail but have focused on their founding and their moments of greatest impact, since these moments reveal the most about the changing nature and uses of policy expertise. I have also found it useful to view expertise from another vantage point, that of the American presidency—though not by any means exhaustively—since the different uses presidents have made of experts provide a way both of gauging our leaders' changing views about political knowledge and of tracking the evolution of practical advisory mechanisms.

While Gulliver described and debunked many of the projectors' ideas in describing the ruin of Balnibarbi, I have not aimed to provide a thorough inventory of the experts' policy ideas nor to praise or blame them. Although experts have become an integral part of American government, unlike Swift, I do not think our modern experts are leading us to ruin. Nevertheless, there is something troubling about the relationship among experts, leaders, and citizens that tends to make American politics more polarized, short-sighted, and fragmented—and often less intelligent—than it should be.

ONE

☆

The Policy Elite

Enter the Experts

Throughout the morning, ominous clouds and intermittent rain threatened to dampen the Labor Day festivities in Buffalo, New York. The year was 1912, and, as it does every four years, the end-of-summer holiday signaled the beginning of another presidential campaign. Only a small crowd of Democratic party stalwarts, working-class families for the most part, had gathered for the political rally and celebrations in Braun's Park, despite the promise that the day's featured speaker would be none other than the Democratic presidential candidate, Governor Woodrow Wilson of New Jersey. The introductions were predictably tedious, but when the former president of Princeton University finally took the podium in the early afternoon, the sun shone and there were, by some newspaper estimates, ten thousand people on hand. Speaking extemporaneously, though with a prepared text in front of him, Wilson gave one of the most skillful orations of his campaign.

Toward the end of his talk on the complexities of monopolies and economic competition, the one-time professor of government and jurisprudence ventured a curious warning to his audience of laborers and tradespeople:

> What I fear, therefore, is a government of experts. God forbid that in a democratic country we should resign the task and give the government over to experts. What are we for if we are to be scientifically taken care of by a small number of gentlemen who are the only men

1

who understand the job? Because if we don't understand the job, then we are not a free people. We ought to resign our free institutions and go to school to somebody and find out what it is we are about.[1]

Coming from any other figure on the American political stage, the words would not have sounded so bizarre. Over the years, countless politicians, few of them readers of Jonathan Swift, had contributed to a venerable national tradition of bashing experts and intellectuals while exalting the practical intelligence and wisdom of the ordinary citizen. Political orators routinely lampooned the wooly minded impracticality of intellectuals. Wilson himself had been heard to complain about the experts' cloudy "rhetoric" and their inability to talk straight, like ordinary men, about the "facts."

As the coda to a political stump speech, Wilson's warning about experts could easily have been dismissed as a disingenuous attempt by a former college professor to place himself squarely on the side of his working-class audience. "I want to say I have never heard more penetrating debate of public questions than I have sometimes been privileged to hear in clubs of workingmen," said the man who, as a graduate student at Johns Hopkins University, had attended seminars by the historian Herbert Baxter Adams and the economist Richard T. Ely. Indeed, for those who knew something about his career, Wilson's words seemed to recant much of what he had worked for as a teacher and scholar of American government.

While at Princeton, Wilson had pushed some of his students toward careers in government, citing the need for more intelligent and better trained civil servants, and as early as the 1880s, he foresaw an expanding public role for the expert-administrator. Yet he drew a sharp line between administrative and political concerns. In a widely known article, written long before he contemplated a political career, Wilson argued that politics and administration were distinct endeavors. "The field of administration," he wrote in 1887, "is a field of business. It is removed from the hurry and strife of politics; it at most points stands apart even from the debatable ground of constitutional study. It is a part of political life only as the methods of the counting-house are a part of the life of society; only as machinery is part of the manufactured product."[2] Like many of his contemporaries during the Progressive Era, Wilson wanted American policymaking to be a more efficient, businesslike process and the execution of policy to be above partisan politics.

In the last decades of the nineteenth century, the university-trained expert was assuming a more visible place in American public life—so much so that by 1912, Wilson's avowal of a deep distrust of experts was less a prescient warning than a worried acknowledgment of the political role experts had already begun to play. At the turn of the century, many of the now-familiar American mechanisms for employing experts and specialists were taking shape. Mayors and governors, as well as Wilson's immediate predecessors in the White House, often turned to experts for informal advice. Professors of economics and law were appointed to investigative commissions and to regulatory and administrative agencies at all levels of government. Research bureaus and legislative reference services were organized in dozens of cities, including several state capitals. Experts were playing a guiding public role in many turn-of-the-century reform campaigns. Indeed, incompetent and corrupt politicians had already felt the political sting of experts' reports and studies that exposed neglected social problems and demanded reforms in tenement houses, factories, and prisons.

Yet as a serious student of government, Wilson saw the growing prominence of experts as a long-term threat to democratic institutions and a potential impediment to full and open political debate. By making public issues seem more complicated than necessary, experts could cause ordinary citizens to lose faith in their ability to rule themselves; government by commissions and regulatory agencies might eventually undermine elected officials and the institutions in which they served. Although we have learned to be more skeptical about the possible extent of expert influence, Wilson's warnings serve to remind us how often our elected representatives have handed over difficult or contentious issues to expert commissions and task forces.

Indeed, despite our avowed democratic disdain for experts, Americans have typically been obsessed with expertise and specialization. We have felt an elemental urge to bring social science and technical skills to bear on policymaking, and our politics has been shaped and reshaped by a yearning to govern ourselves more intelligently—even if doing so means escaping the political process. Expertise in statistics, economics, and other fields of social science, as well as in public administration and various scientific and legal specialities, has been a necessary instrument of modern government, especially as governments at all levels have expanded their spheres of responsibility.

Although Wilson distrusted experts and warned that democratic practices might be undermined by relying too heavily on them, he could not avoid consulting with them. Even the text of his Labor Day speech had been crafted with the help of a Harvard law professor, Louis D. Brandeis, who would later put his indelible mark on Wilson's antitrust policy and the Federal Reserve bill. Nevertheless, Wilson meant what he said about experts and the dangers they posed to democratic institutions.

Although he was a creature of the university and knew what skills bureaucrats and political leaders should possess, Wilson appointed few university-trained specialists to his administration. He was temperamentally incapable of getting along with counselors and advisers, with the notable exception of the shrewd Texan, Colonel Edward M. House. A diligent observer of public affairs and human relations, but too sickly to run for political office or take on full-time official duties, House was content serving in informal ways. Strangely enough, given their intimate relationship, he and Wilson had met less than a year before the election. Eager to advise, House was astute, like Francis Bacon, in his perceptions of the advisory dynamic between counselors and leaders. He even wrote an obscure utopian novel, *Philip Dru: Administrator* (drafted hurriedly in 1911 and published anonymously in 1912), about a West Point graduate who leads a rebellion against the nation's corrupt politicians and their wealthy backers and temporarily establishes a benevolent administrative dictatorship to build a new framework for democracy. However slight his virtues as a novelist, House had a sure grasp of the advisory relationship, and he offered one bit of memorable advice to the would-be adviser: "If we would convince and convert, we must veil our thoughts and curb our enthusiasms, so that those we would influence will think us reasonable."[3]

Wilson was captivated by the colonel (an honorific title) from their first meeting. Yet House was blunt in his later observations about Wilson's personal relations with other counselors. He thought Wilson was odd in isolating himself from cabinet members and concluded that Wilson was simply not able to hear conflicting points of view or weigh the opinions of others before coming to a decision. Wilson, a man capable of friendship with few people, could not confer with those he did not like or fully respect.

Moreover, House thought, the president, though possessing an orderly and analytical mind, made his decisions without much reflection. According to him, Wilson did "not seem able to carry along

more than one idea at a time." On one occasion, Wilson immodestly
remarked to House that one of his great strengths as president, which
he had learned in academic life, was to seek the best advice on any
matter. The colonel confessed that he "almost laughed at this statement." What advice and information President Wilson got came "gra-
tuitously and not by his asking."[4]

But the universe of policy expertise and advising was organized
differently in the early twentieth century than it now is. The only
member of Wilson's cabinet with academic credentials was David
F. Houston, a Harvard-trained economist and former college president. In later administrations, as many as three or four cabinet members at a given moment have progressed from academic and research
institutions to the highest appointive offices. At one time or another
former college professors, deans, and presidents have headed all
the major federal departments and served as ambassadors to the
United Nations. But specialized knowledge played virtually no role
in the selection of cabinet members in the early years of this century;
there were as yet no White House posts, no Council of Economic
Advisers or National Security Council, to which expert advisers could
be appointed. When Wilson chose Houston to be secretary of agriculture, it was not on account of Houston's expertise in agricultural
economics—a field Houston did not know well—but because of his
friendship with House. In fact, House played the decisive part in
selecting many of Wilson's cabinet members, since the president-
elect took surprisingly little interest in the intellectual qualifications
and character of the people he appointed. Wilson also stood aside
while his Secretary of State William Jennings Bryan gutted the foreign
service of its most able diplomats and replaced many of them with
political hacks and cronies.

Walter Lippmann, among others, noted the peculiar irony of
the professor-president's attitude toward specialists. Despite his academic background and his willingness to embrace a number of causes
favored by reformers, Wilson seemed to have inherited his party's
hostility toward intellectuals and experts. According to Lippmann,
this hostility was rooted in the long-standing Democratic opposition
to a strong central government and to large-scale, national business
enterprises. Wilson, who talked of the need to return the government
to control by the people and found politically responsive chords in
his attacks on wealthy and privileged elites, belonged to a party
that was "attached to local rights, to village patriotism, to humble
but ambitious enterprise." As Lippmann said, "its temper has always

been hostile to specialization and expert knowledge, because it admires a very primitive man-to-man democracy."[5]

Some sixty years after Wilson's campaign, another presidential candidate—this time a conservative Republican, Ronald Wilson Reagan—organized three successive campaigns for the presidency, beginning with a futile effort to unseat his party's incumbent in 1976. Reagan's political ideals seemed to harken back to the same vision of rural America in the late nineteenth century that Wilson had known first hand: Reagan was no less devoted to local rights, free enterprise, village patriotism, and "primitive" democracy. Reagan's four years at Eureka College and subsequent career in Hollywood could not compare to Wilson's training at the University of Virginia and John Hopkins and his long academic service at Princeton. Yet despite occasional lapses into the expert-bashing rhetoric that was part of running a campaign in the 1970s against Washington bureaucrats and the "Liberal Establishment," the genial actor-turned-politician genuinely seemed to admire intellectuals and experts, at least those of a particular conservative stripe. The contrast in the way the presidency had come to be organized—and the backgrounds of those who served—could not have been more striking.

Despite the fundamental similarities in their views of American society, the scholar-president and the actor-president relied on different advisory networks. Wilson, alone and sometimes anguished, was his own best counsel; Reagan, apparently detached from the details of policymaking, necessarily depended on conservative intellectuals and academics, while he, in turn, was the most persuasive pitchman for the post–World War II conservative movement's ideas. Reagan's advisory network was extensive. He had conferred with conservative intellectuals regularly in the years before he ran for the presidency and seemed generally familiar with the work under way at conservative think tanks. He took time to appear at banquets and symposia that celebrated the accomplishments of these think tanks and accepted an honorific title, "Distinguished Fellow," from the Hoover Institution. Political associates in California even organized a think tank— San Francisco's still-active Institute for Contemporary Studies—when Reagan left the governorship and was in need of policy advice as he contemplated running for the presidency. More important, Reagan found places for members of conservative academic networks, both among his campaign advisers and within his administration.

The extent of a modern conservative president's network of experts reveals how much the nation's political advisory processes have changed since Wilson's haphazard and often reluctant reliance on experts. It also indicates how vast and well organized the realm of outside experts has become. Reagan's policy coordinator in the 1976 and 1980 presidential races was Martin Anderson—an economist trained at the Massachusetts Institute of Technology, a former professor of business at Columbia University, and a senior fellow at the Hoover Institution. Anderson had come to his own conservative political awakening early enough to have involved himself in Barry Goldwater's 1964 presidential campaign. Like many young conservatives of the late 1950s and early 1960s, he acknowledges the influence of Ayn Rand, as well as that of such economists as Friedrich Hayek, Ludwig von Mises, and Milton Friedman, though he still expresses shock that a graduate student in economics in the late 1950s was not likely to encounter the works of those economists in the formal curriculum.

In 1980, as he had for Richard M. Nixon in 1968 and Reagan in 1976, Anderson put together a campaign advisory team to help Reagan come to terms with the many issues about which he would have to exhibit at least a passing degree of familiarity. He oversaw 25 task forces on domestic and economic policy, and 23 others were convened on foreign policy and national security. All told, more than 450 policy experts and intellectuals were drawn into the campaign.[6] Dozens of the campaign advisers, including Anderson who served as domestic policy adviser during the first year of Reagan's presidency, and Richard V. Allen, who advised Reagan on foreign policy during the campaign and then served a brief, stormy stint as national security adviser, assumed positions in government after the election.

Reagan's decisive defeat of Jimmy Carter in 1980 was almost immediately heralded as a revolution—an intellectual revolution fostered by conservative thinkers. Indeed, the "Reagan Revolution" was a rhetorical and ideological break not merely with the New Deal and its fifty-year legacy, but with an older and more cautious progressivism; in retrospect, the policy legacy of the Reagan administration proved less revolutionary than was first proclaimed. Nonetheless, the revolution brought to the fore new cadres of policy experts— libertarian and classical liberal economists, traditionalist conservatives, Straussian political philosophers, and "neoconservatives." In fact, so many conservative intellectuals had already descended on Washington by the early 1980s that veteran political journalists began to speak of a new "ideas industry" and to assess the role that conservative think tanks, such as the Hoover Institution, American Enterprise

Institute, and Heritage Foundation, had played in Reagan's victory.[7]

Just as the presence of Franklin D. Roosevelt's Brains Trust and John F. Kennedy's New Frontiersmen had sparked debate about intellectuals and technocrats in Washington, the sudden prominence of hundreds of conservative intellectuals—self-described "revolutionaries" in many instances—seemed to point to the changed role of experts, intellectuals, and ideas themselves in American political life. Between the boasting of the individual think tanks, each asserting that their ideas had been the driving force behind Reagan's success, and the perplexity of political observers, who thought they might have missed a story basic to understanding the rise of the conservative movement, talk was heard everywhere about a new "politics of ideas." The practitioners of this new politics were the very experts and specialists that politicians, especially those on the Right, often scorned, but on whom twentieth-century political leaders of both parties had come to rely. Wilson had feared the consequences of a government of experts, whose scientific techniques of administration and analysis might ultimately sap the political vitality and commitment of the citizenry. He had doubtless not imagined a politics of expertise in which the experts themselves would contend so vigorously and so prominently in the political arena.

Experts Ascending

Although experts have historically assumed a progressively larger and more visible role in American politics, ambivalence and, at times, open hostility have accompanied their rise. A visceral populist scorn for intellectuals and experts has always simmered, ready to boil, in American society. Even the most revered of the Founding Fathers drew barbs from their contemporaries. Thomas Jefferson, for one, was bitterly attacked for his overly philosophical turn of mind. The sage of Monticello, "impaling butterflies and insects, and contriving turn-about chairs," was criticized for his timidity, inertness, and doctrinaire embrace of abstract theories. Another critic, giving vent to a democratic prejudice at least as old as Socrates, claimed that Jefferson had been "carried away by systems, and the everlasting zeal to generalize, instead of proceeding, like commen men of practical sense, on the low but sure foundation of matter of fact."[8]

Similar words have been directed at intellectuals in later eras, surfacing with a vengeance in Andrew Jackson's day and erupting episodically whenever politicians and political commentators feel the urge to tap a readily arousable populist resentment against "egg-heads"—Stewart Alsop's famous epithet of the early 1950s. Senator Joseph McCarthy and his followers habitually confounded social science with socialism, adding anticommunist fuel to the embers of an older anti-intellectualism. George Wallace and Spiro Agnew are probably best remembered for their assaults on "pointy-headed intellectuals" and the "effete corps of impudent snobs" who had invented the Great Society programs that they so strongly opposed. In 1988 even a Yale-educated candidate, George Bush, was not above deriding his opponent's ties to Harvard University's Kennedy School and his network of Cambridge-based advisers.

Added to these populist resentments are the modern Luddite suspicions of science and technology that emerged after World War II. Defense intellectuals and nuclear strategists, whose profession was born in the atomic era, have been the most deftly caricatured. Stanley Kubrick's Doctor Strangelove epitomized the figure of the mad scientist who escaped from the laboratory to exercise authority with generals and presidents. Although no such character embodied the domestic social planners of the Great Society, the terms for the locales that housed them—*brain banks, think factories, egg-head row*, and the now-familiar *think tanks*—often had derisive connotations. Even more descriptive terms like *social engineer* and *technocrat*, which first appeared in the 1930s, continued to convey a certain disdain for planners in the 1960s. Indeed, the members of an expert elite will inevitably meet with popular skepticism in a democratic, egalitarian society. Nor is an informed skepticism inappropriate. In the past decade, expert commissions operating outside the public's purview have addressed problems of national importance: social security, Central American policy, nuclear missiles, military bases, and the budget deficit. Such bodies may conveniently take contentious policy matters off the hands of elected leaders, but they seldom serve to inform the public about the issues at stake.

Since Woodrow Wilson's day, the number of experts working on public issues in and out of government has boomed. Two world wars, nearly five decades of Cold War, and periodic economic crises have spurred the creation and growth of an American policy elite, comprised of trained professionals who devote their careers to the study of public policy. Although some may be described as intellectuals, a few crude distinctions are in order. There are many kinds of expertise in modern society, but not all are pertinent to public policy, nor do most wide-ranging intellectual speculations about society and culture bear directly on public issues. Public policy experts (and more of them are experts than intellectuals) are closer to what H. Stuart Hughes called "mental technicians" than to philosophers or critics characterized by "freely speculating" minds. The expert properly so called, as Hughes implies, is more concerned with technical means than with values or ends.[9]

One of the obvious characteristics of modern intellectual life is that it is highly organized. The unattached intellectual, independent of universities, research posts, and foundation grants, is rare in our society; the unaffiliated expert virtually nonexistent. Expertise implies training, certification, professionalization, and other attributes that are dependent on an organized community of knowledge. Policy experts are invariably attached to universities, think tanks, governmental research units, consulting organizations, or foundations; more recently, business corporations have established policy-analysis divisions as well. Accordingly, the story of the policy elite is as much the story of these institutions and their growth as it is of individuals.

Policy experts—and the ambiguous elite they now comprise—did not emerge suddenly. The infrastructure of graduate programs in the social sciences and public administration that now supplies them in such abundance took shape only in the last half of the nineteenth and early part of the twentieth centuries, a period that also saw the rise of organized national associations of social scientists. Professional routes along which their careers might advance—through private research organizations, reform associations, governmental agencies, or universities—have likewise been shaped over many decades. Wilson's career, from graduate student and professor to state governor and president, was made possible only by the new intellectual infrastructure of late-nineteenth-century America. Though none would rise to such high office, countless others would be drawn to the policymaking arena.

The institutional arrangements that connect policy experts to decision-making structures have also taken shape fitfully. They began informally, with a private presidential summons that could easily and swiftly be revoked. Wilson turned—albeit grudgingly—to experts during World War I when the nation confronted the task of mobilization. Economists and statisticians served on the staffs of the War Industries Board and its component agencies; sociologists and psychologists worked to evaluate, train, and organize the troops; historians, geographers, and linguists helped formulate propaganda campaigns to spur homefront morale and to demoralize the enemy; and some

150 social scientists worked quietly in New York in what was mysteriously named "The Inquiry," preparing for the postwar peace conference. Many of the experts sailed with Wilson to France, though he disbanded most of the wartime agencies, and as soon as the war ended, he sent them back to their campuses, research institutes, and business-research bureaus.[10]

Herbert Hoover's attitude was markedly different from Wilson's. As secretary of commerce and later as president, Hoover tapped hundreds of experts for service on ad hoc commissions. A moderate progressive early on, he shared the rational reformer's concern about the dangers of excessive political passion. Hoover thought that social research and analysis could place policymaking on a more objective basis. Accordingly, early in his presidency, with more than half a million dollars from the Rockefeller Foundation, he organized a massive survey of social trends headed by two of the nation's most distinguished social scientists, Wesley C. Mitchell, an economist from Columbia University, and Charles Merriam, a political scientist from the University of Chicago. Hoover hoped, in vain as it turned out once the 1932 election results were tallied, that the mountains of data produced by this committee would guide his policy initiatives during a second term. But the resulting two-volume study, *Recent Social Trends in the United States*, helped neither Hoover nor his successor, Franklin D. Roosevelt, come to terms with the Great Depression.[11]

Roosevelt assembled his Brains Trust early in his presidential campaign (the term coined by a New York journalist has since been changed to Brain Trust). Relying mainly on a trio of Columbia University professors—Raymond Moley, Adolf A. Berle, and Rexford G. Tugwell—he put them to work on the tasks now commonly entrusted to experts: drafting speeches, preparing policy memoranda, and chasing down hastily needed facts. With their help, Roosevelt gradually overcame the widely held impression that he was intellectually lazy and had no clear policy direction, an image summed up cattily by Walter Lippmann, who described him as "a pleasant man who, without any important qualifications for the office, would very much like to be President." Admittedly, even Roosevelt's advisers had initial doubts about his intellectual depth, wondering how much he really understood of what they said to him.[12] In the economic crisis, however, he relied on them, masterfully playing their often-contradictory ideas against each other and grasping more about the political consequences of their proposals than they realized.

Roosevelt, whose byword was "experiment," established various advisory and planning agencies, culminating in the short-lived National Resources Planning Board. His reorganization of the Executive Office in the late 1930s initiated the process that has given his successors a command of vast intellectual resources. Experts also found their way into the new governmental agencies that were created during the New Deal, among them the Social Security Administration, Securities and Exchange Commission, and National Labor Relations Board. They helped design and administer programs, monitor the programs' successes and failures, and collect data that were indispensible to their administration.

Since World War II, the expert adviser and the outside analyst have become fixtures in Washington. In virtually every area of policy, they have provided continuity and have often been visibly identified with a particular program or issue: Wilbur Cohen and social security, Joseph Pechman and tax policy, Herbert Stein or Charles Schultze and economic policy, James R. Schlesinger and defense policy, and scores of others. Expertise provides the cachet for longer and more varied public careers than all but a few elected officials are likely to enjoy. And often expert advisers are now more readily identified with presidents and their policies than are vice presidents, cabinet members, or legislators—as were McGeorge Bundy and Arthur M. Schlesinger, Jr. with President Kennedy, Henry Kissinger with President Nixon, and Stuart Eizenstat and Zbigniew Brzezinski with President Carter.

Though personal relationships will always shape the nexus linking knowledge and political decision making, informal ties have been powerfully augmented by formal research and advisory institutions. Harry S Truman institutionalized a number of presidential advisory mechanisms, including the Council of Economic Advisers and the National Security Council. Cabinet departments have also established and gradually expanded their planning and advisory capacities over the course of the twentieth century. The postwar expansion and wholesale transformation of the nation's international expertise began in 1947 with the State Department's Policy Planning Staff and the reorganization of the nation's intelligence agencies. Planning and research staffs continued to proliferate, especially in the 1960s when domestic research, planning, and evaluation units were created in cabinet departments and often headed by an assistant secretary, a sign of the status that experts by then enjoyed.

Presidents can now call on nearly six hundred policy experts and budget specialists in the Office of Management and Budget. There are usually two or three dozen economists on the staff of the Council of Economic Advisers and some fifty or sixty experts on the National Security Staff, as well as such specialists as those who work on environmental or science policy either in or for the White House. Despite conservatives' proposals to abolish the Council of Economic Advisers, eliminate research and evaluation units in some governmental departments, and drastically cut the economics and social science research budget of the National Science Foundation, the executive branch continues to rely heavily on experts.[13]

Over the past forty years, Congress, too, has substantially augmented its intellectual resources. It built up the staffs of its members and its committees after a major legislative reorganization in 1947; bolstered the policy research arm of the General Accounting Office; expanded the Congressional Research Service of the Library of Congress, which now has a staff of 900; and in the 1970s, created research operations, such as the Congressional Budget Office with a staff of about 200, and the Office of Technology Assessment with a staff of approximately 140. All the while, both Congress and the executive agencies have used contractual relationships to tap the still larger body of experts on university campuses and in such free-standing research institutes as the RAND Corporation and the Urban Institute. Expert advisory structures within the government are thus intimately connected to this much wider network of expert institutions on the boundaries of the public sector.

Though academic degrees are not necessarily a measure of expertise, in the 1970s about one-third of career civil servants and top political appointees had social science degrees, and in the early 1980s a survey of officials in certain policy-coordinating agencies found that over half had graduate degrees in the social sciences. A survey of scientists and engineers by the National Science Foundation counted 28,100 social scientists employed by the federal government in 1988.[14] It is no longer exceptional or especially noteworthy, as it was in Wilson's or even Franklin Roosevelt's day, for cabinet members to have Ph.Ds and to have spent a good part of their careers in universities and think tanks. For some advisory and staff positions—within the Council of Economic Advisers or the National Security Council, for example—graduate training is virtually a prerequisite.

Meanwhile, senior political advisers and appointees to executive agencies, as well as cabinet members in Democratic and Republican administrations (whether liberal, moderate, or conservative), have been drawn in increasing numbers from the ranks of think tanks and universities. Though lawyers as a class have certainly not been supplanted, graduate training in such fields as public administration, economics, international studies, or public policy analysis has become an acceptable route toward a career in the public sector. The law firms and investment banking houses that once were a solid external base of operation for those who came to and went from government no longer provide the clearest routes to responsible policy positions.

Expertise is now a means of advancement for a large proportion of individuals who are actively engaged in making public policy. Yet the powers these experts typically wield and the authority they exercise are peculiarly intangible and diffuse. The power of the expert remains a power rooted in ideas (however one chooses to define the word); it is an authority grounded in the suspect and ambiguous claims of science and professionalism. [15]

Metaphors of Inquiry

The intellectual origins of the American policy elite—and its claims to authority—lie in the long quest to devise an empirical science of society and politics. This search accelerated in the United States in the second half of the nineteenth century as social activists and the first generation of graduate-trained economists, sociologists, and political scientists attempted to understand the changes wrought by industrialization, massive immigration, and urban growth. While the role of the expert is continuously reshaped by the vagaries of political leadership and changing policy aims (as well as by long-term institutional dynamics that have gradually altered the relationship between experts and policymakers), the experts' influence is also linked to attitudes about the nature of scientific knowledge and its public uses.

Indeed, social science inquiry, perpetually insecure about its scientific status, has historically been guided by a succession of metaphors drawn from the hard sciences. Those metaphors have both shaped the methods of investigation and held out the disputable promise that practical benefits would accrue from social research. Whether social scientists have seen themselves as comparable to medical researchers and public health doctors or to physicists and engineers, they have typically looked to the natural and physical sciences to borrow models for their work.

The continuing attempt to apply the results of social science research has also been supported by the fundamentally pragmatic tenor of twentieth-century American intellectual life. The word *pragmatism* characterizes both a political temperament and a philosophical system, and American social science has, from the beginning, been suffused with its spirit. The practical science of society that took shape at the turn of the century was undergirded by the theories of knowledge and action articulated by William James and John Dewey. (The Greek word *praxis*, which is at the root of "pragmatism," conveys the sense of both business and action, affording some justification for Bertrand Russell's comment that pragmatism is the "philosophic expression of commercialism"). James, a scintillating and popular public speaker, the mainstay of Harvard's philosophy department until his death in 1910, challenged the notion that truth was unchanging, an absolute quality inherent in an idea. "Truth *happens* to an idea," he said; "it *becomes* true, is *made* true by events."[16]

James made a famous distinction between the "tough-minded" philosopher who embraced the empirically derived knowledge of the material world and the "tender-minded" thinker who derived knowledge through abstract reason from the realm of ideals. That distinction marked the essence of the budding American social science, with its practical-minded empiricism that rejected older traditions of political theorizing and economic reasoning. James's "radical empiricism" provided a philosophical bolster for the fact-finding impulse of progressive reformers, as well as for the so-called legal realism of Oliver Wendell Homes and his disciples.

James and Dewey arrived at their pragmatism by different routes—and subsequent differences were underscored by Dewey, who continued to write for some forty years after James's death. As the intellectual engagé who churned out an uninterrupted stream of scholarly works and popular essays (usually for *The New Republic*), Dewey touched on every public issue, ranging from industrial problems to questions of war and peace. A critic of capitalism, he embraced the idea of the wider participation of workers in industrial life and endorsed economic planning and schemes for increased social control. For Dewey, pragmatism was not only a philosophical method but a political method. He thought of learning and knowing as problem-driven and active, and believed that the world would be changed in the process of learning about it.

Dewey wrote enthusiastically about developments in the social sciences and their promise of creating new "political technologies." His view of science as an instrument of government was embraced by many others, notably Walter Lippmann, who called scientific thinking the "twin brother" of political democracy. For Lippmann, pragmatism and the scientific temperament were basic tools of governance, the veritable "discipline of democracy." An ethos shaped by facts and an enthusiasm for the possible, pragmatism thus promised to guide democracy toward a "chastened and honest dream."[17]

Dewey's ideas have been all-too-easily caricatured and distorted, primarily because Dewey sought to hold contrasting ideas in a precarious balance. His are notions that inevitably tug against each other as we contemplate the proper role of knowledge in political life: the demands of scientific verification versus practical applications, the ascertainment of facts versus the discovery and articulation of values, the invention of means versus the explication of ends, and the competing claims of knowledge derived from critical reason versus knowledge that results from experimentation.

Dewey understood that our political debates and our approach to public policy are deeply rooted in our methods for knowing the world. And it is not surprising that the tensions which are embodied in pragmatic thought frequently define the fault lines that have periodically rent American liberalism. At times, these tensions have divided technocrats who focus on the means and instruments of government from earnest left-wing activists whose social inventions are vehicles for redefining values. At other moments, as with the neoconservative revolt of the late 1960s—comprised of liberals who were "mugged by reality," in Irving Kristol's famous phrase—the evident deficiencies of policy means and instruments devoid of articulated values have driven some "pragmatic" liberals to the Right. Charles Murray, author of one of the best-selling policy treatises of the 1980s, *Losing Ground*, followed such a path, as did the many social scientists who contributed to Kristol's policy journal *The Public Interest* in the 1970s. Experts who pointed out the unintended consequences of policy decisions have been instrumental in fashioning pragmatism's most potent self-critique. These intramural debates have also dramatized the pragmatists' ongoing struggle to come to terms with the relation between means and ends, as some, like Kristol himself, moved still farther to the right, embracing a more traditional conservativism rooted in philosophical idealism.

From the beginning, pragmatism warred against political abstractions, especially against ideals that have persisted solely because custom, tradition, or religious authority have not been examined. The pragmatists' search for values in this world—and their acknowl-

edgment that values are not timeless and absolute—has been a continual invitation for American conservatives to assail liberalism as being
without values, conspicuously lacking moral bearings, or aimlessly
relativistic. Without a James or Dewey to articulate its ethos, the
pragmatic philosophy undergirding both social science and modern
liberalism has not always been defended or defined convincingly.
Nor is this lack of cogency surprising, given the pragmatists' tendency
toward specialization and concern with the means of policy, rather
than with the articulation of ends.

In seeking to apply the social sciences to public questions, policy
experts and their supporters in foundations, reform or activist groups,
and government have sought and found explicit rationales that are
generally remote from abstract theories of knowledge or ideal conceptions of democracy. As noted earlier, they have discussed their efforts
in terms of metaphors borrowed from the natural sciences. These
metaphors have governed both research and application, and their
attendant rhetoric has served to shape the experts' public role, as
well as the institutions they inhabit.

In the late nineteenth century, for example, social scientists
adopted a persuasive—and still frequently invoked—medical metaphor, describing themselves, like physicians and public health practitioners, as attempting to understand social afflictions and to discover
cures and remedies. The Russell Sage Foundation, the prototypical
think tank, adopted this metaphor when it was founded. But in the
first decade of the twentieth century, this rhetoric of diagnosis and
cure began to compete with another that was derived from the physical
sciences and based on the notion of efficiency. Social scientists, like
physicists and engineers who were concerned with the efficiency of
engines and industrial plants, began to see parallels in the ideal of
efficiently functioning businesses and governmental bureaucracies.
The Brookings Institution, the Twentieth Century Fund, and the
National Bureau of Economic Research were all propelled by this
new metaphor. Indeed, the search for "efficiency" has been one of
the most persistent ways of justifying the heavy, ongoing investment
in the social sciences.

By the 1920s, social scientists were a diverse and increasingly
specialized lot. Most of them worked in universities; fewer were
concerned explicitly with issues of public policy. Yet they gradually
adopted another metaphor to justify and guide applied research; echoing the language of psychology, they propounded a metaphor of "adjustment." Departing from their previous passivity as more or less

detached observers—particularly after the onset of the Great Depression—they assumed an increasingly active role. They saw themselves as specialists who monitored and adjusted the political or economic system to help it withstand the shocks of unexpected change.

World War II created powerful new tools of quantitative analysis, and by the late 1940s, social scientists had begun to see themselves as engineers, designing and evaluating complex systems. The experts at the RAND Corporation, and later those of the Urban Institute and other new research enterprises, employed this metaphor until public disillusionment with the programs of the Great Society and the Vietnam debacle cast new doubt upon their scientific claims of expertise. Suddenly, their proposals seemed incapable of meeting the test of practical results; and their analyses, it seemed, had not been as rigorous as those of other scientific workers. Even their attempts to mount "social experiments" that would test welfare proposals and health care systems dramatized the difficulty of obtaining accurate scientific information about controlled social phenomena.

In fact, the long-promised (ever-emerging) science of society seemed increasingly to be a mere forensic exercise, a form of political argument disguised as detached scientific inquiry and scholarly discourse. With the ultimate unraveling of scientific claims in the late 1960s and 1970s, social scientists soon found their work variously described as ideological propaganda, a marketplace commodity, or intellectual weaponry. Thus, the vocabularies of warfare and marketing now permeate the language of those who work in Washington's think tanks.

The failures of social science went far beyond mere disappointment over specific programs and have had consequences that resonate well beyond the walls of think tanks or university campuses. The loss of faith in the endeavors of social scientists was both a cause and a consequence of the breakup of liberalism. Liberal means— grounded in a technocratic social science—had either worked badly or not as promised. Knowledge itself seemed to have failed. And the political consequences proved to be profound as conservatives, holding different ideas about knowledge and its uses, ascended to power.

Rejecting the absolutism of abstract political ideals, pragmatic social scientists who were interested in policy had sought criteria for political and scientific truth in the realm of action. Policies were considered hypotheses—testable and amendable—a concept befitting a nation that had been conceived as a political experiment. But this pragmatic spirit—typified by the quest for facts, the suspicion of political theorizing, and a belief in the possibility of enlightened compromise—encouraged the expert to focus solely on practical means and to insist on the separation of fact and values. Accordingly, pragmatic social science became increasingly obsessed with means and technique. As early as 1917, the radical critic Randolph Bourne had foreseen how an intelligentsia that was trained in the "pragmatic dispensation" and drawn by the war into governmental service might devote itself to the "executive ordering of events" but remain "pitifully unprepared for the intellectual interpretation or the idealistic focusing of ends."[18] By the late 1960s, a dessicated pragmatism, less capable of addressing questions of value than even Bourne would have predicted, began to yield its intellectual dominion to conservatives. Not long thereafter, the liberal center of American politics gave way.

The Washington War of Ideas

In April 1986, fifteen months into Ronald Reagan's second term, he and other prominent conservatives gathered to celebrate the latest accomplishments of the Heritage Foundation—an institution that had attained preeminence among the many conservative research organizations then operating in Washington. They met especially to congratulate themselves on the impending conclusion of a $30 million fund-raising campaign. President Reagan felt himself to be among old friends when he stepped to the podium, exchanging amiable quips with Clare Booth Luce and Joseph Coors, two of the foundation's long-time boosters.

Addressing a room filled with sympathetic veterans of the conservative movement, the president commended the foundation's promotion of ideas through seminars, conferences, publications, and "its buttonholing of congressmen—for informational purposes only, of course" (a titter of knowing laughter spread through the ballroom as Reagan acknowledged the fine line between research and advocacy in today's political scene). He praised their efforts as both a reflection and a cause of "the revolution in ideas occurring throughout the world." Nevertheless, the president's underlying ambivalence about experts eventually surfaced, even in this distinguished and like-minded company. Experts and pundits, Reagan complained, had often been wrong in the past; sometimes they were simply too close to the facts, concentrating so hard on the superficial ripples that they missed the waves and tides. "Being too close to the data," the

President said, "can sometimes mean missing its significance, and the chance to change it for the better."[19]

As the president reached the end of his speech, he paid homage to paleoconservative Richard Weaver, who along with Russell Kirk, Friedrich A. Hayek, and Ludwig von Mises, had been a pillar of the postwar conservative movement. Weaver, a southerner and a literary scholar who had taught at the University of Chicago, published a book in 1948—*Ideas Have Consequences*—which became a conservative classic.[20] And Reagan knew full well that the Heritage Foundation had adopted the book's title as its motto. "It goes back to what Richard Weaver had said and what Heritage is all about," the president reminded them. "Ideas do have consequences, rhetoric is policy, and words are action."[21]

Reagan and his conservative admirers were not unique in believing that ideas had lately come to play a new part in American politics. A number of defeated Democrats had already asked themselves why their party failed so disastrously in the 1980 election. By and large, they had accepted the conservative premise that liberalism's failure was as much intellectual as it was political; many liberals concluded that they had lacked ideas or had been unable to articulate them with comparable trenchancy. Convinced that conservative think tanks had played a major role in the Republican victory, liberals set up several new research and advocacy organizations in the early 1980s. One of the new progressive groups (the word *progressive* was revived since even on the Left, *liberal* had a taint of disrepute), the Center for National Policy (CNP), was founded only two months after the election. Its organizers were Democrats who were still stunned by the success of the Republican Right. Like many, they had been scarcely cognizant of the conservative intellectual movement, but now felt an urgent need to revitalize liberalism. Slow to fashion an agenda and with no resident staff of researchers, the center was a mechanism for bringing academics and leading Democrats together to discuss issues and programs in the hope of forging a consensus among moderately liberal party activists.

In 1986 the CNP's then president, Kirk O'Donnell, educated in history at Brown University but schooled in practical politics in Boston's City Hall and on the staff of former Speaker of the House Tip O'Neill, expressed the view that his center reflected a fundamental change in the conduct of American politics. Ideas, he observed, were an increasingly significant "political currency." They sometimes seemed to have become even more important than regional, class, or economic interests in shaping political affiliations.[22] But the liberal analysis, at least in the early 1980s, still failed to understand both the sources of the conservative appeal and the nature of liberalism's weakness.

Throughout much of our history, American politics has appeared to all the world as notably free of ideological controversy. Tocqueville summed it up by saying that in America, "differences of opinion are mere differences of hue."[23] Our major parties have been practical, electoral coalitions, and even though our debates are often heated and contentious, pragmatism has been the hallmark of our policymaking processes. Although the abolitionist and civil rights movements, like the temperance and anticommunist movements, gave American politics a fervent moral dimension for a time—as the abortion issue has recently done—our political discussions and policy deliberations as a rule have taken place within a generally accepted framework of values.

That consensus—more enduring than even postwar policy continuities—had unraveled during the twenty years leading up to the election of Reagan. Some political activists, policy experts, and executives of foundations and corporations had come to see themselves as being consciously engaged in a war of ideas, with Washington as the main battlefield. Indeed, the older scientific metaphors that characterized the experts' role in public life were largely supplanted by aggressive metaphors of battle and hard-sell advertising. And it has sometimes seemed that the new "war of ideas" amounts to little more than the aggressive application of the techniques of public relations, marketing, and survey research to the discussion of public issues. But these are only a superficial manifestation of the sometimes strident battle that has brought experts and the institutions they inhabit to center stage in our political life—a battle about the relationship between knowledge and politics that pits different ways of knowing the world against each other.

Few things perplexed Ronald Reagan's opponents more than his cavalier treatment of facts—in particular how rarely, if ever, he paid a political price for his well-documented misstatements. Reagan's gaffes and errors amazed journalists, who dutifully reported them, as well as his Democratic opponents, who nevertheless scored no political points for recounting them. It is not that facts did not matter to Reagan. The telling anecdote and choice detail made many of his speeches memorable and often compelling, but what his audience remembered—and found true—about the facts he did recite was their illustrative power. Facts were true to Reagan if they harmonized with broad political ideals and if they worked, not to build an accurate description of the world, but to guide and shape political perceptions. He understood intuitively that what was missing from the liberal technocratic regime was the appeal to values. (In trying to cast the 1988 election as a choice between "competence" and "ideology," Michael Dukakis also sensed what was at issue and vainly sought to pull the focus back to the terrain upon which liberals and moderates have been most comfortable.)

Central to the long-term political success of the conservative movement has been its revolutionary approach to ideas. On the popular level, it answered the nation's simple yearning for moral clarity after two unsettling decades of social change, failures of foreign policy, and economic uncertainty. Less remarked upon, however, is the recurring or cyclical nature of this so-called revolution. In essence, it is more a *restoration* that seeks to revive the philosophical idealism repudiated by pragmatists at the turn of the century. Thus, while the Reagan revolution is generally considered to have been an assault on the New Deal, the target is, in fact, much older and more venerable. The conservative revolt was really a frontal assault on the pragmatic philosophical assumptions that have been at the core of American politics—and, not coincidentally, of social science expertise—since the turn of the century. The new conservatives rejected the intellectual basis of American policymaking, including the approaches advanced by the progressive reformers, Hoover's technocrats, Roosevelt's New Dealers, Truman's Cold War liberals, and Eisenhower's "modern" Republicans, as well as Kennedy's New Frontiersmen and the architects of Johnson's Great Society.

Reagan's victory was the culmination of a conservative movement that began in the 1940s and early 1950s. Its intellectual lineage is correspondingly diverse; indeed, its variety has made for considerable volatility. It draws on the writings of traditionalists like Richard Weaver and Russell Kirk, classical liberals like Friedrich A. Hayek and Ludwig von Mises, militant anticommunists like Whittaker Chambers and Frank Meyer, and political philosophers like Leo Strauss and Eric Voegelin. These great teachers or their followers built a network of conservative institutions and supplied the ranks of the experts that were called on by the new administration.

But diverse as the sources of modern American conservativism may be, they share a common belief in the primacy of ideas and their historical reality. Ideas precede the talk about policy, shaping responses to the realm of facts, even reshaping the facts themselves, as President Reagan suggested in his speech to the Heritage Foundation. Whether ideas and values, the "permanent things" in Russell Kirk's phrase, are thought to be divinely ordained or derived from historical experience, they exist outside our consciousness and often require interpretation by another sort of elite that is schooled in the fundamental texts. The phrase so often heard in conservative circles, "ideas have consequences," is not a simple truism but an evocation of the conservative idealistic tradition that has been sharply critical of empirical social science and its pragmatic underpinnings.

The story of American political expertise and of the policy elites and institutions that now contend with one another is, broadly conceived, a contest between two ways of understanding the world. Its beginnings may be traced to the late nineteenth century. Pragmatism—a political temperament as well as a philosophical tradition—was the point of departure for both empirical social science and the progressive reform movement that took shape in the late nineteenth century. Social scientists and reformers were convinced that scientific methods of analysis would suggest a course of practical action on which reasonable people would be almost certain to agree. The wisest policies would follow from accurate investigation, not from political infighting or, as they feared in the wake of violent labor disputes, radical political activity, popular agitation, and social unrest. Over the course of the century, we have swung back and forth between the poles of naive faith and exaggerated disillusionment in our approach to expertise and its political uses. We are now at another nadir. The story of America's policy elite and the institutions they have created begins, however, at a moment when the hopes vested in science were at their peak.

TWO

☆

Laboratories for Reform

The Social Science of the Amateurs

Although think tanks have vastly proliferated in the past twenty years, they did not sprout overnight. Their sheer number and volubility make them seem like a new phenomenon, but recognizable prototypes have been tested time and again since the late nineteenth century. In fact, the dynamics that have shaped the experts' role—attitudes toward social science, an infrastructure for graduate training and professional careers, well-organized large-scale philanthropy, and an expansive conception of the state and its functions—were clearly discernible in the decades after the Civil War. Even individual career patterns—readily familiar to contemporary members of the policy elite—were being tentatively traced by such first-generation American social scientists as Richard T. Ely, Lester Ward, and John R. Commons. Moreover, in the contours of the discussions about social science and expertise in the late nineteenth century, one can hear echoes of our continuing concerns about the proper uses of knowledge in policymaking.

The first institutional experiments were in the hands of amateurs. In October 1865, nearly a hundred people met at the Massachusetts State House in Boston. The assemblage included reformers of every stripe from all over the country: abolitionists in search of new causes to replace the one so recently resolved at Appomatox; advocates of public health and sanitation who were justifiably proud of the wartime successes of the U.S. Sanitary Commission; people who were interested in the reform of prisons, insane asylums, orphanages, and schools; and a number of women who had performed charity work during the Civil War and now sought wider political rights for themselves. The meeting attracted writers and journalists; educators from the nation's oldest colleges, as well from as its newest scientific and technical institutes; and governmental officials who were concerned with economic and social improvement.

The Boston conclave was a policy elite of sorts. And for their era, those who attended it were experts, though the word would probably have sounded strange to their ears. Although they were not burdened with years of graduate training or armed with doctorates in the social sciences, they felt comfortable thinking of their interest in social reform as scientific. They were the earliest American partisans of what they enthusiastically termed "social science" (then a singular discipline, rather than the many separate disciplines that make up today's social sciences). Franklin B. Sanborn's letter of invitation had been specific about this science and its scope. The meetings, he said, would explore poor relief, unemployment, public health, the prevention of crime, prisons, and "those numerous matters of statistical and philanthropic interest which are included under the general head of 'Social Science.' "[1] Although they were not the first or most insightful group to think about the relation between science and politics, they set in motion a continuing effort to link systematic research to the sphere of social reform. Professional organizations, such as the American Economics Association and the American Political Science Association, as well as such national reform groups as the National Conference on Charities and Correction, trace their lineage to the Boston gathering.

Those who attended the Boston meeting were all aware that the sweeping social and political transformations they had witnessed were born of scientific and technological developments: steam power, railroads, telegraphy, innovations in manufacturing, and discoveries about hygiene and disease. Many reformers were convinced that the scientific methods that had contributed so much to knowledge, permitting an unparalleled degree of control over the natural and physical world, could be fruitfully applied to social and economic problems.

Such problems abounded in American cities, many of which were being rapidly transformed by immigration from abroad and by the movement of the native born from farming to industrial jobs. The Civil War had underscored vexatious problems that had only temporarily been pushed aside during the nation's long paroxysm over slavery and secession. Draft riots in New York City in 1863 had exposed dreadful conditions in the city's Irish slums. Volunteers, especially women, who nursed wounded soldiers and assisted the soldiers' families had learned firsthand about the condition of the working classes and the desperate situation of thousands of widows and orphans. Long-time abolitionists joined efforts to help the freedmen, setting up charitable programs to deal with the most pressing needs of the former slaves and attempting to supply the kind of training and education that might help them become self-supporting.

The Boston conclave bestowed upon itself an impressive name, the American Association for the Promotion of Social Science (later abbreviated to the American Social Science Association, or ASSA). Its membership was diverse. Unlike our era, the distinctions between the professional "expert" and the knowledgeable "amateur" had not yet hardened. Indeed, the word expert—rooted in the Latin verb experiri, meaning to try or to experience—conveyed less of the contemporary notion of expertise as training and theoretical insight than of practically acquired knowledge. Modeled on a British group formed in 1857 to investigate, advise, and lobby for social reform, the ASSA promised a broadly ambitious program of reform, but one to be carried out primarily in the communities and states in which the members lived, rather than nationally.

The Civil War had offered hints of what the federal government could accomplish in the social and economic arenas. But Americans notably lacked what H. G. Wells would describe several decades later as a "sense of the state." The new breed of scientific reformers, while they spoke of the Nation and the Republic as metaphysical entities and created the first national associations of intellectuals and reformers, were slow to seize on the policy implications of state sovereignty. Indeed, the confused and bitterly ideological debates over Reconstruction left reformers disillusioned and conflicted about the uses of federal power.

Gradually, however, as amateur social scientists gave way to professionals in the early twentieth century, a new sense of government and its spheres of responsibility took shape. These changing convictions were mainly the fruit of efforts by amateur and professional social scientists to devise new techniques of investigation, foster a new awareness of social problems, and create a national arena for the discussion of social and economic questions.

The ASSA had been set up to act as an umbrella organization for reformers, university professors, and governmental officials; its members wanted their discussions to harmonize conflicting opinions among these groups and to uncover "the real elements of Truth."[2] The founders made no bones about their scientific aims or propagandistic objectives. To them, social science, reform, and notions of Christian charitable obligation were virtually synonymous. They all considered themselves scientists in some respect, duty bound to investigate society's most troublesome conditions, and they assumed that science held the key to social remedies. This (to us) naive confidence was epitomized in the proclamation that they would "collect all facts, diffuse all knowledge, and stimulate all inquiry, which have a bearing on social welfare."[3]

A rudimentary scientific spirit also pervaded federal agencies, which made more consistent efforts after the Civil War to improve the collection of social and economic data through such units as the Treasury Department's Bureau of Statistics and an increasingly professional U.S. Bureau of the Census. Following the model of progressive states like Massachusetts, which had created a bureau of labor statistics in 1869, the federal government formed its own bureau in the 1880s.

A great part of the appeal of this rudimentary social science, particularly as labor confrontations turned more violent in the 1880s, was its promise of resolving social conflict. In encouraging scientific investigations, the vigorous charity organization movement that swept through American cities in the late 1870s also fostered contact between the middle-class or wealthy volunteers and the poor. "Not alms but a friend" was their oft-repeated slogan, though critics of the movement, seeing it as harshly moralistic and condescending, thought that "neither alms nor a friend" more accurately summarized its objectives. A verse from Boston's John Boyle O'Reilley summed up the critics' view: "The organized charity scrimped and iced/In the name of a cautious, statistical Christ."[4]

For its middle-class adherents, however, the new social science (and its cousin, "scientific charity") held many attractions. It would help institutions operate more efficiently. It would lead to more rational appraisal of the needs of individuals. It would make for greater social harmony, with factual knowledge helping to reconcile conflicts of political ideology and economic interest. And, in the end, it would provide a surer method of social improvement than reliance on corrupt and partisan political processes. Seeking social facts and institutional data, the nineteenth-century reformers disdained abstractions and theory. The search for hard and certain nuggets of fact expressed a

hope that people with different views would thereby find a firm
ground for agreement and action. An emphasis on theory, it was
feared, would only compound disagreements and harden political
positions.

But the simple investigations by the amateurs soon gave way
to a more professional approach. New graduate programs in the social
sciences—especially at Johns Hopkins, Columbia, Chicago, and Wisconsin—and expanded opportunities for public service in state and
local governments were a promising framework for professional careers. The first generations of trained social scientists (who then
trained more researchers) created a pattern in which teaching and
public service were combined.

Three members of the emerging elite of university-trained
experts helped build even closer ties between experts and the government. Richard T. Ely, a founder of the American Economics
Association, and John R. Commons, who spent much of his career
at the University of Wisconsin, both used their skills as economists
in a variety of advisory capacities. Lester Ward, a pioneering sociologist, spent a good part of his career in the federal government's
scientific agencies before joining the faculty of Brown University.
These three are prototypical members of the policy elite, who made
their way in academic life while seeking to apply their expertise in
the political realm. Their professional credentials reinforced their
claims of scientific knowledge, while their public careers helped shape
the institutions through which governments could tap private expertise. Meanwhile, their conception of science and its political uses
gradually worked to redefine and broaden the responsibilities that
the government assumed.

The First Experts

Had he lived only a generation earlier, Richard T. Ely, born
in 1854 into a family of strict and dour Congregationalists, would
almost certainly have become a minister. But like others of the generation that came of age in the decades after the Civil War, his career
took directions that would have been inconceivable in antebellum
America. After earning an undergraduate degree at Columbia College
in 1876, Ely studied at the Universities of Halle and Heidelberg
where, like other Americans studying in Germany, he was much
taken by the teachings of the so-called historical economists.

The German economists were severely critical of the laissez-faire doctrine that prevailed in Britain and the United States. They assailed what Ely later called the "absolutism of theory" that had always pervaded classical political economy. The Germans thought that the absolute certainties of classical economists were founded on the false belief, that economic laws based on simplistic assumptions about human behavior could hold for all times in all places.

Neither Ely nor his German professors was convinced that there were timeless natural laws, economic or otherwise, that held in every society and on all occasions. Ely saw all around him the forces that were reordering social and economic relations. "We had learned the idea of evolution and never ceasing change as a condition of life," he later wrote. "We thought that by getting down into this life and studying it carefully, we would be able to do something toward directing the great forces shaping our life, and directing them in such a way as to bring improvement."[5] This conception of economic knowledge and its usefulness as a tool for reshaping human relations propelled him into public life.

Ely and other Americans who witnessed the creation of the German welfare state were greatly impressed by the status of German professors. These professors had close ties to political leaders and civil servants and played advisory roles in policy areas as diverse as agriculture, trade, social welfare, and labor. Nor could American students avoid drawing invidious comparisons between the well-ordered life of German cities and the haphazard, corrupt, and amateurish city and state governments in their own country.

Ely's return to the United States after a three-year absence was a jolting experience and remained so decades later when he composed his memoirs. Arriving in New York, he saw a city that depressed him in comparison to stately Berlin. New York was even more unseemly than Liverpool, the raucous seaport from which he had just embarked. It was "dirty and ill-kept, the pavements poor, and there were evidences of graft and incompetence on every hand. Is this my America? I asked myself." Thus, were Ely's reform enthusiasms kindled.

Ely continued his studies and began to teach at Johns Hopkins University, established in 1876 and expressly modeled on the German university. In his seminars and scholarly writing, the young professor preached against the established authorities in Anglo-American political economy and criticized the policies that followed from their teachings. Above all, he could not accept the sharp limits on the role of government that were so fundamental to classical liberal economics.

In 1885 Ely set about organizing an association of younger economists who shared his conviction that the government should be an
active agent of social change. As the number of academically trained
experts grew,* social scientists in various fields began to establish
national organizations with the double aim of raising professional
standards and extending their influence outside the classroom. The
American Economics Association (AEA) (a lineal descendant of the
older ASSA), which early on included a surprisingly large number
of clergymen among the economists, was imbued with the objectives
of reform but was led by social scientists who had received formal
academic training and were busily pursuing university careers. Professional associations like the AEA (political scientists organized their
association in 1903; sociologists in 1905) provided an organized forum
where social scientists could air their views on questions of policy.
In its early incarnation, rather than concerning itself exclusively with
theoretical and discipline-bound questions, the AEA created committees to examine such contemporary questions as trade and tariff policies and labor conditions.

Ely's view of the social sciences carried with it an explicit conception of the state. "We regard the State," he wrote in a draft prospectus
for the AEA, "as an educational and ethical agency whose positive
aid is an indispensable condition of human progress." He and many
of the others who helped found the AEA were skeptical about the
doctrine of laissez-faire, both as a foundation for scientific inquiry
into economic relations and as a guide to policy. To him, it suggested
"an inadequate explanation of the relation between the State and
its citizens."[7] Ely wanted to replace classical economics' universal
abstractions about human nature with an empirical investigation of
human customs, traditions, and institutions. To him, the principal
aim of his science was to aid social progress. And the agent of that
progress would be the state, which in using the emerging social
sciences, could act as a benevolent educator and ethical guide. Thus
was born the modern notion of the social science expert as a political
adviser and a public mentor.

Another who assailed the social and political passivity of laissez-
faire was Lester Ward. Born in Joliet, Illinois, in 1841, the son of a
mechanic, Ward worked in various factory and farm jobs and later

---

* Three American universities awarded three Ph.D.s in political economy in
the 1870s, five institutions awarded eleven doctoral degrees in economics in the
1880s, and twelve awarded ninety-five doctoral degrees in the 1890s.

served with conspicuous bravery in the enlisted ranks of the Union army. One of the great autodidacts of the late nineteenth century, he taught himself Latin, Greek, several modern languages, and the rudiments of science while working at menial jobs. He earned a teaching certificate along the way. After the war, he was first a clerk in the Treasury Department and then worked in various statistical and scientific agencies in Washington, D.C. Upon advancing to the post of chief paleontologist in the U.S. Geological Survey, he joined the pioneering investigations of John Wesley Powell. Ward's learning knew no disciplinary bounds, and out of his capacious mind came another critique of laissez-faire and social Darwinism.

Social Darwinists like Herbert Spencer and his American disciple, the Yale professor William Graham Sumner, tended to view both nature and society as organisms of such complexity that human lawmakers could never successfully direct or accelerate the course of progress. Although Spencer's social science was optimistic about progress in the long term, it remained impassive in the face of immediate social distress and skeptical of the scientific claims of social reformers. Spencer and his followers considered themselves practitioners of a science whose aim was not to guide social change but to demonstrate the limits of human control over natural processes—not unlike the later neoconservatives' complaints about the unintended consequences of social intervention. According to Sumner, it was "the greatest folly of which a man can be capable to set down with a slate and pencil to plan out a new social world."[8]

Lester Ward's critique of Spencer and the laissez-faire economists pointed out some of the facile analogies that social Darwinists had drawn between the operations of the natural world and human society. Invoking the wastefulness of nature's operations—the seeds that did not germinate, the young who did not survive to maturity—Ward argued that the laws of competition and survival of the fittest that described brute nature were unworthy of civilized humanity. For Ward, human progress was the story of the triumph of mind over environment, not a blind competitive struggle or the gradual accumulation of accidents, as the social Darwinists supposed. Progress was the fruit of the purposeful application of an organized, collective intelligence.[9]

Ward also had an answer to the social Darwinists' reluctance to mitigate social and economic hardship. In *Dynamic Sociology*, he described the guiding role of systematic research in human affairs. "Intelligence, hitherto a growth, is destined to become a manufacture," he wrote. "The origination and distribution of knowledge can no longer be left to chance and to nature." Ward advocated the use of statistics in what he termed "scientific lawmaking" and foresaw an institutionalization of scientific methods in government. Carrying his metaphor still farther, he envisioned legislatures that would operate like laboratories, where laws would be enacted as "a series of exhaustive experiments."[10] He called for the creation of a national academy devoted to the study of social problems and to the scientific training of public servants. He spoke of "sociocracy," which implied an active government whose laws were grounded in the emerging discipline of sociology.

Although the utopian institutions Ward imagined in the 1880s were far from realization, by 1900 the rudimentary social science that reformers had practiced since the Civil War had attained greater maturity. The expert was being drawn into political service, helping to collect data and serving on new regulatory commissions; and professors and graduate students were being employed in expert agencies and on special commissions at all levels of government. Richard T. Ely, while still an assistant professor at Johns Hopkins, served on the Maryland and Baltimore tax commissions; Arthur Twining Hadley, a distinguished conservative economist at Yale, was Connecticut's commissioner of labor statistics; Henry Carter Adams served as statistician for the Interstate Commerce Commission while teaching at the University of Michigan; and Walter Willcox, an economist and statistician at Cornell University, worked to improve the operations of the U.S. Bureau of the Census. The ranks of American faculty members had swelled from roughly 5,500 in 1870 to nearly 24,000 in 1900, and the number of doctorates awarded in the United States had increased from 1 in 1870 to nearly 400 in 1890.[11] And many academics were finding a social role for themselves outside the classroom.

Arthur Twining Hadley's presidential address before the AEA in 1898 was a summons for even greater political involvement on the part of economists: "I believe that the largest opportunity in the future lies not in theories, but in practice, not with students, but with statesmen, not in the education of individual citizens, however widespread and salutary, but in leadership of an organized body politic."[12] But Hadley was cautious, insisting that social scientists should limit their advice to specific areas of expertise and should quietly offer it to elected officials rather than use it to arouse public sentiment. He thought the expert should operate behind the scenes, advising on request but neither presuming to make political decisions nor trying to go over the heads of elected officials to appeal to the democratic populace.

Although a number of social scientists were drawn to temporary service in city and state governments and occasionally worked in the federal government, there were still no prestigious or intellectually rewarding career routes outside the university for policy-oriented social scientists. The attractions of the advisory or administrative positions in Washington at the turn of the century were notoriously limited. Bright social scientists with new doctorates would go to Washington for a year or two, working for the census bureau or a cabinet department, but few were happy there. Given the choice between a government career and returning to the university, most chose to leave Washington when they were offered academic positions.

The atmosphere of governmental agencies seemed particularly stifling to Wesley C. Mitchell, who went to Washington after receiving his degree in economics from the University of Chicago in 1899. Some years later he recalled, "The servility of the clerks nauseated me, and the feebleness of the official representatives of economics in the several bureaus where I became acquainted frightened me. I could not live in such a community without having to fight a battle with myself every day for self-control."[13] Mitchell's complaints were typical of his time and were echoed by others who had similar experiences.

Experts Organizing

Throughout most of our nation's history, Washington has not offered a hospitable climate or suitable professional rewards for serious intellectual work. Virtually from the moment the federal government first sought to employ experts for their technical skills and policy insights, it was necessary to invent special mechanisms to obtain the services of the most talented social scientists, with the notable exceptions of the Department of Agriculture and the Federal Reserve Board where research was valued in its own right. For work on commissions, such as the U.S. Industrial Commission and Theodore Roosevelt's 1908 Country Life Commission, or with White House conferences, experts were drawn into service on an ad hoc basis. But for the most part, since able careerists with statistical training were competent to carry on the routine work in federal agencies, the federal government's need for university scholars was minimal in the early 1900s.[14]

More secure institutional frameworks existed for expert advisers at the local and state levels, the most significant arenas for policy activity at the turn of the century. In 1890 Melville Dewey set up a rudimentary reference service to assist New York State legislators. An even more celebrated plan, referred to simply as the "Wisconsin Idea," brought professors from the University of Wisconsin into the political process as researchers and legislative draftsmen through a reference service organized by Charles McCarthy in 1901. Madison, with the state university and capitol only a mile apart, was a uniquely suitable laboratory for this experiment in linking knowledge and power.

John R. Commons, who taught economics for nearly thirty years at the University of Wisconsin, referred fondly to the legislative reference library as "Charlie McCarthy's clipping bureau." Commons first learned its value when Governor Robert La Follette pushed forward a civil service reform law in 1905. "I found that here was an entirely new kind of library," Commons wrote. "It was telegraphic. McCarthy wired to civil service organizations, to state governments, to individuals for statutes, bills before legislatures, clippings, and comments. Within a day or two after La Follette requested my help on the bill, McCarthy had me supplied with everything one could need in drafting that bill. . . . I never before had known such a quick-action library."[15]

Though imitated elsewhere, Wisconsin's legislative reference service was uniquely successful in that progressive state, and it earned a special location in one of the four wings of the newly built state capitol, on the same floor as the state Senate, Assembly, and Supreme Court. But although professors and legislators praised the library for its speed in assembling material on all sides of important issues, lobbyists and lawyers, who resented the academic intrusion in the political process, denounced it as a "bill factory."

Nevertheless, despite complaints from some quarters, the library's services tended to be far more technical than political. More often than not, the experts were simply asked to compile and analyze statistics or to examine legislative proposals from other states. It was important and useful work, but it did not turn professors into politicians, nor did the university usurp the legislature's function. Commons saw the role of the professors as decidedly secondary, pointing out, "I never initiated anything. I came only on request of legislators, of executives, or committees of the legislature."[16]

Even so, Commons was a central figure in Wisconsin's policy

experiments. He worked on the Public Utility Law of 1907 and the Workmen's Compensation Act of 1911, and he advised governors on railroad regulation and tax policy. He also helped set up the Wisconsin Industrial Commission, a group of experts and labor and business leaders who sought to resolve industrial disputes in that neutral arena. In later years, he would sometimes go to Washington as an adviser to the House Committee on Banking and Currency. But his main focus remained the state government. Not until the New Deal, when many of his students were drafted to help with social security and labor legislation, were there better and more permanent governmental mechanisms for bringing academics into the federal policy process.

At different stages in his career, Commons, who had studied under Ely without completing his Ph.D., worked in most of the settings open to university-trained experts at the turn of the century. With another economist, E. W. Bemis, and with financing from George H. Shibley, who had made a fortune selling law encyclopedias and who fancied himself an economist, Commons tried to establish a pioneering Bureau of Economic Research in 1899. The bureau lasted two years, investigating such subjects as municipal monopolies and freight rates from a "nonpartisan but progressive standpoint," as Commons put it. In fact, Shibley was less interested in scholarship than in seeing the bureau's work used by Democrats to attack the policies of President William McKinley.

Anticipating the work of the National Bureau of Economic Research by two decades, Commons tried to create a more rigorous statistical basis for the analysis of economic trends. But when Shibley grew unhappy with the economists' work on price indexes, finding it politically less useful than he had expected, he cut off his financial support and the experiment died. Commons moved on, writing a report on immigration for the U.S. Industrial Commission, which he later described as the "original 'brains trust,'" and then joining the research staff of the National Civic Federation, another institutional experiment.[17] Founded in 1900 and supported by a broad group of reform-minded businessmen, including Andrew Carnegie, E. A. Filene, Gerard Swope, V. Everett Macy, and George Perkins, the federation was the prototypical business research and policy organization. Although it became a vehicle for the militant antisocialist propagandizing of its director, Ralph Easley, after World War I, its early aim was to promote legislation and to effect an accommodation of business and labor by steering a middle course between socialists in the labor movement and unreconstructed laissez-faire businessmen.

There were other attempts to link academic research with policy-making in the first decade of the twentieth century. In 1904 Ely and Commons embarked on a joint venture, setting up the American Bureau of Industrial Research. With support from businessmen and eventually from the Carnegie Corporation, Commons and his collaborators produced multivolume works on labor and industry, including *A Documentary History of American Industrial Society*, noteworthy in its day. In 1906 Ely and other economists joined with reform-minded individuals, backed by liberal businessmen, to create the American Association of Labor Legislation, which sought greater uniformity of state and local laws, and ultimately federal legislation on workers' compensation, minimum-wage, and job-training proposals.

Today's familiar patterns of entrepreneurialism and institution building in policymaking are not new. In the early twentieth century, as now, research institutes and bureaus sprang up out of individual ambition and enthusiasm and could as quickly die when energy and financing failed. Their existence as bridges between research and policymaking has always tended to confuse the lines between disinterested investigation and political advocacy. Commons, however, drew early and valuable lessons from his diverse experiences in private research organizations, governmental commissions, and universities (early in his career he had been fired from a post at Syracuse University for his allegedly radical tendencies). "I learned with Easley, as I had previously begun to learn with Shibley and afterwards with La Follette," he later wrote, "that the place of the economists was that of advisor to the leaders, if they wanted him, and not that of propagandist to the masses." Commons believed that only practical experience could teach politicians how to filter the advisers' advice and that the politicians were accordingly free to use or reject that advice as they saw fit. "They were leaders," he concluded, "I was an intellectual."[18]

Writing self-effacingly in the 1930s about events at the turn of the century, Commons seemed to have accepted a subordinate and largely technical role in the policymaking process. But the modest distinction between "leaders" and "intellectuals" belied his accomplishments in Wisconsin and the real and growing influence of social scientists who would soon occupy prominent advisory positions in Washington. Indeed, as an elderly man, Commons looked with pride on his thirty or more former students, by his estimate, who had been drawn to Washington during the New Deal.

What Commons had not anticipated in the early years of the twentieth century was the invention of a new American institution, the philanthropic foundation, which provided a more secure and permanent link between the emerging national elite of experts and the circles of government. The new foundations and the many research institutes they funded would give added weight to the voices of university-trained social scientists and supply the resources for relatively stable private institutions operating on the margins of government. As a result, the nineteenth-century image of the expert as a fact gatherer and statistician—much the way Commons portrayed his political role—soon gave way to that of the learned doctor operating out of a research laboratory. These social and political doctors had special insights into the prevention and cure of social ills, as well as a secure base from which to diagnose and prescribe.

Experts and the Science of Prevention

Without the legacy of scientific discoveries and practical accomplishments that the natural sciences can point to, the promise of what the social sciences can deliver has often seemed remote. Indeed, the very notion of a "social" science seems ambiguous, since social science deals not with fixed and predictable connections between chemical elements or measurable physical properties, but with malleable human institutions and erratic human behavior. In the end, the very concept of a social science may itself be more a metaphor than a realizable aim. For while our understanding of society may have improved—and even that may be debated—the "scientific" aims of prediction and control that were articulated at its origin seem no nearer to being achieved than they were a century ago.

At the turn of the century, the metaphors that most attracted the reform-minded proponents of social science were drawn from medicine and the related field of public health. The ideals of prevention and cure strongly appealed to those who wanted to address social and economic concerns through scientific means, and as the diagnostic metaphor caught on, it provided a compelling rationale for public intervention in many areas, including the improvement of working conditions, housing for the poor, education, and recreation. The metaphor was particularly important to a handful of wealthy philanthropists and their advisers who began to practice what they termed the new "science of preventive philanthropy."

Frederick T. Gates, a one-time Baptist minister and an adviser to John D. Rockefeller, Sr., expressed this prevailing view when he argued that "disease with its attendant evils is undoubtedly the main single source of human misery," the root of all economic, social, and moral distress.[19] Having devoted much of his summer vacation in 1897 to reading Sir William Osler's *Principles and Practice of Medicine*, which described the retarded development of medical research, Gates returned to New York and outlined a plan for what became the Rockefeller Institute of Medical Research. Patterned on the Koch and Pasteur Institutes in Berlin and Paris, the Rockefeller Institute opened in 1901, bringing together medical researchers who devoted their energies to full-time research. The researchers' swift success in identifying the causes of various diseases and in proposing appropriate treatments strongly suggested to Rockefeller that philanthropy itself should be, in his words, "a search for cause, an attempt to cure evils at their source."[20]

That view profoundly influenced contemporary approaches to social and economic problems. Philanthropists, researchers, and reformers uniformly adopted the metaphors of scientific medicine, speaking of social ills, expressing a reluctance merely to alleviate symptoms, and wanting to explore root causes and find cures and remedies. The parallel discovery that specific germs caused particular diseases—and the resulting possibility of prevention and cure—also led philanthropists and social researchers to think in correspondingly simple terms about cause and effect in the social sphere.

This turn from symptoms to causes, from relief to prevention, from good works to broad social investigation represented a fundamental shift in outlook. Reformers now thought less about alleviating hardship through old-fashioned individual charity than of eliminating collective ills through sustained social research. Their approach embodied an implicit argument for new ways of organizing social investigation and new kinds of research institutions that would not merely investigate the administrative problems of charitable agencies or the moral fitness and economic needs of people who sought assistance. Instead, attention needed to be paid to the broader structural and environmental causes of these problems.

New institutional arrangements for bringing together larger groups of researchers for long-term investigations began to take shape with the backing of the new general-purpose philanthropic foundations. The Carnegie Corporation (founded in 1911) and the Rockefeller Foundation (founded in 1913) brought unparalleled resources to social research, but the Russell Sage Foundation (set up in 1907) pointed the way. The Russell Sage Foundation was a novel institution, innovative in many ways but also rooted in the past. It was a link between the old world of the amateur social investigator and the emerging professional social scientists, operating comfortably in the traditional sphere of state and local policy while helping to create a national policy elite that would increasingly look to the federal government for solutions to the nation's social problems.

A Foundation for "Permanent Improvement"

Upon the death of her husband in 1906, Margaret Olivia Sage, then nearly eighty years old, became the wealthiest woman in the country—perhaps the world. She had devoted much of her life to charitable and educational work, teaching school after her graduation from the Troy Female Seminary; working for the U.S. Sanitary Commission; and serving as one of the three chief administrators, though a volunteer, of Women's Hospital in New York City. She quickly seized the opportunity to apply her vast fortune of $70 to $90 million to the many social causes that intrigued her. She gave away some $35 million in the twelve years before her death. She also cast around for a mechanism to organize some of her contributions to social welfare.

Many of her peers, including her lawyer Robert deForest, a member of an old New York family who headed New York's Charity Organization Society, had already seen the need for a well-funded national organization that would devote itself through research and writing to what the Sage Foundation's charter called "the permanent improvement of social conditions." In 1907 Mrs. Sage gave $10 million to create the foundation named (some think with more irony than affection) for her husband, a man not renowned for his charitable enthusiasms.

The Russell Sage Foundation helped shape social research, policy prescription, and public debate in the waning years of the Progressive Era, forging a new national arena for the discussion of policies.[21] In virtually every respect, the foundation, which still supports a program of social science research and publishing, was the prototypical organization for research on and the advocacy of social policies. Its goal was not knowledge for its own sake or basic social science research, but the application of research to the solution of social ills. As one adviser to the foundation put it, "I am impatient to get results from the facts already at hand" and to get further facts, that we may get more results."[22]

After unsuccessful efforts to tap university-based researchers for projects (they were chronically late with their work), the foundation assembled a cadre of researchers at an elegant, Renaissance-inspired office building in New York City. There the researchers undertook investigations through departments whose names ring quaintly of the era: Child-Helping, Child Hygiene, Recreation, Women's Work, and Charity Organization. At the outset, their links were closest to the charitable organizations operating in cities throughout the country, and their initial recommendations were aimed primarily at improving these organizations' work. Private charitable agencies could be made to operate more efficiently; charity workers could benefit from better training; books, pamphlets, and journals could be more widely distributed among reform groups; and there was much to teach the public about poverty and disease and the prevention of both.

The experts assembled by the Russell Sage Foundation—most had gained their research skills through practical experience, rather than from advanced graduate training—were eager to disseminate their findings to the public. The metaphor of prevention that shaped their self-conception demanded vigorous public education campaigns. The hundreds of pamphlets, brochures, and articles that poured from the foundation contained practical advice on feeding babies, finding jobs for expectant mothers, organizing children's dispensaries, building healthful outdoor sleeping porches, teaching games to children, and landscaping urban settings.

The foundation took on some of the most pressing concerns of the day, including child welfare, tuberculosis, and women's working conditions. It took every opportunity to link social research to public reform campaigns and, unlike many older groups, it operated with a national perspective. Its researchers collected data and made the data available to reformers across the nation. Until the 1930s, the foundation also served as a clearinghouse for state legislation and drafted model bills on such diverse subjects as loan-sharking and juvenile court systems.[23]

The foundation's most promising approach to research was honed in an early project on Pittsburgh. From time to time, New York's Charity Organization Society had sponsored writers who wanted to explore social problems outside New York. The society hired a young writer and editor, Paul U. Kellogg, to survey industrial conditions in Pittsburgh. The project, funded by the Russell Sage Foundation, lasted eighteen months and produced a six-volume study of Pittsburgh's housing, sanitation, and working conditions. Kellogg and his associates wanted a "human measure" of social conditions that would prod the government of Pittsburgh to solve the city's problems. Thus, the survey mingled quantitative data with case studies, combining a rudimentary research report with a readable journalistic narrative; it was illustrated with photographs by Lewis Hine and sketches by Joseph Stella.

Organizers of surveys in the 1910s and 1920s, particularly those engaged in general surveys of cities like the one in Pittsburgh, had a clear idea of the public role their research would play. The surveys were conceived as a collaboration between professional investigators and community leaders. They were usually conducted under the supervision of citizens' committees, church federations, chambers of commerce, or civic improvement associations. These groups then relayed the findings of the technical experts to the public who, enlightened by the facts, were expected to mobilize public opinion and press for appropriate reforms.

The actual political results seldom lived up to the organizers' expectations, however. Assessing the direct impact of his survey on Pittsburgh, Kellogg confessed that it was modest, limited to a few improvements in workers' housing. But indirectly the survey advanced various state campaigns for the passage of workmen's compensation laws.

Nevertheless, surveys patterned after Kellogg's came to be the most widely used tool of social research during the first three decades of the century, a tool that combined social research and popular education in an attempt to bring about political change. After the final volume of the *Pittsburgh Survey* was published in 1914, the foundation was inundated with requests to fund similar surveys. Eager to nourish the survey technique, but unable to finance so many projects, the foundation established a department to provide technical advice and, in general, to "foster the spirit of inquiry into local conditions by the people of localities." From 1900 to 1928, approximately 2,700 such surveys were undertaken in the United States, ranging from general citywide surveys to focused studies of education, recreation, public health, and crime.[24] Very different from the policy research of today, this early research enterprise brought together technical experts with private citizens and officials of municipal governments across the country.

Like the first generation of amateur social investigators, the new professional social scientists were mainly interested in gathering factual evidence. But they had also begun to devise standards and units of measurement that at least hinted at explanations of and cures for social ills. Cubic feet of air per person per apartment provided a measure of the healthy or unhealthy conditions in tenements. Pupil-teacher ratios indicated something about the standards of schools. The ratio of the square footage of windows to the area of a factory floor was one way to judge working conditions. In these and countless other measurements, the professionals presumed that there were causal relationships and, thus, implicit remedies for social problems. But the surveys usually explained much less than met the eye. In reality, they were less an instrument for testing hypotheses and designing reforms than for arousing a community's conscience and "quickening community forces" for reform, as one staff member of the foundation put it.[25]

The findings of most surveys in this period were published in books or summarized in pamphlets; they were widely publicized in newspaper and magazine articles and dramatized in public exhibitions that were the centerpieces of local educational campaigns. The Russell Sage Foundation provided technical assistance and spent considerable sums to design traveling exhibitions that made the rounds of state and county fairs or circulated to public libraries and schools. Specialists in graphic design and "visual education" joined the survey department to make sure that the results would be comprehended by a wide audience. Researchers were expected to address church groups and gatherings of civic-minded people. Though books were published, pamphlets proved to be the easiest way to disseminate practical information; 250 to 300 pamphlets were distributed by the foundation from 1907 to 1917.

Usually, however, the immediate benefits were few. The organizers of surveys and community leaders could claim only that the surveys had a momentary impact, alerting the public to local problems. According to an editorial writer in Topeka, Kansas, where a civic group conducted a so-called improvement survey, the project "awakened a larger and more sympathetic popular confidence in systematic and organized methods of welfare work, as well as a deeper consciousness of municipal responsibilities and capabilities, a profounder sense of the city's unity." In Springfield, Illinois, a minister concluded that in his "somewhat ultra-conservative community" the survey's value lay "not so much in what has been done, but in the spirit which it generated—in the social awakening which has taken place." The idea of the survey so captivated Illinois poet Vachel Lindsay that he volunteered to read its findings aloud at civic meetings. Afterwards, Lindsay wrote *The Golden Book of Springfield* as a dramatic commentary on the survey's data.[26]

Committed to educational and propagandistic work—many social scientists believed that their statistical research was a means to educate and arouse the conscience of docile communities—the researchers within the foundation's orbit nevertheless thought of themselves as scientific investigators. They were, as one observer put it, a "faculty of experts" comparable to that of any great university, but housed in a different kind of institution, one "that would benefit the 95 percent who do not receive a college education."[27] And indeed the foundation was a new kind of institution—a well-endowed research entity with a national perspective and a permanent body of investigators—and proved to be the most successful policy research institution in the quarter century before the Great Depression.

Mary van Kleeck was one of the foundation's most prominent "faculty" members. After graduating from Smith College in 1904, she began her career working for a settlement house in New York, where she surveyed the conditions of working women. She joined the foundation staff and in 1909 became head of its Department of Industrial Studies. She and her colleagues produced volumes of data about the wages, hours, and working conditions of women who were employed in the bookbinding and millinery trades and in the making of artificial flowers. Her work at the foundation opened the way for her participation in governmental research projects in the Department of Labor during and after World War I, and those projects ultimately led to the creation of the U.S. Women's Bureau. Though she spent her career at the foundation, her work, like that of other members of the policy elite, spanned the spheres of both public and private research. The utility of her work at the foundation spurred the government, not for the last time, to set up parallel research efforts.

More routinely, steps were being taken to make research findings useful to policymakers in state and local governments. New York's Factory Investigating Commission relied on Mary van Kleeck's survey reports along with its own data, to promote the passage of legislation in 1913 to forbid women from engaging in factory work at night. In 1914, when the commission considered introducing wage legislation, it turned again to the foundation, this time for data on the millinery industry. But while their avowed goal was to improve social conditions, researchers in this period did not view themselves as proponents of class or partisan interests. Rather, they saw themselves as facilitating democratic processes by means of competent research. According to van Kleeck, research was undertaken in the faith that the "community itself must discover its own program of action." Van Kleeck and her colleagues viewed themselves as neutral experts seeking facts that would rouse the public to intelligent action.[28]

Indeed, social science at the turn of the century took a community's values for granted and was little concerned with theories. The truths it sought were to be found in application. "Our problems should come to us from contact with life as it is lived today; from the needs and incongruities of that life," wrote Mary Richmond, head of the foundation's Charity Organization Department and the author of *Social Diagnosis*, the pioneering treatise on social work.[29] But while this early science of society was limited to dispassionate investigations of social phenomena, it nevertheless began subtly to alter the political environment in which it operated and to change its own assumptions.

Gradually, the accumulated social investigations of the reformers—undertaken through Charity Organization Societies; state Boards of Charity; governmental commissions; reform associations; settlement houses; university research institutes; and, most notably, the Russell Sage Foundation—disclosed the weaknesses of activities in the private sector. Researchers increasingly identified the fundamental causes of distress in a social environment that was not always susceptible either to charitable relief or to greater individual efforts. Ultimately, in a subtle shift of far-reaching importance, explanations of poverty, unemployment, and ill-health began to focus not on the moral failings and responsibilities of the poor nor on the deficiencies of the private institutions that sought to help them, but on the broader interplay of social phenomena.

Furthermore, although the early social scientists were still committed primarily to the idea of public education, their work created an intellectual environment that demanded yet more systematic investigations by professionally trained researchers. Their growing number and increasing specialization soon altered the ways experts interacted with one another—and with the public. As social scientists withdrew to universities or worked on regulatory and investigative commissions, the relationship between the expert and the public was transformed. Once the complexities of social and economic phenomena became apparent, social science research became more narrowly focused and less easily communicated to the ordinary citizen. And finally, as the metaphor of prevention lost its hold on social scientists, experts seemed less willing to attempt to communicate with the general public. Rather, they sought a new public role for themselves, not as doctors seeking to prevent and cure social ills, but as scientists of efficiency, experts in the techniques of institutional management.

THREE

☆

Efficiency Experts

The Gospel of Efficiency

"A city is a great business enterprise whose stockholders are the people."[1] With that terse observation, John Patterson, founder of the National Cash Register Company, summarized the view of many middle-class reformers who wanted to make city governments more efficient. Businessmen like Patterson had led civic reform efforts in the 1880s and 1890s, knowing that tangible economic benefits resulted when city governments were well run. Paved streets, urban transportation, electric lighting, harbors, and wharves were costly new amenities, but essential for a city's economic success. As cities expanded the scope of their public services in the late nineteenth century—and as the legitimacy of those functions came to be accepted—social reformers and businessmen found a common ground in their quest for more efficient municipal administration. In the early 1910s their efforts were rewarded when many cities adopted commission and council-manager forms of government.

Among social reformers in the early 1900s a new scientific metaphor competed with the metaphor of prevention: the ideal of efficiency. A notion drawn from physics, efficiency supplied a new rationale for the use of experts and redefined their participation in government, acting as a lodestar to reorient the claims of expertise in policymaking.

The passion for efficiency that took hold of this country in the first two decades of the twentieth century has been likened to "a secular Great Awakening," affecting businesses, factories, hospitals, schools, churches, homes, and every level of government.[2] The new vocabulary came into wide political currency in the 1910s and began to displace—without eliminating—the metaphor of preventive medicine as a guide for policy. The quest for efficiency motivated the founders of graduate schools of business, public administration, and social work. It also inspired the early backers of the oldest surviving policy research organizations, including the Brookings Institution, the Twentieth Century Fund, and the National Bureau of Economic Research. Soon experts, as proponents of efficiency, entered into a new relationship with both governments and citizens. They were employed at first like business consultants and then like corporate managers. Citizens—like stockholders—were expected to defer to the experts' informed decisions, passing judgment only periodically on the experts' performance.

The ideal of efficiency has always held a revered place in American life. It was, of course, an old-fashioned, Franklinesque moral virtue. Charity workers and social reformers talked about problems of organizational efficiency when they confronted the depressions of the 1870s and 1890s. But the term acquired a more rigorous meaning at the end of the nineteenth century when the newly discovered laws of thermodynamics were used to analyze the energy input–output ratio of the steam engine. Thanks to the mathematical and technical calculations of mechanical engineers, "efficiency" attained quantitative precision and began to be applied to the industrial workplace and elsewhere.

Frederick Winslow Taylor, who had toiled since the 1880s to uncover the scientific principles of managerial efficiency, was the new gospel's most famous preacher. As he stood with notepad and watch in hand, carefully observing workers at their daily tasks, he saw possibilities for making their work more rational and scientific. He wrote about the "science of shovelling" and the "law of heavy laboring," in the belief that every act of every workman could be reduced to a mechanical principle and made more efficient. His principles of scientific management were rooted in observation and experiment and motivated by the search for general laws that paralleled the laws of nature. A greater "conservation" of human effort would maximize the output of a factory or business with a minimum input of labor.

Sharing the conviction of reformers and philanthropists that science could foster harmony and cooperation in the workplace and throughout society, Taylor thought that the adoption of scientific methods of management would eliminate the causes of disputes between workers and employers. He found his answer to Karl Marx and other prophets of the class struggle not in laws of historical development or in major structural changes of the economic order but in the laws of physics as applied to every American worker, from the most menial stevedores to skilled machinists and clerical workers. According to Taylor, all work relationships could be organized more productively and the fruits of labor shared so that the interests of workers and owners would become identical.[3]

With violent labor confrontations in the streets of Lowell, Massachusetts, and the mining camps of Ludlow, Colorado, among other places, Taylor's vision of harmonious relationships appealed to many middle-class reformers. But his system required full-time planning, observation, on-the-job experiments, extensive record keeping, heavy training of the work force, and constant exhortations to sustain the pace of work. Furthermore, the experts—as planners and managers—would always be dominant in Taylor's scheme. The worker would have to give up to the expert most of the responsibility for determining how a specific task would be performed. Fully realized "efficiency" would drive the worker to the limits of physical endurance, as so comically portrayed by Charlie Chaplin racing to keep up with the relentless assembly line in *Modern Times*. But Taylor predicted that acquiescence to the judgment of experts would yield such dividends in productivity that greater harmony was bound to follow between managers and workers. Precisely how these dividends would be apportioned was not clear.

If concepts of efficiency could be applied to men, machines, and money in the business environment, it was not long before political reformers thought of adapting the concept to society and government. Reformers concluded that democratic government might be improved if it adopted more of the centralized and hierarchical traits of the modern business corporation and if better trained managers took over its administrative tasks. Expert administrators would make decisions not on the basis of patronage but according to criteria of competence and efficiency, defining the public interest in ways that elected officials, through partisan processes and back-room deals, could not. The tension between the experts' methods of defining the public interest and the politically cumbersome procedures for ascertaining it were obvious.

Although still conducting broad investigations designed to arouse and lead an enlightened citizenry toward reform, experts were simultaneously carving out a permanent place for themselves within the bureaucratic domain of government. In many cities, reform-minded citizens, usually with the backing of prominent businessmen, set up bureaus of municipal research to advance the cause of efficient government. These bureaus—sometimes private and viewed skeptically by elected officials and sometimes quasi-public and operating with the cooperation of local governments—sprang up in forty to fifty American cities. The bureaus operated locally, but most also saw themselves as striving to advance a valid general science of administration that could be applied anywhere.

Henry Bruere and William H. Allen helped organize the best known of the new agencies, the New York Bureau of Municipal Research, which was incorporated in 1907. Bruere—a student of Thorstein Veblen at the University of Chicago who had also studied political science at Columbia University and had a law degree from Harvard—was one of the new breed of social science professionals. He began his career in the personnel department of the McCormick Harvester Corporation and then moved to research positions in private reform organizations. Bruere met Allen at New York's Association for Improving the Condition of the Poor (AICP), an old-line group for research on charity and reform that was established before the Civil War. Allen, who held a Ph.D. from the University of Pennsylvania (where he had studied with the brilliantly quirky economist Simon Patten, described by another student as a "twister of the tail of the cosmos") was another of the new graduate-trained professionals. After a stint with the AICP, Bruere and Allen set about creating a research bureau that would make fuller use of the skills of professionals who were trained in social science, accounting, administration, and law and that would insulate them from politics and the vagaries of reform movements.

Breure had been psychologically crushed when Mayor Seth Low, who had rallied the city's reform elements in 1902, lost a bid for reelection in 1904 and was turned out of office after a single fruitless term. Reflecting on his experience of political defeat and the frustrating search for the "great administrator, great by instinct and personality," Bruere expressed the disillusionment felt by many reformers when he concluded that the ideal administrator "wasn't found because he doesn't exist."[4] Allen voiced similar complaints when he remarked that "almost without exception, so-called reform governments have emphasized goodness rather than efficiency." As Allen saw it, a political research bureau should depend "neither upon politics nor *average* [*sic*] public intelligence. . . . The Supreme need is for an Intelligence center that will substitute facts for calamity or scandal."[5] Some of the city's most prominent businessmen were won over by their arguments, among them John D. Rockefeller, Andrew Carnegie, J. P. Morgan, E. H. Harriman, and the banker R. Fulton Cutting.

By 1910 the New York Bureau had a staff of 46 and a then-sizable annual budget of nearly $100,000 (contributed by 64 individuals). Its researchers might be spotted standing at curbside taking notes while municipal employees filled potholes. They might be found in city offices going over ledgers or designing new forms to report on expenditures. Tammany Hall politicians were quick to dub it the "Bureau of Municipal Besmirch," but the heads of several city departments nevertheless called on the bureau for advice. Concentrating principally on budgetary and accounting methods, the bureau won acceptance among city bureaucrats and by 1911, it was running the Training School for Public Service, the first in the United States dedicated to public administration and the lineal ancestor of the Maxwell School of Citizenship and Public Affairs at Syracuse University. Its research inspired the creation of similar research bureaus across the country; even the socialists who controlled Milwaukee's city government in the 1910s set up a Bureau of Efficiency, asking John R. Commons to head it. Playing a prominent national role throughout the 1910s and 1920s, the New York Bureau was renamed the National Institute of Public Administration in 1928.

Across the country, experts working in municipal research bureaus brought methods of accounting, rudimentary cost-benefit tests, and the careful reporting of agencies' performance to city governments. But efficiency meant more to them than merely providing civil servants with green eyeshades, sharp pencils, standard voucher forms, and ledgers. It implied a fundamental change in the notion of citizenship. The New York Bureau produced hundreds of pamphlets and reports with elementary titles on impossibly complex topics— *How Manhattan Is Governed* was the first—but its principal publication between 1907 and 1913 bore the incongruous title *Efficient Citizenship*.

The bureau's staff viewed efficiency as the prerequisite for political accountability. Without criteria for judging the government's performance, citizens could not make intelligent decisions in the voting booth. An independent, nonpartisan agency, staffed by administrative experts who were not mired in political bureaucracies, clearly had a place in any well-conceived political system. Scientific expertise, as Walter Lippmann argued in *Drift and Mastery*, was needed to provide "the discipline of democracy," setting objective standards, advising agencies on new administrative techniques, and determining whether the criteria of efficiency were being met.

Experts in municipal research bureaus maintained that theirs were scientific, not political, endeavors. They sought only the facts, they asserted. But efforts to inform the public and judge the performance of governments inevitably compromised such claims. Reports on waste or fraud in a department of finance or public works had political consequences. Campaigns to create new agencies, such as a Bureau of Child Hygiene proposed for New York City, were often taken as indictments of a specific mayoral regime.[6] Administrative expertise ineluctably encroaches on political authority. Meanwhile, the efficiency experts sometimes betrayed the fact that they were as concerned with political ends as they were with administrative means. Bruere, for one, thought that progressive goals would never be attained until governments operated more efficiently, while Allen explained that the movement for efficiency in government should not be seen as "a penny-saving or penny-pinching proposition" but, rather, as "a movement to make democracy a living, vital thing, because it showed how people could get done what all the time they had really wanted to get done but didn't know how to do."[7] Allen clearly believed that the expert had sufficient insight to interpret and translate the popular will into political action.

At all levels of government, experts forged an alliance with the executive branch, vaunting the ideal of an efficient, rational administration over the chaos and confusion of the legislative process. The "efficient" citizen, the new experts claimed, would simply have to accept that the complexity of modern government demanded special training and techniques and recognize "the need for professional service in behalf of citizen interests," as Bruere ingenuously put it.[8] His ideal image of an efficient democratic society, in which independent experts would help public officials to act rationally and would guide the public to choose wisely, suggests a modern Platonic Republic, in which a special class of Guardians would be schooled in techniques of accounting, economics, and public administration. Meanwhile, with many cities striving to achieve economy and efficiency, the experts increasingly turned to Washington as the federal budget exceeded the unheard-of sum of $1 billion and the federal debt, following the Panic of 1907, attained mountainous proportions.

First Watch on Washington

Budgets obsessed the reformers. No process was more labyrinthine than the federal budget, a maze of more than two dozen congressional committees that practically invited waste and corruption. Recognizing the problem and knowledgeable about the work of urban reformers, President William Howard Taft set up the Commission on Economy and Efficiency in 1910, obtaining a $100,000 congressional appropriation to finance it. Taft knew what he wanted from the commission. He named Frederick Cleveland of the New York Bureau of Municipal Research chairman and filled the commission with other advocates of an executive-controlled budgetary process.[9]

The commission issued twenty reports on the financial and accounting practices of federal agencies, including, in 1912, a six-hundred-page volume entitled *The Need for a National Budget*. The report reflected the fiscal concerns of the moment, while retreating from the progressive social concerns that had motivated Bruere. It called for greater governmental savings and a new executive Budget Bureau that would centralize planning and allow the president to present a comprehensive budget to Congress.

Taft, who left office in 1913, did not have time to act on the proposal, and Woodrow Wilson, though avowing interest in budgetary reform, was never an enthusiastic advocate of this Republican-initiated measure, which would, in any case, encounter opposition in a Congress controlled by his own party. The proponents of budgetary reform, retreating to the New York Bureau of Municipal Research, sought to keep their ideas alive in Washington by establishing in 1916 the private Institute for Government Research, which would later be expanded and, in 1927, be renamed the Brookings Institution.

Unlike the municipal bureaus, which had depended on donations from local businessmen, the Institute for Government Research flourished thanks to the newly created philanthropic foundations. The trustees of the Rockefeller Foundation, casting around for new ventures in the early years after its establishment in 1913, briefly considered creating an Institute for Social and Economic Research modeled after the Rockefeller-financed Institute for Medical Research in New York or the Carnegie Institution in Washington. But the foundation's corporate and philanthropic activities had been under intense scrutiny for a number of years and the foundation approached the arena of public policy warily.

A series of legal battles leading to the dissolution of the Standard

Oil Trust, settled by the Supreme Court only in 1911, had exposed the inner workings of the Rockefellers' interests. The foundation, which John D. Rockefeller and his advisers had been trying to organize since 1910, was still reeling from a bitter controversy surrounding its efforts to obtain a federal charter. In 1913, the Rockefellers had attracted even more scathing criticism in the aftermath of strikes and violence in southern Colorado involving a company in which the family held a significant financial stake. The Walsh Commission on Industrial Relations heard testimony from John D. Rockefeller, Jr., and other Rockefeller associates, which further embroiled the family in public disputes.

Following so hard upon the various controversies, the Institute for Government Research was seen at first by some as a plan by the Rockefellers to turn the tables on the federal government—to investigate governmental agencies and to counter the Walsh Commission's investigations. It seemed part of a sinister web of political and economic influence woven by Rockefeller money. Indeed, Jerome D. Greene, the foundation's secretary, had been worried as he drafted the prospectus for the new research bureau in Washington. Several Rockefeller associates were involved in setting up the bureau, but Greene knew that it would have to function as a separate entity. With advice from Taft's onetime private secretary, Charles D. Norton, Greene invited a distinguished roster of American businessmen and educators to serve as trustees, confident that such a prestigious board would protect the foundation from populists who were eager to sniff out another Rockefeller conspiracy.

The sponsors of the Institute for Government Research intentionally sought to assemble a board that would represent a balance between liberal and conservative, businessman and academic, and even east and west. The trustees included such notables as the New York financier R. Fulton Cutting; Charles W. Eliot, former president of Harvard University; Eliot's successor A. Lawrence Lowell; Felix Frankfurter of Harvard Law School; Arthur Twining Hadley, president of Yale University; Mrs. E. H. Harriman, a philanthropist and member of the Walsh Commission on Industrial Relations; railroad executive James J. Hill; New York banker Frederick Strauss; Theodore Vail, president of American Telephone and Telegraph; and Charles R. Van Hise, president of the University of Wisconsin. Less prominent, but soon to take on a major role, was Robert S. Brookings, a retired St. Louis businessman who was then president of the Board of Trustees of Washington University. The institute's chairman was

Frank Goodnow, a distinguished scholar of public administration (having held the first American chair in the field at Columbia University) and president of Johns Hopkins University.

Even this group was not above attack by some politicians and journalists who labeled them the "Rockefeller Inquiry." But the allegations dissipated quickly when the institute set about its mundane tasks of advising governmental agencies on administrative routines. Such work was neither sinister nor likely to attract sustained public attention. Although Rockefeller associates like Norton and Greene maintained a close interest in the institute, they and the board sought to insulate its research program from outside control by foundations or individual funders. The prestigious board also helped to shield the Rockefeller Foundation from public attack.

The close but circumspect relationship between the Rockefeller Foundation and the Institute for Government Research set a pattern that other foundations would follow. The staff and trustees of American foundations remained leery of political controversy, and when potentially divisive social issues called for study or recommendations, they often preferred to work through intermediary organizations. Only a handful of endowed foundations, such as the Russell Sage Foundation and the Twentieth Century Fund, were set up to conduct their own research programs. For the most part, the large funders of policy research have fostered intermediary groups, using grants to create new research centers and the hundreds of private commissions and task forces that have carried out various assignments in policy research.

No less a figure than the revered Charles Eliot of Harvard was concerned about the initial relationship between the Rockefeller Foundation and the new Institute for Government Research, which seemed to him like subterfuge, a contrivance intended to give cover to the work of the foundation. Since the foundation had been involved in organizing the new Institute for Government Research and given financial support, Eliot thought that it might as well assume full responsibility for the institute by making it a department of the foundation. The foundation, he wrote, should "meet any attacks that may hereafter be made on it, itself do the good and get the good will which in time will result from it."[10]

Far from treating it as an unwelcome attempt by private interests to exert undue influence, federal agencies actively sought the new institute's assistance from the moment it moved into its temporary quarters on Connecticut Avenue. Many requests were mundane appeals for help in organizing filing systems, writing personnel manuals, or improving accounting methods. Others were for general studies on administration. In its early years, the institute focused on the narrow problems of the functional efficiency of federal agencies, rather than on the policies and goals the agencies pursued.

The institute's narrow notion of efficiency reinforced the old Wilsonian assumption that politics and administration were separable. Moreover, the hiring of university-trained and technically inclined political scientists, rather than long-time activists in the cause of good government, underscored the institute's claim that its neutral experts could serve any administration. Gradually, a network of formal and informal relationships linked the institute's staff with officials in executive agencies, a pattern that has been sustained for some seventy-five years.

The first director, William Willoughby, was a typical governmental researcher. He came from Princeton University, where he had been a professor of government, but his practical experience in government made him one of the first of Washington's "in and outers." After graduating from Johns Hopkins in 1884, he had been a statistician for the Labor Department, held various colonial posts in Puerto Rico, and worked for both the U.S. Bureau of the Census and the Taft Commission on Economy and Efficiency. Willoughby was outspoken in his dislike of partisan politics in which, he complained, greed and corruption were the norm. He thought majority government "little better than mob rule" and maintained that the qualified expert was suited not only for administration but for legislative duties. Unlike the earlier generation of social scientists, Willoughby placed little faith in an enlightened citizenry or even in broadly educated elites. Government ought to be the preserve of trained specialists, he thought, the fewer and more specialized, the better. Unlike his one-time Princeton colleague, Woodrow Wilson, Willoughby applauded the growing reliance on expert commissions for the regulation of railroads, banking, and health care and welcomed research bureaus as sources of intelligent legislative proposals.[11]

Although he preferred administrative solutions to legislative ones, Willoughby and his colleagues did not shy from opportunities to draft legislation, especially when it came to creating the long-hoped-for Bureau of the Budget. In 1919 Willoughby helped organize congressional hearings on budgetary reform, drafted a bill for the House Appropriations Committee, and lobbied hard to get the bill passed. When Wilson vetoed the act, concerned that the president did not have sufficient power to remove the comptroller general,

Willoughby went back to the drawing board. He conferred with Wilson's successor, Warren G. Harding, soon after Harding took office. Moving into the arena of public opinion, he also took the exceptional and potentially dangerous step of hiring a public relations man to seed newspapers with favorable stories and editorials.

In 1921 Harding signed the Budget and Accounting Bill, and the Institute for Government Research celebrated one of its great victories. Though it had hardly remained above the political battles surrounding budgetary reform, the institute nevertheless avowed its commitment to neutrality and to the separation of the administrative and political domains. Budgetary reform, so the institute's staff reasoned, could be considered an administrative reform. The staff saw themselves as advocates of a change in the framework within which political decisions were made, but not as partisans; they believed they were seeking to improve administrative procedures and accountability but not to shape the outcomes of policies. Their sincere belief in the Wilsonian distinction between politics and administration allowed them to lobby for administrative reform without feeling that they had overstepped the boundaries circumscribing the participation of experts in the legislative process.[12]

Mr. Brookings Goes to Washington

World War I had provided the first national test of what the experts could accomplish, and the lessons of their wartime service would be summoned up as models over the next thirty years. The jobs to be done in Washington's various emergency bureaus, from the Commission on Training Camp Activities to the Central Statistical Bureau, drew thousands of "dollar-a-year" business executives, as well as lawyers, social workers, and professors out of their ordinary spheres of activity and into the war effort. Both social workers in the orbit of the Russell Sage Foundation and university-affiliated psychologists dealt with the education, testing, and training of military recruits. Researchers studied the adaptation of women to their new roles in the work force. Economists and statisticians collected data on industrial production for the War Industries Board, on trade for the Tariff Commission, and on labor conditions for the War Labor Board. Psychologists and historians worked with journalists and advertising executives on the Committee of Public Information to whip up popular fervor for the war. Proponents of administrative efficiency from municipal research bureaus and schools of public and business administration tried to integrate the operations of the hastily created boards, commissions, and bureaus.

The experience of organizing for war was brief but intense. The experts did what the emergency called for. They set up shipping routes and schedules; tried to make the railroads run on time; inventoried the production of shoe leather, textiles, and weapons; organized songfests, baseball games, and lectures on health in training camps; watched prices; and monitored the demand for factory workers. The social scientists' contributions during World War I had little to do with theory or method and left little in the way of an institutional legacy in Washington. But their work did leave a general impression that the social sciences could be made even more useful. The war both demonstrated the weakness of the federal bureaucracy and pointed the way toward repairing those weaknesses through a greater reliance on business managers and academic social scientists. One of its most important legacies was the bringing together of businessmen and scholars.

Robert S. Brookings was among the businessmen who went to work in the hastily created wartime agencies. Already in his late sixties, white haired and with a neatly trimmed beard and mustache, Brookings sat on the War Industries Board and chaired its Price-Fixing Committee. Born in Maryland in 1850, he had made his fortune in St. Louis, moving there in 1866 to join his brother as a clerk in the firm of Cupples and Marston. He quickly became a star traveling salesman and was made a partner of the firm, which acted as an agent for manufacturers of basic household items, from woodenware, clothespins, and willow baskets to twine, paper bags, and wrapping paper. There were many households to supply west of the Mississippi, and Brookings traveled a vast territory in the 1860s and 1870s. By the time he was thirty, he had made his million. "I chased fortune and knifed my competitors," he later said, "Today they would put us in jail for the things we did then."[13]

Fighting fatigue and mental breakdown in his early forties, Brookings took a year-long break from business to travel and study the violin in Europe, where he quickly learned that his musical talents were not up to a professional level. After returning to St. Louis to battle briefly with old business rivals, he retired in 1895 at age forty-five to pursue wider interests in education and philanthropy. He helped build Washington University in St. Louis and joined Andrew Carnegie as a trustee of several organizations, including the Carnegie Endowment for International Peace, which was founded in 1910.

He had served on the Taft Economy and Efficiency Commission and was appointed to the original board of the Institute for Government Research, but not until his appointment to the War Industries Board did his interest in government truly develop.

Brookings's term of service left him with more detractors than admirers. Bernard Baruch, a fellow member, dismissed him as a "lady-like old bachelor." Another observer wrote, "Mr. Brookings is a very fine person, of high intelligence; but by universal consent, he lacks . . . speed." But the most frequent complaint of those who knew Brookings was simply that he talked too much; they described him as "fussy and tiresome" with a ceaseless flow of "pointless and commonplace remarks."[14]

Deciding to stay in Washington after the war, Brookings became chairman of the board of the Institute for Government Research in 1919. At seventy, he turned his energies to building the institution that now bears his name and that has become the model of private expertise organized for public ends. His first task was to raise enough money to secure its immediate future, which he did by again traveling the country, persuading his acquaintances that the only way to lower taxes and reduce the deficit was to make government more efficient. "He would tackle anyone for money," said a friend, "and if you had any that wasn't nailed down, Brookings would likely get it . . . he never let up on a man; and just wore people out."[15]

In 1922, Brookings approached his friend Henry Pritchett, then head of the Carnegie Corporation, with an idea for a new economics institute. Brookings had learned on the War Industries Board how little economic data governmental administrators had at hand when making decisions. Ever the businessman seeking greater efficiency, Brookings complained about the many sources of waste and friction in the economy. His new institute would assemble and interpret economic data, study the reasons for waste, and try to eliminate them. Most notably, he reflected a new view of efficiency, not as a criterion applied to the individual firm or governmental office, but as a general standard that was applicable to the overall functioning of the economy.[16]

The Carnegie Corporation contributed $1.65 million over ten years to set the new institute in motion. Convinced that economic theory was adequate (and that other institutions were engaged in advancing theoretical research), the Carnegie Corporation wanted the institute simply to apply knowledge of economics to questions of policy, ascertaining the facts and making them clear to both decision makers and the public.[17] The Institute for Government Research and the Institute of Economics shared both staff and board members, occupying offices a block from the White House on Jackson Place. Brookings looked, as he put it, for "conservatives or capitalists" (making no significant distinction) to serve on the board, and bankers were especially well represented on it. To head the new institute, the board chose Harold G. Moulton, an economist from the University of Chicago. Moulton, thirty-nine years old, had written well-received books on banking and finance and had recently completed a study on the adjustment of war debts. When Brookings met with him to discuss the new institute, Moulton was hesitant, wary of the board's business connections and the institute's philanthropic backers. He did not want to head an organization that would merely echo the amateurish enthusiasms of its founder and trustees or that might resemble the National Industrial Conference Board, a business group funded by large manufacturers whose research Moulton dismissed as partisan and predictable.[18] Moulton wanted written assurances that the staff would have full independence; the bylaws accordingly stated that the primary duty of the trustees was to make it possible for scientific work to be done, not to express their views about the research the institute would undertake.[19] Brookings, though often impatient with the pace of research, abided by the charter, deferring to Moulton and the institute's other professional economists. Soon, however, the institutions Brookings presided over faced unavoidable and novel questions about the proper advisory role of supposedly neutral research institutions operating so near the government. They also had to face perennial questions about the training and education of those who aspired to govern and advise.

Brookings was convinced that the government needed better-trained civil servants—"efficient workers," in his language—but he was not certain that the workers' training should be bound by academic disciplines. Nevertheless, in 1923, he endowed a graduate department of government and economics at Washington University, St. Louis, whose curriculum reflected his fascination with the practical problems of government. Students were required to spend time at the two Washington research institutes, under the supervision of staff members. In 1924, however, because of problems with Missouri tax laws, the graduate program had to be reincorporated as a separate entity in the District of Columbia. It was the third Washington institution chaired and sustained financially by Robert Brookings's efforts.

During its brief life—though it was officially disbanded in 1927, it continued to award degrees to students who were already enrolled until well into the 1930s—the Brookings graduate school was a highly innovative educational experiment that focused more on social and political issues than on academic training in particular disciplines. There were no formal courses, credits, or majors. Instead, students participated in seminars and were expected to work with the institutes' staffs on practical projects, which accorded with Brookings's aim of teaching students to solve contemporary problems, rather than simply transmitting accumulated knowledge.[20]

But observers and critics, including William Willoughby and some of his colleagues at the Institute for Government Research, were not impressed with the evolving curriculum. The students apparently were not interested in preparing personnel manuals, studying accounting methods, or writing administrative histories of federal agencies. They were only slightly more eager to work with the institute's economists. Instead, they flocked to hear lectures or take short seminars from visitors like Charles Beard, Johan Huizinga, and Harold Laski.

In time, friction grew between the specialists in public administration, the economists, and the teachers in the graduate program. Although the issues often seemed like petty battles over academic turf, they signaled budding disagreement over the role of the expert in government and the intellectual tools that would influence policy. The experts in public administration, inheritors of the "mugwump" and progressive disdain for partisan politics, wanted students to master accounting and public finance, expressing continued faith in scientific methods and nonpartisan expertise. The economists were exploring a broader range of issues, including the disposition of international war debts, tariff and trade policies, and agricultural policy, and were publishing books designed to guide policymakers through these complex topics.

Gradually, the notions of efficiency and nonpartisanship, which had once united progressives, began to mean different things to different people in the two research institutes. The scholars of public administration and the political scientists at the Institute for Government Research focused on questions of functional efficiency, eschewing any concern with the ends toward which governmental agencies worked. They dealt with federal retirement policies, personnel classification systems, administrative structures, and civil service examinations. Willoughby avoided making pronouncements about policies; such matters were the proper concern of elected officials, he thought. "Nonpartisanship" meant helping any elected administration efficiently pursue its chosen aims. But the economists saw ways of applying standards of efficiency to policies, evaluating alternatives in terms of the allocation of resources and opportunity costs. Policy itself might therefore be shaped by the technical considerations of experts, whose methods promised to yield criteria for decision making. Although the fault lines between these two groups could be glimpsed in the mid-1920s, the fissures did not widen until later.

In 1926, Brookings asked Harold Moulton to head a committee to study the possible merger of the graduate school, the Institute of Economics, and the Institute for Government Research; in the process, questions about the role of experts and private advisory institutions naturally came to the fore. The administrative researchers criticized the graduate school for its focus on history and theory and its neglect of applied government. Brookings complained that the granting of the doctorate brought "less mature students," most of whom wanted to teach rather than serve in government. The graduate school was "a long way in its results from the direct service I have always had in mind."[21] Without Brookings's backing, the graduate school could not survive for long.

The school's dean, Walton Hamilton, had different notions about graduate training for public service. He thought that both experts and the public had first to ask what policies ought to be carried out before turning to administrative questions. And policies, he knew, rested on political assumptions and moral choices. Hamilton defended the graduate school as "a distinctive venture" in graduate education, concerned with "the direction of national life." He advanced an even more heretical criticism of Willoughby's Institute for Government Research and the old convention of distinguishing between politics and administration. Questions of efficiency were too narrowly drawn. For Hamilton, policy, politics, and administration were inextricably intertwined. Moreover, Hamilton challenged the view held by Moulton and others that nonpartisan experts could determine the public interest. He argued that unacknowledged choices among values always lurk beneath the surface and that the policymaker therefore needed broad training in the liberal arts to learn what values were at issue and how to order them.

Hamilton's view of the proper training for public service, grounded in history, political theory, and philosophy, proved irreconcilable with the "neutral" expertise esteemed by Willoughby and Moulton.[22] In the end—over the bitter protests of faculty and students and despite public appeals and legal threats (the students sought counsel from both Oliver Wendell Holmes and Louis D. Brandeis)—

the graduate school was closed. The two research centers were merged and renamed the Brookings Institution in December 1927. Moulton became its first president, a post he would hold until the early 1950s.

Brookings and his associates envisioned a center of practical research that was to be neither a university nor an advocacy and reform organization, but a pool of disinterested experts serving the public good. The institution promised to fill a void in Washington, and although it would never become a prestigious national university capable of training public servants, as some had hoped, it has served for much of its history as an unrivaled national center for applied research in the social sciences.

Perhaps the supporters of the Brookings Institution were prescient, or perhaps developments in American academic life had already passed them by. But they saw their institution as a needed remedy to the emerging patterns of "educational specialization" that were already afflicting the universities, rendering social science "increasingly impotent in the service of society."[23] Thus, the paths of academic and applied policy research, though parallel, began to move farther apart. While the institution made solid contributions to the understanding of vexing public issues in the late 1920s, intellectual developments in the social sciences were increasingly focused in universities.

The Brookings Institution had begun as an effort to make federal agencies more efficient. Over the years, it has kept a steady eye on budgetary and tax policies, international trade and economic issues, agencies for international cooperation, and the conditions of federal employees. Throughout, it has continued to pose questions about the efficiency of government and the economy. Indeed, the language of efficiency still undergirds debates about policy, shaping the questions that are asked about political institutions, the allocation of resources, and the success or failure of governmental programs. In many respects, American public policy is a mere gloss on the changing concept of efficiency. But shifting definitions of expertise reflect the changing analytic skills that give "efficiency" its meanings, and no discipline has done more over the past sixty years to define and redefine the notion of "efficiency" than has economics.

The Economists' Laboratory

Wesley C. Mitchell was one of those who entered governmental service during World War I. "Sworn in—part time $300 per month," he noted tersely in his diary in early 1918. At forty-four, Mitchell, already one of the nation's most influential economists, had written books on monetary theory, prices, and the business cycle. A colleague would later describe him as "the most representative economist of the first half of the twentieth century" and said he was "symbolic of the ushering in of the age of research in the social sciences."[24] If an institution is the lengthened shadow of a man, the National Bureau of Economic Research, set up in 1920, was Wesley Mitchell's. Its evolution exemplifies the maturation and increasingly problematic use of social science expertise by those in government, and it illustrates the growing schism between researchers who emphasized theory and method and those who wanted timely policy-relevant results.

Mitchell had been in the University of Chicago's first entering class in 1892. Torn between economics and philosophy, he studied with the leading lights of both departments: Thorstein Veblen (his lectures were like "vivisection without an anaesthetic," Mitchell wrote), J. Laurence Laughlin, John Dewey, and George Herbert Meade. In four decades of teaching and writing at the University of California at Berkeley, the New School for Social Research (which he helped found), and Columbia University, Mitchell sought to make economics a matter of close statistical work and to bring both quantitive and theoretical rigor to the study of business cycles. It was the patient accumulation of facts that drove his work.[25]

In Washington during World War I, Mitchell worked within the orbit of the War Industries Board, serving as chief of the Price Section and writing memos on such arcane subjects as the availability of canned meats, manganese, and New Zealand lamb skins. Frustrated by the lack of statistical data and reduced, as he put it, to "tall guessing," he and a wartime associate, Edwin F. Gay of Harvard's decade-old School of Business, worked to set up a comprehensive statistical agency. By early summer 1918, the newly formed Central Bureau of Planning and Statistics, under Gay's direction, became the federal clearinghouse for economic data. Mitchell hoped it would become a permanent agency for economic planning and coordination, but he and Gay were unable to prevent President Wilson from abolishing it, along with the other temporary wartime agencies.

For Mitchell and other economists, the war experience revealed how vast the productive capacities of the U.S. economy were. But although the government's wartime interventions in the economy had worked in the heat of crisis, they had also exposed how inadequate knowledge of the national economy was and how essential better

statistical data were for sound planning and efficient economic management. The war experience convinced Mitchell and others that economic statistics could lead to "the guidance of public policy by
quantitative knowledge of social fact." Moreover, in the face of revolutions in Europe and a "red scare" at home, social science seemed
to offer a framework for gradual reform and social peace. Even before
the war, Mitchell had expressed mild irritation with amateurs, the
charity organizers and social workers, who "putter with philanthropy
and coquette with reform" but act without understanding the causal
connections among social phenomena.[26]

As he watched the veterans come home and the economy return
to peacetime production, he was troubled that social change would
once again proceed fitfully as a result of class strife and political
agitation. The fragile wartime cooperation between management and
labor might shatter, returning the nation to the divisiveness and
violence typified by the prewar strikes. "Are we not intelligent
enough," Mitchell asked rhetorically, "to devise a steadier and more
certain method of progress?"[27] Mitchell foresaw that economists would
deal not with mere institutional reform but with broader social and
economic planning.

Despite their conviction that it could be of service to society,
Mitchell and other economists—unlike the amateurs of the late nineteenth century—did not believe that social science could offer immediate solutions to specific social ills. Wartime service taught them that
they could help make the economy work better, although the bout
with postwar inflation also revealed how limited their intellectual
tools were. The social sciences now seemed to promise something
less than instant cures and remedies, yet something more than mere
efficiency. If social scientists were ever to live up to their promise
as scientists, they would have to improve their methods. One day,
perhaps, social science could guide human progress, making social
change a matter of technique, rather than a grudging response to
upheaval—but not yet.

Mitchell and other social scientists knew how young their disciplines were and how little they understood social and economic processes. The best of them were cautious about their scientific claims;
Mitchell worried that social science might turn out to be closer to
metaphysics or theology than to mechanics or chemistry.[28] When
the war ended, he and Edwin Gay wondered whether economics
could ever become a true science, and Gay mused that it could
take "fifteen or twenty generations" of hard work and perhaps five

hundred years of statistical studies "before the base line is long enough to make statistical deductions from social measurements."[29]

But if social scientists aspired to the precision and mathematical rigor of the physical sciences, what did they have to offer to those who were confronting practical questions? What kind of policy advisers could they be? Mitchell explicitly retreated from the metaphor of "cures," saying that social scientists had not done enough laboratory work to equal that of medical researchers. But he still believed that even elementary research could be useful. His tempered wisdom is instructive. Even without understanding all the causal interconnections underlying the performance of the economy or social behavior, he believed that social scientists could measure changes as well as observe events with sufficient acuity to begin to grasp the connections. Disciplined observation and reporting, even if they could not promise immediate solutions, could improve the decisions of governmental officials. Mitchell's efforts called for a new kind of research institution—one that would collect the data that the government did not have at hand and whose empirical investigations would yield both theoretical insights into the economy and practical, albeit tentative, guidelines for policymaking.

The idea for a bureau of economic research had been discussed in academic, business, and philanthropic circles for a number of years. Malcolm Rorty, an engineer and statistician who worked for American Telephone and Telegraph, where he prepared monthly surveys of business conditions, talked with a number of people, including Mitchell, about such a national bureau during World War I. Like other observers of economic trends, Rorty was worried about the unequal distribution of income in the United States. Industrial conflict could not be resolved and a degree of social harmony restored, he thought, until reliable data on the nation's income and its distribution had been gathered. In 1916, he discussed the problem of income distribution with his friend, Nahum I. Stone. "Here we are considering a most important question which deeply affects the lives of every man, woman, and child in this country," Rorty remarked, "and despite a large fund of statistical data, there is no agreement on the purely arithmetical question of what part of the national income goes to each element of society. Would it not be a great step forward if we had an organization that devoted itself to fact finding on controversial economic subjects of great public interest?"[30]

Rorty and Stone agreed that such an organization would have to represent all schools of economic thought, "from extreme conservative to extreme radical," and include representatives of all the country's major organized interests. The founders of the National Bureau of Economic Research thus enlisted representatives from various constituencies, and from the beginning, they avoided making specific recommendations on policies. Their aim, echoing the long-standing faith that factual evidence could be separated from value judgments, was simply to establish an objective ground on which reasonable people could begin to discuss the alternate courses of action. The bureau would not take the next step of recommending what that action should be.

Nonetheless, the bureau's founders did not think that even the most honest and self-critical researchers could ever transcend their biases, since "no such creature as a perfectly impartial man" seemed to exist.[31] Thus, they established a collective review apparatus. Manuscripts were submitted for comment, and if critical views could not be accommodated in a revision, dissenting directors were allowed to publish their opinions. The aim was an institution that would produce disinterested research and begin to foster a consensus on policies. According to Mitchell, the bureau sought to raise the discussion of policy to a higher level, replacing subjective impressions with objective facts, teaching those with divergent opinions that they could agree, and thereby contributing to the "working methods of intelligent democracy."[32]

The business cycle was a subject of urgent concern in the wake of the recession that had begun in 1920. It was also the field in which Mitchell had earned his scholarly reputation with his pioneering 1913 work, *Business Cycles*. Mitchell now envisioned a statistical study of these processes that would chart the fluctuations of factory production, orders for goods, hirings and firings, demand for credit, capital expenditures, repayment of loans, and all the other complex interactions that make up the episodic rise and fall of the economy. Though Mitchell and his colleagues were reluctant to draw either theoretical or practical conclusions from their work, the data they assembled promised to supply a conceptual framework that others would find useful in approaching the tasks of economic management.[33]

The practical promise of economics was great. Some observers began to envision a "New Era," as the decade of the 1920s has been termed. Economic management was at the core of the New Era—and it depended upon the empirical investigations of the economists, the speedy communication of data, and the cooperative response of business managers and public officials. The belief that the economy could be manipulated, rather than left to the blind operations of immutable economic laws, bolstered the already-robust empiricism of American social science. Facts, in the form of economic statistics, could help business executives time their capital investments or purchases of inventory and governmental officials schedule expenditures for public works. And both business and political leaders would work together to temper the business cycle. But strong links between empirical research and action on economic policies had yet to be forged.

Herbert Hoover and the Policy Connection

Finding a way to transform economic data into policy was not Wesley C. Mitchell's central concern in organizing the National Bureau of Economic Research. But Herbert Hoover, who became secretary of commerce in 1921, did begin a decade-long experiment with ways of making the connection between research and policy, and throughout his tenure at the Commerce Department and later as president, he constantly asserted that the nation badly needed better data and a deeper understanding of the economic cycle. Hoover's views reflected a basic consensus among enlightened business leaders, economists, and philanthropists. These people had begun to see the business cycle and irregular employment not as inevitable features of capitalism—one the result of natural processes of overproduction, the other providing a necessary pool of surplus labor—but as aberrations. They were signs of economic waste and inefficiency.

Ideas now converged in several fields of social science. Eliminating waste and improving production were goals upon which social workers, reformers, business managers, engineers, academics, and governmental researchers could agree. Mary van Kleeck and her colleagues at the Russell Sage Foundation had shown, in studies of particular industries, that poverty and poor working conditions were a consequence of irregular and unstable employment. And economists like Mitchell who had studied business cycles came to see the rise and fall of the economy as a sequence of events that might be predicted and stabilized by well-timed adjustments.[34]

But social scientists were much less certain about what instruments could make the national economy work more efficiently. World War I had left no clear lessons about the government's role in this respect. Bernard Baruch, the courtly chairman of the War Industries Board and an elder statesman of high finance, believed the war had

forced a shelving of outmoded laissez-faire traditions.[35] Most businessmen were not willing to be directed by the government, despite its
recent success in mobilizing the nation's productive capabilities. If
any lesson could be drawn from the brief wartime planning experience,
it would tend to reinforce a conviction that only voluntary cooperation
among business, government, and labor—based on persuasion—could
make the economy function smoothly. Historian Ellis Hawley describes this cooperative pattern as an "associative state," with private
groups, not the federal government, at the center of policymaking
activities.[36]

The war experience held out the prospect of establishing a
uniquely American way of managing the economy and confronting social problems. An approach grounded in voluntary cooperation would
be neither as anarchic as laissez-faire competitiveness nor as stifling
of individual freedoms as collectivism and statism, the insidious European tendencies that troubled many Americans. Few Americans took
the lessons of wartime planning and voluntary cooperation more to
heart than did Herbert Hoover. As secretary of commerce from 1921
to 1929 and then as president, Hoover systematically worked to build
a cooperative commonwealth rooted in social science expertise. He
did so by summoning experts to participate in commissions, committees, and conferences. In his first months at the Commerce Department, during the 1921 recession, Hoover convened the Conference
on Unemployment; at the end of his presidency, he released the
massive report of his Research Committee on Social Trends. In all,
he assembled 30-odd conferences and commissions during his term
as president, on such topics as education, housing, public lands, oil
conservation, law enforcement, and waste. Many of the conferences
were huge collaborative research efforts. The White House Conference on Health and the Protection of Children alone included 2,500
delegates and issued 35 volumes of research.

Hoover believed that an enlightened individualism, less selfish
and more aware of long-term, cooperative goals, could be awakened
through education, publicity, and persuasion. The academic working
groups were a fundamental instrument of his vision of a harmonious,
smoothly working capitalist system—a rational republic. According
to Hoover, expert commissions would assess scientific information
and come to an agreement on how to resolve specific problems,
insulated from pressure from the public. The commissions' reports
would be used to shape public opinion and to mobilize support for
the policies that would emerge from quiet, dispassionate deliberation.

Private philanthropic foundations typically put up the money for the projects (Hoover was a shrewd and adept fund-raiser), and most of the experts conducted their research through private research institutions and universities.

Hoover was more optimistic about the uses of expertise than were many of the experts he tapped. When he assembled his Conference on Unemployment, the nation faced the immediate problems of emergency relief and the creation of jobs, but Hoover's real goal was to develop means for averting cyclical economic disruptions.[37] When the conference set up its first research committee, it called on the National Bureau of Economic Research (NBER) to study the 1921 depression and to evaluate various proposals for reducing unemployment. NBER completed its report within the allotted six months. But Wesley Mitchell and his staff were sorely troubled by the haste demanded of them. Mitchell complained that his staff stopped its work only because a deadline had been reached, not because the investigations had been completed.[38] His innate scientific caution was at odds with political urgency, and, in Mitchell's view, the standards of a nascent social science had been jeopardized by an imprudent emphasis on timeliness.

Nevertheless, the hopes vested in social science as a tool of "fact-based" policymaking remained high throughout the 1920s. Hoover relied on his commissions to mobilize the experts' intelligence and publicized the commissions' findings with the hope that voluntary cooperation could be won so the government would not have to legislate solutions. As long as the experts could fashion a consensus, he believed, the American economy would regulate itself and the scope of governmental activity would not widen.

In 1927, in the midst of a minor recession, Hoover again approached the New York foundations, this time with plans for a study of the economy. The resulting Committee on Recent Economic Changes assembled much the same cast as the earlier Conference on Unemployment and again relied on financing from private foundations and the work of private research groups. The NBER played the leading role once more, but several dozen universities assisted, along with governmental agencies and business, professional, and labor organizations. Issuing its report in early 1929, the committee applauded what appeared to all as a decade of progress in economic management.[39] Businesses seemed capable of smoothing out seasonal and other minor economic fluctuations, and there was little reason to doubt that statistical knowledge and intelligent cooperation had begun to give the nation considerable control over its economic life. The great stock market crash of the autumn and the ensuing depression quickly reduced this optimistic report to an ironic commentary on the exuberance and confidence of the 1920s. But Hoover's faith in social science was unshaken.

As president, Hoover expanded the techniques of research and policy formulation he had employed as secretary of commerce, and in late summer 1929, he assigned one of his staff members, French Strother, to organize a huge survey of national trends. The president initiated the idea and met privately with many of the people he wanted to enlist, including executives of the Rockefeller Foundation whom he asked to fund the project. Meanwhile, whatever reservations Mitchell and other social scientists might have had about joining another of Hoover's committees, they would not miss the opportunity to enhance their standing as policy advisers.[40] Hoover envisioned the committee's work as "the first thorough statement of social fact ever presented as a guide to public policy," and he fully expected the report to shape the policies of his second term. Enthusiastic about research, Hoover did not expect the federal government to have to pay for it. In the end, he obtained over half a million dollars from the Rockefeller Foundation to support his survey.[41]

An old-school progressive who was more deeply committed to rationally plotted social change than were most of his experts, Hoover saw science as the antidote to the unsettling excesses of democratic politics. Although he was forthright in expressing his conviction that science could temper popular passions, what Hoover did not reckon with were the depth and hardships of the Great Depression and, almost as intractable, the perplexing politics of social science research. The new professionalism of university-based research and the growing concern with technique and method in the 1920s had placed an intellectual wedge between many academic social scientists and those like Hoover who still saw science as the "cure" for partisan politics and a useful tool for government. Notably, the social scientists who gathered and presented the facts for Hoover's Research Committee on Social Trends often did so with greater interest in the abstract problems of data collection and theory building than in what those facts revealed about social and economic problems.[42]

The committee's 1,500-page report was front-page news on its release in January 1933. While the basic work of fact-finding was praised by many reviewers, considerable hostility was directed toward technocrats and planners. To the editorial writers of the *Richmond*

Times Dispatch, the report was a rational guide for avoiding a social and economic revolution. The *Cleveland Plain Dealer* thought the report would correct "haphazard groping" and supply "a textbook of facts for immediate practical guidance." For the *Washington Post,* however, the report proposed nothing less than socialism as a remedy to the economic crisis; others also saw frightening ideological overtones in what was described as "an essay on technocracy" mixed with "Communist doctrine . . . the lamentations of Jeremiah . . . and a dash of the book of Job." To other journalists and editors, it was "Alice-in-Wonderland nonsense" or even the "work of the Anti-Christ." The typical reactions, however, were more restrained. The report was seen as comprehensive, analytic, and unbiased, but not likely to have much impact.[43]

Among its more attentive readers was Adolf A. Berle, a professor of law at Columbia University and coauthor of an influential study of wealth and corporate power in America, *The Modern Corporation and Private Property.* Berle, who had signed on as a campaign adviser to Franklin D. Roosevelt in spring 1932, became a central figure in Roosevelt's so-called Brains Trust. He observed that the report was characterized by the "barrenness of quantitative theory and statistical measurement." It described what was happening in the society but made no attempt, Berle complained, to answer the question of whether the depression had to continue. Berle concluded that the academic community had failed to draw out the consequences of the data and that the desire for objectivity had been carried to excess. The report's authors had simply not used their research to point the way out of the depression. In the end, the report would require a "master" to turn it into a "serviceable tool."[44]

Berle's commentary on Hoover's academic research enterprise hinted at the new, more active role the expert was about to play in the New Deal. Indeed, the depression was a watershed for social scientists. The confidence of the 1920s—and the shared assumptions about the framework of policymaking—gave way to perplexity about the policies that would lead the country out of the depression and about the experts' public role.

The experts could not agree on a diagnosis, much to the frustration even of those who had been involved in Hoover's study of social trends. Edward E. Hunt, the committee's executive secretary, thought the report evaded the entire tragedy of the depression, complaining that he had to wade through fifty pages before the depression was even acknowledged. "If the economic and social system is sound," he said, "let the Committee say so in the first sentence. If it is unstable, let the Committee say so . . . let the Committee stake out its claim in the first paragraph and say 'thou ailest here and here.' "[45]

The report's "barren" uselessness exposed how wide the gap still was between knowledge and its applications to policy, and, indeed, the gap widened as the economic troubles worsened. The social and economic systems were afflicted, it seemed, by something more serious than mere inefficiency. And the experts' accumulations of data did not offer either clear remedies or a framework for discussing whether the system needed to be repaired or more fundamentally restructured. In moments of crisis when systemic flaws are revealed, the experts' long-standing explanations are inevitably exposed as deficient. The value of their knowledge is questioned. But in times of crisis, experts also find opportunities to test new insights and hypotheses. Marginal intellectuals may move to center stage; debates among experts intensify. And, as in every crisis, the opportunities for public service expand when political leaders, who have grown dependent on the analyses of experts, draw on wider circles for advice. Backing Roosevelt in 1932, though with deep reservations about so "amiable and impressionable a man," Walter Lippmann worried "that almost everything depends upon the character of his advisers."[46] Indeed, experts soon put their mark on the New Deal.

FOUR

Experts Advising

Trust in Brains

Franklin D. Roosevelt often unnerved and confounded the experts who advised him. He was intellectually inconsistent, embraced contradictory ideas, and held to a "try anything" philosophy that frustrated anyone of determined policy views. He preferred talk and debate to reports and memorandums, and the circle of those who had access to him was always wide and informal. Nearly a hundred people could gain entrance to his office, which no doubt accounted for some of the intellectual excitement that many felt in Washington. As H. G. Wells observed of him in 1934, "He is, as it were, a ganglion for reception, expression, transmission, combination, and realization, which I take it, is exactly what a modern government ought to be."[1]

Roosevelt clearly delighted in playing his advisers off against each other, using their disputes as a means of screening and developing policy ideas while retaining control of what truly mattered—the political power to decide. Lavishing abundant personal charm on the people who counseled him, he evinced their highest loyalty and effort. But even as he drew fresh hordes of experts and intellectuals to Washington and engaged them in new ways in government, he constantly kept them off balance.

Rexford G. Tugwell described a meeting with Roosevelt during the early stages of the presidential campaign in 1932. Sounding more like a love-struck teenager than a forty-year-old professor of economics, Tugwell said, "I was taken out of myself . . . meeting him was somewhat like coming in contact with destiny itself. It was a tremendous unnerving experience, only to be realized and assimilated over a long time."[2] During the campaign, Tugwell, together with Adolf A. Berle and Raymond Moley, became charter members of the Brains Trust ("brain trust" in later usage), a group set up when Samuel Rosenman (the shrewd lawyer and judge who advised Roosevelt when he was governor of New York) realized that he and their long-time associate, the old politico Louis Howe, needed intellectual help for the campaign.

Rosenman called on Moley, then in his mid-forties and a specialist in criminal justice at Columbia University who had served on the New York State Commission on the Administration of Justice, to coach the candidate on the issues. Moley, drawn into politics as a follower of Henry George and Cleveland's reform mayor Tom Johnson, idolized Woodrow Wilson and thought he could follow Wilson's route from academia to politics. After teaching in Ohio, he became director of the Cleveland Foundation and, in time, moved on to Columbia.

Moley brought with him his colleagues from Columbia: Tugwell, an expert on agricultural policy, and Berle, a specialist in corporate law and finance. Rosenman turned to these professors as something of a last resort, having concluded that members of the business community and other national leaders had produced no promising proposals for dealing with the depression. The professors, he thought, "wouldn't be afraid to strike out on new paths just because the paths are new."[3] The core Brains Trusters, assembled during the early months of the campaign, were soon augmented by a cluster of experienced political advisers.

People with ideas about policies generally find an opening in the early moments of a campaign: Arthur Laffer's "supply-side" economics was incubated and hatched in the 1980 Reagan campaign, and even Woodrow Wilson was receptive to help during his campaign. Candidates are usually like eager pupils cramming for final exams. They must develop cogent and appealing proposals for policies in areas they might never have contemplated, and it is during the campaign that these ideas are generally given their most coherent formulation by advisers who do not need to weigh bureaucratic interests or the immediate prospects of legislative compromise.

The economic crisis of the early 1930s presented an unparalleled opportunity for experts to peddle solutions. In spring and summer 1932, Roosevelt's discussions with his academic advisers touched on many of the programs that would take shape in the first hundred days of his administration. And there was considerable competition to win the candidate's ear, with Moley jealously guarding his access. Proposals for responding to the depression—the relief program; the public works projects; higher corporate and individual taxes; and the regulation of public utilities, banking, and the securities industry—were all laid out in broad terms by the professors. Conceding that some of the New Deal legislation was impromptu, Tugwell still maintained that virtually all the important ideas had been discussed at length during the campaign. Indeed, the professorial adviser, though charmed by his imposing student, saw his role as a political Pygmalion, transforming the "well-informed amateur" who thought of policy in "oversimple" ways into a formidable candidate of "all-around competence" on the issues. Moley was similarly pleased with the experts' impact on the president's thinking, remaining convinced that the general framework for the relief and recovery programs of 1933, as well as for later legislation, including the Social Security Act of 1935 and the Fair Labor Standards Act of 1937, had been devised in planning sessions at the governor's mansion and in the ensuing months of transition.

Roosevelt was an odd pupil for the professors, however, and as the 1932 campaign reached its climax, Tugwell learned some of the pitfalls of campaign advising. Roosevelt was not especially interested in intellectual abstractions and seemed to detest economic theorizing (John Maynard Keynes would also comment on his paltry understanding of economics). Tugwell recalled that the advisers were "uneasy" about Roosevelt's policy inconsistencies despite the best efforts of his experts. Late in the campaign, the candidate promised a 25 percent reduction in governmental expenditures, while remaining committed to a costly program of relief for the unemployed. "This was about as contradictory as it was possible to be," wrote Tugwell.[4] The advisers knew that the economic figures simply could not be made to support both positions. It was not the last time Roosevelt would shock their academic sensibilities and it foreshadowed the selective way he would use their advice, guided not so much by his advisers as by his political instincts. On one occasion, when Moley presented two radically different options and Roosevelt could not choose between them, Roosevelt simply instructed him to weave the two together.

Roosevelt, wrote Moley, "loves the stimulation of unorthodox ideas." He seemed particularly drawn to Tugwell, who was adept at explaining economic issues to the president, especially complex ideas about agricultural policy. Tugwell's "range of interest provided [Roosevelt with] a sort of intellectual cocktail." Roosevelt himself offered one of the most telling comments on his Brains Trust. Knowing that the description of an advisory trust was politically loaded, he remarked to Berle that he had no Brains Trust but, rather, "trusted in brains."[5]

In the end, the Brains Trust was short-lived, but the term stuck as a symbol of Roosevelt's receptiveness to new ideas. It certainly captured something about the president and his unusual appeal, both to peddlers of political nostrums and to serious academics and intellectuals. The term also captured the skeptical public attitude toward the professors, as a "trust" with the potential to monopolize ideas, as well as to control the president. Indeed, Moley, the first of the members to write of his role as a member of the trust, did much to portray Roosevelt as a creature of his advisers.

What Roosevelt sensed in 1932 was a national eagerness, born of desperation, for new ideas, caring not for their consistency, but only their success. As he said in a famous and revealing campaign speech at Oglethorpe University in Atlanta (written, curiously, not by one of the Brains Trust but by a journalist, Ernest K. Lindley, who was covering the campaign): "The country needs and, unless I mistake its temper, the country demands bold, persistent experimentation. It is common sense to take a method and try it; if it fails, admit it frankly and try another. But above all, try something."[6] Necessarily, he reached out to the experts for something to try. But Roosevelt's experimental impulse had little to do with science and everything to do with the exigencies of taking action at a moment of unprecedented national crisis. The contrast with Hoover was clear. Hoover, the engineer, was so deeply committed to scientific methods of fact-finding and deliberation that he could not act until the evidence was in hand. Roosevelt, though his language was sometimes that of the experimental scientist, was not testing methods, but striving for results.

Roosevelt's proclivity to act was immediately apparent to people in Washington and had a profound effect even on those outside his immediate circle. "I had lived in a world in which, for practical purposes, there appeared to be no government, in which there was an almost demoralized people who had the feeling that there was no one to whom they could turn," recalled Milton Katz, then a lawyer at the Reconstruction Finance Corporation and later on the faculty of Harvard University. With Roosevelt's arrival, he said, the change was "virtually physical."[7] Washington became a magnet. Indeed, Felix Frankfurter thought the most significant early achievement of Roosevelt's administration was that it "stirred the imagination of younger people of the adventure of, and the durable satisfactions to be derived from, public service."[8] Among those so inspired were two of Frankfurter's students at Harvard: Benjamin Cohen and Thomas Corcoran, who drafted the legislation regulating securities, the stock market, and holding companies.

The clarion calls for "action and action now" and for "bold, persistent experimentation" were a boon for experts. But it is misleading to look at the Brains Trust or Frankfurter's students and see experts in the 1930s primarily as originators of ideas or intimate advisers of the president. A number of them were, indeed, political participants, devising political strategies and programs, drafting bills, and writing speeches. But of the thousands of experts who came to Washington in the 1930s, most would serve as administrators of programs, rather than as developers of innovative policies. In 1933, however, there was still something insecure about the role the experts would play; no one quite knew as yet where to put them.

Doctors of the New Deal

Although many experts had served Roosevelt during the campaign, it was not obvious whether he would have any use for them after the election. Even his closest campaign advisers did not know where they might land. Louis Howe, never comfortable with the professors, hoped and expected that they would finish their political sojourn and go back to their universities after the transition. Raymond Moley told Roosevelt on more than one occasion that he did not want a job in the administration. Saying that he preferred university life, Adolf A. Berle returned to New York, though he did find time to help with legislation during the Hundred Days and was later given other political assignments. Tugwell assumed the position of assistant secretary (later under secretary) of agriculture and survived four difficult years in that department. In short, Roosevelt's Brains Trust was powerfully symbolic—but only symbolic—of the changes then reshaping the public role of the policy expert.

One reason for the dispersal of the Brains Trust was simply that in 1933 there were no obvious places for them to serve. No formal advisory structure existed within the White House, nor was there much of an administrative apparatus to assist the president.

Indeed, Herbert Hoover had caused a small sensation by doubling his senior administrative staff from two to four, making use of two military aides and as many as forty typists and clerks. Roosevelt entered office with the authority to appoint an administrative assistant and three secretaries (Howe filled one job, Stephen Early was appointed press secretary, and Marvin McIntyre was named appointments secretary). The posts were reserved, as their titles suggest, for the day-to-day needs of the White House, not for planning policies.

Roosevelt had litle choice but to find positions for his experts in cabinet departments. Though Moley was his closest policy adviser, the president chose not to make him an administrative assistant for fear of upsetting Howe. Moley finally (and reluctantly by his account) accepted a position as assistant secretary of state, but with the clear understanding that he would work directly with the president in developing policies. Moley lasted only six months in the job, but during that time, he was a highly visible figure, at the center of almost every legislative proposal. He was the "one-man reception committee" through whom all policy ideas had to pass, according to a *Newsweek* article. He worked as a liaison with Congress and recruited the legislative draftsmen who prepared the relief-and-recovery program.

The awkward incongruity of an assistant secretary of state serving as a White House aide quickly undid Moley. Internal policy disputes and an impolitic memorandum at the London economic conference were politically fatal to the first Brains Truster. When the president had to choose between his politically prominent Secretary of State, Cordell Hull, and the professor who was nominally his assistant, he sided with Hull. Moley, the adviser with a broad intellectual portfolio but no political base, was expendable and knew it. When the opportunity presented itself, he moved on to publish a news magazine, *Today*. In time, he became one of the sharpest critics of the New Deal.

But other experts had been at work in Washington long before Roosevelt's arrival. The Brookings Institution had moved to a new and larger building on Jackson Place, and Harold G. Moulton, president of Brookings, was eager to help the incoming administration. During the transition period, Brookings volunteered its services. The offer had little chance of being rebuffed, since Frederick Delano, the chairman of the board of Brookings and a major figure in city and regional planning circles, was also Roosevelt's uncle. Roosevelt was known to have an interest in administrative and budgetary matters, and Brookings was the logical place for a new president who had promised a program of governmental economy during the campaign to look for advice. In the rush to draft recovery legislation, the Brookings staff were also enlisted, though they ultimately broke with the administration over price-setting provisions in the version of the National Industrial Recovery Act that was finally passed. They soon became one of the most recalcitrant centers of opposition to the New Deal.

During the legislative rush of 1933, the demand for knowledgeable researchers was virtually insatiable. Staff members of the Russell Sage Foundation and the National Bureau of Economic Research (NBER) were lured to Washington to serve in emergency agencies, where they helped devise data-gathering procedures and monitored new programs. Economists from NBER helped devise economic statistics for the Commerce Department, with Simon Kuznets taking the lead in setting up a federal system of national income accounting. The researchers from Russell Sage studied the programs of the Federal Emergency Relief Administration and examined the Works Progress Administration and the evolution of labor policy under both the short-lived National Recovery Administration and the later National Labor Relations Board.

Although it had initially been difficult to find official positions for the president's key intellectuals, new legislation soon created thousands of jobs for social scientists. Unlike the positions their predecessors had filled in the hastily built and quickly dismantled wartime bureaucracy, many who came to Washington in the 1930s were willing to stay. By 1938, with most of the New Deal programs in place, the Civil Service Commission counted roughly 7,800 social scientists working in the federal government, over 5,000 of them economists. There was excitement and satisfaction in joining the lengthening roster of professionals at work in the alphabet soup of acronymic federal agencies, from the AAA (Agricultural Adjustment Administration) to the WPA (Works Progress Administration). Ambition led talented young people to Wall Street in the 1920s, but it took them to Washington in the 1930s.[9] And as federal programs expanded, experts were increasingly employed in collecting data and monitoring and administering programs. Interest in research in its own right or as a tool of planning varied from agency to agency. The Social Security Administration was one of many new places where economists, statisticians, and demographers could be found. There, the staff was able to do research that private agencies could not, collecting social and economic data on a huge scale, analyzing programs, and looking at the long-term needs of the elderly, children, and the disabled. Research in older federal agencies like the Bureau of Agricultural Economics, the Children's Bureau, and the Women's Bureau also acquired new impetus.

Most experts served in the burgeoning bureaucracy, but many were closely identified with the formulation of policies. Experts operated much closer to the policy process under Roosevelt than was possible in Herbert Hoover's time. Hoover had conscientiously kept his experts at a distance from executive decision making, setting up various commissions and conferences through which they might advise. Roosevelt drew highly visible experts directly into the government and its political and deliberative processes.

The new roles were sometimes dangerous. Experts, no longer functioning behind the scenes, could become embroiled in political controversies. Tugwell's position as assistant secretary of agriculture and later as undersecretary and director of the Resettlement Administration gave him opportunities to work on farm-recovery legislation, soil conservation, and food-and-drug legislation and to administer a program designed to relocate fifteen thousand poor farm families onto land owned by the government. He was publicly identified with specific bills, especially a 1933 bill to reform the Food and Drug Act that set stricter standards for the labeling and advertising of drugs. The press unofficially dubbed it the Tugwell Act. The controversial bill turned him into one of the chief whipping boys for anti-Roosevelt business groups that were skeptical of the New Deal. By 1936 Hearst papers were denouncing the "Tugwell Bolsheviks" around the president, and the Saturday Evening Post portrayed Tugwell as the chief instigator of what it termed the president's "class-hate and anti-business policies." In effect, the modern expert had assumed another role, often played by courtiers and advisers in earlier times, of deflecting criticism from political leaders.

The presence of the experts soon affected the intellectual framework of deliberation about policy. Often lines of disagreement followed academic rifts in the advisers' professional background and training. There were many such splits, but none so well known (and by now overemphasized) as those between the economic planners, who were comfortable with a degree of corporate concentration, and those who feared "the curse of bigness" and sought to restore free-market competition. Tugwell, an institutional economist who had studied with Simon Patten and Scott Nearing at the University of Pennsylvania and who was profoundly influenced by the works of Thorstein Veblen, was the most ardent proponent of planning. Berle, professor of law and scholar (with Gardner Means) of corporate concentration in the United States, shared many of Tugwell's ideals. As a rule, Felix Frankfurter's lawyerly protégés—Benjamin Cohen, Thomas Corcoran, James Landis, David Lilienthal, Max Lowenthal, and Charles Wyzanski, among others—were in another camp; they were more cautious about planning, gradualist in their embrace of policy measures, and more attuned to constitutional niceties.

By the end of the 1930s, federal activism had also transformed the wider public arena for debates about policies. The national focus of discussion moved from states and localities to Washington. The journalist John Chamberlain was among the first to describe the transformation in the late 1930s, terming the federal government a "Broker State" whose mission was to oversee the contest among organized groups as they made their bids for wealth or competitive advantage.[10] Correspondingly, a budding sector of private-interest lobbies and social activist organizations directed their attention to Washington. Although the executive branch had accumulated considerable intellectual resources (and would draw even more people into governmental service by the end of World War II), organized interest groups began to build their own cadres of researchers, analysts, and public relations experts. Those interest groups that failed to enlist experts who could engage governmental economists and lawyers on terms of intellectual equality made little headway in Washington. The National Association of Manufacturers and the U.S. Chamber of Commerce, for example, were slow to add economists to their Washington staffs and thus were often relegated to the margins of debate in the mid-1930s. Indeed, one of the founders of the U.S. Chamber of Commerce, Edward A. Filene, resigned over its failures to modernize its research and advisory apparatus.

J. H. Willits, long-time head of the Rockefeller Foundation's social science division, foresaw problems as "the group" became the framework for intellectual activity. Scholars who were drawn to Washington had sacrificed their independence, allying themselves with partisan politicians (whether supporters or opponents of New Deal programs). Furthermore, they were being compelled as advocates to think not in terms of testable, amendable hypotheses but of policy arguments with political consequences. Willits decried the growing partisanship of the Washington intellectuals, their work as propagandists, and their resulting "blindness to inconvenient facts."[11]

In this environment, it was impossible to maintain that the expert was a detached and politically neutral participant in the policymaking process or to view research as a "value-free" pursuit transcending politics and pointing the way toward an objective definition of the general interest. Even the independent private research institutions, trying early to offer administrative help to the new federal agencies, found themselves entangled in bureaucratic politics; the researchers at Russell Sage became outspoken critics of federal relief policies, and the economists at Brookings assailed the recovery program. While experts were winning political and administrative places for themselves, they did so at the cost of their claims as scientific and politically neutral practitioners.

A Crisis of Confidence

Ironically, the experts won their place at a time when public confidence in their science was faltering. There was especially deep despair among those who had contributed the most during the 1910s and 1920s to building the nascent enterprise of social science research. In 1931 Edmund E. Day, director of the Rockefeller Foundation's social science division, announced his growing disillusionment: "We do not know enough to deal wisely with the forces wreaking havoc in this world of ours. We are essentially unprepared. No situation of this generation has made so clear our lack of genuine social intelligence." With unintended irony, Day concluded that faith in science was precisely what was lacking. "There must be faith that there is an effective means to every social end," he said, "and that the means is necessary to that end."[12] His was surely a pragmatist's faith, trusting in the means, rather than appealing to the ends.

And it was the scientific means that troubled many of those in philanthropic foundations and research organizations. Trustees and staffs of foundations met in worried conferences throughout the early 1930s, debating how best to respond to the depression and wondering what their tens of millions of dollars in expenditures on research during the 1920s had really yielded. Among the large foundations that supported such research, Carnegie and Rockefeller principally, the immediate urge was to move away from research and to experiment freely with the knowledge already at hand. The trustees seemed to find the energy that was emanating from Washington to be infectious. The fact of human suffering, after all, seemed self-evident; to call for yet more studies at a time like this was merely to justify further delay and inaction. Members of the board of the Carnegie foundation proceeded to cut funding for economic research. They were particularly embarrassed by NBER's participation in Hoover's Research Committee on Economic Trends, hinting that the bureau had somehow succumbed to political pressures and failed to foresee the depression.[13] The trustees of the Rockefeller Foundation, having grown impatient with their talented but research-minded staff, set up a committee to deal with the "special problems" of the depression, hoping to shift the foundation's work from basic research to experimental applications. Meanwhile, Russell Sage, its endowment eroding with the stock market (the annual budget slipped from $700,000 to $500,000), was torn between continuing to do research and using its resources to alleviate economic hardships.

The sense of intellectual failure was palpable. At Russell Sage, the research program finally gave way to practical help—advising cities, states, and private relief agencies; examining new federal programs; and fostering traditional self-help activities. The foundation encouraged such practical schemes as subsistence gardens and work-barter arrangements. Having been founded in an era when private organizations and states and localities were the focus of policies, it struggled to grasp both the national economic dynamics of the depression and the radically changing federal role.[14]

Both Brookings and NBER found themselves under severe financial pressures in the 1930s. NBER's budget fell by 60 percent in five years, to just over $100,000. Some of its staff moved to the Commerce Department, while Wesley C. Mitchell, always taking the long view, wrote calmly to his foundation patrons: "When the current depression is over, we expect to complete an intensive examination of the peculiar features of the business cycle which began in January, 1928."[15] Uncomfortable as always with the idea of advising about policy, the bureau shifted to more academic questions about the structure of the labor market (in time their research improved the era's abyssmal measurements of unemployment) and the relationship between technology and unemployment (through which Mitchell hoped to dispel some of the popular misconceptions that technology caused the depression). NBER continued to move away from the business of advising about policies and to evolve into an institution that coordinated collaborative academic research. In the end, Mitchell was not as pessimistic about the long-term benefits of research as he was about the political misappropriation of its findings.

At Brookings, long-term grants from the Carnegie Corporation and the Laura Spelman Rockefeller Memorial expired, and the institution's long-time fund-raiser, Robert Brookings, having given a total of $1 million to the institution, died in 1932. A pledge by the Rockefeller Foundation to match $2 million from other sources lapsed when the amount could not be raised, a sign both of hard times among the wealthy and of the crisis of faith in social science. Brookings, its $300,000 annual budget fast shrinking, was forced to take on contract research for state governments and consultancies with the U.S. Chamber of Commerce and American Federation of Labor. It also did research on the nation's transportation system for the National Transportation Committee, which was funded largely by financial institutions that had invested heavily in railroads. With support from Pittsburgh's Falk Foundation, Brookings began its most substantial research project of the 1930s—a series exploring the "productive capacities" of the American economy and hence the presumed causes of the depression.

While the depression caused hardship and uncertainty for established research institutions, the changed environment for policy in the 1930s provided opportunities for a different kind of research organization—the Twentieth Century Fund. Though operating out of Boston and New York, the fund adapted to the new pace and tenor of policymaking in Washington more quickly than did the others. Edward A. Filene, its founder, was a dapper, onetime department store magnate from Boston and an ardent progressive. A founder of the Good Will Fund and the International Management Institute, a prime mover behind the U.S. Chamber of Commerce, and a backer of credit unions and cooperatives, Filene had devoted a portion of his fortune in 1911 to the establishment of a research organization that was interested in workers' cooperatives, appropriately named the Cooperative League. Broadening its scope in 1919, the organization was renamed the Twentieth Century Fund.

Filene was one of Franklin D. Roosevelt's most outspoken supporters. "E.A. is surer of the New Deal than the President himself," wrote Lincoln Steffens.[16] Filene's sensibilities had always been attuned to the needs of consumers. He had created the department store's famous Automatic Bargain Basement, where prices dropped each week on unsold goods until the last unwanted shoes, shirts, and dresses were given to local charities. Thus, while manufacturers and industrial engineers worried about the costs of production, Filene remained concerned with consumers and the distribution of goods. He was also more sympathetic toward workers than were many other businessmen.

Filene thought that the depression was part of a second industrial revolution, brought about by the application of scientific management techniques to business organization, and that, like the first industrial revolution, it had brought its own excesses, dislocations, and suffering. The revolution was now "menaced by certain dangers" that it was the duty of "business statesmen" to recognize and solve."[17] According to Filene, the task for social research—especially at the Twentieth Century Fund, over which he presided until his death in 1937— was to anticipate the problems of this new industrial revolution so that society might avoid a renewal of the "radical agitation" which had been both "costly" and "fruitless." Social science seemed to hold out the prospect of relieving social conflict, but purely academic research was not Filene's goal when he gave a small initial endowment to the organization and continued to support it with gifts of roughly $100,000 per year. Filene wanted research that would lead to "intelligent and effective action."[18]

Usable knowledge, he thought, was acquired through a combination of laboratory research and practical experience. "Business diagnosis is a strange hodge-podge of 'hunches,' guesswork and personal opinion checked only here and there by sporadic research," Filene remarked. In 1930, he invoked the old model of medical research, which had inspired earlier philanthropists and still shaped the views of the seventy-year-old Filene. He called for the fund to take the lead in "a great practical movement in scientific social therapeutics" that would diagnose and treat the various ills of the "social organism."[19] Whatever he meant by that statement, Filene's fund turned its attention toward examining recommendations for public policy especially those under consideration at the federal level. Filene chose a journalist, Evans Clark, to head the enterprise, and journalists have continued to direct the fund for seventy years.[20]

In contrast to the scholarly investigators at NBER, the fund wanted the bulk of its studies to propose a course of political action— even though the fund's chief researcher, J. Frederic Dewhurst, was a respected economist. The phrase, "not just research but the next steps forward" has continued to echo at the fund's board and staff meetings, making at times for awkward relations with cautious scholars who are tentative about proposing solutions to policymakers. Unlike the Russell Sage Foundation, the fund was not enmeshed in a network of private organizations. And in contrast to Brookings, it was not leery of federal intervention in economic life.

In the 1930s the fund closely tracked the legislative agenda of

the New Deal, examining the legislation on the stock market the
securities industry, the social security programs, and labor relations.
Its method was to assemble large committees of prominent scholars,
businessmen, and public officials to oversee teams of researchers
and writers, who typically produced hefty compendia of expert opinions on policy issues, rather than original research. Usually, the recommendations were formally conveyed to the president and officials of
the executive branch; occasionally, information was provided to members of Congress. While the causal matrix linking research and analysis, policy proposals, and legislative action is complex, the discussions
at the fund helped to shape agreement on general goals and methods.
In its studies of the stock market, labor relations, problems of the
elderly, health, and the internal debt structure of the United States,
the fund served as a broker of ideas, provided a forum for winnowing
proposals, and functioned as an instrument for building an elite consensus on policy.

In time, however, Filene became impatient and skeptical that
the fund's books were mere "documentation," too far removed from
the activism that had always been a part of his life. The fund was
in New York, Filene was in Boston, and the locus of action had
shifted from state and city governments and private reform groups
and research organizations throughout the country to Washington
and its executive agencies. A private institution, even one whose
members believed in federal action, found it hard to keep abreast
of federal policymaking. The outside expert could no longer act as
a doctor who was called upon for diagnosis and cure, nor could the
outside efficiency expert propose administrative reforms that would
simply realign old organizations to operate more smoothly. The new
order in Washington demanded that experts conceive of their role
in a new way.

Adjustment and Planning

The language of experiment suffused the rhetoric of both social
science and politics in the 1930s, though neither the experts nor
the politicians who arrived in Washington during the depression
were truly experimental scientists. Genuine social and economic experimentation—with controls and testable hypotheses—would not
emerge until the late 1960s. The experimental rhetoric in the 1930s
simply evoked old images of the nation as a continuing experiment
in self-government. At a time when both the intellectuals' theoretical

knowledge and the politicians' practical experience offered no certain policy guidelines, the open-ended language of experiment allowed policymakers to act quickly and even inconsistently, unencumbered by the weight of precedent. The language of experiment and trial were reassuring when the success of any policy seemed uncertain.

While the experts serving at the Social Security Administration, National Resources Planning Board, or Securities and Exchange Commission were indeed part of national policy experiments, they were not experimental scientists. Two related terms—*adjustment* and *planning*—served better to define and justify the experts' presence in Washington. Drawn from the new science of psychology—and reinforced by a biological corollary, adaptation—the notions of adjustment and maladjustment cut across the fields of economics, anthropology, sociology, and politics. The language was already discernible in the 1920s. Harold Laski recalled the old habit of social scientists to borrow terms and concepts from the sciences—from Isaac Newton in the eighteenth century and Charles Darwin in the nineteenth century. In 1928, he noted that it had already become "fashionable for the observer to apply to the social process the latest discoveries of psychology."[21]

Adjustment so suffused the language of social scientists and policymakers that it was taken for granted. The lack of adjustment was "the source of untold human misery," wrote Robert Crane, president of the Social Science Research Council, and was "greatly increased by the rapidity of social change and by the growing complexity of modern society." Another observer of social science research, Jerome D. Greene, told an audience at Brookings that "the present maladjustment of production and consumption, supply and demand" was at the heart of calls for greater planning.[22]

Roosevelt the candidate had also expressed the themes of adaptation and adjustment in a speech in San Francisco that was drafted by Adolf A. Berle. Declaring that the "day of the great promoter or the financial Titan" was over, Roosevelt now saw the task of government to be the "less dramatic business" of administering existing resources, reestablishing foreign markets, "adjusting production to consumption," and "adapting existing economic organization to the service of the people."[23] If economic problems were construed merely as matters of adjustment, then the crisis need not seem so dire. "Adjustments" were far less worrisome than were diagnoses that called for radical transformations of the economy. The nation's economy had not failed, Roosevelt was telling the voters; markets were simply out of balance. Ample raw materials, industrial capacity, and a willing work force were available; they were simply not functioning in their proper relationship. Tempering the business cycle demanded measures to adjust productive capacity and demand; international trade and tariffs called for adjustment, and farm problems would be dealt with through the aptly named Agricultural Adjustment Administration; meanwhile, the pathological behavior of individuals and groups would be remedied by techniques of psychological and social adjustment.

The idea of adjustment supplied ample justification for summoning the expert to the government. It was a way for both academic and governmental experts to view their work as scientific but without the heavy burden of prediction and control. Implying tentative measures, rather than sweeping change, *adjustment* suggested retraceable steps, a shift in the opposite direction if the first moves did not work. It answered the question of how a chastened social science might contribute to public action; coincidentally, it also required the continuing presence of experts in the government to monitor and adapt federal programs to new needs. Moreover, the notion of adjustment provided a handy rationale when Congress delegated broad powers to executive agencies. Broad legislative mandates could be passed; the expert administrators could work out and adjust the details (it was precisely such delegation that caused the National Recovery Administration to be declared unconstitutional).

The notions of balance and adjustment that suffused contemporary policy discussions appeared most clearly in the New Deal's farm policies, especially in the writings of Henry Agard Wallace, the Iowa-born secretary of agriculture and a serious student of both the genetics of plants and agricultural economics. Dedicated to science and economic statistics, Wallace was also something of "a spiritual window-shopper," in one journalist's phrase, a man fascinated by Christian mysticism and the occult. When he arrived in Washington in 1933, he moved into the same small apartment and the same governmental office that his father, Henry Cantwell Wallace, had occupied a decade earlier as the secretary of agriculture under Presidents Harding and Coolidge. But the younger Wallace, though well liked by his associates in the department, did not move comfortably in administration circles. As one politician noted, "Henry's the sort that keeps you guessing as to whether he's going to deliver a sermon or wet the bed."[24]

For Wallace, the farm problem was rooted in an imbalance between city and country, with the purchasing power of the farmer far more depressed than that of the city dweller. And the remedy—the Agricultural Adjustment Act of 1933—was, in many respects, the culmination of a decade of deliberation by experts about farm problems. Wallace, Tugwell, and economists in and out of government, principally John D. Black, Mordecai Ezekiel in the Department of Agriculture, and M. L. Wilson of Montana State University, worked out a system of allotments for domestic crops and sold it to the president. In 1932 Wilson explained that the plan "applies to agriculture fundamental ideas of adjusting production to consumption, as exemplified in industry by the Swope plan and the plan of the United States Chamber of Commerce for stabilization and continuity in business."[25]

The act (the bill was drafted primarily by Wallace, Ezekiel, and the lawyer Jerome Frank) sought to adjust farm prices to production levels and to balance the role of agriculture in the wider economy. Rejecting the voluntary planning that Hoover had embraced as a remedy for cyclical economic swings, the act traded farm price supports for controls on production to harmonize price and supply. For Wallace, economic adjustment and democracy went hand in hand: "An enduring democracy can be had only by promoting a balance among all our major producing groups, and in such a way as does not build up a small inordinately wealthy class." Although Wallace asserted that he did not consider the act and other recovery measures to be permanent, he did believe the market had broken down and required new rules to establish harmonious relationships between prices, margins, profits, and distribution of income. Roosevelt conceded to Congress that the measures represented a new and untrod path, but he explained that "an unprecedented condition calls for the trial of new means."[26]

The notion of adjustment went to the heart of the efforts to understand the causes of the depression and the measures needed to escape from it. But the language of adjustment was broad enough to accommodate several explanations of the nation's economic woes. Early in the depression, those who thought downturns were inevitable and self-correcting phenomena could argue that markets would naturally act to adjust costs and prices; however, the idea of a natural economic adjustment was less persuasive after 1932. Others who saw the depression as an international crisis, rooted in international debts from World War I and the failure of financial mechanisms, spoke in terms of adjusting international debts. Yet others, like Wallace and Tugwell, saw fundamental structural imbalances in the American economy, and their calls for adjustment presumed a need for fundamental structural realignments.

Another concept, no more precisely defined, also had a wide appeal—national planning. Ideas about planning were a part of the managerial legacy of progressivism and were rooted in concerns about conservation, the management of natural resources, and public ownership of utilities. Specific planning schemes, such as the Tennessee Valley Authority, were grounded in the regional planning efforts devised by economists, engineers, and urban planners during the 1920s. During the depression, still broader ideals of planning were endorsed by many leading intellectuals, including Herbert Croly, Thorstein Veblen, Charles Beard, and John Dewey, who were worried about the fate of American liberalism as it struggled to come to terms with the depression.

Dewey was explicit about the link between liberalism and planning. The historic connections between individualism and liberalism were undergoing a transformation. The rugged individualism of the nineteenth century had derived meaning and focus within small local communities. But in the mass society and national economy of the twentieth century, the individual required a new point of orientation. According to Dewey, the new individualism had to work through the government, rather than in opposition to it. Though not specific about the appropriate mechanisms, he argued that society could not function if it depended only on the unplanned actions of millions of individuals who were seeking private advantage. Rather, planning would supply the goals and structures to direct society toward liberal ends.[27]

Planning schemes abounded in the early 1930s, many of them variations on the short-term approaches that had seemed so successful in World War I. Nor did all the schemes emanate from the Left. According to a researcher at the Twentieth Century Fund who was hired to keep track of such ideas, six legislative proposals for a central planning body circulated in Washington between 1930 and 1933; another nine were being promoted by private groups. Schemes were also proposed by labor leaders in such notoriously unstable industries as mining and clothing manufacture. John L. Lewis of the United Mine Workers and Sidney Hillman of the Amalgamated Clothing Workers wanted a national economic council to chart policy for the country. At the same time, businessmen like Gerard Swope of General Electric and Henry Harriman of the U.S. Chamber of Commerce advanced their own schemes for cooperative planning that would

make use of trade associations. Historian Charles Beard spoke of
five-year plans and urged the creation of a national planning board.
Another popularizer of the ideal of planning was the journalist Stuart
Chase. More liberal than most of the others, he blithely asked, "Why
should the Russians have all the fun of remaking a world?"[28]

With interest in planning spanning much of the political spectrum, the National Planning Association (NPA), still in operation
today, was set up in the mid-1930s. The NPA studied proposals for
a national planning mechanism that ranged from explicit calls for
the nationalization of industry to more timid suggestions for the creation of economic research groups. Inevitably, however, ideas about
national planning foundered when formal mechanisms and specific
goals began to take concrete shape. The proponents of national economic planning, with all that such mechanisms of whatever form
might have meant for the use of experts in government, left no
enduring institutional legacy. Whether the model was the conservative trade-association approach of the National Recovery Administration (NRA) denounced by the Hearst press as "absolute state socialism"
and declared unconstitutional in 1935 or the more comprehensive
planning espoused by the National Resources Planning Board, abolished by Congress in 1943, advocates of planning saw only short-
lived success.

The NRA, the New Deal's first venture in joint business-govern-
ment planning that sought to control industrial production and levels
of employment, was the most conspicuous failure. Businessmen in
large corporations who were eager to end "destructive competition"
had embraced it at first; liberal intellectuals and labor leaders had
seen it as a possible means of improving working conditions and
wages. While the two-year planning experiment touched some five
hundred industries, it died, for the most part unmourned, when
the Supreme Court declared it unconstitutional. Not the least of
the reasons for its failure, concluded Mordecai Ezekiel of the Department of Agriculture—aside from the complexity of the economy it
sought to plan—was the lack of a trained staff and adequate data.
According to Ezekiel, it would have taken ten years for the NRA to
build up a professional staff that would have been able to carry out
its planning role in various economic sectors.[29]

The ideal of planning gave shape to the New Deal's approaches
to policies on agriculture and natural resources and to public works
projects. Planning spurred the hiring of experts. The most significant
effort to institutionalize the expertise of planners in the 1930s was

the often-renamed and frequently relocated National Resources Planning Board (NRPB). Never securely rooted in Washington's bureaucratic firmament, the NRPB underwent four name changes during its ten-year life, migrating from the Interior Department, where it began as an agency for planning public works projects, to the Executive Office of the President, where, with a president eager to put specialists to work on natural-resource planning, it had the potential to become a central policy planning body.

Roosevelt enthusiastically greeted the NRPB's 1934 document, *A Plan for Planning*, endorsing its tempered view. Planning, the authors stated, "does not involve the preparation of a comprehensive blueprint of human activity to be clamped down like a steel frame on the flesh of the community." Rather it involves "readjustment and revision" that are sensitive to the emergence of new situations and problems. The report called for a more permanent planning body (like many New Deal agencies, the initial planning board was set up only under an emergency legislative provision). The staff of the permanent body would serve as a "general staff" for the president—gathering data, coordinating policies, and planning new initiatives.[30]

With strong support from Roosevelt in the mid-1930s, the planning board's 50-member staff (at its peak in the early 1940s, it employed some 250 full-time staff members and about 250 consultants) issued reports on pollution, natural resources, and public works, gradually expanding its range of reporting to include economic issues, demographic trends, and the impact of technology. It spent about $10 million during its life span. Strong relations with the president were assured, since Frederick Delano, Roosevelt's uncle, chaired it for the duration and Charles Merriam, a political scientist from the University of Chicago who earned the affectionate title "Uncle Charley," remained the key board member during its ten-year odyssey. Through the NRPB, the Roosevelt administration tapped outside experts, working with the Social Science Research Council and the Public Administration Clearing House, as well as individual scholars.

But popular suspicions both of planning and of presidential power were deeply engrained. They had surfaced when Hoover's experts issued their benign report on social trends in 1933 that contained no policy schemes; they were even more vehement when an activist president was visibly allied with a group of expert advisers. The *New York Times* condemned the "cult of planning." And even Roosevelt's cabinet members grew restive at the threat of White House experts encroaching on their bureaucratic turf.[31] In the end, the

NRPB was unable to survive the covert efforts to undermine it from within the administration and the public scorn of critics who characterized its "shell-pink and dreamy visions" as the entering wedge of socialism.[32]

Although the board was brought closer to the president when the Executive Office of the President was expanded and reorganized in 1939, it could not be saved. Some of its failure was its own doing. It never clarified the relationship between research and policy planning, remaining an enclave of research within the executive branch that exerted only sporadic influence on presidential policy. The experts in the NRPB also proved vulnerable to the president's congressional opposition.

The conservatives' dislike of the NRPB intensified when the board hatched plans to extend the New Deal. The massive 1942 report *Security, Work and Relief Policies*, oftened likened to Britain's Beveridge report in its call for a more comprehensive social insurance network, was a challenge to the opponents of New Deal programs.[33] In 1943 the board was killed, quickly and efficiently, by a Congress that was hostile to the growing powers of the chief executive and by the long-standing opposition from such bureaucratic bastions as the Army Corps of Engineers, the Forestry Service, and the Bureau of Reclamation.

The tentative experiment with a national planning body came to an abrupt end in the midst of World War II, at the very moment when wartime economic controls and planning were in full force, but exercised by bodies of a clearly temporary nature. There was considerable irony in NRPB's demise. Experts in both the social and natural sciences were proving invaluable to the war effort, and a broad national debate on the dimensions of postwar planning was just getting under way. The decade of economic crisis and the beginning of the war had drawn experts to Washington in unprecedented numbers. The experts' analytic skills had helped them find useful places, administering programs and gathering data in many governmental agencies. But the role of social scientists as policy advisers with a formal, institutional role in government did not fully mature until a new set of advisory relationships took shape after World War II.

Knowledge for What?

The arrival of experts in Roosevelt's administration had been symbolized by the Brains Trust, but the real work was carried out in hundreds of cramped offices, far from the innermost advisory circles. Nonetheless, the highly visible experts, particularly Tugwell, captured the popular and journalistic imagination. Though the Brains Trust ceased to function as a "privy council" after the 1932 campaign, the phrase continued to appear, suggesting a growing public perception of their power. "The 'brain trust' completely overshadows the Cabinet," wrote a journalist in the *Chicago Tribune*. "On a routine administrative matter you go to a Cabinet member, but on matters of policy and the higher statesmanship you consult the professoriat."[34] But these assessments were wide of the mark and were designed to discredit Roosevelt as much as his advisers. Tugwell, was closer to the truth when he said in 1932 that the Brains Trust simply gave "the voice of learning" to the president's speeches. The professors had learned "the trick of moving with [Roosevelt's] mind and supplying its needs," he said, but the "the tapestry of the policy" was guided by a conception "not made known to us." Clearly, the experts who were closest to the president knew that they could not usurp or even share Roosevelt's political leadership.[35]

But what had happened to the experts' claims to intellectual authority as they moved closer to the source of political and bureaucratic power? Before the New Deal, their authority had rested on their assertion of detachment from partisan wrangling. The independent institutions they had created and the advisory patterns that had evolved tried to preserve this respectable distance by presenting the experts primarily as fact-finders who were seeking to reconcile ideological or "value" differences. But the 1930s had brought some experts into political advisory positions and many more into positions as planners and administrators of governmental programs. Accordingly, their expertise began to operate on the political process in a different way. Instead of a disinterested knowledge that fostered a consensus on policy solutions, theirs was now a knowledge that served political actors, justifying policies and rationalizing political convictions. No doubt, experts and intellectuals in power had always been tempted by power. But with the modern demands for expertise so great—especially after a decade of crisis—the distance between knowledge and power was being bridged routinely. And as the gap between experts and the political leaders was closed and the experts were drawn into roles as administrators and policy planners, knowledge began to look less like a form of higher intellectual counsel than simply another instrument of political power.

As social scientists gained prestige and proximity to power, at least one voiced the fear that they had narrowed their field of vision in the rush to be useful. Robert Lynd, professor of sociology at Columbia University, was concerned about ultimate political ends and questions of value at a time when most other social scientists were struggling with questions of political means. Lynd asked the elemental question, *Knowledge for What?* in a book published in 1939.

The son of a midwestern banker, Lynd graduated from Princeton University in 1914, and his career proceeded in stages that neatly paralleled the evolution of social science in the early twentieth century. After working for four years as managing editor of *Publishers Weekly*, Lynd enrolled at New York's Union Theological Seminary. A summer of fieldwork in Wyoming exposed him to the deplorable living conditions of workers employed by Standard Oil of Indiana. He complained directly to John D. Rockefeller, Jr., son of Standard Oil's founder, and then wrote a series of stinging articles for *The Survey* and *Harper's* in 1923. Lynd's critique intrigued some of Rockefeller's philanthropic advisers, and he was asked to undertake a research project for the Rockefeller-funded Institute for Social and Religious Research. The study, which began as a general survey of the possibility of cooperative social work among the religious and charitable institutions of a small American town, became the sociological classic *Middletown*, a survey of life in Muncie, Indiana.

The Muncie survey challenged the prevailing pragmatic assumptions of social research by trying to go "beyond the institutional level" to explore what Lynd called "the vital moral and spiritual factors, issues and values of life." The surveyors wanted to learn about "the actual ethical and spiritual experience of the inhabitants of a community; to evaluate their habitual activities from the ethical viewpoint."[36] In short, Lynd wanted to know how values arose and what institutions nourished them.

Rather than discrete and fragmented institutional facts, Lynd took business and working-class cultures as the essential fact of urban life. In thus challenging the traditional survey with its emphasis on institutional efficiency, Lynd raised provocative and uncomfortable questions about the values underlying social science research. Nor did he please the study's sponsors, who thought his work had overstepped the bounds of objectivity.

Lynd returned to those troubling questions in 1939, a decade after the publication of *Middletown*, with a blunt and powerful critique of the social sciences. *Knowledge for What?* raised doubts about the scientific claims of social science, and therefore its utility for policy, by asking whose interests were actually served by a discipline that sought "disinterestedly" to inquire into social conditions. What was the problem with the social sciences? "Is the difficulty, as the social sciences maintain, that they do not have 'enough data'? Or do we have data on the wrong problems?"[37] These factors and others were partly to blame for the confusion of the social science enterprise, he concluded; but to Lynd, it was, above all, the specialization and "atomism" of modern social science that had limited its capacity to understand society and to probe human values.

Lynd had specific targets in mind, including his friend Wesley C. Mitchell. He was highly critical of the strictly empirical studies undertaken by Mitchell's NBER. While admitting that the bureau represented the best contemporary research on economics, he took issue with its "tacit assumption" that private enterprise and the profit incentive alone could guide the application of technical skills to problems of production and supply. The NBER did not question or "go substantially beyond the core of the folkways." It did not challenge customs and habits or reexamine accepted social values. Lynd also criticized the Brookings Institution, whose studies of America's production and consumption capacities, despite their modest arguments for redistributive economic policies, allowed "the traditions of business enterprise to define the situation for it."[38]

At the least, most social scientists had tacitly accepted the prevailing value system. Their customary obsession with facts had often been an explicit way of avoiding such questions. Fearing that differences in the sphere of values would be hopelessly divisive, the nineteenth-century founders of the American Social Science Association, as well as the more recent incorporators of the NBER, had placed their faith in facts in the hope of thereby muting disagreements over values and attaining a political consensus. Lynd, however, called for a social science that would cast its net more widely, seeking to integrate the understanding of specialists, rather than to produce fragmented bits of knowledge. Only if they were conceived as the study of culture, especially of human wants and needs, could the social sciences find "the common frame of reference" missing from more specialized empirical work.[39]

But social science still required an explicit set of values to help it determine its selection of problems to study. Lynd urged his fellow social scientists to articulate their "tacit criteria of the 'significant' " and advised them to look beyond their own culture, as the "natural and inevitable" source of values, to explore the more basic values rooted in a people's needs and longings. The question social scientists should ask about human beings, he said, is "How do they crave to live?"[40]

Lynd directed his critique at a social science that, as he saw it, had grown detached from genuine social concerns in the pursuit of scientific certainty, professionalism, and service to power. Too often, the problems it set itself were mere puzzles of technique and method that were shaped by the immediate concerns of government and business. Social science, he concluded, "must have the courage to fight for its freedom from the dragging undertow of a culture preoccupied with short-run statements of long-run problems."[41] Lynd expressed an early and fundamental dissatisfaction not only with the evolution of American social science, but with the technocratic and managerial emphasis of the progressive tradition.

Despite his worries about the research institutions and governmental offices that enabled social scientists to serve the political order, Lynd remained within an intellectual tradition that was committed to rationalism, experimentation, and planning. His conception of values, although it sounded the note of passionate moral concern, was really rooted in the material wants and needs of the citizen and based in a pragmatic tradition that saw changes in the physical environment as preceding "adjustment and adaptation" in the realm of values. His was still the progressive's faith in the perfectibility of man and the power of the rational intellect to guide political progress.

Nevertheless, Lynd raised troubling questions about the role of the expert and intellectual, anticipating issues that would surface again in the postwar period. Social scientists had crossed a line in their service to government and business that inhibited the more searching inquiry into the prevailing alignments of power and benefit. Indeed, Lynd doubted whether social scientists were asking significant questions at all. The sovereign concern with technique—whether in respect to research methods or managerial techniques—rendered social science irrelevant in discussions of social and political ends.

FIVE

☆

Technocratic
Faiths

Doctor Win-the-War

The playwright Robert Sherwood, who labored as one of Roosevelt's speech writers in the early 1940s, viewed the New Deal as something like a domestic dress rehearsal for World War II. Franklin Roosevelt and Harry Hopkins, whose wartime relationship was the focus of Sherwood's superb Washington memoir, had used the New Deal to prepare themselves and the American public for the "gigantic efforts" of a global war. "Spiritual preparedness for coping with powerful evil was required," he wrote, "before it began to occur to people that some tanks and bombers and aircraft carriers might also be helpful."[1] Roosevelt put it another way. With the outbreak of hostilities, Doctor New Deal had to step aside so that Doctor Win-the-War could get to work.

War embraces many contradictions. It is hugely destructive while accelerating social change. It is irrational and chaotic while spurring whole societies to organize their efforts in fundamentally new ways. It is atavistic and primitive while pushing humankind to new technological and scientific inventiveness. One of the greatest ironies of World War II was that the horror and destructive force of modern methods of warfare restored the public's faith in the possibilities of scientific progress.

Agreeing on the urgent end—to win the war—scientists and politicians learned what organized science could accomplish. They applied the scientific means that were at hand when the war began, and in the hothouse environment of wartime research agencies, they invented new scientific and technological tools. By the time the war was over, the goal of defeating fascism had given way to the equally urgent postwar domestic goals of sustaining employment and production, as well as the military and political aims of combatting Communist advances. Broad agreement on the ends of policy allowed experts to focus on the technical means of accomplishing those aims. For economists—the domestic policy experts par excellence—this postwar policy consensus, grounded in the theories of John Maynard Keynes (a consensus that began to unravel only in the 1960s) marked a new high point of their influence. For the new generation of Cold War strategists, the two decades after World War II were also a moment of intellectual exhiliration in which new rational, quantitative and systematic ways of thinking about policies were conceived and applied to all sorts of problems. If scientists felt a twinge of unease, it lay mainly in their doubts about the political and social means of controlling the nuclear technologies they had unleashed.

The atomic bomb, the most epoch-shattering result of wartime research, was only the most dramatic scientific contribution to the war. Radar, the design and propulsion of aircraft, optics, synthetic materials, and electronic computing were among the war's other technological offspring—the outcome of federally coordinated research projects managed by the Office of Scientific Research and Development and of hugely increased wartime expenditures for research. In 1940, the last prewar year for the United States, the federal government spent $75 million to $100 million on research and development, about a third devoted to agricultural research, a quarter to military research. By 1945 these sums had increased roughly fifteenfold to approximately $1.5 billion, mostly for research on atomic weapons.[2]

The modern military-scientific-industrial complex, so often decried by the New Left and its offspring, was conceived during the war. The success of contract-research arrangements and government-run research laboratories established new models for harnessing scientific and technical expertise to political needs. Although the most prominent actors in the wartime drama were the physicists and mathematicians working in Los Alamos to build the atomic bomb or perfecting radar at the Radiation Lab on the campus of the Massachusetts Institute of Technology, social scientists also played a considerable supporting role in the war effort.

Although numerous social scientists had moved to Washington

during the New Deal as policy advisers, program planners, and administrators, they did much more to demonstrate their usefulness during the war. The economic crisis, as urgent as it was, had been little more than a trial run for their wartime performance. In the first months of mobilization, social scientists from all fields flocked to the newly created governmental agencies, their number doubling by one estimate, in the first six months of 1942, to more than fifteen thousand. Historians, geographers, linguists, anthropologists, economists, sociologists, and psychologists served ably in the State Department, Office of War Information, War Production Board, Office of Strategic Services, Bureau of Naval Personnel, Army Information and Education Division, and countless other wartime boards and agencies. Their practical contribution to the war effort included economic analyses, public opinion surveys, intelligence testing, examinations of the stress of combat, and explorations of group dynamics.[3]

Scattered in many governmental agencies during the war, however, social scientists could not point to any decisive intellectual breakthroughs on the magnitude of the atom bomb; nor did they ever seem so vital to the wartime effort as the physicists and engineers. Indeed, army psychologists and sociologists were sometimes ridiculed by draftees and career soldiers. Responding to complaints from the officers, Secretary of War Henry Stimson issued a short-lived ban on polling soldiers, on the grounds that surveys undermined the cohesiveness of the army.

Nonetheless, psychologists in the Bureau of Naval Personnel managed, among other things, to devise personnel tests that enabled the navy to classify and assign new sailors, most of whom had never been at sea. When a crew had to be picked for a newly launched battleship, the U.S.S. *New Jersey*, psychologists worked out the duty assignments; their success astonished the veteran naval officers. Members of army research teams prepared training programs, including such delicate assignments as surveying race relations and producing such films and pamphlets as *The Negro Soldier* and *Command of Negro Troops*, designed to help white officers assume the responsibilities of their command. Anthropologists in a research unit set up by the War Relocation Authority studied the attitudes of Japanese internees, both as a tool for administering the camps during the war and for understanding how dislocated communities in occupied Japan might operate. Scholars with expertise in particular regions of the world were also drawn into service early in the Ethnogeographic Board, which worked out of the Smithsonian Institution, and later in various military and diplomatic intelligence-gathering units.

These social scientists paved the way for continuing service after the war. Research units, though considerably pared down, survived in the armed services, and new contractual arrangements, pioneered during the war, kept university-based scholars at work on military research. New governmental advisory bodies were also established after the war, including the National Security Council, the Policy Planning Staff in the State Department, and the Central Intelligence Agency, further institutionalizing the presence of advisers in Washington and incidentally reflecting the new prominence that social scientists had gained.

No single field increased more in stature during the war than economics. Although they might be blamed for production bottlenecks, cumbersome price controls, and rationing schemes, economists could take credit, as they had in World War I, for much of the success in organizing production and deploying military and civilian personnel. Early in the war, policymakers had fitfully groped their way toward an organizational structure for managing the economy. The National Defense Advisory Commission, set up in mid-1940, was followed by the Office of Production Management in early 1941 and the War Production Board in 1942. Together with the Office of Price Administration and the Supply Priorities and Allocation Board, through their various changes of name, location, and structure, these were the most important planning agencies.

The productive powers of the American capitalist system, which had seemed no match for the superefficient fascist war economies in the 1930s, quickly surpassed them. Tanks and bombers rolled off the assembly lines in unprecedented number. By 1944 the levels of military production alone approached the nation's entire gross national product for 1929. At the war's end, industrial production was 2½ times the prewar level, and unemployment was slightly over 1 percent. Paul Samuelson, one of the many young Keynesian economists who were drawn to Washington in the late 1930s, believed that just as some had thought of World War I as the "chemist's war," World War II could be considered, without too much exaggeration, the "economist's war."[4]

Under constant pressure to meet military deadlines, the economic planners set production priorities and worked out schemes for price controls and rationing. With inadequate data, despite the advances made by governmental statisticians in the 1930s, and with little time for sustained analysis, the governmental economists oversaw the expansion of military production while they struggled to keep the price and supply of civilian goods under control.

Haste and necessity spawned new techniques and, in time, new insights into the functioning of the economy. The Bureau of Labor Statistics and the U.S. Bureau of the Census were forced to undertake more frequent statistical surveys, devising new sampling techniques and relying on newfangled computing devices. Often having to deal with volatile public attitudes about rationing and prices, the Office of Price Administration (OPA) sponsored surveys of consumer sentiments and public opinion. Along with their colleagues in such agencies as the Office of War Information and the War Labor Board, where public attitudes had to be gauged in structuring war-bond campaigns, exhorting workers to produce, and bolstering civilian morale, social scientists made genuine advances in survey research and in understanding how the economy behaved.

The efforts to set prices and devise rationing schemes, even when they did not work, taught economists a great deal. "The experience of being disastrously wrong is salutary," John Kenneth Galbraith observed some forty years later, reflecting on his own war-induced education. Having written a well-circulated paper on price controls, Galbraith had been picked in April 1941 by Leon Henderson, the head of the OPA, to oversee the office's pricing policies. Within a year, Galbraith was forced to conclude that "the extraordinarily logical model of wartime economic management that had brought me my considerable and welcome power was proving itself a disaster."[5] There were simply too many products and prices to be able to control them individually. After April 1942, however, when the General Maximum Price Regulation (or General Max, as it was called) went into effect, prices were fixed and inflation was virtually halted. Not until controls were lifted at the end of the war did prices bounce upward. Perhaps the economists' most substantial contribution to the war was to exorcise the specter of the rampant inflation of World War I and its aftermath, which was still fearfully remembered.

Although credit and blame for management of the economy during the war can be endlessly debated, economists could point to the nation's hugely expanded productive capacities and to their role in seeing that the Arsenal of Democracy was fully stocked. Social scientists thus emerged from the war with greater confidence and their reputations enhanced—largely because they demonstrated something through their wartime service that they had not always been able to do during the 1930s. Social scientists proved their worth not simply because they, as individuals, possessed substantive knowledge of a subject (or knew how to learn things quickly) but because, as members of individual disciplines, they had valuable skills and analytic methods that could be applied to questions of policy.[6]

Especially with the embrace of the Keynesian ideas of demand management, the tools of economic analysis would begin to have a direct bearing on economic policymaking after the war. Economics, not merely economists, began to exert a tangible influence on the thinking of governmental officials and businessmen, giving rise to new research organizations in and out of government and shaping policy in ways that mere advisory relationships could not. Social scientists and their techniques were employed in ways that made them an integral part of the policymaking process.

Economists Ascendant

The nation's productive capacity had expanded enormously during the war, but memories of the depression—a crisis that had been brought on by industrial overcapacity to many minds—were still alive as Americans contemplated a return to peacetime production. Especially vivid were the cruel disappointments when the economy had faltered in 1937, just as it seemed that the corner had been turned toward renewed prosperity. Anxiety about sustaining wartime levels of employment once military production ceased and the troops had been demobilized sparked a national debate over the shape of the postwar economy. Federal spending accounted for over half the gross national product in 1944. What would happen when military spending was curtailed? How would 30 million jobs be found—10 million for returning servicemen and 20 million for civilian employees in war-related industries?

The older policy research groups—Brookings, the Twentieth Century Fund, and the National Bureau of Economic Research— were concerned with how the nation could avoid slipping back into an economic depression. Although scholars who were affiliated with these organizations accepted the notion that levels of employment and production ought to be maintained within a "mixed economy," the composition of that mix was far from obvious. What tools could the government employ to intervene in economic affairs? What should the limits of such intervention be? The choice of particular policy instruments would inevitably shape the role that economists might play. Under the leadership of Harold G. Moulton, Brookings took a conservative stance, throwing in its lot with opponents of the New Deal, both in Congress and in the business community, and bitterly resisting the emerging Keynesian wisdom. The Twentieth Century Fund, which had sponsored a series of popular books by the writer Stuart Chase, was most closely identified with formal planning schemes and liberal interpretations of Keynes. The Russell Sage Foundation, falling under the sway of academic sociologists in the mid-1940s, would have little to say about the shape of postwar policy. As the lines of debate took shape, a major new research institution was born—the Committee for Economic Development (CED).[7]

The debate over the government's economic role was well under way in academic circles before the war. Alvin Hansen, an economist at Harvard, was the leading interpreter of Keynes to the American audience. Author of a widely circulated pamphlet for the National Resources Planning Board (NRPB), *After the War—Full Employment*, published in 1942, Hansen was a favorite target of conservatives who adhered to the old gospel of maintaining a balanced budget. He and a group of economists who were clustered around the NRPB argued, beginning in the late 1930s, that the nation's economy had reached a state of "maturity," anticipating a later generation's argument that the world had reached the "limits of growth." Examining the sources of economic growth in the nineteenth century—territorial expansion, a growing population, and technological innovation—these economists concluded in the 1930s that the prospects for continued future growth were dim. They foresaw nothing but prolonged stagnation. Consequently, during the economic downturn of 1937–38, Hansen called for income-generating governmental expenditures to move the economy forward, even if it meant a greater federal debt. As the economy accelerated, he argued, governmental spending could be curtailed.[8]

With the war winding down toward its inevitable end, businessmen, too, came to be caught up in the debate about the national economy. Manufacturers and industrialists had practical worries about the fate of American capitalism if it did not make a swift and successful transition from military to peacetime production. Yet, however eager businessmen might be to end wartime controls, the war's cost-plus contracts had been profitable and the transition presented enormous uncertainties. The prospect of canceling governmental contracts for planes, rifles, and uniforms; converting factories from tank to automobile production; ending price controls; and all the other steps that would have to be taken to disentangle the government from business added urgency to the growing debate.

No research organization played a more important role in shaping this debate—and sustaining the postwar consensus on economic poli-cymaking—than did the CED, a business research group founded in 1943. The CED's founders were businessmen, most of whom had gotten to know each other while serving on the Commerce Depart-ment's Business Advisory Council, set up in 1933 during the first heady days of government-business cooperation under the National Recovery Administration. The council, a group of roughly fifty chief executives of large corporations, met periodically at the Commerce Department and enjoyed a quasi-official advisory status (the govern-ment did not pay the council's expenses but gave them office space and staff assistance). The scores of memorandums and statements on economic policy, as well as private meetings with governmental officials, gave big business a powerful voice in the early phases of the New Deal.[9]

Several members of the Business Advisory Council had planned to create an independent research group on the eve of the war. In 1940 Paul G. Hoffman, the gregarious and energetic president of Studebaker, and William Benton, founder of the Benton and Bowles advertising agency and publisher of the *Encyclopedia Brittanica*, met for this purpose with Robert Hutchins, president of the University of Chicago. Hoffman, who had spent a year at the University of Chicago before his father's financial difficulties made tuition too great a burden, sat on the university's board of trustees. Benton, who had abandoned advertising for a University of Chicago vice presi-dency, was a close friend of Hutchins.

Sensing an opportunity to involve the faculty more directly in national political affairs, Hoffman proposed bringing together scholars and leading businessmen in a research and advisory forum. With the help of political scientist Harold Lasswell, the partners tried to organize a group called the American Policy Commission, in which fifteen or twenty "literate" businessmen would meet with the universi-ty's faculty every few months in an effort to "close the gap between knowledge and policy."[10] In 1940 their principal topic was the proper balance between private enterprise and government in a mixed econ-omy; their aim was to turn the contentious debate about government and business into a more constructive dialogue between economists, businessmen, and policymakers.

With the United States on the verge of entering the war, the university-based plans stalled, only to reemerge within the Business Advisory Council of which Hoffman was vice chairman. Jesse Jones, the secretary of commerce, wanted to draw businessmen into postwar planning, mainly to stave off the more liberal plans taking shape in the NRPB. Calling on members of the Business Advisory Council, Jones sponsored the organizing committee that spawned the CED in September 1942. For political reasons Jones and others downplayed the connections between the two groups, since many small businessmen and conservatives no longer considered the council to be their voice in Washington. The new CED was a research and planning body, hatched in the Commerce Department but designed to be independent of the government. Like so many other policy research groups now operating within the private sector, its genesis was hybrid. Both governmental officials and private individuals often have found it useful to have organizations that span the two sectors.

While conservative and business publications quickly and accurately identified the CED trustees as among the more liberal-minded American businessmen, most of the national press saw the CED as conservative and isolationist—in short, as something other than it claimed to be, perhaps a revival of the old National Industrial Conference Board. The CED was tolerated largely because it was initially set up as a temporary body to do practical research on the most immediate problems of economic reconversion—terminating contracts, converting factories, and firing and hiring workers—subjects that no other research group was so well equipped to study.

These were matters of considerable urgency as the war came to an end. Beardsley Ruml, a CED mainstay who had left the world of philanthropy and academia to work for Macy's Department Store, spoke for many businessmen in CED's orbit when he said that unless the problem of unemployment could be tamed, private enterprise would be "supplanted by some other arrangements" for the production and distribution of goods and services.[11] Analysts worried that if postwar business activity fell to the level of 1940, some 15 million workers would be unemployed after the war. The goal, as they saw it, was to keep production at 35–40 percent above the 1940 levels and to provide 7–10 million more jobs in the private sector. But although the CED researchers took on a number of short-term studies of economic conversion, Paul Hoffman and his colleagues quickly realized that their focus on immediate problems would not guarantee a long-term role for the business community in shaping broader economic policies.

Hoffman, whose leading role in the CED helped propel him after the war to posts directing the Marshall Plan and presiding over the Ford Foundation, believed wholeheartedly in the value of research, remarking in 1944 that if business had spent $5 million on policy research in the 1920s, it could have saved $50 million on lost production in the 1930s. He and the other leaders of the CED— Benton; Ruml; and Ralph Flanders, head of a Vermont toolmaking firm and later a U.S. senator—wanted to turn their short-term research operation into something that could rise above the parochial views of either the National Association of Manufacturers or the U.S. Chamber of Commerce. They were a most unorthodox assemblage of businessmen; none represented large business enterprises and all had academic ties of one sort or another. Denouncing the "pressure group economy" and the partisanship of policy research, Hoffman stated that the CED would demonstrate "that business men are not afraid of light."[12] The light they had begun to find was Keynesian, and they would refract it in directions that were acceptable to American business.

The CED was a new kind of policy research organization. Although it was not a captive of any single industry, it was run by businessmen and funded directly by business, rather than by endowed foundations in which decision making had fallen increasingly into the hands of administrators whose backgrounds were generally as academic as those of the scholars they chose to support. The businessmen who set up the CED respected the professional expertise of economists and sought to put academic research into the service of policy formulation. A resident staff of economists, under the direction of Theodore Yntema of the University of Chicago, was hired, and the organization was willing to employ other university-based scholars when their expertise was needed. The CED established a pattern of publishing the scholarly work of individual staff members, while reserving for the business membership the prerogative of issuing institutional policy statements. In its first decade, the publishing program yielded fifteen books and some thirty policy statements. The CED's directors knew that for businessmen to play a substantial part in the policy process, they would need new arrangements for conducting research, gathering information, keeping abreast of theory, deliberating with expert counsel, and ultimately expressing their ideas. They saw the CED setting a new pattern by creating a forum to bring "business thinking" together with representatives of governmental agencies and the most eminent scholars from American universities.[13] The CED was thus to be the businessman's bridge to both professional economics and governmental policymaking—a bridge built more on academic expertise than on dogmatic assertions of principle and narrowly conceived economic interests.

The CED's credo—"The Economics of a Free Society: A Declaration of American Economic Policy"—issued in 1944, readily conceded that the depression had demonstrated some of the shortcomings of classical economic theory. The CED acknowledged the inability of the competitive market to answer all the society's needs and declared its willingness to accept the new role of the government in collective bargaining and old age and unemployment insurance. Most important, the CED acknowledged that it was the task of the federal government, through its tools of fiscal and monetary policy, to mitigate the extremes of the business cycle.[14] Somewhat cryptically, it called for "intelligent handling" of the national debt, meaning that the CED members would tolerate federal deficits in times of recession as a necessary instrument of policy.

The declaration of principle—and the CED's work in educating business leaders—helped define a middle ground for economic policy, moving many businessmen away from free-market fundamentalism. In the late 1940s, the CED struck a policy course between orthodox fiscal conservatives, who persisted in calling for an annually balanced budget and minimal governmental intervention, and the liberal inter-preters of Keynes, who had concluded that the economy was so prone to stagnation that continual governmental spending was needed to keep it going. The Keynesian ideas that undergirded American economic policy for at least the next twenty years (Herbert Stein, a CED economist who later chaired the Council of Economic Advisers under President Richard M. Nixon, called them "Keynesianism with a Chicago spin") relied primarily on monetary policy, tax reduction, and a relatively passive fiscal policy.[15] The CED helped settle the debate on the acceptable instruments of postwar economic policy, though there would still be discussions of when and how particular measures would be used.

The older ideal of national planning—embodied in the NRPB's concern with civilian public works projects, natural resources plan-ning, and the steady expansion of social welfare measures—was amor-phous as an intellectual concept and, to many people, deeply unsettling in practice. The wartime planning apparatus, with its production and price controls—justified by President Roosevelt as emergency measures—was quickly dismantled by President Harry S Truman.

Keynesian techniques had an appeal that planning did not. They were grounded in theory, and they suggested certain limits to govern-mental intervention. Rather than focusing on the performance of particular economic sectors, with the cumbersome idea of adjusting production in each industry as the National Recovery Administration and the Agricultural Adjustment Administration were designed to do, postwar economic policymakers would use the broader tools of federal spending, interest rates, and (on occasion) tax policy to stimulate or restrict aggregate demand. These managerial techniques limited the scope of direct governmental involvement in the economy and set the boundaries for serious discussions of policies in the two decades after the war.

The Keynesian approach also determined the main kinds of expertise (training in macroeconomics) and the sorts of analysis (aggregate economic analysis) that would be given the most weight in public policy debates. Postwar policymakers defined a much narrower economic role for the federal government than advocates of national planning had foreseen in the 1930s, but the effect was to create a much more secure place for economists in the government and to justify their advisory role not in terms of generalized knowledge, but as a consequence of specific professional skills. The economist's theory and analytic techniques were directly linked to policy measures that required the ongoing presence of economists in the government. For the first time, intellectual consensus on a social science theory of how the economy functioned had yielded broad agreement on the policy implications. By 1946 theoretical insights had become the basis for a law—the Employment Act—and theory thus determined where some economists would sit as governmental advisers.

Insiders Institutionalized

The Employment Act of 1946 established the Council of Economic Advisers and required the president to issue an annual economic report. As a statement about policymaking, the Employment Act reflected the anxieties of a generation that had witnessed the failures of economic management during the 1930s.[16] Striking an uneasy compromise between those who wanted to restrict governmental intervention and those who feared the instability of competitive markets, the act defined the federal government's responsibility for tempering the business cycle while accepting the most conservative Keynesian tools for creating fiscal and monetary policies as the best means of attaining economic stability. Edwin Nourse, who had been at Brookings for twenty-three years, became the first chairman of the Council of Economic Advisers. He described the Employment Act as a milestone in establishing a "scientific" basis for the formulation of national economic policy.[17]

The Employment Act of 1946 signaled the economists' arrival

at the center of the postwar American presidency. The creation of
the Joint Economic Committee (originally the Joint Committee on
the Economic Report), also established by the act, gave economists
a significant presence in the legislative branch as well. The resulting
institutionalization of expertise was perhaps the most significant development of the postwar period, though the presence of advisory institutions is no guarantee that they will be used wisely or well. "After
the lapse of little more than a year," as Edwin Nourse wrote bitterly
in 1947 of President Truman's failure to consult the advisers in any
matter of national economic policy, "there is no clear evidence that
at any juncture we had any tangible influence on the formation of
policy or the adoption of any course of action or feature of a program."[18]

Nonetheless, President Truman—the first to enjoy such an intellectual asset—praised the Council of Economic Advisers as an "eminently qualified" group. The praise was not surprising, since he had
chosen its members himself, and according to his memoirs, the council
was especially useful, because the members he had picked were
not of one mind.[19] But, in fact, Nourse's observations were closer
to the truth. Truman used the council sparingly in the early years
of his presidency, turning to it only after Leon Keyserling had succeeded Nourse as chairman in 1950. Keyserling, who ironically did
not have a degree in economics, championed policies of economic
growth that suited Truman's preferences. He also seemed to understand the president and his advisory needs better than did his predecessor, remarking of Nourse, "He could never understand that the
president of the United States has too many things to do to engage
in long bull sessions on economics of the kind that take place at the
Brookings Institution."[20]

Whereas Roosevelt had drawn experts and intellectuals into the
government and seemed to revel in a disorderly policy process, Truman and later Dwight D. Eisenhower were both uncomfortable with
such informal lines of advice and debate. Whereas Roosevelt had
fostered conflict and personal rivalry among his experts, Truman
and Eisenhower institutionalized the various advisory roles, trying
to reduce conflict by devising more systematic methods for weighing
alternative policies.

Truman, although awed in many ways by the man he succeeded,
had little regard for Roosevelt as an administrator. His approach to
the office was different. Roosevelt cultivated chaos. Truman gathered
the information he needed and generally decided on the spot. Averell
Harriman, briefly Truman's secretary of commerce, as well as director

of the European recovery efforts and later a special assistant to the president, recalled, "You could go into his office with a question and come out with a decision from him more swiftly than from any man I have ever known."[21] Truman was never a man to deal in abstractions or multiple levels of complexity. He simply decided, sometimes, as it seemed to Henry Wallace, in advance of careful thinking. But Truman did institutionalize expert advisory relationships in ways that Roosevelt was not inclined to do.

Even as a senator, Truman had criticized the fragmented nature of military and diplomatic intelligence gathering. Reports came from the army and navy, the State Department, the Federal Bureau of Investigation, and the Office of Strategic Services. When he became president, therefore, Truman set up a coordinating body, creating the Central Intelligence Group by an executive order in January 1946. The National Security Act of 1947 went even further and established a permanent presidential advisory body, the National Security Council (NSC). In language appropriate to a onetime store clerk, Truman said the NSC would keep "a running balance and a perpetual inventory" of American policy interests and would be staffed by specialists noted for "objectivity and lack of political ties." He also emphasized that the NSC was intended not only to serve him but to assure the continuity of policies from one administration to the next.[22]

In some policy areas Truman was his own best expert. The federal budget was one of his "serious hobbies," as he put it, an interest stemming from his ten years on the Senate Appropriations Committee. Truman met at least twice a week with his budget director, James E. Webb, sometimes in all-day sessions when the budgetary cycle demanded it. Webb became one of the president's most trusted advisers, screening legislative proposals for him and, at times, using the Bureau of the Budget almost as an extension of the White House staff in preparing legislation. Taking pride in his command of relevant details, Truman delighted in meeting with journalists for two- and three-hour "budget seminars," in which he went over spending plans page by page.[23]

With more experts beginning to occupy positions on specific advisory bodies, the president needed more staff members and a system for coordinating the work of the experts. Among his intimates, two men stood out as policy coordinators: Clark Clifford, who served as special counsel between 1946 and 1950, and John Steelman, who bore the title special assistant. There were others, too: the Missouri cronies and hangers-on, "big-bellied, good-natured guys who knew

a lot of dirty jokes," as I. F. Stone described them. Unlike many of
the Missourians in the White House, Clifford distinguished himself.
Trained as a lawyer, he was the most urbane, a genuinely talented
and hard-working staff member, who took charge of issues of international and national security.

Steelman, a jovial, somewhat bombastic man, was an Arkansas-
born economist who had studied at Vanderbilt, Harvard, and the
University of North Carolina. His experiences in the 1930s had been
typical of the onetime academics who were drawn to the government.
Having met Secretary of Labor Frances Perkins at a conference, he
left his position at Alabama College for Women and took a job in
her department, soon rising to head the Federal Conciliation Service.
Truman appointed him director of the Office of War Mobilization
and Reconversion and then brought him into the White House in
early 1947. In the White House, Steelman concentrated on domestic
policy, though he did not impress many people with his intellectual
gifts.

The president was gradually learning how to draw on this new
wealth of executive advice. Just as he learned to use Keyserling
and the Council of Economic Advisers, Truman also abandoned his
early suspicions and turned to the staff of the NSC during the Korean
War. A rudimentary planning board emerged so that memorandums
on security policy could be drafted in the White House, rather than
by the agencies. Although the president found use for the statutory
advisory bodies, the proliferation of expertise seemed also to require
that the president have his own intermediaries, generalists such as
Clifford (special assistants were also beginning to develop their own
staffs), who could help translate the experts' contributions into policy.

President Eisenhower continued this practice, setting up even
more formal procedures for dealing with both advisory bodies and
cabinet departments. Tidy organization and well-delineated lines of
authority mattered to both men, but Eisenhower was more skillful
in holding to formal hierarchical lines in the White House than was
Truman. Truman was, in most respects, his own chief of staff, chairing
the morning staff meetings, making the daily assignments, and even
overseeing the White House budget. He was by nature too informal
and accessible to inhabit a box at the center of an organizational
chart. He knew how much information he needed and he organized
the White House in a way that let him gather and absorb it. Time
and again, however, he insisted that decisions came from him; advisory
bodies such as the NSC were used only to supply recommendations.

As he put it, "the policy itself has to come down from the President, as all final decisions have to be made by him."[24] Truman's eagerness to involve himself in decisions and his impulse to decide quickly sometimes seemed at odds with the advisory ethos.

By the late 1940s, the executive branch could tap many sources of expertise through the Council of Economic Advisers and other federal departments in which economists were clustered. Sources of expertise could also be found within the staff of the NSC, the policy planning staff of the State Department, and the Central Intelligence Agency. The new institutionalized presidency thus proved a boon to experts. It not only created formal advisory posts for people with academic specialties, it opened the way for greater contact between advisers who were working in the government, whatever their specialties, and the vast array of experts who were working outside it on questions that might bear on public policy decisions. Thus, the practice of institutionalizing advice inside the executive branch, far from displacing the outside advisers in universities and think tanks, managed to open up new opportunities while incidentally helping to legitimate the value of academic inquiry into social, economic, and international issues.

One of the most important new developments for the growing number of experts who were concerned with policy issues was the system of contractual arrangements through which governmental officials could tap outside researchers. The new global burdens of the United States, especially the permanent danger of warfare in the atomic age, quickly suggested a new rationale for channeling federal funds into scientific research. Indeed, to political leaders, the need for expertise was more urgent than ever. New federal agencies—foremost among them the National Science Foundation and the Atomic Energy Commission—were created to fund research in universities and private research centers, though pure research in social science would not be a significant part of the National Science Foundation for some years. The individual military services and the Defense Department also became major funders of research. Experts in and out of government benefited hugely from the new largesse.

Advice by Contract

The creation of postwar contract research organizations fundamentally altered the relationship between experts and public policy making. Almost any governmental agency was now able to have semipermanent reservoirs of outside experts at their command. Although there had been similar contractual arrangements before the war, the remarkable contributions of wartime scientists led to new institutional arrangements. The prototype was the RAND Corporation, founded at the end of World War II, its name an acronym for "research and development." The success of the RAND model inspired a flock of other new research firms whose work throughout the 1950s and 1960s was performed largely at the behest of and by contracts with governmental agencies.[25]

When the war came to an end in 1945, the commander of the U.S. Army Air Forces, General Henry Harley ("Hap") Arnold, foresaw that military research funding would soon lapse and that government scientists would accordingly drift back to their comfortable niches in universities and private industry. Arnold believed that the next war would be won or lost by the nation's scientists. In a world already made considerably smaller by technology, the scale of warfare in the late twentieth century was likely to be global, its speed supersonic, and its destructive power thousands of times greater than in the war just ended. The old pace of industrial mobilization—a year or two to gear up for full war production—would no longer be adequate for the nation's security. And with huge advantages going to those who made the first breakthroughs in offensive weaponry, the nation's research and technological resources would have to be permanently harnessed to the needs of national security.

As early as 1944, Arnold had written to Theodore von Karman, director of the Air Force Scientific Advisory Group, proposing that the members of that body step back from the immediate problems of winning the war against Germany and Japan "to investigate all the possibilities and desirabilities for post war and future war's development." Among other projects, Arnold expressed an interest in whether some new device might replace the airplane or if remote-control and "television assisted" rockets and atomic propulsion were possible.[26] These were not questions that air force officers were trained to answer or even to ask; yet they were the very questions upon which immediate congressional appropriations for the military—and hence the long-term shape and survival of the air force—would depend.

During the last two years of the war, others in the War Department, especially scientists in the Office of Scientific Research and Development, had also asked how the successful partnership between the military and scientific communities might be maintained. Contractual relationships with researchers were routine for that office during the war, and a number of direct links with university laboratories had been established, including one with the Radiation Lab of the Massachusetts Institute of Technology, which, in its work to develop radar, had made one of the most spectacular contributions to the war effort.

Edward L. Bowles, a scientist at the Radiation Lab, and two engineers from the Douglas Aircraft Corporation, Arthur Raymond and Frank Collbohm, had worked together on projects using the new analytic techniques of operations research. Looking at the uses to which the B-29 was being put in the Pacific, for example, they found that the planes could operate more effectively if they were stripped of some of their armor and allowed to fly higher and faster, outrunning Japanese fighters. Such tactical contributions impressed the air force high command, including Curtis Lemay and Hap Arnold. "We have to keep the scientists on board," Arnold said to von Karman, "Its the most important thing we have to do."[27]

Bowles thought a research organization should begin to explore rocketry and intercontinental warfare. And Collbohm recommended to Arnold that the Douglas Aircraft Corporation assemble a civilian research group to do the work for the air force. Arnold embraced the idea, and borrowing a presidential plane the day after his meeting with Collbohm in September 1945, flew to San Francisco's Hamilton Field, where he met with the principals from Douglas. Arnold agreed on the spot to finance the project with $10 million in unexpended funds for war research, and in March 1946, a small team began work in a section of Douglas's Santa Monica plant.

As the research project grew, however, it became more than Douglas wanted to manage, perhaps even a hindrance to winning more lucrative air force contracts. The research staff, which had grown to 150 by 1947, also saw benefits in cutting loose from their corporate overseers. In 1948, with the blessings of the air force and loan guarantees from the Ford Foundation to assure its survival, Project RAND was severed from Douglas and became a free-standing nonprofit organization, the RAND Corporation.

Out of the initial air force contract would grow one of the nation's largest and best-known nonprofit think tanks, a different creature from the policy research organizations that were created before the war. In fact, RAND and *think tank* are virtually synonymous, the term having been adapted from wartime slang and applied after the war to RAND and other military research-and-development organizations. RAND became the prototype for a method of organizing and financing research, development, and technical evaluation that would be done at the behest of governmental agencies, but carried out by privately run nonprofit research centers. The contractual arrangement placed the expert in a relationship to the government that was neither fully dependent nor completely free. Loosed from the constraints and procedures of a governmental bureaucracy, the researcher now had to take account of the client's needs and preferences. It required considerable boldness to issue a bad report. Though operating outside the government, the contract researcher was, in many respects, more dependent on the client in the short-term, since contracts were perpetually being sought or coming up for renewal.

The RAND model flourished in the 1950s, spinning off competitors and causing the other military branches to set up similar units. Such groups as the Mitre Corporation, the Systems Development Corporation, Analytic Services, the Center for Naval Analyses, the Research Analysis Corporation, and the Institute for Defense Analyses have given military planners routine and sustained access to researchers with advanced scientific and technical skills. Although much of the work was and is highly technical—including evaluations of weapons, analyses of engineering problems, or the development of specialized computer systems—nonprofit advisory organizations working under contract to specific governmental agencies soon began to play a larger role in policymaking, conducting studies the agencies did not have the resources to undertake and informally advising their counterparts within the governmental bureaucracy. Indeed, far from supplanting outside researchers, the experts in government sought expanded links to universities and institutes, employing financial resources far larger than those available to private foundations and individuals.

By the end of the 1950s, a huge, government-funded market for expertise had begun to take shape in which experts would begin to speak more routinely of client-agency relationships than of public responsibility. Reports and studies typically responded to the questions raised by policymakers and their staffs. To survive, the research organizations, dependent on contractual relationships, now had to "market" their services to the government. Ideas were "sold" and research "products" were supplied to the contractor. And for the individual researcher working in this environment, skills and methods had to be developed that were useful, that is to say, "marketable," in addressing a variety of problems.

Systems Thinking

RAND not only became the model for the new generation of think tanks, it played an important role in developing new analytic methods. The old patterns of survey research, institutional analysis, and aggregate statistical study had earned a secure place in the policy process, but the new techniques of systems analysis employed at RAND promised much more. Drawing upon cost-benefit analysis, linear programming techniques, game theory, and more, systems analysis was ideally suited to the needs of contract firms for which methods of general analysis were more useful than was narrow substantive expertise.

From the beginning, the researchers at RAND had conceived of themselves somewhat high-mindedly as thinkers who were "fundamentally interested in and devoted to what can broadly be called the rational life."[28] The quantitative reasoning of mathematicians, engineers, and physicists shaped their perspective, and as RAND expanded from working on precisely defined technological problems to fields involving nuclear strategy and national security policy, its researchers embraced a style of rational analysis that would indelibly define an era in American policy.

Systems analysis, an offspring of operations research, was one of the less tangible intellectual by-products of World War II, and the researchers at RAND adopted its language and methods, regardless of their original disciplinary training. Though less dramatic than the weaponry and other technological marvels of the war, operations research nevertheless played an important part in the military victory by providing quantitative measures for determining how best to use particular weapons. At what level would an exploding depth charge be most likely to destroy an enemy submarine? Where should radar systems and antiaircraft batteries be best deployed to defend a target? In what formations should airplanes fly? Are heavily armored aircraft more likely to succeed in their mission than are light, speedy ones?

Operations researchers attached in the last stages of the war to many combat units in the Army Air Force had usually focused on the specific technical and tactical considerations surrounding a particular weapon and its limitations. With new weaponry being developed after the war, the questions grew more complex. E. W. Paxson, a mathematician who joined RAND in 1947, posed the problems that postwar military planners were facing: If the objective is to destroy a submarine or attack a particular target, what kinds of weapons will accomplish the mission? How much will it cost to destroy a given set of targets? What weapons will fulfill the mission at the least cost?[29] Paxson, operating outside the framework of RAND's departmental structure and trying to integrate the work of physicists and engineers, was soon called the "systems analyst" by his colleagues; his quantitative methods were accordingly termed "systems analysis."

The question of what new weapons to build opened up more complicated problems. Complex mathematical manipulations were required for the design of still-emerging technological systems, and systems analysis, with roots in all three fields, helped to bridge the different concerns of engineers, economists, and mathematicians. As RAND has employed researchers trained in an expanding array of disciplines, systems analysis has continued to evolve and unite its research teams.

A variable set of analytic tools, so eclectic that it often seems more an attitude than a fixed methodology, systems analysis is, at its core, a cluster of procedures for determining how to choose among policy means—a problem of greater and greater weight as the costs of both weapons systems and social programs have grown. Because of the focus on choices among means, the methods of the systems analyst often overwhelm the consideration of ends. Systems analysis is, thus, a fitting tool for the contract adviser, for it limits the adviser's role to evaluating the ways to accomplish ends set by the client.

While Paxson's linear equations demonstrated the potential of the systems approach for analyzing weapons, John von Neumann's work on game theory raised it to another level as a tool for sorting out the strategic choices that nations would confront in the nuclear age. From early concerns with rocket propulsion, aircraft design, and operations-research problems, RAND evolved during the 1950s into the nation's leading center for nuclear strategy, drawing into its orbit such thinkers as Bernard Brodie, Herman Kahn, William Kaufmann, Thomas Schelling, and Albert Wohlstetter.[30]

Von Neumann, a Hungarian-born mathematician who arrived in the United States in the 1930s, was one of the guiding minds of the Manhattan Project during the war. Afterwards, with his friend Edward Teller, he tried to grasp the mysteries of the new fusion weapon, the hydrogen bomb. He was also a pioneer in electronic computing whose work led to a huge acceleration in the speed of computers. While on the faculty at Princeton University, von Neumann served as a consultant to RAND and the weapons laboratory at Los Alamos. But his work on the theory of games had the greatest impact on strategic thinking. Game theory is a method of mathematically calculating rational strategies in the face of uncertainty about what an opponent will do. Assuming that both players in a game are acting rationally—a large assumption to be sure—game theory enables a strategist to calculate an opponent's best moves with mathematical rigor and to anticipate accordingly.

Von Neumann's voluminous *Theory of Games and Economic Behavior*, published with Oskar Morgenstern in 1944, pointed toward far-ranging applications in the economic and social spheres. It seemed especially well suited for analyzing the strategic uncertainties of international conflict. In a world devoid of trust, where heavily armed opponents faced each other across an ideological divide, game theory offered a consoling mathematical method for calculating strategy. In tune with the spirit of the times, game theory was at once pessimistic and hopeful. It assumed that the nuclear players were sufficiently rational to choose to avoid destruction; if they were not trustworthy, therefore, the opponents were at least predictable.

As it evolved, game theory made systems analysis an even more powerful tool for weighing strategic choices, and it gave RAND a means to broaden out from purely technological research to speculations about nuclear strategy and defense policy. One of the earliest RAND practitioners to demonstrate its uses in this sphere was Albert Wohlstetter. A onetime student of philosophy and a keen logician and mathematician, Wohlstetter came to RAND in the late 1940s after serving on the War Production Board as a quality-control specialist. He was not especially enthusiastic when Charles Hitch, head of RAND's Economics Division, asked him in 1951 to work on a study for the air force on overseas bomber bases. It did not look to Wohlstetter like interesting work: "dull, full of nuts-and-bolts, the kind of thing one normally associates with logistics."[31]

But when Wohlstetter saw how the air force had formulated the problem, he discovered a fundamental, but strikingly obvious strategic dilemma: The closer the bombers were placed to the target, the more vulnerable they were to enemy attack. The air force seemed to conceive of a third world war as a problem not unlike those confronted during the strategic bombing campaigns at the end of World War II—a matter of selecting targets and choosing routes. They had not asked what might happen if the bombers never left their bases, if the Soviet Union landed the first blow. Wohlstetter, whose wife Roberta was then working on a study that would become a classic account of the surprise attack on Pearl Harbor, had not forgotten how World War II began for the United States. Although he did not work with the mathematical sophistication of such colleagues as Kenneth Arrow in his elaboration of game theory, Wohlstetter had absorbed the theory's basic premise: The best strategies of one's opponents have to be taken into account in planning for war.

Intensely and urgently curious, a prodigious worker, known for staying all night in his office, Wohlstetter began to corner RAND's other experts. He asked about air defense systems and the technical capabilities of aircraft, as well as about tactics and the problems of refueling, maintenance, and repair. Wohlstetter's inquiries confirmed his suspicion that the forward-basing strategy rendered the bombers exceedingly vulnerable; a Soviet nuclear attack, using some 120 forty-kiloton bombs, could destroy about 80 percent of the nation's bomber force. Accordingly, Wohlstetter and his team recommended in 1953 that early-warning systems be improved and that supply depots and fuel-storage areas be strengthened to withstand nuclear blasts; they then made the radical suggestion that overseas installations be used only for refueling and repair, not as permanent bases.

Their study, known among RAND projects simply as R-266, became an essential, defining part of RAND's institutional ethos and is still touted as an example of what systems analysis can accomplish. Researchers at RAND like to say that their first step is to make sure that the right question has been asked, and, as Wohlstetter's study demonstrated, the beginning of wisdom lay in the proper formulation of the problem. But analysis, no matter how persuasive, does not determine policy. Much depends on how a study is communicated, the timing of its presentation, and whether it agrees or conflicts with the agendas of the political executives and bureaucrats who eventually determine its impact.

Wohlstetter and his team (three others shared authorial credit with him) published a top-secret report of more than four hundred pages, which was condensed into a forty-five-minute briefing that could be presented with charts, maps, and graphs. When Wohlstetter first rehearsed his briefing in front of colleagues—a customary practice at RAND that was intended to test the product in front of a critical audience—its implicit challenge to the air force high command was obvious. One of his colleagues remarked after the briefing: "The impact of this study will be the greatest that RAND has ever had. If, Albert, General LeMay stays in the room after your first two sentences."[32] At the conclusion of the first briefing in 1953 to top officers in the Strategic Air Command (SAC) in Omaha, LeMay's deputy, the highest-ranking officer present, remarked tersely, "Very interesting," and hastily marched out of the room. But he had sat through to the end. More briefings followed—ninety-two in all.

The SAC command, especially General LeMay, seemed reluctant to spend money to protect the bomber force. The answer to the bombers' vulnerability, from their perspective, was more bombers and ultimately new, longer-range intercontinental bombers. The SAC command, which reported directly to the Joint Chiefs of Staff, rather than to the air force staff, was also wary of accepting proposals from a cadre of outside consultants hired by the air force.

Wohlstetter's recommendations might easily have been thwarted by the air force bureaucracy, but he persisted. RAND arranged a briefing for the acting air force chief of staff, who took the report seriously and soon began to implement some of its suggestions by reducing the reliance on overseas bases. But even a briefing at the highest level might not have proved persuasive if the explosion of a Soviet hydrogen bomb in August 1953—a bomb far larger than the weapons on which Wohlstetter had based his assumptions—had not confirmed the vulnerability of American bombers (so, too, had a tornado that swept over Carswell Air Force Base in fall 1952, damaging more than eighty bombers parked on the airfield).

The impact of the study was not necessarily its specific recommendations. SAC remained more interested in getting its planes off the ground and on their way quickly than in preparing to withstand a Soviet attack. But the report focused attention on the problem of potential military weakness and made strategic vulnerability a matter of relatively precise calculation. The concept of vulnerability, rather than any specific recommendation, was what gave the report its long-term influence on thinking about policy. Furthermore, it was not the written report, but the ninety-two briefings that drove home the message. Wohlstetter's intellectual work was impressive, but it was really the assurance and persistence with which he communicated his findings that commanded attention.

By the late 1950s, economists, mathematicians, and strategists had evolved sets of analytical tools and assumptions for thinking about the principal questions facing policymakers—economic growth and nuclear strategy. Fearsome as the stakes were, those tools were the source of extraordinary confidence in policy making. The expert was about to attain new heights of prestige and political influence. As confidence in social science methods grew in the 1960s, the expert enterprise, both within and outside government, burgeoned.

SIX

☆

Action
Intellectuals

Ivory-Tower Activists

John F. Kennedy explained to campaign audiences in 1960 why he was running for the nation's highest office: "I want to be a President who acts as well as reacts—who originates programs as well as study groups—who masters complex problems as well as one-page memorandums." He vowed that he would be "a Chief Executive in every sense of the word—who responds to a problem, not by hoping his subordinates will act, but by directing them to act."[1] The imagery of action clearly evoked the tone of Franklin Roosevelt's presidency; it also served implicitly to criticize the elderly and, to all appearances, passive President Eisenhower, a man whose ornate staff-advisory system and highly structured cabinet meetings struck Kennedy as self-imposed impediments on the president's freedom of action.

On the face of it, Kennedy's promise of presidential activism and the gentle dismissal of study groups and orchestrated deliberations by staff did not bode well for all those experts who had obtained advisory posts within the increasingly institutionalized presidencies of Truman and Eisenhower. As part of a bureaucratic chain of command, the expert had clear lines of communication and a formal place in executive branch deliberations. Kennedy's promises of action suggested a return to the freewheeling days of Roosevelt's professors. Cultivating an image of cerebral activism, however, Kennedy managed to attract a breed of academic experts—"action intellectuals," in Theodore White's memorable phrase—whose Washington careers have shaped the modern mythology of the policy intellectual. If Camelot had its handsome young king (and its beautiful and gracious queen), it also had to have its wizardly Merlins and intellectual Round Table.

Kennedy was not the leading presidential choice within the academic community in the early months of the campaign. In January 1960, a poll of prominent academics and writers in *Esquire* showed Kennedy well behind Adlai Stevenson, Hubert Humphrey, and Richard Nixon. Stevenson was obviously the liberal intellectuals' sentimental favorite. After his failed and rather amateurish 1952 campaign, Stevenson had been encouraged by a number of Democrats to put together a more permanent policy-planning group to prepare for 1956. "As the party of the well-to-do, the Republicans do not hesitate to use their dough," John Kenneth Galbraith wrote in 1953. "As the party of the egg-heads, we should similarly and proudly make use of our brains and experience." Under the direction of Thomas K. Finletter, former secretary of the air force, the so-called Finletter Group funneled position papers and advice to Stevenson. Stevenson used their work in his speech making and met many of the academics individually as he traveled the country, but, curiously, kept his distance from their meetings. Early on he wrote Galbraith, "I am eager to avoid any impression that this is a Stevenson brain trust operation." The most scholarly sounding twentieth-century aspirant for the presidency knew he could not afford the further taint of too close an association with intellectuals.[2]

Though not the first choice of the nation's intellectual elite, Kennedy was not an unknown quantity to some of those who later served him. Throughout his rather undistinguished senatorial career, Kennedy had called upon Harvard acquaintances for occasional advice. From time to time, he had telephoned Galbraith when he had questions about economic issues, especially agricultural problems that might understandably perplex a senator from a northern industrial state. Galbraith, like the other intellectuals who had served Stevenson in the 1952 and 1956 campaigns, seems to have been won over slowly by Kennedy, whose lack of scholarly distinction as an undergraduate still nettled some members of the Harvard faculty. Many at Harvard, as Galbraith confessed in a volume of memoirs, "had difficulty in believing that the Kennedy brothers are in the very first league, wholly worthy of the Harvard badge and blessing." But recalling occasional Saturday-night dinners at the Locke-Ober Restaurant with

Kennedy and Arthur Schlesinger, Jr., his tenor softened. "His conversation was wide-ranging and informed," remembered Galbraith; "my respect and affection grew."[3]

But Galbraith also saw in Kennedy a streak of impatience and restlessness that, as president, sometimes caused him to cut off discussion and often kept his wordiest advisers from fully expressing their views. The impatience was doubtless a mark of mental quickness; it was also a sign of his eagerness to get things done. Though notably ineffective as a legislator and apparently unwilling to master the Senate's cumbersome political procedures, he fully understood how the forms of executive branch decision making might help or hinder him as president.

The nation's political elites were afflicted by great uncertainty about national goals. At the end of the 1950s, many Americans seemed to believe that the nation was adrift. General confidence in the country's scientific and technological estate, particularly its educational system, had been dramatically shaken by the early failures of the American space program and by the Soviet Union's surprising success in launching Sputnik in 1957. Many also worried about the so-called missile gap, a spurious issue it turned out, but one that played on real concerns. Beyond these technological concerns, Arthur Schlesinger, Jr., had struck a responsive chord with talk about the "qualitative" deficiencies of American life.

Toward the end of his term, President Eisenhower summoned a national commission to assess the nation's performance and chart long-term goals. With the 1960 election approaching, *Time's* publisher, Henry Luce, commissioned and edited *The National Purpose*, a volume of essays by ten prominent Americans who were worried about a nation that they characterized as lost, becalmed, adrift, and without bearings. Several of the authors looked toward a new style of presidential leadership. "We are waiting to be shown the way into the future," wrote Walter Lippmann. "We are waiting for another innovator in the line of the two Roosevelts and Wilson."[4]

With his coolly rational style, Kennedy appealed to liberal intellectuals, though less because of any explicitly articulated ends than because of the simple and often-repeated promise "to get the country moving again." The candidate, sounding the themes of "vigor," movement, and activism, gradually won the support of intellectuals during a generally unedifying presidential campaign. The intellectuals' growing sympathy for Kennedy was obvious enough for his opponent, Richard Nixon, to make an issue of their support; he sought to stir up the anti-intellectual passions of one southern audience by labeling the Democrats "the party of Schlesinger, Galbraith and Bowles."

After winning the election by a hair, Kennedy designed his political appointments as much to reassure his detractors as to reward his supporters. C. Douglas Dillon, a Republican investment banker, was appointed secretary of the Treasury Department; Luther Hodges, a former governor and businessman, went to the Commerce Department; and Abraham Ribicoff, a respected Connecticut governor, was picked to head the Department of Health, Education, and Welfare. Only two cabinet appointments seemed to break with traditional patterns or to signal the emerging high-level alliance with the nation's intellectual elite. Kennedy chose Dean Rusk, president of the Rockefeller Foundation and a man with extensive prior service in the State Department, to be secretary of state; he did, however, surround him with much better known and more politically powerful undersecretaries. He also selected Robert McNamara, a former professor of business and recently named head of the Ford Motor Company, to run the Defense Department.

In his chronicle of White House service, Kennedy's longtime congressional assistant and White House special counsel, Theodore C. Sorensen, claimed that the president-elect had sought to create nothing less than "a ministry of talent." Sorensen noted that Kennedy had appointed more academics to important positions including (as he dutifully recorded) fifteen Rhodes scholars, than had any of his predecessors. But these "action intellectuals" were not located in the cabinet (except for McNamara and Rusk) or even among the senior White House staff (except for Schlesinger, McGeorge Bundy, and Sorensen). Rather, they were scattered in many subordinate positions throughout the government.

The real difference with past administrations lay in the concern with second- and third-tier appointments and in the personnel assigned to work in the various advisory and regulatory agencies. Kennedy, whose planning for the transition was shaped by studies under way at the Brookings Institution, as well as by memorandums prepared by political scientist Richard Neustadt, clearly understood that the control of such low-level appointments would offer the greatest leverage for policymaking (an insight the Reagan revolutionaries would revive in 1980). And Sargent Shriver, who was given the job of chief talent scout, cast his net widely in recruiting people for the administration.[5]

The White House staff arrangements under Kennedy were much

less formal—conscientiously so—than they had been under Eisenhower's hierarchically organized system. Cabinet and staff meetings were rare, and the staff secretariat was abolished. The president's special assistants worked more or less as equals, operating with small staffs in the White House and enjoying considerable access to the president. Kennedy described the White House as "a wheel and a series of spokes" with himself at the hub. When necessary, the spokes reached far into cabinet departments. But for the most part, Sorensen, who coordinated domestic policy, relied on staff work done in the Bureau of the Budget and the Council of Economic Advisers. Meanwhile, in foreign policy, McGeorge Bundy and his small national security staff, with its own area specialists and ad hoc task forces, were able to supersede the State Department's advisory apparatus. With several hundred policymaking positions to fill in executive agencies, expertise tended to be widely diffused in the bureaucracy and could be called upon as needed. Perhaps for the first time, one could also discern the ways in which advisory institutions—not merely individual advisers—were in contention with one another.[6] "Action intellectuals" were less likely to be adjuncts to a formal deliberative process, as in Eisenhower's White House, than intellectual insurgents seeking to shake up the administrative bureaucracy. McNamara's band of defense intellectuals recruited from the RAND Corporation were the most notable.

In this environment, the outside expert, whether drawn from life in academia or the think tanks to work full time in the government or merely consulted while employed in a university or think tank, could play a major part in shaping policy. When James Tobin of Yale demurred at the suggestion that he join the Council of Economic Advisers, modestly describing himself as something of an "ivory-tower economist," Kennedy reportedly won him over by responding, "That's all right—I'm something of an ivory tower President."[7] But, in truth, Kennedy was interested in ideas mainly when he could see their practical consequences. And he knew that most intellectuals, however much they might disavow an interest in the active, political life, were drawn to service not because he appealed to their "ivory-tower" sentiments but because he promised them proximity to action—the opportunity to employ their ideas. And, indeed, many of them were experts whose notion of an idea was no less practical than his. They were technocrats and social engineers, people primarily interested in crafting the instruments for getting things done. At the same time that the action intellectuals descended on Washington, however, some Americans had been contemplating the end of ideas as a driving force in politics.

The End of Ideology

In becoming a political adviser and intimate participant in policy-making, the expert had little choice but to serve as a problem solver and technician. While historians like H. Stuart Hughes and Richard Hofstadter distinguished between intellectuals and mental technicians, sociologists coined the oxymoronic term "bureaucratic intellectual" to characterize the role of experts working in governmental agencies. Robert K. Merton described how some experts adapted to their new dependence on policymakers and bureaucratic superiors: "This sense of dependency, which is hedged about with sentiment, is expressed in the formula: the policy-maker supplies the goals (ends, objectives), and we technicians, on the basis of expert knowledge, indicate alternative means for reaching those ends."[8] The formula may have been new, but the underlying assumptions were not. The pragmatists' retreat from abstract theories and absolutes at the turn of the century had set this course for intellectuals and experts. The policy expert in the United States was primarily a technician of means.

The experts' move into the inner circles of political power in the 1960s was paralleled by a steady diminution of the interplay of ideas in political life. The then twenty (nearing thirty) years war against fascism and communism had strongly reinforced long-standing American suspicion of ideological systems (especially among those intellectuals who had flirted with one or the other before the war). Writing in the 1950s, the so-called consensus historians—principally Daniel Boorstin, Richard Hofstadter, and Louis Hartz—proclaimed an underlying homogeneity in American political and intellectual life. Whether the absence of serious intellectual differences was explicitly nonideological—traceable to the primacy of the struggle for survival in settling a new continent, as Boorstin saw it—or was simplemindedly ideological in accepting a cluster of Lockean dogmas, as Hartz maintained, Americans were generally not inclined to reflections on ultimate values. As historians, adherents of the consensus approach thus expressed their generation's skeptical view of the older Progressive idea of conflict as the driving force in history; as witnesses to the domestic and international turmoil wrought by the depression,

World War II, the Cold War, and McCarthyism, they were expressing, perhaps less consciously, a need to find and reassert the fundamental unities of American society.[9]

Like the historians, some social scientists—most notably Daniel
Bell and Edward Shils—had grown wary of abstract ideas. Nazi concentration camps, the Moscow trials, and the brutal repression in
Eastern Europe offered evidence that ideas were dangerous political
instruments, apocalyptic in their consequences. Ideology as a means
of converting ideas into "social levers," in Bell's phrase, had lost all
intellectual appeal and, therefore, had come to a historic end. Bell—
labor editor of *Fortune* during the 1950s and a frequent contributor
to *Encounter* and *Commentary*—argued that ideologues lived not
for contemplation and thought but for action; indeed, the latent function of ideology was simply to arouse emotion and direct it toward
political ends. Few "serious minds," according to Bell, could be
persuaded either by left-wing utopian blueprints or by predictions
that the welfare state and governmental involvement in the economy
led to serfdom, as resurgent voices of classical liberal economics
such as Friedrich A. Hayek had begun to argue. In his essay "The
End of Ideology in the West," Bell saw the emergence of "a rough
consensus" that included an acceptance of the welfare state, the desir-
ability of decentralized power, and a commitment to a mixed economy
and political pluralism.[10]

Robert Lane, a political scientist at Yale, whose previous studies
had focused on American business and public opinion, traced this
"politics of consensus" to the nation's growing affluence and the apparent ability of the government to tame the business cycle. The political
style of the late 1950s had become less acrimonious than that of the
depression or the McCarthy era. Lane explained the period's optimism
by noting that people felt "less at the mercy of chance and more in
control of their lives." Significantly (and ironically from the vantage
of the fundamentalist revival of the 1980s), he discerned a lessening
of the power of religious institutions and dogmas. He was wide of
the mark with other predictions, too. He said that individuals were
becoming more trusting, both of one another and of government.
And he predicted that the growing struggle for racial equality would
be made easier by the nation's rising affluence.

Lane predicted the emergence of a nonideological politics that
"deals less with moral absolutes and becomes more a discussion of
means than of ends." Ideology would be of less significance in a
society that had undergone what he called a "second scientific revolu-

tion," namely, the vast postwar expansion in the resources devoted to research on social, economic, and political problems. For Lane, the intellectual resources devoted to the social and policy sciences had brought about a change in the very nature of political decision making. He posited a distinction between a domain of "pure politics," in which decisions are determined by calculations of influence, power, or electoral advantage, and a domain of "pure knowledge," in which decisions are made rationally and efficiently about implementing agreed-upon values. In his view, the domain of pure knowledge was expanding and the domain of pure politics was shrinking. Political leaders were seeking better counsel, using rational criteria, and relying on better evidence for their decisions.[11] Thus, forever seeing the end of something, by the early 1960s intellectuals had pronounced an end to conflict, ideology, and even politics.

President Kennedy took up the twin themes of knowledge and political action when he addressed Yale's graduating class of 1962. He, too, celebrated the era of diminished ideological passions, echoing the widely shared conviction that there was now a broad consensus on liberal values. The central domestic issues of the time, said Kennedy, "relate not to basic clashes of philosophy or ideology but to ways and means of reaching common goals—to research for sophisticated solutions to complex and obstinate issues." Sounding like one of Lane's graduate students, Kennedy stated that the problems of the 1960s, unlike those of the 1930s, posed "subtle challenges for which technical answers, not political answers, must be provided." Outdated clichés and myths and a distracting "false dialogue" had to be cast aside, he said. Kennedy was no doubt looking beyond his immediate academic audience toward members of the business community in the wake of that April's bruising battle over price increases in the steel industry. "What is at stake in our economic discussions today is not some grand warfare of rival ideologies which will sweep the country with passion but the practical management of a modern economy. What we need is not labels and clichés but more basic discussion of the sophisticated and technical questions involved in keeping a great economic machinery moving ahead."[12]

Kennedy, suspicious of abstractions, was more concerned with managerial efficiency and expertise, and he was generally confident about the benefits of applied technology. A familiar Progressive commitment to nonpartisanship and a reliance on politically neutral expertise resonated in the sentiments he expressed at Yale, already reflected in his political appointments. Whether Kennedy, who was, after all, a tough professional politician, rather than an intellectual, agreed entirely with Lane's rosy predictions, he certainly believed that policy-making demanded subtlety, complexity, sophistication, and technical virtuosity. The men he chose to serve under him seemed to share his belief that knowledge could serve the goals of policy in highly refined ways—through "flexible response" to military threats and economic "fine-tuning," for example.

Thus, the vaunted "idealism" that Kennedy's administration tapped was really an expression of faith in the powers of rational intelligence and technical virtuosity to overcome social and economic problems.[13] At its core was a conviction that policymaking is a pragmatic endeavor, driven by knowledge; seeking to solve specific problems; and devoted, when necessary, to experiment. And especially in its Cold War struggles against a formidable technological enemy, the country needed public servants who were technically competent, quick, and imaginative about political means. The ends and ideals of political life appeared as self-evident truths, too obvious to require examination.

Experts on Tap

The word *think tank* was not yet secure in the popular lexicon when Kennedy was elected. But journalists were quick to note the existence of a cluster of so-called brain banks and think factories along Massachusetts Avenue. Far and away the most prominent was the Brookings Institution, which had established its imposing new Center for Advanced Study a block from Dupont Circle in 1960. In reporting on the center's official opening only two weeks after the election, the *Washington Post*, offering editorial encouragement, expressed the hope that "men of learning and ideas have taken over our government again." The *Washington News* was more circumspect, however, describing the affair under the headline "Eggheads See Sunnyside." Less than a year later, *The Economist* described the Brookings researchers as Kennedy's "experts on tap" and hailed "the educated approach to government" as a characteristic feature of the new administration.[14]

Experts inside government inevitably look to experts outside. The ties are often casual. Such links were established early on with Brookings. With no official space for the Kennedy transition team to work (later legislation setting aside federal funds for presidential transitions was a direct outgrowth of Brookings studies of the problems of transition), some members found not only offices, but a library and meeting rooms at Brookings. The transition "task forces" consulted widely. They relied heavily on the nearly one hundred scholars (counting affiliated university researchers) who were working on policy issues for Brookings. One of the most useful was Laurin Henry, whose work on past presidential transitions guided the Kennedy team.[15]

The researchers and analysts at Brookings and RAND typified the new policy intellectuals of the 1960s. And these institutions, more than any others, came to symbolize the era's technocratic style. For both, the means of their influence were diffuse and hard to measure. Brookings had the advantage of being the premier organization for policy research in Washington, with a research program covering many fields and having long-standing ties to the federal bureaucracy and congressional staffs. RAND, a continent away and focused on defense research, not only had contractual ties with the air force and other governmental agencies, but was the principal recruiting ground for Robert McNamara as he sought to gain control over the defense establishment. Its influence was largely through the people it sent into the government and the methods they brought to policy analysis.

Robert Calkins, president of Brookings since 1952, had seen the institution through a major expansion and building program. None too secure financially when he took over and with a reputation as a cranky opponent of New Deal and Fair Deal policies in the 1930s and 1940s, Brookings restored its ties to the government during his tenure with its Advanced Study Program for senior federal executives and its hiring of a solid research staff. Like his predecessor, Harold G. Moulton, Calkins was trained as an economist. He had been chairman of the fractious economics department at the University of California at Berkeley and dean of Columbia University's School of Business. A onetime labor mediator, he had also worked for the War Labor Board and directed the General Education Board, one of the oldest Rockefeller philanthropies. He had come to Brookings somewhat reluctantly and against the advice of friends like Beardsley Ruml, who thought the institution had been in decline for so long that it could never be resuscitated. From the vantage point of New York's foundations, on whose largesse any expanding institution would have to depend, Brookings seemed out of the political mainstream in the early 1950s and isolated from the most promising developments in social science in the universities.

After a careful inspection of the situation, Calkins accepted the challenge of resurrecting Brookings. Within a year, he had reduced the staff by nearly half and put together an advisory committee of outside academics. Haunting the offices of New York foundations, he repaired relations with the philanthropic community, most significantly the Rockefeller and Ford foundations, where the rumblings about the intellectual quality of the work at Brookings had been the loudest.[16] Acknowledging some of the foundations' complaints, he set about hiring a core of first-rate scholars.

It was a slow task, and many turned him down, but Calkins managed to create a solid and experienced nucleus for the Economic Studies Program. The new fellows included Joseph Pechman, who had worked for the Committee for Economic Development, the Council of Economic Advisers, and the Treasury Department, and Walter Salant, who had studied with Keynes and Hansen and held a number of governmental posts, including work for the Office of Price Administration and the Council of Economic Advisers. The programs in Government and Foreign Policy studies proved more difficult to build, but by 1960, with a budget of about $2 million, a staff of approximately forty senior researchers and sixty research associates, and expanding links to the universities, Brookings was poised to play an important new role in Washington.[17]

Throughout the 1960s, seventy to one hundred research projects were continuously under way. Though not primarily a contract research organization, Brookings responded to projects initiated by governmental agencies and foundations. Between 1955 and 1967, one foundation, Ford, gave some $39 million to Brookings. Its aim was to create what a staff member at the foundation described as "a private intelligence unit for government operations."[18] The Ford Foundation financed much of the cost of a new building, contributed to Brookings's endowment, and gave long-term funding to research projects. The connections among governmental agencies, foundations, and research centers were informal, much less constrained by the competitive processes for submitting proposals and formal mechanisms for determining accountability. In 1964, for example, the State Department wanted a memorandum to outline U.S. policy options with regard to new technical assistance programs of the United Nations. State Department officials told the Ford Foundation that they needed outside help; the Ford Foundation agreed to pay for it, and Brookings had staff members who were already studying the United Nations who were willing to prepare the report. On another occasion, the Ford Foundation approached Brookings (after conversations with members of the Council of Economic Advisers) and suggested that the institution study the impact of the 1964 tax cut. Soon, with many governmental agencies seeking its services (and the administrators at Brookings complaining that there were more requests for research than they could ever undertake—a far cry from the competitive search for funds a decade later), the Brookings program expanded into many fields.

Economic Studies, the largest and consistently regarded as Brookings's strongest research division, centered its work on policies for economic growth and stabilization, the effects of industrial concentration, fiscal and tax policy, and international competition. It produced studies on automatic economic stabilizers, governmental investments, and the individual income tax, as well as on monetary policy, all subjects that were of interest to the Keynesians who dominated the policy debate. In 1960, with a Ford Foundation grant of more than $2 million, Brookings began a series of studies of governmental finance under Pechman's direction, which would ultimately yield more than thirty books.[19]

The researchers in Brookings's Government Studies division produced book-length reports on the higher reaches of the civil service and on the government's personnel policies. Calkins's new staff broke with the older managerial traditions of public administration, moving from nuts-and-bolts concerns to projects that examined the political contexts shaping the work of governmental bureaucrats. They also began to study politics, focusing on presidential nominations and the electoral process and exploring the legislative branch by looking at the job of the congressman and the need for new rules and organization on Capitol Hill.[20] Meanwhile, Brookings continued to look for practical ways of improving the skills of bureaucrats, setting up training seminars and ultimately the Advanced Study Program for senior government employees, whose successor, the Center for Public Policy Education, is now Brookings's largest operating unit.

Researchers on foreign policy studied the United Nations, international economic development, and the administration of U.S. foreign assistance programs, especially in Latin America after Kennedy initiated the Alliance for Progress. They were also interested in the training of political leaders and managers in developing countries, spending several years on an advisory project in Vietnam. In addition, they analyzed the role of education in less developed nations.[21]

Each year Brookings's annual reports tallied up the diverse advisory roles played by its researchers, but the core of the institution's work was still its book publishing program. The staff grounded their work in book-length studies; advising was secondary because all seemed to agree that long-term influence lay in books. Brookings, which had issued eight to ten books a year in the late 1950s, was publishing twenty-five a year by the end of the 1960s. Opportunities for consulting and advising, whether through personal contact or the preparation of brief memorandums, did not as yet provoke much reflection on the nature of a policy research institution's influence and the best strategies for increasing it.

In the 1960s policy researchers must have shared Robert Lane's convictions that the domain of knowledge was expanding and that of politics contracting. Opportunities to serve, formally and informally, were plentiful. And often, it was governmental officials who were seeking assistance, not the institutions that were pushing their services on the government. Clearly, however, a market for professional services was taking shape that would restructure the environment in which the older think tanks, such as Brookings, had operated and that would change the career opportunities and professional incentives of the expert. Although Brookings expanded considerably throughout the 1960s, it was dwarfed by the RAND Corporation.

Tools of the Trade

There was much in the Kennedy style that appealed to the analytic ethos of the RAND Corporation, just as there was much about the RAND style that seemed to appeal to Kennedy. Some of RAND's analysts had forwarded memos to the Kennedy campaign and provided material for speeches as early as 1959. Their opposition to the doctrine of massive retaliation, their idea that the "missile gap" was growing, and their proposals to build up conventional war capabilities struck resonant chords with the candidate and his inner circle of advisers.[22]

After the election, RAND's direct influence increased as its staff and alumni accepted governmental posts. Kennedy selected Robert S. McNamara as secretary of defense and McNamara, in turn, picked a number of budget analysts, economists, and strategists from RAND as the nucleus of his team of so-called Whiz Kids. McNamara, who at age forty-four had only recently been named president of the Ford Motor Company, was no stranger to systems analysis. During the war, he had been a member of an operations research group that helped the air force solve logistical problems—getting planes, men, and equipment to the right place at the right time. After the war, McNamara and some of his associates banded together to sell their services to American industry. Hired by Henry Ford II, they began to apply the new analytic techniques to the troubled automobile company.

The group McNamara assembled when he left the Ford Motor Company included men like Charles Hitch, the first head of RAND's Economics Division who was hired as the Pentagon comptroller; Alain Enthoven, deputy assistant secretary for systems analysis; and Henry Rowen, a deputy to the assistant secretary for international security affairs. Consulting relationships allowed many other RAND disciples to contribute to defense decision making. Their employment was based not on broad knowledge but on confidence in the specific analytic methods with which they were skilled.[23]

McNamara and his team put weapons systems to the cost-benefit test, looking at the defense budget in its entirety, across the services and with broad goals for national security in view, as RAND analysts had tried to do for a decade. Hitch, as comptroller, asked questions that RAND analysts were trained to ask: "What weapons system will destroy the most targets for a given cost? What weapons system will destroy a given set of targets for the lowest cost?"[24] Such questions often had concrete policy consequences, providing evidence that could be used against dubious proposals for weapons. Cost-benefit analyses wreaked havoc on the air force's plans, raising doubts about both the B-58 and the B-70 and questioning the worth of half a dozen missile systems.

But analysis is inevitably embedded in the political process, and once in the government, the RAND analysts quickly learned about the limits of their analytic tools. McNamara asked Hitch and Enthoven to determine how many intercontinental ballistic missiles (ICBMs) the nation needed. No stranger to quantitative analysis, McNamara thought that roughly 400 ICBMs would inflict sufficient damage on the Soviet Union to deter an attack. Enthoven's calculations generally concurred with McNamara's assessments, and both saw no justification for the 2,400 missiles the air force requested. Some analysts at RAND thought the vastly lower figure was a post hoc calculation to justify the direction in which the administration already leaned. But when the decision was finally made, analytic premises and careful calculations had to yield to the reality of pressure from the military services and Congress, leading the administration to commit itself to build 1,000 ICBMs.

RAND analysts set out to apply system and method to problems in which new technologies and budgetary decisions intersect. Procurement decisions, long-range planning, and measures to control a huge and complex budget seemed to lend themselves directly to the quantitative rationality of operations research and economic analysis. But even in areas that are most susceptible to quantitative analysis—the acquisitions of weapons, budgeting, and logistical decisions—there are no guarantees that analysis will shape the outcome of events. Nor can there be full proof that analysis determines the outcome, even when the decisions conform to the analysis.[25]

RAND's relationship with the air force had not always been smooth in the 1950s, especially when analysis challenged a much-sought weapons system or standard operating procedures. The systems analysts found much more resistance from the Pentagon in the 1960s, primarily because some officers disdained their lack of military experience. General Thomas White, on retiring from his position as chief of staff of the air force, wrote: "I am profoundly apprehensive of the pipe-smoking, tree-full-of-owls type of so-called professional 'defense intellectuals' who have been brought into this nation's capital." He characterized the McNamara appointees as over-confident and arrogant young professors, stressing their youthfulness and lack not only of military experience, but of "worldliness." The analysts' knowledge was abstract and academic, and they had little understanding of actual warfare; they also had a tendency to disparage military men. "The term 'defense intellectual,' " he concluded, "conveys a nice, cozy, unwarlike and non-military feeling, as though modern war could be settled on a chessboard in an ivy-covered Great Hall."[26]

More than twenty years later, some veterans of RAND conceded that they were probably naive about what their methods could accomplish. Gene Fisher, who had been at RAND since 1951, moved to the Pentagon to help Charles Hitch set up the so-called planning-programming-budgeting systems that were at the center of McNamara's attempted managerial revolution. Fisher quickly and painfully learned that analytic methods—even those that seemed well suited for aiding budgetary decisions—often had little or no effect on the outcomes of policies. "We were all naive," he ruefully observed in a 1986 interview. Neither complex bureaucracies nor politically astute policymakers proved easy to move by quantitative analysis. Yet despite the acknowledged limits of their methods, the RAND researchers made systems analysis the *lingua franca* of the policy elite.

The American approach to social science had always been linked to statistical methods and quantitative analysis. But the mathematical sophistication of the systems analysts was a compelling contribution. Systems analysis was the most sophisticated tool of a technocratic liberalism that sought to reduce politics to a quantitative science. Social scientists seemed, at long last, to possess the tools for a *policy* science and to have willing patrons in political life who were eager to have the tools tested. The hyperrational analysis cultivated at RAND proved neatly compatible with the style and aspirations of both the New Frontier and the Great Society. And for a brief moment, the new quantitative methods gave policymakers and their advisers a confidence they had not known before.

Lacking the wisdom of earlier social scientists who had experienced the failures of their methods, the new systems thinkers either made huge claims about what their technical skills could accomplish or let misconceptions flourish among political leaders. Nevertheless, in the early 1960s, some RAND analysts were already wary of the tools they had created. R. D. Specht of RAND's Mathematics Division noted that RAND analysts had always sought to represent the world with a single mathematical model "to produce a neat solution from which conclusions and recommendations could be drawn." These analysts found their computers more intriguing than they did the underlying context and assumptions, which they thought of as "givens," the concern of the political leader rather than of the analyst. But they were not really analyzing problems "with a given and definite context" in which "simple optimization procedures" might work, Specht warned. Even the objectives might not be clear-cut. With his unusual understanding of the difference between analyzing a narrow problem and designing policy measures, Specht was prescient in his warning of what analysts might face as they tried to design systems that would operate in the unpredictable world of political reality.[27]

The experts who were drawn to Washington in the early 1960s acknowledged—even celebrated—the complexity of domestic and international problems. Rather than speaking of cures for social ills or adjustments to imbalances in the social and economic order, as earlier experts had done, they found a new metaphor for thinking about the political uses of knowledge. They spoke of "systems" and "design," adopting the language of engineers and employing the most refined tools of mathematical and economic analysis. Systems analysis and computer modeling were rooted in engineering, while theoretical developments in game theory, input-output analysis, and linear programming linked engineering to economics and broadened the application of its conceptual tools.

The systems analysts promised to see social and economic processes as a whole and, in designing policies, to explore the complex relationships among a system's components. More often, however, they reduced the whole to a set of mathematical common denominators. A world seen through models and systems often confused the artificial order of mathematical relationships with the disorderly world. The promise of solving problems too easily became an exercise in redefining problems in ways that seemed amenable to technical solution. Answers could be dismissed if they were not quantifiable, and problems could often be ignored if they were not measurable. Quantitative virtuosity began to win out over the less certain conclusions derived from experience and tempered judgment. But the aim of scientific technique has seldom been to enhance political judgment. Rather, it has been to remove contentious issues from the realm where judgment is necessary. Pragmatic social science began as an attempt to engage the world as it is, rather than seeing it through philosophical abstractions. It had treated action as inherently adaptive. Over roughly sixty years, it had evolved into a hyperrational attempt to impose a quantitative order on the world. Thus, the flight from abstract political and economic theory that had begun a century earlier had come full circle by the 1960s, arriving at a destination no less abstract and often a great deal farther from reality.

The experts and their political partners enjoyed a short-lived era of confidence. Their attitudes about expertise and its relation to policy, which culminated in Lyndon Johnson's Great Society, bore the seeds of the subsequent popular rejection of experts and the retreat from political complexity and from liberalism itself. They had little time or patience for public education, the nurturing of popular constituencies, or the fostering of a sustained political commitment. "Complexity" appeared to mean that fewer efforts needed to be made to communicate their findings and prescriptions to the public; thus, unwittingly—and tragically—the experts abandoned one of the main concerns of turn-of-the-century progressives.

RAND and other contract research organizations, as they always had, produced reports for particular clients, not for the public. But even those institutions that had once aspired to wider influence now committed themselves to serving relatively narrow subcommunities of policy professionals and political decision makers. Both Robert Calkins and Kermit Gordon, who succeeded him as president of

Brookings in 1967, saw their audience as a group comprised mainly of policymakers, university-based experts, and other members of the policy elite. Among the older groups, the National Bureau of Economic Research produced technical studies for economists, while Russell Sage worked increasingly within the framework of academic sociology, engaged primarily in studies of the methods and techniques of social science. Only the Twentieth Century Fund, where journalists August Heckscher and his successor, Murray J. Rossant, directed the program, remained committed to publishing books that might engage a wider public.

As the national research enterprise expanded during the 1960s and found eager clients in the government, problems of technique and methodology led discussions farther from political ends and values and the assumptions that underlay policy. As experts reveled in their technocratic skills, they grew more and more detached from even the educated public. Knowing how valued their skills were in the government, the career expectations among the policy elite began to change as well. The Kennedy appointments suggested that there were any number of academic routes to public offices. Deanships, foundation presidencies, prestigious teaching appointments, and writing on public issues had opened the way not merely for informal advising but for a period of highly visible public service. Roosevelt's Brains Trusters (Raymond Moley, Rexford G. Tugwell, and Adolf A. Berle) had been uncertain about their role after the election, preferring to return to their academic careers and let the politicians deal with the official chores of government. And Roosevelt himself had not been sure where he should use them. But there were fewer such uncertainties for those who went to Washington in 1961. Knowledge and power seemed comfortably joined. For aspiring members of the policy elite, the new analytic techniques, as well as the new institutional structures for professional advancement, helped to define policymaking as a career, rather than as a series of fortunate accidents.

The sudden ascent of the expert in the 1960s was the result of a rare coincidence of favorable circumstances—public officials set a tone by emphasizing technical competence and intelligence in addressing issues of public policy, a receptive president brought experts and academically inclined generalists into important positions, apparent agreement on national goals produced a focus on the technical means of attaining them, analytic techniques and insights from social science seemed on the verge of making political decisionmaking more rational, governmental agencies were willing to fund research, and a period of sustained national prosperity created hefty endowments for foundations and produced generous grants for public policy research institutions. Nonetheless, Lyndon Johnson's use of the experts quickly exposed both their pretensions and their weaknesses in serving power.

The Labyrinth of Power

"Is our world gone?" Lyndon Johnson asked in his 1965 inaugural address. "We say farewell. Is a new world coming? We welcome it, and we will bend it to the hopes of man." Relying on the straightforward queries and declarative sentences drafted by special assistant Richard Goodwin, Johnson captured the simple optimism of the American spirit of reform. He blithely dismissed the past, while confidently asserting that the government could bend and shape the future to conform to America's highest ideals.

A man with limited oratorical skills (yet so amply endowed with a Texan's capacity for exaggeration that the term *credibility gap* was coined to describe his efforts to persuade the public), Johnson nevertheless effectively used the power of words to drive and control the policy process. His awkward gestures and studious delivery sharply contrasted with his uncanny and typically overbearing private powers of expression. Goodwin, who wrote many of the president's major speeches during 1964 and 1965, instinctively grasped the way Johnson used language. Johnson knew, Goodwin observed, that "in exchange for words—only words—many men would make concessions, yield their will to his, enhance his power."[28]

Johnson's *Great Society* and *War on Poverty* were captivating terms that encapsulated a whole administration and its aims. They linger more insistently than have any terms coined by speech writers to describe subsequent administrations. They embody his ambitions for the simple reason that speech writing and policymaking were not viewed as separate functions in the Johnson White House. In fact, nine of Johnson's eleven special assistants could wield words skillfully enough to contribute to the writing process (Nixon moved his writers to the Executive Office Building and his successors left them there, thus symbolizing a widening gap not only of personal credibility but of political speech and action).

The term *Great Society* was first worked into the fabric of a presidential speech at the commencement ceremonies at the University of Michigan in 1964 after several months of casting about for a theme and rationale that would link the new administration's myriad bills and programs, express its aims, and, ultimately, suggest a progressive course distinct from the New Deal obsession with relieving material want. Goodwin had proposed the phrase, conscious of its resonance with Walter Lippmann's *The Good Society* (1937) and Graham Wallas's *The Great Society* (1914), an influential Fabian-socialist document. What was initially "a fragment of rhetorical stuffing" for an unimportant speech grew into a phrase that Goodwin (encouraged by Johnson) used in the commencement address to epitomize the president's ambitions.

The idea of a military struggle against poverty had emerged four months earlier, in the 1964 State of the Union message, when Johnson still lacked a coherent program. Although many antipoverty proposals had been under consideration in the Council of Economic Advisers—where Walter Heller, the chairman, had begun work on a poverty program several months before John Kennedy's assassination—the formal declaration of war preceded any detailed battle plan. Throughout his presidency, whether driven by militant rhetoric or the grandiose ambition to construct a Great Society, Johnson's experts constantly raced to devise programs that would keep pace with his rhetorical commitments or supply the rationale for legislative initiatives that had already been announced. At Michigan, he acknowledged that he did not have the answers, but he promised to assemble the "best thought" for dealing with the problems of cities, education, and "natural beauty" (the term "environment" was not yet widely used). A few days later, still exuberant about the audience's cheering response and the overwhelmingly favorable reaction by the press, Johnson reportedly told Goodwin, Bill Moyers, and Jack Valenti, "Now it's time to put some flesh on those bones. . . . Let's get to work, bring in all those experts and put it all together. And don't worry about the politics. I'll get it done."[29]

The Great Society was not intended to evoke images of material prosperity as much as to summon Americans to deal with the qualitative and spiritual dimensions of life. However grand the project of constructing a Great Society sounded, it was to be a structure fashioned from many small pieces of legislation, rather than a few stolid pillars. And for all Johnson's military rhetoric, the so-called War on Poverty was neither lengthy nor hard fought as most wars go. The major legislative campaigns were mapped out and won in a brief two-year period that saw the passage of the Economic Opportunity Act, the Voting Rights Act, and the Elementary and Secondary Education Act, and the creation of Medicare and Medicaid, all in 1964 and 1965. The pace was rapid fire. From 1964 to 1968, roughly four hundred pieces of domestic legislation were passed, and by the time Richard Nixon took office in 1969, more than 400 domestic programs were in place—ten times more than when Eisenhower left office in 1961.

But the most protracted battle of the War on Poverty has been the bitter intellectual conflict over how to interpret its successes and failures and in what ways to apportion the blame for the perceived excesses of American liberalism. The legacy of the War on Poverty has been one of the most keenly disputed subjects of the past twenty years, shaping the ideological contours of conservatism, liberalism, and their "neo" variations in the 1970s and 1980s. Indeed, the political success of the conservative claim to be the party of "new ideas" is best explained by the wide perception of the breakdown in domestic policies that occurred in the 1960s.[30]

Among the most serious casualties of the official War on Poverty were the many policy experts who left the field with wounded reputations. Indeed, some of the first critics of the Great Society programs had been the programs' architects, suddenly skeptical of the weapons they were using to combat domestic problems and even of the political role they had chosen to play. The recriminatory passions unleashed by these struggles ultimately raised doubts about the experts' claims to neutrality; their knowledge of politics, economics, and human behavior; and the analytic weapons in their arsenal.

The social science enterprise—in government; in universities; and in various think tanks, contract research organizations, and consulting firms—had blossomed during the 1960s. Theodore White watched it unfold during the Kennedy years, and in 1967, with much of the Johnson legislation complete, he proclaimed the emergence of "a new power system in American life . . . [a] new priesthood, unique to this country and this time, of American action intellectuals." Their ideas seemed to propel the whole machinery of government and politics, shaping defense, foreign policy, and economic management; redesigning schools and cities; and planning to reshape entire regions of the country. White and others had already noted the number of cabinet members, under both Kennedy and Johnson, who were onetime college professors. But White also observed a new reliance on think tanks, university-based research, foundations, and expert commissions; the presidency had become "almost a transmission belt packaging and processing scholars' ideas to be sold to Congress as a program." When the early reports on Johnson's domestic programs came in, White was poised to ask the perennial questions about experts and intellectuals: "Do social scientists yet know enough to guide us to the very different world we must live in tomorrow. Do they offer wisdom as well as knowledge?"[31]

Though the transformation of ideas into policy could hardly be described as a smoothly running conveyor belt, social scientists and policy experts had been among the most significant purveyors of the optimistic mood that launched the decade, a mood that helped to justify wider governmental intervention in American social and economic life. But what contributions had they actually made to public policy? How much had they really contributed to the design of specific policies and programs? And, balancing the decade's accomplishments and disappointments, how much had their failures done to undermine the confidence that any social goal could be accomplished by government?

Lyndon Johnson drew eminently talented people into governmental service (though they were less heralded as intellectuals than were those on the Kennedy team), while managing to retain a handful of Kennedy's appointees. In the inner circle, Bill Moyers, Harry McPherson, Richard Goodwin, Douglas Cater, and Horace Busby were skillful writers and, for the most part, comfortable with experts and intellectuals. Johnson's inner circle sifted and filtered ideas and turned them into legislative initiatives.

Others brought more specific analytic tools to the job of crafting the president's legislative program, among them Kermit Gordon and Walter Heller, two economists who had early won Johnson's trust. Gordon, a former member of the Council of Economic Advisers who served both Kennedy and Johnson as budget director, and Heller, chairman of the council, were the architects of bills on tax reduction and the budget. Heller also shaped the early antipoverty proposals. Although he was a lawyer, Joseph Califano, who had assisted Robert McNamara at the Defense Department, brought a familiarity with systems analysis into the domestic policy circles of the White House. Those techniques were embraced with typical enthusiasm in 1965, when Johnson issued an executive order requiring all governmental agencies to use the so-called planning-programming-budgeting system. It was a "very revolutionary system," in his words, which he claimed would make the decision-making process "as up-to-date as our space-exploring equipment."[32]

Johnson was genuinely interested in the technical advice the community of policy experts could give him, but he also viewed them warily—as an important political constituency that was not inclined to support him. He would ask his staff to solicit their advice and in the same breath condemn "the Harvards" and other intellectuals for their superior airs. His unsurpassed mastery of detail and strategy awed those who served him directly (aides were continually astounded by his formidable memory). Still, he desperately craved the respect of a wider intellectual community, the very group to whom his civil rights initiatives ought to have appealed most. Yet from the beginning of his presidency, he was uncomfortable and inconsistent in his dealings with them. "This Administration feels no discomfort in the presence of brains," he felt compelled to tell one early gathering of domestic policy thinkers.[33] To the contrary, the graduate of Southwest Texas State Teacher's College and onetime high school teacher always seemed uneasy in the company of Ivy League professors. But Johnson knew he needed the professors, as much for their influence on public opinion as for their policy expertise.

Among the intellectuals Johnson turned to was Eric Goldman, a historian at Princeton who specialized in twentieth-century American history. Summoned to Washington as a presidential "special consultant," Goldman served for more than two years as Johnson's principal emissary to the American intellectual establishment. Johnson's ambivalence toward having an intellectual in the White House was palpable. At first, he insisted that Goldman's consultancy be kept secret (Goldman was even discreetly advised not to hang the document commissioning him on his office wall). Moreover, not wanting Goldman to appear to be playing the same visible role that Schlesinger had played for Kennedy, Johnson explicitly forbade him from occupying Schlesinger's former office.

Goldman spent much of his time assembling task forces and distinguished advisory groups for Johnson. Johnson preferred to see even these groups functioning as secretly as possible, which compounded Goldman's problems of recruitment. It is not surprising, then, that the groups were never used, in Goldman's view, to great effect. The domestic policy group had significant influence on only two substantial programs and a lesser role in another, although Goldman identified neither in his memoirs. As Goldman saw it, outside experts and intellectuals could wield only limited power in the intimate circles in which policies are made, particularly for a hard-driving political force like Lyndon Johnson. But he also conceded that the experts he recruited were probably not up to the task of policymaking. "Over the long pull," he observed, "instant ideas were not their specialty; indeed, men of this type have little use for them."[34]

The role of Goldman's advisory groups was further complicated by the president's compulsion for secrecy when mounting a legislative campaign. Although an expert's ideas might find their way into his special messages to Congress and the ensuing legislative initiatives, any deliberative scheme of advisory commissions or task forces proved difficult to implement, given Johnson's personality. Planning processes moved rapidly and erratically, and ideas were always mediated by those closest to the president. Goldman, a self-described loner, politically unskilled and meeting rarely with the president, echoed the dismayed assessment of anthropologist Margaret Mead who, after serving on one of the task forces, described government as a "labyrinth compounded by human beings." Johnson, the master of the legislative labyrinth, did not need social scientists to design a program or craft a bill. Nor did he particularly trust them.

Moreover, the "politics of haste," as biographer Doris Kearns noted, typified Johnson's style, undercutting the work of his advisory task forces and other planning and deliberative mechanisms.[35] When ideas were adopted, it was not because they were intrinsically sound or well-thought-out, but because they filled an immediate political need. Haste and urgency were Johnson's trademarks, and his capacity to outrace the intellectuals was evident in his instinctive decision to move ahead with the War on Poverty. Like Roosevelt, Johnson's view of an idea was different from the scholar's. When he called for an idea, he wanted something that could be done immediately. "An idea," wrote Goldman, "was a suggestion, produced on the spot, of something for him to do tomorrow—a point to be made in a speech, an action, ceremonial or of substance, for him to take promptly, a formula to serve as a basis for legislation to be hurried to Congress."[36] Jack Valenti's kind but shrewd recollections of his White House years echoed Goldman's account. Presidents are always demanding ideas. They "need to be constantly offered ideas with a possible fit to a specific problem, whether it be an appointive vacancy, a gristly crisis, a need to be filled, or a charting [sic] to be explored."[37]

SEVEN

☆

At the Limits of Liberalism

Poverty Wars

The day after John F. Kennedy was assassinated, Lyndon Johnson called Walter Heller, chairman of the Council of Economic Advisers, into the Oval Office for a general briefing on the economy. Heller had been pushing Kennedy for some time to mount an attack on poverty, and Kennedy was becoming more enthusiastic about the plans in the month or so before his death. When he heard of the plan's broad thrust, Johnson did not have to be pushed or persuaded. He saw immediate opportunities and sensed his power to take the legislative initiative in the wake of the assassination. According to Heller, Johnson "expressed his interest in it, his sympathy for it, and in answer to a point-blank question, said we should push ahead full-tilt on this project."[1]

Poverty had not been high on the nation's agenda in the 1950s. The postwar boom seemed to be lifting black and white Americans alike out of poverty, and those who remained seemed largely confined to "pockets" in Appalachia and elsewhere. Kennedy had sought to address the problems of regional poverty early on, beginning with the Area Redevelopment Agency, set up in 1961. But for the most part, discussions of economic policy in 1962–63 focused on the need for general economic stimuli, notably Heller's proposal for a tax cut. Influential works of general social criticism, the most famous being

146

Michael Harrington's *The Other America,* were then just beginning to rouse the liberal conscience.

When Johnson told Heller to move quickly on the antipoverty proposals, both knew that they did not yet have a coherent program and that they faced serious political, bureaucratic, and intellectual hurdles. Heller was in the midst of reviewing fifty-eight different proposals culled from various governmental agencies. After talking with Johnson, he enlisted help from the Bureau of the Budget as well, and began looking for a thread that might link as many as three dozen separate initiatives. In the concept of "community action," Heller and his associates believed they had found a solution to a number of problems. It had the sheen of a new idea and was capable of both explaining poverty and of suggesting practical and inexpensive means for lifting people out of it. Moreover, the means in question—local community development groups who would determine how funds should be spent—were politically appealing and could be sold to both Congress and local officials.

The theory had its origins in the academic work of Richard Cloward and Lloyd Ohlin, academic researchers and social activists who had been studying juvenile delinquency in New York City since the late 1950s. Arguing that adolescents turned to crime mainly because society had foreclosed other alternatives, Ohlin and Cloward had tested their theoretical formulation and possible remedies in a Manhattan social service agency they founded called Mobilization for Youth. In their opinion, neighborhood-based organizations were the key to opening up opportunities for delinquents.

Though Ohlin and Cloward did not push the connection, their "opportunity theory" had broader implications for dealing with poverty. It resonated in Ford Foundation programs aimed at the increasingly obvious problems of urban ghettos. The idea also shaped the thinking of the President's Committee on Juvenile Delinquency, which had become a pet project of Attorney General Robert Kennedy, doling out grants to a number of community groups.

As Heller looked for ways to assemble the pieces of an antipoverty program into a coherent intellectual whole, the idea of "community action" may have appealed to him because of its vagueness; more certainly, it was appealing because it reinforced old-fashioned convictions about self-help and local initiative. "Action" could mean whatever the community might need or want. Some types of action would involve coordinating existing programs and making them more efficient and responsive. Others would take the form of grants to local groups, but these grants would be short term, for fixed purposes, and inexpensive, thus overcoming Johnson's concerns about spending too much money, since he was emphatic about holding the federal budget under $100 billion.

Nevertheless, despite the budgetary constraints, Johnson had large ambitions. Heller's cautious plan to start small with ten community action groups quickly gave way to Johnson's expanded goal of agencies in seventy-five communities. In the end, community action may even have reminded him of his glorious early days as head of the National Youth Administration in Texas. An untested theory of delinquency and proposals based on it thus became the framework not for tentative experiments in social policy, but for the "unconditional war on poverty" that Johnson declared in his 1964 State of the Union message.

Many of the appraisals of the social scientists' contributions to the War on Poverty have focused on community action and the haste to embrace it. In 1969, while serving as urban affairs adviser to Richard Nixon, Daniel Patrick Moynihan, the most successful professorial politician since Woodrow Wilson and the first to ground a political career in the analytic powers of the modern social scientist, looked back at the role played by social scientists in promoting the idea. He issued one of the first indictments of the role of social scientists in *Maximum Feasible Misunderstanding*, a play on the notion of "maximum feasible participation" which described one aim of the community action programs. As an assistant secretary in the Department of Labor, responsible for the Office of Policy Planning and Research—one of the many research departments created in domestic agencies during the 1960s—he, too, had been infected by the rash optimism of his fellow social scientists. But looking back, he judged that a "desperate desire for success" had induced him and his peers to abandon their critical instincts, understate difficulties, overpromise results, and ignore evidence of impending problems.[2]

Peter Marris and Martin Rein, two sociologists who also examined community action programs, saw a fundamental incompatibility between research and political action. While policies and programs were inevitably "tentative, non-committal and adaptive," serious research had to adhere to a definite course of action until a theory could be proved or disproved.[3] For Moynihan, the failure of the whole establishment of experts during the War on Poverty "lay in not accepting—not insisting upon—the theoretical nature of their proposition." Indeed, he argued tellingly, "to proceed as if that which only might be so, in fact was so, was to misuse social science."[4]

However, the abuse lay not solely with social scientists, but with the politicians who had embraced their ideas so readily and who used them to rationalize and justify the political choices they had already made. And that, fact should not have been seen as new or surprising. The disillusionment with social science, though made worse by the excessive expectations fostered by social scientists and politicians in the 1960s, has persisted because of the lingering perception that social scientists cannot agree on what had been accomplished and what had failed to work. And those disagreements were the result of a change in the uses of social science in policymaking. Social scientists, in and out of government, were increasingly serving as critics and evaluators of programs—using their skills to criticize governmental undertakings.

Step by step, the social science enterprise expanded with the social initiatives of the Great Society. In 1965, federal agencies spent about $235 million on applied social research; by 1975, the expenditures had grown to roughly $1 billion. Defined more broadly, expenditures on research and development in social science reached nearly $2 billion by the late 1970s.[5] In many respects the social science enterprise, in focusing its attention on the evaluation of policies and programs, had become a source not of ideas but of institutionalized skepticism—and potentially a more conservative political force.

The Power to Evaluate

For decades, social scientists had devoted themselves to studying broad social and economic phenomena. Some had also sought to devise policies and to create the political instruments for addressing social ills or the tools for tracing social trends and problems. By the late 1960s, the growth of government demanded a more rigorous scrutiny of governmental programs, especially as domestic budgetary commitments began to compete with military ones. Johnson accelerated this development by ordering all agencies to adopt the techniques of the planning-programming-budgeting system in 1965.

The president explicitly addressed the question of the uses of social science by government on the occasion of the Brookings Institution's fiftieth anniversary in 1966. In a speech apparently written by Harry McPherson, Johnson said, "We have seen, in our time, two aspects of intellectual power brought to bear on our nation's problems: the power to create, to discover and propose new remedies for what ails us; and the power to administer complex programs in a rational way. But there is a third aspect of intellectual power that

our country urgently needs . . . less glamorous . . . less visible
. . . the power to evaluate . . . to say about public policies and
private choices: This works, but this does not."[6]

The increasingly obvious need for government to evaluate its
programs—often mandated in the enabling legislation—gave a tremendous new push to the social science enterprise, both in and
out of government. Experts and policy analysts were asked to turn
their attention from society to government, redirecting the "critical
facility" from broad social and economic phenomena to discrete governmental activities.

Domestic agencies hastened to set up analytic bureaus, and several cabinet departments placed assistant secretaries in charge of
research, planning, and evaluation. By the end of the decade, research
in government—primarily evaluation research—was more widely diffused than it had ever been. An estimated eight hundred analysts
were at work by the late 1960s in sixteen domestic policy research
agencies; in 1971 the Office of Management and Budget compiled a
partial list of thirty-six agencies that were engaged in planning and
evaluating policies.[7]

The energies of thousands of people were now devoted to evaluating new governmental programs, and the data they collected became
the instrument for rethinking what the government could accomplish.
Overall, the data engendered disillusionment and reinforced a feeling
of skepticism about governmental initiatives, and the attitude spilled
over onto the social sciences themselves. Somewhat ironically, the
cost-benefit techniques pioneered by defense-budget analysts contributed to what Clark Abt, founder of Abt Associates, called "the
widely held opinion that social research is essentially negative, destructive, and not particularly helpful to society."[8] Thus, the very
expansion of the research enterprise led both to mounting disappointment with governmental initiatives and to a general retreat from
the technocratic values underlying American reform. Research went
a considerable way toward undermining some of the deeply held
convictions that inspired reform legislation. The research process,
suggested Henry Aaron, a scholar at the Brookings Institution and
former assistant secretary of the Department of Health, Education,
and Welfare (HEW), seems inevitably "to corrode any simple faiths
around which political coalitions are ordinarily built." When research
proves inconclusive or is superseded by new findings and when scholarly debates undermine public certainty about expertise, political
will and vision grow dim.[9]

The intellectual undoing of American liberalism and its patterns of piecemeal reform began as a crisis from within, long before conservatism offered its alternatives. Almost from the first legislative salvos, the poverty warriors expressed doubts about the means by which the war was being waged. They also knew that it would not be won as quickly as the president's rhetoric suggested. As early as 1966, staff members at the White House felt that the management of domestic policy was in disarray and that much needed information could not be supplied by the executive agencies that were charged with administering new programs.

In March 1967, when Johnson delivered a message to Congress on urban and rural poverty, he called on Robert Weaver, secretary of the Department of Housing and Urban Development, to encourage the establishment of an "Institute of Urban Development."[10] Echoing recommendations of a 1964 presidential task force on urban problems, this suggestion was the seed from which the Urban Institute, now one of Washington's largest policy research organizations, would grow. Plans for the institute accelerated when Johnson's advisers realized that domestic policies had proceeded too hastily and that departments and agencies were too fragmented to coordinate the rush of new programs. Furthermore, the domestic budget was beginning to run up against the mounting expense of the war in Vietnam and, accordingly, the least successful programs would have to be pared or eliminated.

Joseph Califano, then a White House special assistant with the major responsibility for domestic social programs, assumed the leading role in planning the new research institute. The RAND model for a nonprofit contract research organization was not far from his mind, though he saw the new institute working under contract to many different federal agencies, rather than relying on a single major client.

Having spent eighteen months at the Pentagon as special assistant to the secretary of defense, Califano witnessed McNamara's efforts to rationalize the planning of military policies. On moving to the White House, he had assumed that data on domestic issues would be readily available, but he was dismayed to learn how little the government knew and how hard it was for planners to find the needed information. Califano was especially put out when he could not even learn from the secretary of HEW how many Americans were on welfare. The facts he wanted proved surprisingly hard to dig out of the federal bureaucracy. "We had a lot of data, he recalled, "but

we didn't have the kind you need to make major policy recommendations to the President."[11] The obstacles to analysis and evaluation
were even more serious, forcing policymakers to set up one ad hoc
group, interdepartmental committee, or task force after another.
Moreover, both Johnson and Califano distrusted the federal agencies
on which they depended for information on programs. Califano bluntly
concluded that "the guy who starts the program isn't going to be
able to give you the answer" when asked to assess it.[12] Accordingly,
he pushed ahead with plans for an institute that would supply more
reliable, objective, and timely data than that provided by interest-
bound executive agencies.

In late autumn 1967, Califano assembled a group to incorporate
the new institution. The group included Robert McNamara, recently
appointed head of the World Bank; Arjay Miller, president of the
Ford Motor Company; Irwin Miller, chairman of the Cummins Engine
Company; and Cyrus Vance, a New York lawyer and sometime Democratic political appointee. The Urban Institute came into being in
April 1968, with initial support from a half dozen federal agencies,
though understandably none had leaped forward to provide money
for an organization whose purpose was to act as a critic and goad to
their programs. McGeorge Bundy, who had left the White House
in 1968 to become president of the Ford Foundation, promised $1
million in general support to give the Urban Institute additional
working capital and to guarantee it a degree of autonomy, not only
from the governmental bureaucracies, but from academic researchers.
Nonetheless, to survive, the Urban Institute would have to sell its
analytic services to the cabinet departments that were involved in
implementing domestic policies.[13]

William Gorham, one of McNamara's Whiz Kids, who was in
his mid-thirties, was selected as the institute's president—a post he
still holds. He had worked previously at the RAND Corporation,
the Defense Department, and the Department of HEW, where he
had been the assistant secretary in charge of the planning and evaluation office. Gorham accepted the job knowing that the Great Society
programs were in trouble. "By 1968 the early returns were coming
in," he wrote in 1971. "Although the tracking ability of the federal
government was—and still is—weak, the success stories, judging
from what could be seen, were very few."[14] Gorham deplored the
slim intellectual foundations on which most of the legislative initiatives
had been built and denounced the patchwork systems for gathering
information about existing programs and the failure to devise appropriate tests before rushing headlong into major commitments.

At the outset, the Urban Institute's program focused on the distribution and redistribution of income, urban governance, unemployment and inflation, alternative housing for the poor, and welfare reform, grounding its reports in the methods of cost-benefit analysis. Among the earliest major projects, however, was a comprehensive examination of the federal government's ability to evaluate its own social programs. Other early studies appraised some of the major legislative measures of the Great Society, the Elementary and Secondary Education Act of 1965, and the Model Cities program. Despite the growing climate of skepticism about these and other governmental initiatives, the institute did not appear to question the role of government. Instead, it concentrated on "several domestic problems which might be alleviated if greater information were available and increased government action were applied."[15] In almost every case, the study's conclusions would sound the call for more evaluation, field testing, and experimentation and for yet more extensive technical assistance to the administrators of programs.

The results of the institute's initial research suggested that much of the legislation of the mid-1960s had been hasty, ill-planned, and inadequately administered. Nevertheless, the research program—with its faith in quantitative knowledge and cost-benefit and systems analysis, and by its evident conviction that the government could in the end be supplied with adequate tools to finish what it had begun—embodied the assumptions on which the technocratic reforms had been predicated. Although the government had not performed well, more technical knowledge could make it work.

In 1970 Kermit Gordon, president of Brookings, took note of the "waning faith in government" and called attention to the "widely shared verdict" that billions of dollars had been wasted in trying to solve the nation's social and economic problems. Anticipating later, much harsher critics like conservative Charles Murray, Gordon thought that, in some cases, social problems had indeed been worsened by governmental intervention. The failures pointed to the "endemic disabilities" of the government—the absence of market tests for governmental actions, the president's limited managerial authority, bureaucratic inertia, and the relative inexperience of the government in confronting the social problems it had tried to solve. But Gordon—like the analysts at Gorham's Urban Institute—called for yet more evidence, more testing and experimentation, and more research, not an abandonment of faith in applied research or in the capacities of the government to act when guided by knowledge.[16]

Although some policy analysts and social scientists conceded that their knowledge was deficient, their calls for more research and data were not satisfactory to critics on both the Right and Left. Some of their peers were becoming more and more skeptical of the entire course of liberal social science. Several new institutions emerged in the 1960s to challenge conventional wisdom and the organization of professional social science and policy analysis. They signaled the fragmentation of the liberal intellectual enterprise.

The Hudson Institute and the Futurist Scenario

No one did more to fix the popular stereotype of the think-tank "type" than did Herman Kahn, the man who thought the unthinkable about nuclear warfare while an analyst at RAND in the 1950s and who founded his own think tank, the Hudson Institute, in suburban New York in 1961. Kahn's full beard, capacious girth, and restless intellect typified the popular image of the think-tank intellectual—the crackpot genius, absent-minded misfit, and Strangelovian strategist—and supported the notion of the think tank as the home of odd intellectual specimens.

"Herman stories" abound among Kahn's former associates at the institute, over whose freewheeling seminars he presided for more than twenty years until his death in 1983.[17] They talk of him riding through snowstorms with the top of his red convertible down and several wool hats piled on his head like a character out of Dr. Seuss. They tell of a famous appearance before a college audience with his beard and hair a brilliant green after a swim in an overchlorinated pool. Kahn's obvious delight in shocking and outraging other people makes it difficult to say how much of his persona was calculated and how much was indeed the result of professorial absent-mindedness.

Clearly, Kahn was a man of captivating personality and large intellectual gifts. His mathematical skills were prodigious, and some contend that he had total recall of what he read, at least early in his career. At the same time, he was so chaotic and disorganized, his habits so undisciplined, that he was sometimes at odds with his superiors at RAND and at best an indifferent administrator at Hudson. Financially troubled at his death, the institute he founded has undergone several wrenching transitions in recent years, including relocation from the estate it occupied in New York's Westchester County to a new headquarters in Indianapolis.

With only a bachelor's degree in physics from UCLA and graduate courses in applied mathematics and physics at the California Institute of Technology, Kahn joined RAND's Physics Division in 1948 while still a student. He never finished his doctorate and harbored a certain disdain for those who insisted on plodding down the path toward an advanced degree. At RAND he was assigned to diverse projects, ranging from the development of a nuclear powered airplane to studies of construction materials. He also dabbled in mathematical theory. In time his interests gravitated toward questions of nuclear strategy and civil defense. Former RAND colleagues describe him as endlessly curious about the work outside his own department, a rare trait among members of the Physics Division, which, in the 1950s, tended to be aloof and somewhat isolated from other departments. His shirttail always escaping from his pants, Kahn wandered the corridors, appearing in offices to talk about whatever had captured his fancy. Time and again, those who conversed with him describe his conversation as "seductive," his rapid talk filled with concrete images, arresting metaphors, and striking phrases.

But by the late 1950s, Kahn had become unhappy with the bureaucratic constraints of a large contract research organization. RAND's president, Frank Collbohm, was equally unhappy with Kahn's lax administration of projects and his inability to meet deadlines—bad habits that Kahn never overcame. Their disagreements festered, and Kahn left RAND in 1961, a year after the publication of *On Thermonuclear War*, the book that brought him into the national spotlight as a premier defense intellectual.[18] While Kahn might easily have settled into a university teaching position, he chose to establish his own research institute at Croton-on-Hudson, New York, assembling a maverick group of analysts who were initially interested in nuclear strategy and civil defense.

The Hudson Institute was founded at a propitious time. Kahn, whose reputation (and notoriety) had been bolstered with the publication of *Thinking about the Unthinkable* in 1962, found research contracts relatively easy to come by in the early 1960s.[19] By 1965 half the institute's $1.2 million annual budget came from contracts with the Department of Defense, one-quarter from the Office of Civil Defense, and the rest from other governmental agencies and private contributors. The expansion of Great Society programs further boosted the levels of available research dollars; by 1970 half the institute's work concerned domestic matters. Forty permanent fellows and one hundred consultants made up the stable of researchers who gathered at the institute's twenty-two-acre estate overlooking the Hudson River.

Relatively few of them came from conventional academic backgrounds or held doctorates. Kahn hired on instinct, choosing people he found stimulating, though none was ever as outrageous or provocative as he. He told one prospective colleague that he wanted "paranoid megalomaniacs" at the institute, on the grounds that such types "may have a high false alarm rate, but sooner or later they cover every corner of the subject."[20] Kahn believed deeply in the insight and imaginative freedom of the amateur. He did not want colleagues with stifling, discipline-bound academic interests or victims of the "trained incapacity" (to borrow Thorstein Veblen's phrase) to see beyond their own narrow professional parameters. Above all, Kahn saw it as his mission, and Hudson's, to explode accepted opinions. "The conventional wisdom is always wrong," he said over and over, in a phrase that might well stand as the institute's motto and that ultimately became its own brand of conventional wisdom.

Kahn's primary method was talk. He justified the endless conversations by arguing that talk kept ideas from being prematurely fixed. Accordingly, the staff convened loose groups of researchers, as well as unofficial kibbitzers so that no single author's preconceptions or assumptions would shape a research report. It created a giddy sense of being provocative and unconventional. Often, however, the atmosphere of collegiality in the context of a never-ending seminar left no one with final responsibility for writing the reports; thus, projects were not completed on time. And meanwhile Kahn, his curiosity abated, moved on restlessly to the next intellectual puzzle.

During the 1960s, significant work was done at Hudson—and books were published—on civil defense, missile defense systems, nuclear strategy, and the perplexities of Vietnam strategy.[21] But by the early 1970s, the institute had developed a reputation among its clients of not always delivering its reports or of finishing them a year or two behind schedule. Sometimes the work seemed frivolous; sometimes it simply restated the obvious. An assessment by the General Accounting Office (GAO) of Hudson's work on civil defense marked a more general tightening of its auditing procedures and a scaling down of governmental contracts that affected most contract-research organizations. The GAO report still rankles the few remaining Hudson staff members from that era, who contend that it was an unfair evaluation of the substance of their work, though correct in faulting the institute for delays and other administrative shortcomings (just as the GAO found fault with other contract research groups).

By the mid-1970s, the six-figure contracts that had once been so easy to win were much harder to come by. Procedures that allowed the government to sign exclusive agreements were curtailed, and Hudson, along with other contract research firms, found itself in a much more competitive environment as funding for research shrank and governmental agencies suspended "sole-source" contracts. Clients also demanded stricter standards of performance and greater accountability, and the institute's reputation for unpredictable research results—"kicking people in the ass with their own money," as Kahn put it—meant that foundations and governmental agencies were not eager to sign long-term agreements with Hudson. Kahn had never been an effective administrator and he was not especially adept at planning the institute's long-term finances, as both he and the board members realized. A succession of administrators came and went as the institute struggled from one fiscal crisis to another in the 1970s and early 1980s. But with Kahn as its resident genius, Hudson never failed to be provocative and continued to attract national attention.

Meanwhile, Kahn's interests had broadened in the late 1960s from defense issues to the global context in which American policy was necessarily embedded. Accordingly, the institute began to look systematically at scenarios for the world's future. While other research organizations evaluated programs, looked at current issues, and cast their thinking in a three- to five-year time frame, Hudson boldly tried to look twenty-five and fifty years ahead. Kahn's characteristic method combined data on social, economic, demographic, and other quantifiable trends with broader speculations about historical patterns. By instinct, Kahn was a macrosociologist concerned with historical periodization and the causes of the large underlying shifts from epoch to epoch. He was not a forecaster or extrapolator of trends, but a man whose sweeping perspective led him to spin out speculative visions. Future scenarios, Kahn wrote, "can often play the same role as historical allusion; they are useful tools for making historical predictions concrete because they force the writer to relate events to one another in narrative form."[22]

Kahn was not trying to predict the future. He did, however, offer a contrary view to those who foresaw a gloomy era of shortages and limits, views typified by the Club of Rome's report on the *Limits to Growth*. The Club of Rome, an organization of international business leaders and academics, based its projections of the future on complicated computer models and predicted an entropic world of unrelenting shortages. In contrast, Kahn relied not on computers but on discussion and imagination. He began with a "surprise-free" pattern of development, imagining the changes that were most likely to occur in the absence of such unforeseeable upheavals as wars, depressions, or other kinds of turmoil. This "least improbable" or "standard world," became the base scenario against which other variants were measured. Underpinning Kahn's projections of the future, described in books like *Toward the Year 2000, The Next 200 Years,* or *The Coming Boom,* was a secular optimism that oddly belies his image as a prophet and philosopher of nuclear destruction (he remained optimistic enough to think we might survive a nuclear war).[23] His perspectives on the past convinced him that human progress and technological advance were inevitable.

Kahn's faith in human ingenuity was linked to his conviction that overall, free-market arrangements had worked well. He and his colleagues saw the energy shortages of the early 1970s not as a harbinger of future crises but as aberrations of the market. Though he was not a free-market ideologue, his faith in progress and the long-term rationality of markets set the tone for the institute's work in the early 1970s; he looked relentlessly ahead with an optimism that most liberals could no longer muster. He lacked the simmering resentment that animated many neoconservatives, but nonetheless foreshadowed their concerns.

Unable to adapt to the considerably more competitive research funding environment, however, Hudson's budget plummeted in the early 1980s to $3 million ($500,000 coming from Kahn's speaking fees, which he relinquished to the institute). Morale suffered, resignations increased, and Kahn's death in 1983 at age sixty-one might easily have meant its demise. Deeply in debt, the institute sold its Hudson River estate, hoping to find a new home and a generous patron. Negotiations to move the institute to Arizona, Ohio, or Texas fell through, but in Indianapolis, a consortium of local business leaders and foundation executives, backed by the Lilly Endowment, made an offer that Hudson could not refuse. The consortium agreed to finance the institute's relocation and provide upwards of $750,000 per year in financial support. The local business community, as well as the state and local governments appeared eager to tap Hudson's expertise, and by 1985, the budget for its Indianapolis operations approached $7 million, with another $21 million from the Center for Naval Analyses, a Washington-based federally funded contract research center that has been managed by Hudson for the government since 1983.

Closer now to the tributaries of the Wabash than to the Tappan Zee, Hudson lost many of its staff members during the transition and has had a succession of presidents. Some of its best work since the move has focused on education, the work force, and international trade, and it has found governmental and corporate clients throughout the Midwest. It is poised to play a role as a regional research center, but still faces an intangible problem of sustaining the intellectual vitality and spirit with which Herman Kahn endowed it. Those who worked with Kahn want to sustain his spirit of serious intellectual play, taking the long view of human events and confronting policymakers with the reality that alternative futures ought to be examined systematically.

What Herman Kahn understood is that the knowledge on which a policymaker must act is never likely to meet strict standards of scientific or legal proof, and he was generally more forthright about the nature of uncertainty than were the scientific-minded analysts who were searching for one more set of data or the results of one more study. Kahn thought that policymakers often face a "Scotch verdict" on events; that is, they must deal with cases that are plausible but uncertain of proof. He looked skeptically at the claims of expertise and at passing intellectual fashions, though he was not immune to his own enthusiasms. Nonetheless, his quirky genius challenged the assumptions of technocratic analysts by sheer force of personality, while his view of long-term historical processes and faith in markets anticipated critics of liberalism from the Right and gave Hudson a conservative bent in the 1980s.

Reinventing the Left: The Institute for Policy Studies

In 1961 Marcus Raskin and Richard Barnet, among the youngest of the "action intellectuals," were, in many ways, typical of the scholarly policy thinkers who were drawn into the foreign policy establishment. Graduating with bachelor's and law degrees from the University of Chicago, in the last years of the Eisenhower presidency Raskin was drawn to Washington, where he worked for a group of congressmen who were intent on launching what they termed the "Liberal Project." Anticipating a swing of the political pendulum after eight years of Republican control of the White House, the project attempted to formulate policies that would go beyond the framework of economic programs set up during the New Deal.

After the Kennedy victory, Raskin was chosen to serve on the staff of McGeorge Bundy's National Security Council because of his focus on issues of defense and disarmament and his solid connections with liberals on Capitol Hill. Raskin was only in his mid-twenties when he took the White House post, and he played the role of gadfly, finally resigning in 1963. After leaving the White House, he began to voice more public criticisms of the administration's policies; Bundy, exasperated with his former assistant, once told him to "please stop identifying yourself as a former White House aide."[24]

Richard Barnet, five years older than Raskin, had earned a BA and LLB from Harvard, practiced law, and spent a year at Harvard's Russian Research Center. The author of *Who Wants Disarmament?* (1960), Barnet joined Dean Rusk's State Department in 1961, but moved quickly to the Office of Political Research of the Arms Control and Disarmament Agency. Though both men were trained in the law, they would later say that they came to Washington with faith in the analytic tools of social science and a textbook conviction that American institutions were capable of responding to public pressures for reform.

The two founders of the Institute for Policy Studies (IPS) first met in 1961 at a planning conference on disarmament. John J. McCloy, one of the Wise Men of postwar foreign policy, had been summoned back into public service from his senior partnership at the law firm of Milbank Tweed to advise Kennedy on arms control. He addressed the conference of weapons and policy experts, saying "If this group cannot bring about disarmament, then no one can." Raskin and Barnet caught one another's eye and stifled their laughter, profoundly skeptical that a group of generals and defense analysts whose careers had been shaped by the Cold War could ever bring themselves to challenge the military underpinnings of postwar foreign policy. Indeed, they had both already concluded—only a few months into the Kennedy administration—that they did not belong in government. They needed an intellectual perch from which to criticize the experts who served the government and over the next two years, they mapped out plans for an independent research institute that would be free from the bureaucratic constraints of government contract work.

Their scheme for creating a Washington-based institute with a small resident staff and links to outside scholars seemed conventional enough. They had even talked over their plans with staff members at Brookings, who thought seriously about hiring one or the other of them. They also made the rounds of foundations. When he talked to executives of foundations, in the early 1960s, Barnet was careful to explain the need for a new institute with greater independence from the federal bureaucracy and more extensive connections to university-based research centers. Brookings and RAND were comfortable in their role as expert advisers. IPS sought greater intellectual distance and a more critical dialogue with those in power. The institute's "public scholars," as they termed themselves, were suspicious of the claims of a "value-free" social science that could direct policy.

After many discussions, the money for the new IPS came from a handful of wealthy families with liberal sympathies. Sears's heir, Philip Stern, provided $200,000. James Warburg of the banking family gave a considerable sum. The Samuel Rubin Foundation (Rubin was the founder of the Faberge line of perfumes and a longtime backer of liberal causes, including Henry Wallace's 1948 campaign) and Rubin's daughter, Cora Weiss, were early and consistent contributors as well.

The new institute opened in October 1963.[25] The board reflected the institute's strong initial ties to universities. It included former New Dealer and lawyer Thurman Arnold, author of *The Folklore of Capitalism;* David Cavers of Harvard Law School; Freeman Dyson, a physicist at Princeton; Hans Morgenthau, a political scientist at the University of Chicago; Steven Muller, director of Cornell's University Center for International Studies and, later, president of Johns Hopkins University; and sociologist David Riesman of Harvard. Although Barnet's and Raskin's views were to the left of the Kennedy and Johnson administrations, the two men were not out of the political or intellectual mainstream of the period.

The deep fissures that would rend American society during the civil rights movement and the Vietnam war were barely discernible in 1963, but the New Left was already taking shape to challenge the "Old" Left's assumptions about communism and the Cold War. In book after book over the next quarter century, Barnet would offer a revisionist account of the origins of the Cold War and the beginnings of America's "national security state" and its permanent war economy; Raskin would devote his intellectual energies to a series of books criticizing the relationship between knowledge and political power in this country.

At the outset, however, IPS seemed like a scholarly alternative to Brookings—situated to its left but not out of touch with those in power. Raskin, Barnet, Arthur Waskow, and the other intellectual activists who gathered at IPS raised fundamental objections to the ways in which organized knowledge and bureaucratic power were conjoined in Washington. They were skeptical of piecemeal social and economic reform and of an economy so heavily dependent on military spending. The Vietnam War crystallized their opposition to American foreign policy. Indeed, one of IPS's early publishing successes was *A Viet-Nam Reader*, edited by Raskin and Bernard Fall, a French journalist who had spent many years covering the French debacle in Indochina. It was the basic text for the teach-ins that marked the beginning of opposition to the war in Vietnam by students and faculty at the universities. Through the late 1960s and early 1970s, IPS was a center of antiwar discussion and organizing activity, and its fellows found a friendly reception among senators and congressmen who were opposed to the war. As early as 1967, Raskin was urging Senator George McGovern, who later became both a fellow and a board member of IPS, to mount a presidential campaign. In 1968, after the violence of the Democratic convention in Chicago, he tried to organize the New Party around the themes of antimilitarism and anti-interventionism.

IPS has attracted scholars and writers, whose training and professional pursuits are different from those at other think tanks. For example, documentary filmmakers like Saul Landau and Paul Jacobs have been senior fellows who have used film to explore such subjects as the Cuban and Nicaraguan revolutions and the government's deception about nuclear fallout in the 1950s. Writers and critics, such as John Berger, I. F. Stone, Ariel Dorfman, and Rita Mae Brown, have been affiliated at various times with IPS. And scholarly activists on the Left, including Paul Goodman, Roger Wilkins, and Barbara Ehrenreich, have been based at IPS.

Throughout its history, IPS has been committed to experimental projects, attempting to combine the quest for knowledge with activities for social change. In the 1960s IPS helped to start community development organizations and cooperative food stores in Washington's black neighborhoods and experimented with ways of organizing community health services. The institute also held seminars and courses on various topics—sometimes for children, more often for adults. Its educational programs evolved into IPS's Washington School, which enrolls several hundred people in its courses and draws many more to its lectures. In the 1960s IPS also spawned institutional offshoots, including the Bay Area Institute; Atlanta's Institute for Southern Studies; and the Cambridge Institute, which was founded by two former fellows, Christopher Jencks and Gar Alperovitz.

In 1973 IPS set up the Transnational Institute with outposts in

London and Amsterdam. Along with its affiliate, IPS explored North-South issues, especially revolutionary movements, violations of human rights, and the role of multinational corporations. Revolutionary events touched IPS directly in 1976. The institute's most tragic hour came in the wake of the military coup that overthrew Chile's elected socialist president Salvador Allende. Orlando Letelier, Allende's for-eign minister and ambassador to the United States, became president of the Transnational Institute. In 1976, while he and a young IPS staff member, Ronni Moffitt, were driving to work in Washington, they were killed by a car bomb that had been planted by assassins hired by the Chilean government. Although the conspirators were indicted by a federal grand jury, the Chilean government refused to extradite them for trial.

The murders marked the beginning of a difficult period for IPS. Funding had never been easy, and the institute's dependence on only a handful of major backers made it vulnerable. As the Left in general fragmented into contending constituencies, organizing around gender, race, ethnicity, or sexual identity, IPS found it more difficult to meet the claims of specific groups. And the institution, which operated according to an ethos of participatory democracy, could neither set intellectual priorities, agree on hiring new fellows, nor resolve paralyzing internal disputes over governance. One faction broke away to set up a new institute, taking with it nearly $500,000, roughly one-third of the IPS endowment. As the nation turned more conservative, IPS was not in a position to rally intellectuals on the Left.

Ironically, throughout the era of conservative ascendance, IPS has continued to obsess some members of the militant anticommunist right. One conservative writer argued that IPS has created "a network of interlocking directorates" in its pursuit of "the Soviet line." Another characterized its activities with the term "communophilism," suggest-ing that IPS is consistently sympathetic to communist revolutions, but absolving most of its staff of actually being card-carrying members of the Communist party. In fact, it is difficult to discern an IPS line, party or otherwise, or to give credence to the right-wing's efforts to portray the institute as a politically powerful and subversive force in the United States or the world. The assaults on IPS from the Right say more about the conservative mind and its demons—and about the irresistible urge to stigmatize opponents—than about the nature of the contemporary American Left or the intellectual roots of IPS.[26]

Barnet and Raskin have concerned themselves with liberal principles, focusing on how knowledge and change are connected. Necessarily, they have been critical of experts and technocrats ("megadeath intellectuals," in one of Raskin's phrases of the early 1960s). They have viewed the community of experts as being unable intellectually to transcend the framework into which policy choices are generally cast. Over the years, they have drawn on eclectic intellectual sources—the indigenous pragmatic thought of John Dewey and William James, which inspired their efforts to synthesize knowledge and action; the French existentialists, who encouraged their passionate embrace of new social movements; and the Marxian theorists, who supplied a critique of economic relationships between the First and Third Worlds—to reactivate liberal thinking.

In Being and Doing (1973), which may be considered the institute's apologia, Raskin developed a "philosophy of reconstruction" and a theory he called "existential pragmatism."[27] Calling for a new kind of knowledge, Raskin declared that "empathy and verification" must replace "the meaningless facts of unshared authority and hierarchy" as guides to social action. According to Raskin, social science in its present form had come to serve the bureaucratic ends of stability and control, bolstering, rather than challenging, institutional authority. Returning to Dewey and James, Raskin and his colleagues sought to recover a social science of direct experience and experimentation. In a more fundamental sense, they tried to rescue pragmatism as an instrument of progressive social change.

Raskin's discourse on epistemology, grounded in eclectic sources, rings quaintly at times of the intellectual indulgences of the late 1960s and early 1970s. In Being and Doing, Raskin exhorted readers to discover what they felt and sensed in order to overcome the deadening effect of performing bureaucratic tasks in large hierarchical institutions. This numbing of the senses is a prerequisite for "pyramidal power," he contended. Echoing Noam Chomsky, who denounced the "new mandarin" class in American life, he argued that bureaucracies foster "the idea of expertise" in political and moral affairs, with the result that "only the few get to share in judgments of everyone's concern."

Raskin was particularly critical of operations research, labeling numerical calculation and quantitative analysis "deceptive modes." "Through abstractions and 'objectivity' we find that the mandarin group has developed a ritualistic language whose social consequence is the exclusion, exploitation and manipulation of other people." Needless to say, he concluded, these experts and their analytic tools were antithetical to the ideals of participatory democracy.[28]

Being and Doing—the title evoked both Dewey and Jean Paul Sartre—sought to explain the institute's commitment to knowledge and action. Raskin and his colleagues believed that knowledge could be gained only from "participation, empathy and experimentation." Accordingly, their projects, or "social inventions," have always combined study and political engagement. IPS challenged the liberal consensus of the 1960s—the conviction that all problems were matters of technocratic complexity—by questioning not only policies but the way expertise, knowledge, and public debate are organized in a modern democracy. While pragmatic methods of social inquiry had been basic to the ways Americans thought about policy and framed alternative means, IPS tugged at the institutional framework that had evolved. "When a body politic can no longer deal with the simple, the human and the obvious," Raskin wrote, "when its structure is beyond human scale and dimension, and people believe that there is no human or natural necessity that causes things and relationships to be ordered or authorized as they are, the body politic and the institutions within it first wobble and then collapse."[29] They wobbled, but predictions of collapse were premature.

In challenging the constraining intellectual bounds of technocratic pragmatism, a pragmatism of means that seemed incapable of contemplating ends and values, the founders of IPS wanted to recover the radical activist spirit of American pragmatism in which ends are discovered and refined in action. Radicals of both the Left and the Right agreed that liberalism, as it confronted domestic issues, was no longer a political philosophy but a set of tools and programs. And whether it dealt with domestic or foreign affairs, liberalism had reached an impasse, unable to articulate its basic values, to defend itself in the arena of public discourse, or to fashion a vision of the future.

The liberalism of the late 1960s was a political philosophy rendered inarticulate by its commitment to technique and expertise. Incremental change within a programmatic structure that was set during the New Deal; technical adjustments, rather than a searching reassessment of the ends of policies; the conviction that complexity required expert analysis and judgment; and the suspicion of uninformed (and perhaps uninformable) popular opinion detached liberalism from both its intellectual and popular foundations. Moreover, the experimental spirit of liberal reform, Roosevelt's "try-anything philosophy" and Johnson's compulsive legislative activity, seemed also to have drained liberalism of a coherent policy direction. Historian Allen Matusow concluded that "liberalism had experimented with so many programs and intellectual reformulations that it seemed less a creature of the past than of mere mood."[30] Liberalism and the century-old research enterprise that had attempted to link knowledge to policymaking was particularly vulnerable. Its world of complexity and expertise was far removed from the passionate simplifiers on the Right. Conservatives knew what they knew with certainty, and their conceptions of knowledge and ideas in politics challenged the older institutional framework of policy expertise.

EIGHT

☆

The Ideological
Divide

The Conservative Counterestablishment

Political campaigns may tap people's enthusiasm for an autumn, but they can rarely be considered epoch-defining events. Yet observers of Barry Goldwater's 1964 presidential campaign sensed that there was something unusual about it. Though brief and unsuccessful, it seemed more like a social movement than an electoral campaign. As Theodore White noted shortly afterward, the campaign touched upon "something deep, a change or a reflection of change in American life that qualified as more than politics—it was history."[1] It was, in fact, the first political expression of a rising conservative movement that was grounded in moral and intellectual outrage and determined to repudiate nearly a century of national policy, as well as the established framework of thinking and talking about policy.

Goldwater, the movement's square-jawed spokesman, possessed the traits of an intellectual manqué. An indifferent student, he had left the University of Arizona after one year to run his family's department store and carry on its interest in local politics; an uncle had founded Arizona's Democratic party, and Goldwater first campaigned for the Phoenix City Council on an independent ticket. Elected to the U.S. Senate in 1952, a Republican hanging on to Eisenhower's coattails in a largely Democratic state, he soon found his closest congressional allies within the right-wing opposition to Ike's "me-too" Republicanism. With a talent for publicity and pithy phrasemaking, Goldwater seemed an ideal conservative spokesman.

Like many others who have acquired political or religious convictions late in life, Goldwater embraced abstractions like "individualism" and "liberty" with far greater passion and conviction than have those who were trained early on to be more skeptical or to consider them in contrast with alternative ideals. Goldwater, "with mechanical precisions and fixes entirely unreal," as White described him, was like "a Trotsky of the far right."[2] Actually, he was more like a medieval Platonist who believed that ideas were real, permanent, and timeless, not mere names affixed by people to denominate experiences. "The laws of God and nature have no dateline," he avowed in his *Conscience of a Conservative* (1960), a campaign book brokered by Clarence Manion, a pillar of the Old Right, and written with the aid of L. Brent Bozell of the *National Review*.[3]

Goldwater served as a broker between the nascent postwar conservatism and Washington's policy circles. And his skills as a popularizer of political ideas were considerable. Setting forth the axioms of conservative politics, his tract found a sympathetic audience, selling 700,000 copies in its first year. Advocating "complete victory over the forces of international Communism" and an end to federal programs that overstepped the rights of both states and individuals, Goldwater laid out an agenda that challenged a bipartisan foreign policy based on the Cold War "containment" doctrine and a domestic policy of incremental advances in social welfare.

The ideological conservatives who seized the machinery of the Republican party in the early 1960s and nominated Goldwater at the party's convention in San Francisco's Cow Palace were newcomers to partisan politics, most of them unknown even to the Republican leaders in their states. But during the convention, they were organized down to the finest detail, urged by the movement's leaders to read Goldwater's convention newsletter, watch Goldwater's television broadcast three times a day, and listen to Goldwater's radio program heard five times a day.[4] The new conservative activists understood the power of mass communication. They also believed passionately in the power of ideas.

As an intellectual movement, modern American conservatism had been in the making for some twenty years. The partisan activists of 1964 drew upon intellectual capital supplied by men like Russell Kirk, Richard Weaver, and Peter Vierick, traditionalists who were nostalgic for the fixed order of preindustrial societies. Many supporters of Goldwater had also read the classical liberal economists, the Austrians Friedrich A. Hayek and Ludwig von Mises and the American Milton Friedman. And they had drawn their fervor from the anticommunist polemics of disillusioned, apostate leftists, such as Whittaker, Chambers and Frank Meyer, who were as ardent in their assault on "weak-kneed" liberals as they were on Communists. This "conservative" intellectual mix, no more a consistent political ideology than is American liberalism, has always been unstable. But it has typically found common cause in assailing a dominant liberal tradition. While liberals have not always taken conservatives seriously, conservatives have generally taken liberalism all too seriously—as a systematic ideology and a dominating presence in American life.

Conservatives often speak of the Liberal Establishment (sometimes, populist westerners think of it as the Eastern Establishment), comprised of the nation's major foundations, Ivy League universities, New York publishing houses, research institutions, newspapers, and the broadcast media, which maintains the supremacy of liberal ideas and policies. An "Establishment" is, of course, the opposite of a movement. The concept implies stasis, control, and a self-sustaining group of institutions. Imported from England in the 1950s, the term was the subject of a seriocomic essay by Richard Rovere in *The American Scholar*.[5] Rovere named names: John J. McCloy was probably the Establishment's chairman, while Lyndon Johnson, Richard Nixon, Edward Teller, and Duke Snider were definitely not members.

Goldwater's campaign assailed most of the political ideas that the Establishment appeared to represent. He rejected the New Deal, the Fair Deal, and Eisenhower's "Dime-Store New Deal." Themes propounded by Ronald Reagan in the 1980s had already been laid out with biting wit and conviction by Goldwater—strict construction of the Constitution; reducing the size of the federal government and restoring political power to the states; opposition to the federal government's involvement in civil rights and education; hostility to unions; the pursuit of military superiority over the Soviet Union; opposition to arms-limitation agreements, including the 1963 Nuclear Test Ban Treaty; support for anticommunist "freedom fighters"; and suspicion of the United Nations. But unlike Reagan's, Goldwater's campaign in 1964 never caught fire. Apart from organizational difficulties within the party and Lyndon Johnson's deft exploitation of every political advantage—as if they were not enough—Goldwater's candor and uncompromising articulation of his views cost him the election. Unlike most presidential candidates, Goldwater did not shift his campaign toward the center; he thus frightened moderate Republicans and the business community, capturing only six states and less than 39 percent of the popular vote.

In their search for explanations, conservatives believed that the towering Liberal Establishment accounted for the failure of their intellectual appeal. Conservatives took the reality of the Establishment for granted. It is "an empirical thing, out there . . . guiding the lives and destinies of the American people," wrote the conservative editor and author M. Stanton Evans in 1965. Evans tried to explain Barry Goldwater's overwhelming defeat as a result of the Establishment's power to "direct and instruct" popular opinion. Slightly less conspiratorial was William Buckley's description of "the intellectual plutocrats of the nation" with "vast cultural and financial resources" at their disposal.

In the face of this united opposition, the embattled conservative minority, however intellectually diverse, would have to construct new, albeit beleaguered redoubts.[6] Hence, the conservatives redoubled their institution-building efforts, knowing that their main job was to win minds by propagating the conservative faith. Accordingly, they turned from the tasks of political organizing to those of building an intellectual infrastructure. Over the next decade, such institutions as the Hoover Institution on War, Revolution, and Peace and the American Enterprise Institute were among the beneficiaries of the conservatives' philanthropic largesse, and by the early 1970s, new institutions, including the Heritage Foundation and the libertarian Cato Institute, had also been organized.

If conservatives have banded together in the face of mutual enemies, they have also been linked by one common intellectual filament—a shared view of the role of ideas in history and political discourse. Libertarians and classical liberals, Burkean traditionalists, and "new" conservatives, as well as militant anticommunists, took ideas and intellectual abstractions more seriously as a dynamic force in history than had the midcentury inheritors of pragmatism and liberalism. Liberals had always found abstractions to be divisive. The conservatives were not afraid of invoking large ideals and of setting them in sweeping historical contexts in which grand ideas clashed and struggled.

Though there were fundamental rifts within the conservative ranks, the leading conservative intellectuals seemed to share one strong conviction: Intellectual error—much of it to be found in the social science disciplines—was the root of modern problems. Conservative writers rejected the liberals' optimistic theories of historical progress, finding instead decisive and unfortunate intellectual turning points in Western history. Friedrich A. Hayek based his economic analysis on a denunciation of rationalist efforts to comprehend and improve society. In his view, the beginning of a progressive, reforming tradition lay in the embrace of Cartesian rationalism.[7] Leo Strauss, a political theorist at the University of Chicago, assailed the historicist thinking of the nineteenth century and sought to revive the ancient tradition of natural right. For Strauss, the philosophical turning point came when Niccoló Machiavelli rejected the ancient political thinkers and abandoned their lofty dialogue about human nature and the best political order. Machiavelli, with his stark realism and systematic redefinition of political virtue, lowered the sights of political leaders from the contemplation of transcendent ideals to the harsh calculations of practical statecraft; he believed that necessity, not moral purpose, should determine political ends. Machiavelli "limited his horizon in order to get results," argued Strauss, making him sound like nothing so much as a precursor of William James and John Dewey.[8]

Richard Weaver, whose *Ideas Have Consequences* (1948) has long been celebrated by conservatives, located the beginning of modern intellectual troubles in a battle among fourteenth-century philosophers, when the so-called nominalists, convinced that ideas were mere names, routed philosophical idealists from medieval universities. At that moment, the Western intellectual tradition took a positivistic turn. Modern science was unleashed, turning the human mind toward investigation of the natural world, rather than toward the contemplation of higher ideals. The resulting obsession with acquiring knowledge of the material world implied an "abdication of the intellect." Western man, in Weaver's words, had become a "moral idiot."[9]

Russell Kirk, who set out to recapture the conservatives' intellectual patrimony in *The Conservative Mind* (1953), saw the turning point a little later, asserting that Western society had rushed headlong down a deviant path during the Enlightenment, whose ideals were given political force by the ensuing French Revolution. Kirk sided with the revolution's critics, the most notable of whom, Edmund Burke—the founder of what Kirk called the "true school of conservative principle"—believed that divine intent rules society and that political problems are fundamentally moral and religious. A thoroughgoing traditionalist, Kirk also defended custom and "sound prejudice" as necessary restraints on human will and its impetuous desires, while claiming that a stable society needed orders and classes and strong leadership.[10]

Whether grounded in religious faith or in a "great tradition" of Western political thought, the conservative intellectuals mounted a serious (yet scarcely perceived) philosophical assault, not merely on left-wing liberals but on the intellectual core of pragmatic liberalism. The conservatives attacked rationalism, "moral relativism," and the liberal obsession with scientific and technical solutions. To them, the most intractable problems of the modern world had not arisen because of deficient knowledge about how economies and societies functioned, and they would not be solved or managed by gaining more of the same kind of knowledge. The pragmatists' emphasis on understanding economic and social forces was no substitute, the conservatives argued, for attending to fundamental ideals and principles.

It is true that American liberals had usually been more comfortable searching for facts than contemplating moral values. From the beginning, they had sought institutional and managerial solutions, rather than a more fundamental refashioning of the social and economic order, leaving themselves open to critics on both the Left and Right. But liberalism was so deeply engrained that it had seldom bothered to answer its critics, as Louis Hartz noted in *The Liberal Tradition in America* (1955). Hartz's influential book helped shape the academic wisdom of the day and, like Clinton Rossiter's treatise on American conservatism, infuriated conservatives for its dismissal of their views.[11]

Hartz contended that American society was liberal to the core. Liberal ideals were so deeply engrained that they required little articulation and needed no political movement or party to give them force. Identifying the link between the deep-rooted liberal faith and the ethos of pragmatism, he accurately remarked, "It is only when you take your ethics for granted that all problems emerge as problems of technique."[12] Liberalism was natural to Americans, Hartz argued, a native frame of mind, and to the extent that they were conservative at all, what they sought to conserve were their liberal values. But liberalism's very naturalness in the American context had placed it beyond self-examination.

The liberal discomfort in discussing ideals and values was nothing new. Robert Lynd had underscored the problem in *Knowledge for What?* in the late 1930s. After the war, others recalled the faltering intellectual defense of liberal values in the face of earlier challenges from fascism and communism, and in the postwar world, liberals remained divided about how to confront communism in Europe and Asia. At times, they were neither sure of what they believed nor fully believed what they knew about liberal democracy. Though there might be temporary agreement on specific prescriptions for policies, the means sometimes seemed intellectually deficient and inattentive to more fundamental values. Trying to remedy the incoherence of liberal thinking—which nonetheless was appealing enough to shape a "vital center" of American politics—Arthur Schlesinger, Jr., conceded in 1947 that, "the 'liberal' analysis today is predominantly wishful, sentimental, rhetorical."[13]

In the face of this liberal muteness about values, traditionalist conservatives like Weaver and Kirk urged a return to moral absolutes. But when conservatives in the postwar years said "ideas have consequences," they were not just affirming philosophical idealism. They were also consoling themselves, while looking to a distant future when their ideas would make a political difference. The conservative revival in the decade or so after World War II remained a scattered and marginal intellectual movement, dismissed by liberals and centrists as aberrant, well outside the mainstream, and even pathological. Like any group that feels itself outside the framework of public debate—since public debate is most often about means rather than about ends—conservatives had no choice but to argue that ends and values were absent from the debate.

If the terms of the debate were such that no possible outcome would satisfy conservatives, then clearly their task was to change the terms and recast the debate. The beginnings of conservative advocacy organizations and the ideological infrastructure of magazines and journals, societies and associations, and foundations and research institutions can be discerned in the plaintive traditionalist and libertarian voices of the immediate postwar period. The conservatives had persuaded a substantial enough cadre of activists that by 1964, they could seize the machinery of the Republican party and nominate an uncompromising conservative candidate. But Barry Goldwater's resounding defeat taught many of them that their intellectual infrastructure was still too fragile to combat pragmatic liberalism. The twenty-year-old conservative project was still too young and immature to disrupt and dislodge the well-entrenched liberalism and its pragmatic habits of mind. They accelerated their efforts in the 1960s to build an institutional framework for the dissemination and propagation of the conservative faith and to create a set of institutions to counter the power of the Liberal Establishment.

Business Fundamentalism: The American Enterprise Institute

The New Deal had struck many businessmen and Old Guard Republicans as outright heresy. Lewis H. Brown, president of the Johns-Manville Corporation and an influential spokesman for the business community, was one of its more temperate critics, but he remained convinced that Americans lacked "sound ideas" about the economy. Having assumed the presidency of Johns-Manville in 1929, only months before the crash, Brown's longstanding commitments to scientific management and welfare capitalism were put to the test during the depression. What went through his mind as he saw a growing number of workers embracing radical ideas was that businessmen had failed to communicate with labor. Specifically, they had failed to teach their employees how corporations and the economic system actually worked. Brown and others in the business community agreed that the work force needed to understand more about what they called, without irony—even in the midst of the Great Depression—"economic fundamentals."

During the 1930s, Brown instituted an innovative corporate educational program at Johns-Manville, supplying his employees with annual reports on the business climate and pamphlets describing the company's policies on wages, hours, and working conditions. Other corporations followed suit in establishing educational programs for their employees in the forthright hope that they could thereby "break down class consciousness and the battle spirit" that divided business and labor.[14] But Brown also realized that business must change its attitude toward government. Business could not advocate a return to the freewheeling 1920s. Like the men who had organized the Committee for Economic Development, Brown gave credit to the Roosevelt administration for its actions during the economic crisis. Yet, he tried to define the limits of governmental intervention. He opposed public works projects, lectured against redistributive policies, and denounced the incursions of the federal bureaucracy. However, his acceptance of the New Deal did not lead him to embrace Keynesian deficit spending, wartime wage and price controls, or other policies that he thought undermined individual incentives and the work ethic. He believed, as he put it, in the multiplication of wealth, not its division.

Brown was the leading figure among a group of like-minded businessmen who established, in Washington in 1943, an organization they named the American Enterprise Association. The aim of the organization was to educate the public about business and to provide Congress and other interested parties with analyses and evaluations of pending legislation. During the late 1940s and early 1950s, the American Enterprise Association remained an unobtrusive and obscure organization, supported by business corporations but greatly overshadowed by the Committee for Economic Development (CED). With only a small administrative staff, the organization was run directly by Brown and the board, who reviewed and approved every publication and relied primarily on lawyers, often drawn from the general counsel's office of the firms that supported them (a young lawyer named Adlai Stevenson had been asked to draft some early legislative briefs). The legislative analyses, though possibly of use to some understaffed congressmen, left no discernible trace on the debates about policies in this period. While the CED had thought long and hard about its role as a "business-research group" and hired a cadre of well-regarded professional economists, the American Enterprise Association was largely ineffective, both as a business-propaganda organization and as a center of policy research. Looking back, several economists then at Brookings and the CED recall that even as late as the mid-1950s, they were only vaguely aware of the organization.[15]

The board members, well aware that their organization was nothing but "a high-level luncheon club" (in the words of one longtime staff member), were on the verge of shutting it down, but in 1953 they decided to make one final attempt to resuscitate it. A. D. Marshall, chairman of General Electric, agreed to serve a term as chairman of the organization. His first step was to hire two staff economists from the U.S. Chamber of Commerce, W. Glenn Campbell and William J. Baroody. Campbell and Baroody, the former with a Ph.D. from Harvard and the latter with an MA from the University of New Hampshire, spoke the language of the policy community. Abandoning its lawyerly approach to legislative analysis, the organization assembled a board of academic advisers that included some of the nation's most respected conservative economists: Milton Friedman and Gottfried Haberler of the University of Chicago, Paul McCracken of the University of Wisconsin, and G. Warren Nutter of the University of Virginia.[16]

Baroody, one of the shrewdest and most energetic men ever to preside over a Washington research institute, was a fundamentally new type in the world of think tanks. Neither a businessman with an interest in politics, like Edward A. Filene or Robert Brookings, nor an academic with a commitment to a particular analytic method, like Wesley C. Mitchell, John R. Commons, or Harold G. Moulton, Baroody was a policy entrepreneur, and his career was accordingly inseparable from that of the institution he set out to build.

The Idea Broker

Born in 1916, Baroody was the son of a Lebanese stonecutter who had immigrated to Manchester, New Hampshire. Devout Melkite Christians (a sect that observes a rite of the Eastern Orthodox Church), the family made its way in schools and neighborhoods in which Irish Catholics always seemed to have the upper hand. A careful listener could even discern a bit of an Irish brogue in the English that Baroody's father had learned to speak from his fellow laborers. The son stayed close to home, marrying another Lebanese immigrant's daughter at age nineteen and working his way through St. Anselm's College. His rise as an intellectual entrepreneur had its improbable beginnings deep in the recesses of New Hampshire's Unemployment Compensation Agency, where he worked in the 1930s. Moving to Washington after the war, he took a job with the federal government's Veterans Administration Readjustment Allowance Service, heading its research and statistics section.[17]

Baroody left the relative security of his governmental post in 1950 to become executive secretary of the U.S. Chamber of Commerce's Committee on Economic Security. There he first met A. D. Marshall who, on becoming chairman of the board of the American Enterprise Association in 1954, named him executive vice president. Baroody became the chief fund-raiser for the faltering organization, as well as its principal research administrator, and he vigorously applied himself to the slow and tedious task of expanding its base of support. By 1960, the organization had twelve full-time employees and an annual budget of $230,000. The money came primarily from large business corporations, but Baroody also tapped the funds of the relatively few foundations that were then interested in either conservative causes or economic research, including the Earhart, Falk, Kresge, Pew, and Sloan foundations. In 1960 he also persuaded the board to change the organization's name to the American Enter-

prise Institute for Public Policy Research (AEI). The word "association" impeded fund-raising suggesting that it was simply another of
Washington's many trade groups—a lobbying organization, rather
than a research center.

Baroody, who, along with such colleagues as Karl Hess, had
advised and written speeches for Barry Goldwater in 1964, embroiled
the AEI in a public controversy that ultimately propelled it in more
academic directions. A House select committee, wanting to learn
whether the involvement of AEI's staff in the campaign violated
the institute's tax-exempt status, subpoenaed its financial records,
prompting a two-year investigation by the Internal Revenue Service.
Although no wrongdoing was uncovered, the investigation left
Baroody scrupulously cautious about engaging in overt political activities and persuaded him of the need to open the institute to scholars
of more divergent views.

And if he had not fully realized it before, Baroody soon learned
that long-term survival depended on creating an academically respectable institution. Like many fledgling institutes, AEI was still less a
place for full-time scholarly research than a structure for convening
conferences, publishing the proceedings of seminars and policy papers, and linking like-minded academics. Its publications—legislative
analyses (not even the AEI's library has all of them today), position
papers, and a long-running series of handbooks prepared for high
school debate teams—were also short-lived.

Baroody's institution-building strategy reflected the conservatives' belief in the power of ideas, as well as the frustration that
they felt while trying to win a hearing for their views. If conservatives
wanted to become an intellectual force that would be capable of
holding its own against liberalism, they would have to build competing
institutions. The conservatives' conviction that ideas had consequences did not mean that ideas would be carried into play by the
currents of history alone; ideas would have to be promoted by able
spokesmen, who would require a solid base of operation. Baroody's
pitch to funders was that conservative ideas were locked out of the
policy dialogue. In fact, he claimed, there was no real debate; free-
market ideas and the concept of limited government had no defenders
in Washington. Baroody also complained about what liberal social
scientists had wrought; they had, he said, created the tools for expanding governmental administration and thrown in their lot with the
bureaucrats.

Applying his economic conservatism to the policy-making process, Baroody saw the process as a marketplace in which the best ideas should win out, but too often did not. He likened the intellectual marketplace to a monopoly that shut out competition. Indeed, where some conservatives saw the Liberal Establishment, Baroody saw an industry of vertically integrated liberal ideas that stretched from the social science departments and schools of public policy and public administration of universities, where the raw intellectual resources (ideas) were mined, to the Washington research institutes and governmental agencies, where they were refined and manufactured, to the publishing and media outlets, where they were marketed and sold to consumers. This vision bore a certain crude resemblance to the actual links that had evolved between the universities, policy research organizations, and governmental agencies over the past fifty years. But in calling it an ideological monopoly, Baroody gave too much credit to the foresight and consistent ideological motivations of social scientists, executives of foundations, philanthropic-minded businessmen, and administrators who had built such places as the Russell Sage Foundation, the Twentieth Century Fund, the Brookings Institution, and the RAND Corporation.

Whatever its basis in fact, Baroody found the image of a liberal intellectual monopoly useful as he tirelessly made the rounds of foundations and corporations. "A free society," Baroody would say over and over, "can tolerate some degree of concentration in the manufacture of widgets. But the day it approaches a monopoly in idea formation, that is its death knell."[18] Finally, after years of fruitless meetings with executives of the Ford Foundation, Baroody parlayed those arguments into a $300,000 grant from an institution that conservatives had long regarded as a bulwark of liberal values, and Baroody used it to open doors to other foundations.

Baroody knew that conservative ideas could not be peddled by small-time operators; they had to be promoted by institutions with technical skills in public relations and marketing, as well as with large financial resources and solid academic reputations. Baroody knew what kind of institution he wanted—a conservative Brookings— and in setting out to build a rival, he chose to portray Brookings (with little regard for its origins in the early movement for efficiency and economy or its bitter opposition to the New Deal) as a bastion of liberal thinking. By the 1960s, what Baroody mainly saw was Brookings's comfortable working relationship with the federal bureaucracy. Brookings's economists consulted for the State Department, the Agency for International Development, the Treasury Department, and other agencies; its political scientists worked for the Bureau of the Budget and the Agriculture Department; and its experts on foreign policy consulted for the State Department, the United Nations, and various foreign governments. Brookings also enjoyed magnanimous support from the nation's largest foundations—Rockefeller, Carnegie, and (since the mid-1950s) Ford. And although most of its staff members did not enter full-time governmental service, a handful—notably economic advisers Kermit Gordon, Charles Schultze, and Arthur Okun—came to be publicly identified with the Kennedy and Johnson administrations.

Those established institutional relationships and Brookings's staid academic respectability, far more than the policy content of its research and recommendations over the years, symbolized to conservatives the tight-knit operation of the Liberal Establishment and went a long way toward explaining why the conservatives' ideas had not been heard. Labeling Brookings "liberal" provided AEI with both a venerable rival and a sense of institutional mission. It also helped to rally more contributors.

Baroody's assiduous efforts bore fruit in the early 1970s. The institution took a "great leap forward" in fall 1971, according to Robert Pranger, a former vice president of AEI.[19] That year, Melvin R. Laird, then the secretary of defense and a longtime supporter of AEI, kicked off a $25 million fund-raising campaign. A number of officials of the Nixon administration (as well as Baroody's son and successor, then an assistant to Laird) were present in the Pentagon dining room where the campaign got under way. With a staff of only 18 and a budget of slightly more than $1 million in 1970, the institute spurted ahead. By the early 1980s, AEI had a staff of 150 (some 50 to 60 of them engaged in research and writing) and an annual budget of well over $10 million (the budget seems to have peaked at $13 million to $14 million in 1982 and 1983 before financial mismanagement sent it spiraling back down to less than $8 million in the late 1980s).[20]

Ironically, the unraveling of the Nixon administration and the defeat of President Gerald R. Ford in 1976 gave AEI one of its greatest boosts. Ford signed on as an AEI "Distinguished Fellow," drawing a $40,000 salary and participating in seminars and conferences. Two former members of the Nixon cabinet assumed part-time affiliations: Laird, who supervised a study of energy policy, and William Simon, onetime energy "czar" and secretary of the treasury, who oversaw a project on tax policy.

Through part-time arrangements, visiting fellowships, consultancies, grant-funded research projects, and resident fellowships, AEI placed itself at the center of an expanding network of conservative academics. Economists Arthur Burns and Herbert Stein joined AEI on leaving the government; Jeane J. Kirkpatrick worked on Latin American politics and policy; Murray Weidenbaum and James Miller studied regulatory policy; Lawrence Korb analyzed defense issues; Michael Novak wrote about religion and the voluntary sector; and Irving Kristol, editor of *The Public Interest* and professor of social thought at New York University, made AEI his Washington base of operations.

Baroody's success in attracting this impressive cadre of scholars and former officials reflected the maturing of the older conservative movement as an institutional force. But it also reflected the arrival of new intellectual allies, the so-called neoconservatives. The two developments were not unrelated. The neoconservatives gave a new twist to conservative complaints about the unresponsive Liberal Establishment. Irving Kristol, in particular, serving as a broker between conservative funding sources and the Washington-based research organizations, supplied new arguments—if they were really needed—for supporting AEI and similar research endeavors.

A Conservative Counterelite

Borrowing Lionel Trilling's notion of an "adversary culture," Kristol argued that universities and foundations had been hostile to American values, especially those underpinning the capitalist system. Painting his portrait of American philanthropy and the policymaking role of academics and researchers in think tanks in broad strokes, Kristol linked "utopian rationalism" and "utopian romanticism," socialism and a modernist aesthetic, in attempting to discredit the social sciences. The social sciences "absorbed" the antibourgeois socialist traditions, he asserted, with " 'the study of society' coming quickly and surely to mean the management of social change by an elite who understood the verities of social structure and social trends." Kristol branded this elite both subversive and heretical—undermining fundamental American ideals and institutions and indulging in the worship of statistics that amounted to a "silly kind of capitalist idolatry."[21] Kristol himself wanted not science and rationalism, but a new faith or, rather, a renewal of the old faith in capitalism.

Salvation would come both by grace and good works, specifically

through the philanthropy of corporations and conservative foundations. Kristol and other neoconservatives infused conservative intellectuals, executives of foundations, and corporate donors with a
missionary zeal. He announced to his readers, in an essay in the
Wall Street Journal (provoked by the resignation of Henry Ford II
as a trustee of the Ford Foundation), the "fact" that most large foundations and major universities "exude a climate of opinion wherein an
antibusiness bent becomes a perfectly natural inclination." With a
polemical style that managed simultaneously to accuse and retract,
he conceded that foundations and universities "are not homogeneous
or totalitarian institutions" but that they tended to be populated by
a "New Class" that was hostile to the private sector and more sympathetic to the public sector.[22] This "New Class," a term borrowed
from Milovan Djilas's analysis of the Communist party functionaries
who controlled the economies of Eastern Europe, seemed in the
American context to mean primarily those white-collar professionals
whose careers depended on the public sector. Kristol included scientists, lawyers, city planners, social workers, educators, criminologists,
sociologists, and public health physicians whose hidden agenda, he
discerned, was to propel the nation toward an economic system "so
stringently regulated in detail as to fulfill many of the traditional
anticapitalist aspirations of the Left."[23]

The battle had to be engaged on the plane of ideas and within
the intellectual bastions of the New Class, Kristol argued. Universities, think tanks, and foundations were the "idea-germinating" and
"idea-legitimizing" institutions. Defenders of the capitalist ethos
would have to wage war both by creating their own counterparts
and by taking the battle inside the university and, in time, the political
bureaucracy. Kristol asked whether it was in the long-term interest
of corporations to continue to support institutions that had proved
so hostile. He appealed for a more discriminating corporate philanthropy that would identify and support those academics and intellectuals who believed in a strong private sector. Though they were few,
they could be found, he insisted. And through the Institute for Educational Affairs, which he and William E. Simon founded in 1978,
financial resources were directed toward sympathetic scholars and
the research projects of think tanks.[24]

In the early 1970s, executives in a handful of traditionally conservative foundations redefined their programs with the aim of reshaping
the public policy agenda and constructing a network of conservative
institutions and scholars. The John M. Olin Foundation, for example,

had directed its money primarily to antilabor organizations and to educational programs on free enterprise in undistinguished colleges. But in the 1970s, its patterns of giving became more sophisticated and more closely attuned to the potential of grantees for influencing debates on national policies.[25] The J. Howard Pew Freedom Trust, part of the Pew Charitable Trusts (whose assets totaled roughly $1.5 billion in 1985), gave to many of the conservative think tanks, providing nearly $6 million to AEI between 1976 and 1981. The Smith Richardson Foundation and Scaife philanthropies added their resources as well.

Avowing that ideas were the only weapons able to overturn the establishment and working diligently to build an establishment of their own, conservatives founded and strengthened scores of institutions. The new conservative policy enterprise, like a film run on fast forward, compressed and accelerated developments that had taken place over many decades in the social sciences, universities, and older policy research institutions. It also worked to formulate more explicit policy goals, since conservatives had joined in an ideological struggle against liberalism, whether liberals had noticed it or not.

With the arrival of Kristol and other neoconservative reinforcements in the 1970s, the conservative movement gained potential voices that were also highly professional in their approach to philanthropy and able to cast their arguments in the analytic and quantitative language of the social sciences. Baroody himself relished public debate. The experts he gathered at AEI were not diagnosers of social ills, technocratic managers, or social engineers; they were professional researchers and policy intellectuals who were self-consciously engaged in arguments about fundamental values.

Furthermore, the battle would no longer be fought exclusively on the terrain of abstract ideas; it would be extended to the arenas of public opinion, where neoconservative polemicists—though few— were far more comfortable than were liberal technocrats. As AEI gained national prominence during the 1970s, it was obvious that its marketing and promotional strategies set it apart from the more established policy research centers. Baroody, who had always been intrigued by the raw competition of ideas, sponsored debates among proponents of various views of policy that not only gained public— especially the media's—attention but enhanced AEI's reputation for fair-mindedness even among those who did not share its free-market predilections. AEI also continued to issue short, timely publications on pending legislative matters (about twenty each year) and began to produce programs for distribution on public television and radio stations. While Brookings published books for scholars and the classroom, AEI published a cluster of periodicals—*Regulation, Public Opinion, Foreign and Defense Policy Review,* and *The AEI Economist*—aimed not only at Washington's policy community but at journalists, business executives, and other opinion leaders. For all their assaults on the liberal media, the new conservative institutions understood the dynamics of journalism.

American journalism, in fact, had matured in the same narrowly empirical tradition that shaped twentieth-century social science. Reportage is woven out of webs of discrete facts, which is not to say that points of view do not emerge but, merely, that journalists prefer to focus on concrete events, confirmed statements, or bits of data. Analyses and interpretive frameworks are either not stated or are attributed to others. Expert opinion thus becomes another kind of fact to be reported. And since journalists adhere to a simple notion of objectivity, in which one opinion is balanced against a contrary point of view, their appetite for predictable commentary by experts is virtually insatiable.

The more probing and skeptical journalism that took shape after the Vietnam War and the Watergate scandal worked to the advantage of those research centers that understood the needs of journalists. The media looked to them for opposition voices who could turn a memorable phrase, reply to the president or a governmental official, and argue for or against current policies. Far from simply acting as a megaphone for liberal ideas, the press provides a forum for skeptical voices at either end of the political spectrum. It therefore added to the stature of the new conservative organizations.

The Washington media themselves have expanded, providing a growing arena for "authorities," whose claims to expertise are rarely scrutinized by the press. New policy ideas can gain a quick hearing and research institutes can attain an instant standing through the mass media. That insight came easily to Baroody and his colleagues at AEI. Baroody's son and successor also thought that skills in public relations had helped "telescope" the emergence of AEI as a national institution. And Kristol knew that publicity was inseparable from fund-raising, especially among corporate funders whose donations were often treated as an adjunct to advertising budgets.[26]

Baroody's entrepreneurial approach did much to transform the environment in which policy research institutions operated. During the 1970s, Baroody built and oversaw a solid competitor to Brookings, while offering aid and counsel to fellow conservatives as they constructed a robust intellectual infrastructure, comprised of dozens of research institutions in Washington and elsewhere. He placed a premium on publicity and public outreach, which shook the quiet networks of professional expertise that had evolved over the preceding fifty years. By pitting the experts against one another in the media, however, Baroody helped to make them more visible while subverting their intellectual authority, already badly shaken by the failures of Vietnam and the Great Society programs. Thus, by relentlessly asserting that ideas were marketable wares, Baroody and his fellow conservatives began to make the consumer somewhat warier of all intellectual commodities.

Mr. Hoover's Legacy

While Baroody toiled in Washington, his onetime colleague, W. Glenn Campbell, constructed another conservative institution on the West Coast. In his successful bid to turn a library and archive on the Stanford University campus into a major policy research center, Campbell mined old veins of wealth among the aging Old Guard Hoover Republicans and managed to tap into the new conservative enthusiasms of Barry Goldwater's supporters in the Sun Belt.

The Hoover Institution on War, Revolution, and Peace, as it is now known, is decidedly different from the other conservative institutes. It is more a center for advanced study than a participant in day-to-day policy debates. During more than twenty-five years as Hoover's president, Campbell assembled a group of roughly seventy social scientists and historians, including Milton Friedman, George Stigler, Kenneth Arrow, Thomas Sowell, and Seymour Martin Lipset. It is the best endowed of the policy research organizations and the only major one that operates autonomously within the framework of a university, although Hoover's emergence as a focus of the conservative revival has sometimes proved nettlesome to members of the university community.

Herbert Hoover instigated both the original library collection and the institute's later turn toward public policy. The library's evolution thus reflects his personal intellectual and political odyssey.[27] Like many other prominent businessmen, Hoover readily volunteered for public service during World War I. Living in London and witnessing the war from close at hand, not from offices in Washington's jerry-built bureaucracy, he organized the Commission for Relief in

Belgium and later served as director general of postwar relief and as a member of the Supreme Economic Council that oversaw the recovery efforts.

In 1914 Hoover crossed the North Sea on one of his many wartime passages. An accomplished amateur historian, bibliophile, and collector, he was struck by one historian's lament about the difficulties of studying the French Revolution once war, revolution, and the passage of time had wreaked havoc with documentary materials. This comment stimulated Hoover to collect and preserve the records of the Great War. An alumnus of Stanford, he gave $50,000 to the university in 1919 to set in motion a project to collect documents related to World War I and the postwar situation. E. D. Adams, a historian at Stanford, organized a group of young scholars who traversed Europe in search of historical records. Over the next three years, a collection of public and private documents was assembled, including those of the Commission for Relief in Belgium and the American Relief Administration, that covered the war, the revolutionary upheavals of 1917–19, and the emergence of new states after the peace conference. In the early 1920s, historians from Stanford University traveled with relief teams in the Soviet Union and Eastern Europe, where they were able to ferret out and preserve materials on csarist Russia, the Provisional Government, and the early years of the Bolshevik regime. The Hoover War Library (as it was originally called) also gathered material on postwar reconstruction, the League of Nations, and the league's mandates in the Middle East and Africa. Soon, as new political and social movements swept Europe in the 1930s, the library began to collect materials on fascism. At the end of World War II, Hoover encouraged systematic efforts to expand the collection's Asian holdings. He saw the collection as recording "the suffering, the self-denial, the devotion, the heroic deeds of men."[28]

For nearly forty years, the Hoover War Library operated quietly, often in straitened financial circumstances, as a division of Stanford University. Research fellows performed curatorial duties, and the publishing program was tied closely to the archival collection. In the 1920s, with support from the Rockefeller Foundation, the library began the nation's first systematic studies of the Soviet Union. In the late 1940s and early 1950s, the Carnegie Corporation provided funding for studies of revolution and international relations. In sheer quantity over the years, scholarly bibliographies and edited collections of documents have far outweighed research that is of immediate relevance to policymaking.

In the late 1950s, however, Hoover and some of his associates began to plan a more active political role for the institution, and in 1960, the eighty-six-year-old Hoover declared that the institution's research and publications must "demonstrate the evils of the doctrines of Karl Marx—whether Communism, Socialism, economic materialism or atheism—thus to protect the American way of life from such ideologies, their conspiracies, and to reaffirm the validity of the American system."[29] This declaration sparked the first of a series of controversies over the propriety of housing a research institution with an ideological mission in the university community. An ad hoc faculty committee protested that Hoover's statement violated the basic principles of scholarly investigation. Questions about the institution's relationship to Stanford have simmered ever since.

In 1959 the library's status was formally redefined, and the library became an independent institution, operating without reference to faculty or faculty committees and reporting directly to Stanford's board of trustees through the university's president. Much of the controversy between Stanford and the institution over the years has focused on questions of governance and control, but these problems have been aggravated by the uncompromising conservativism of the institution's longtime director, W. Glenn Campbell.

Born in Ontario and trained in economics at Harvard, where he studied with Gottfried Haberler in the mid-1940s, Campbell spent three years on the research staff of the U.S. Chamber of Commerce and six years as research director of AEI. He was Herbert Hoover's personal choice to take the institution in its new direction; in one of the ironies of the shifting intellectual networks in the United States, his name was suggested to Hoover by none other than Raymond Moley, the key member of Franklin Roosevelt's Brains Trust and architect of the early programs of the New Deal.

Campbell cannot be called a charismatic leader. "Dour" and "prickly" are adjectives often used to describe him. But, over the past thirty years, he has also been the most effective institution builder in the conservative movement. Like Wesley C. Mitchell of the National Bureau of Economic Research or Robert Brookings of the Brookings Institution, Campbell has left an enduring institutional legacy and has won the admiration of fellow conservatives by confronting liberalism within the university. Just as Baroody made an adversary of Brookings to win support, Campbell could argue that the Hoover Institution was creating a principled alternative to a mindlessly tolerant, "anything goes" campus liberalism.

Campbell's immediate task was to continue to build the research collection and stabilize the library's finances. Having come from Washington and AEI, he was also committed to Hoover's plan to make it a major conservative voice in public policy circles. Drawing on the former president's conservative friends and associates, he began to raise the necessary funds. The institution was also an early beneficiary of wealthy western conservatives, many of whom had been drawn into politics by the surge of activity surrounding the Goldwater campaign. Campbell convinced these conservatives that an intellectual center, such as the Hoover Institution, could keep the conservative faith alive through hard times. Given its locale at Stanford University and the presence of so many leading conservative economists, the institution was also an early favorite of conservative foundations.

An admiring colleague fondly describes Campbell as a "penny-pinching Scot," saying that his success in raising an endowment was a matter of appealing to conservatives early on and managing programs tightly with an eye to the long term. In that respect, Campbell differed markedly from Baroody, whose organization fell deeply into debt in the mid-1980s. Campbell deserves full credit for building the Hoover Institution into a major national research center. The institution's corps of scholars increased from six in 1960 to about seventy in residence in the late 1980s. It has grown from a financially pressed library and archive with a $2 million endowment and an annual budget of about $370,000 (only $50,000 of which supported research) to a research institution with an endowment of over $125 million and a $17 million budget, over $7 million of which supports research. Roughly 25 percent of the budget is supplied by the university, while 75 percent comes from endowment and outside contributions. The institution's growing wealth has been no small part of the controversy on the campus, with Campbell complaining in 1988, the last year before his not-altogether-voluntary retirement as the institution's director, that Stanford was attempting another takeover of the institution. Certainly, the institution was slipping from his control after nearly three decades; as the 1989 academic year began, John Raisian took over as acting director.

In some respects, there were two Hoover institutions. One was composed of the conservative administrators around Campbell and a cluster of policy-oriented scholars who shared his ideological convictions; the other was a core of scholars, including distinguished historians and social scientists, who were fortunate enough to land in a well-endowed research institute, free (if they wanted to be) from classroom teaching. For the former group, Hoover was a locus of intellectual activism in which policy-related scholarship and political connections could be combined; for the latter group, it was a comfortable place to do research that could as easily be done on other campuses.

The Hoover Institution has differed from university departments in its critical mass of conservative fellows, some obviously selected for ideological reasons, and in the institution's sophisticated methods of promoting op-ed essays, appearances on radio or television, and opportunities to meet policymakers. It has been as skilled as any Washington operation in its public relations and promotional activities. Hoover's ideological inclinations and promotional activities have not pleased a number of faculty members at the university, but the majority have not seemed to be overly upset in recent years about the institution's alleged political biases. Many concede that there has been more diversity at Hoover than the stereotype of a "Reaganite" institution suggests. In fact, one poll of the senior fellows at the institution found that they were fairly evenly split between Republicans and Democrats.[30]

Though clearly a haven for conservative scholars, the institution seems to be tempering its political work and, through joint academic appointments, becoming better integrated into the university community. "We've been gradually taking Hoover away from Campbell," observed one fellow even before Campbell's departure. Hoover has followed a political trajectory similar to those traced by other maturing research institutions as they deviate from the fervor and sense of clear mission that drove the original founders. Pulled by the gravity of a major research university and the weight of its own library and archives, Hoover seems destined, since Campbell retired, to move into a more tightly circumscribed academic orbit.

Nonetheless, the Hoover Institution's role has often been misunderstood by both supporters and critics. Some of the misunderstanding has been fostered by Hoover's (like many other research institutions') grandiose claims about its policy influence when appealing to donors and its inflated assertions about its influence in policy circles. Annual reports and newsletters from Hoover and many other think tanks are generally full of ceremonial photographs of staff members huddled in conference with cabinet members or shaking hands with the president, or of black-tie dinners at which notables of the current administration praise the think tank's contributions, or of Congressional hearings at which researchers report their findings and deliver pronouncements about policies to a rapt audience.

Campbell likewise made much of Hoover's closeness to Ronald Reagan. Reagan's selection as an honorary fellow (Alexander Solzhenitsyn and Friedrich A. Hayek hold the same title), the president's several testimonials to the institution's influence on his thinking and his summons to public service of thirty scholars, trustees, and former fellows (most on part-time governmental commissions) have been cited as evidence of Hoover's influential public role.[31] But the institution's exploitation of these claims seems equally related to the tightening competition for funds once a victorious conservative administration took office and the fervor of longtime donors began to wane.

A more careful assessment of the role of the various conservative think tanks is in order. The public claims made when Hoover or other research organizations seek financial support inevitably exaggerate the immediacy of their contributions to the formulation of policies. Day-to-day operations at a center for advanced study are hard to promote and celebrate among potential funders, as the heads of most think tanks will attest. It is easier to point to political connections and to foster crude notions about how influence works than to look carefully at how such institutions really operate in the American political culture.

Hoover has given a "home and shelter" (in one scholar's phrase) to a number of conservative academics over the years. Some of them had already attained distinction in major universities. Many of the younger scholars would not likely have fared so well in the competitive academic job market of the 1970s and the more penurious environment of research funding of the 1980s and early 1990s. Hoover and a handful of other institutions have enabled a new generation of conservative scholars to pursue academic work and enjoy considerably more public success than would have otherwise been possible through conventional university careers. Whether universities were actually inhospitable to conservatives (especially economists), Campbell and Baroody acted on the assumption that they were and created alternative institutions through which members of a burgeoning conservative policy elite could pursue their careers. When Ronald Reagan campaigned for the presidency in 1980, he had hundreds of experts whom he could tap for advice.

NINE

☆

The Marketplace
of Ideas

Book Mongers

Mikhail Gorbachev had no doubt about the intellectual influence of one conservative think tank. Indeed, his vehement protest to a group of visiting American politicians took them aback: "Your Hoover Institution says our society is falling apart. Let me tell you, you're the one with the deficit, not us." During separate meetings in 1985, first with Speaker of the House Tip O'Neill and later with Secretary of State George Shultz, he complained about a compendium of essays by the Hoover Institution, entitled *The United States in the 1980s.* He took this book, which emanated from the institution where the U.S. president held an honorific title, as something akin to a pronouncement from the Politburo—nothing less than the blueprint for the Reagan administration's policies. Gorbachev reportedly lectured Shultz, "We have read this book and watched all its programs become adopted by the Reagan Administration." The combative general secretary clearly saw it as proof that "right-wing forces" were in control of U.S. foreign policy.[1]

O'Neill and his companions were especially perplexed. Leaving the room, O'Neill turned to a staff member and muttered, "What the hell is this Hoover Institution?" It is no small irony that a leading American politician had only just heard of an institution with which the Soviet leader was already obsessed, for it suggests how removed think tanks sometimes are from the real world of American government, yet how large their influence seems when viewed from a distance. No one who was traveling with O'Neill had read the book—nearly nine hundred pages—or could tell him anything about its contents.

Shultz must have known considerably more about the book, which had been planned and edited by Martin Anderson, a Hoover fellow and long-time adviser to Reagan. Shultz had, in fact, served on an early advisory committee for the project. But the book was hardly a policy-planning document. Rather, it was more a codification of ideas than a statement of new policy initiatives. Reagan was aware of the book and had received a copy, but Anderson, the president's onetime domestic policy adviser, was not sure that he had ever bothered to read it.[2]

Gorbachev, however, seemed actually to have studied the volume (or been well briefed about its contents). Indeed, no research center could hope for a more attentive reader or a more compelling testimonial, for that matter. All think tanks hope to have their "products" bruited about in the marketplace of ideas, regardless of whether the market is a free one or centrally administered. And Gorbachev's comment, though unsolicited, was just the sort of celebrity endorsement that could never have been engineered by a publicist.

The book was simply one of many thousands of policy publications that compete each year for the attention of policymakers and experts in the robust marketplace of publications by think tanks. Books and reports are the most tangible intellectual product of the modern think factory. Efforts to come up with appealing ideas for books and to promote the books after they are published are central concerns of those who administer such organizations, for their marketplace of ideas is, at the most basic level, a matter of selling policy books.

It is a marketplace that has changed in fundamental ways over the years. At the turn of the century, only some 6,000 books, fiction and nonfiction alike, were published each year. Now nearly 60,000 books are published annually, over 6,000 in the fields of economics and sociology alone. When the Russell Sage Foundation was set up in 1907, its founders knew that theirs was one of the only programs to publish books and pamphlets on contemporary problems. In the mid-1980s, the twenty-five largest policy research institutions contributed an annual total of approximately 250 books and over 1,000 reports, conference proceedings, lecture series, and papers, not to mention countless op-ed pieces and news articles (some of the larger think tanks generate 200 or more op-ed pieces per year). Many now publish journals as well, ranging from the scholarly *Brookings Papers on Economic Activity* to the more polemical *Policy Review*, published by the Heritage Foundation.[3]

Thus, the so-called marketplace of ideas is at times a real book market in which some think tanks have met with considerable success. Charles Murray's *Losing Ground*, a critique of the social programs of the Great Society, was one of the best-sellers of the 1980s. A project of the Manhattan Institute for Policy Research, *Losing Ground* sold over 30,000 copies in hard cover, an exceptional figure for a serious book, especially one that makes heavy use of statistics. The book argued pointedly, and controversially, that poverty had actually been made worse by welfare programs, and its findings naturally struck a responsive chord among those who sympathized with Reagan's policies and thus who were eager to dismantle welfare programs.

But the book was also skillfully handled by the Manhattan Institute. William Hammett, the institute's president, had shrewd insights into the audience for the book and knew how to generate talk and controversy to keep it in the public eye for many months longer than a publishing house typically commits itself to a book. Hammett knew that advertising and book tours would not sell a book like Murray's, and in that sense he contends that the book was not a "marketing" success. At first, it even proved difficult to get some journalistic outlets to review it. Hammett and Murray's strategy was to generate talk about the book among influential people over the course of many months. They saw the book as a way of forcing debate on the poverty programs—"another *Other America*," as Hammett put it. Signed copies of the book were sent to hundreds of influential people; Murray lectured to business and economic groups around the country. And in the end, talk penetrated the popular press and the broadcasting media. The book sold, and as Hammett readily admits, "If *Losing Ground* had failed, we would not be here today. It was a big gamble."[4]

For new institutions, as the Manhattan Institute then was, books draw attention and supply a certain scholarly credibility. For older institutions, they may contribute as much as 5 to 10 percent of the annual income. Old or new, institutions define their audience and mission through the kinds of books they produce. The single-author volume is usually the most durable and serious product, as well as the most costly to produce. An institution can easily expect to spend $100,000 or more to support an author through two or three years of full-time research and writing. Collections of essays, conference papers, and task-force reports can be done at far less expense and in a more timely fashion, though their impact typically is more ephemeral. They are less likely to be reviewed, to find their way into the academic literature, or to be adopted for use in the college classroom.

The impact of books—and thus of the think tanks' principal product—is hard to measure. Sales reveal little about the impact of books on policies. Nor are initial reviews and coverage by the press much of an indication of a book's impact on public opinion. Some of the all-time best-sellers for think tanks—Mary Richmond's *Social Diagnosis* for the Russell Sage Foundation, Gunnar Myrdal's *Asian Drama* for the Twentieth Century Fund, Arthur Okun's *Equality and Efficiency: The Big Trade-Off* for the Brookings Institution—do not prescribe policies; they are works of theory, description, or argument. And like the most successful publications of think tanks over the long term, it is the college classroom that sustains their sales. Indeed, at Brookings, where detailed publishing records have been kept and roughly 200,000 books are sold each year, colleges account for 40 to 50 percent of the total.

The market in which think tanks operate is not exclusively a book market. Indeed, the market for ideas is an odd bazaar in many ways. Books are, at times, more symbols than actual vehicles for the transmission of ideas. In themselves, most books and reports doubtless remain unread by busy policymakers. They do, however, spark talk and further writing. A book's ideas are more likely to be encountered in reviews, editorials, broadcast interviews, op-ed pieces, and magazine articles crafted from the book; they may also be heard in legislative testimony, briefings, and lectures or even receive a sentence or two in newspaper articles when journalists assess the opinion of experts on particular topics.

But whether a book is read or not, it is still a necessary artifact in contemporary policymaking circles. It is emblematic of the policy expert's stature and seriousness of purpose. A book endows its author with credibility to speak on a particular subject and perhaps supplies the visibility that will one day lead to a political appointment. A book will also give foundation and corporate sponsors a tangible sign that their money was not ill-spent.

Yet to ask what impact books, articles, and research reports might have on policymaking and public opinion reveals how difficult it is to untangle the general issue of the influence of policy research institutions. Books and reports seem far removed from the give and take of policy. Many people in policy positions readily concede that they have no time to read books and reports; memos and action papers demand immediate attention. The average congressman, reports one study, spends only eleven minutes of the day reading. Typically, the public official relies on the expertise of others and lives off intellectual capital accumulated over the years.[5]

The market metaphor, however deficient as a way of understanding the impact of think tanks, has taken on a reality of its own; it is a strategy not merely for promoting books, but for selling an institution. Over the past fifteen years, marketing and promotion have done more to change the think tanks' definition of their role (and the public's perception of them) than have any other phenomenan. The metaphors of science and disinterested research that informed the creation and development of the first think tanks, naive as they sometimes were, have now given way to the metaphor of the market and its corollaries of promotion, advocacy, and intellectual combat. And the market metaphor has brought professionals in public relations and marketing onto the staffs of most think tanks, while drawing a new breed of policy entrepreneur into the political scene.

Policy Entrepreneurs

Some of the most skillful intellectual impresarios were hard at work in autumn 1980. Ronald Reagan was on his way to the White House after a victory that promised fundamental changes in the ideas that would shape official policies and programs. Ebullient talk about ideas and political power resounded in Washington, but especially in a think tank located in the District of Columbia's Northeast quadrant, not far from the Capitol. There, in a grayish white brick building that only a few years earlier had housed a Korean grocery and a halfway house for drug addicts, the crisply articulate president of the Heritage Foundation, Edwin J. Feulner, spoke urgently about the political opportunities that he and his fellow conservatives saw before them.

Though Reagan's election was still being hailed as a stunning success, Feulner thought that there was precious little time for celebration and no time to be complacent. The first sixty to ninety days are crucial for any new administration, and Feulner told a *New York Times* reporter that conservatives had to act quickly: "Move in there and make some dramatic changes. Send forth as many initiatives as possible."[6]

Feulner's Heritage Foundation burst into the national political arena with an energy that stunned other research and activist groups on both the Left and Right—and made them not a little worried. Only a week after Reagan's landslide, Feulner delivered to Edwin Meese, head of the White House transition team, a 1,000-page volume called *Mandate for Leadership*, distilling nearly a year's work by some 250 conservative scholars, writers, and activists. The staff of the Heritage Foundation thought that the transition team should get their bearings with the help of this hefty tome on governmental departments and agencies. Remembering Nixon's transition, Feulner believed strongly that new appointees needed guidance from sources other than those individuals they were about to replace.[7]

Mandate for Leadership was a blueprint for conservative activists who were coming in from long years in the political cold. Focusing on immediate tasks—the appointment of new personnel and executive orders that could be issued in the first ninety days—the report was also meant to reflect what Feulner called "a whole new mindset" among conservatives that would be constructive instead of reactionary. "In the past so many of our activities have been against things," he said to a newsman. "Now how do you start thinking more positively in terms of conservative initiatives?"[8] In fact, most of the proposals had already been circulated and were familiar to conservatives; but the encyclopedic compilation; the outlining of concrete steps for action, often by executive order; and, above all, the skill with which the report was promoted were novel and unique.

In the moment of transition, with portents of a more dramatic reorientation than the country had seen since Franklin Roosevelt swept into Washington with his Brains Trust, the Heritage Foundation's report seemed to be a guide to what would follow. Accordingly, reporters and commentators who had scarcely heard of the Heritage Foundation now scrutinized *Mandate for Leadership* for clues to the new administration's policies. One reporter characterized the report as a "blueprint for grabbing the government by its frayed New Deal lapels and shaking out 48 years of liberal policies." Another described it as an "owner's manual for the Federal Government."[9] For a few weeks, at least in Washington bookstores, *Mandate* was something of a best-seller.

The Heritage Foundation had stolen a march on the older, more established research organizations and other would-be counselors, introducing itself as the font and source of conservative policy and gaining a tactical advantage, in large measure, through the skillful orchestration of the report's release. These tactics, which became a model for the promotion of ideas, are a compelling demonstration of how a relatively obscure organization can suddenly become—with a well-promoted book—a major player in national policy.

In the weeks before the report's release, the foundation had arranged advance briefings for a handful of sympathetic reporters. Portions of it were systematically leaked to journalists who were interested in particular areas of policy. Herb Berkowitz, who heads Heritage's public relations program, later explained that the early leaks were intended "to create a snowball effect . . . to have members of the national press corps fighting over the bits and pieces of the study we were ready to release." The strategy worked well. Once the first wire-service articles appeared, Heritage was inundated with requests from other news organizations.[10] The foundation knew that it could count on the competitive zeal of journalists to put its ideas into play. It also exploited the journalistic weakness for political prediction. By thus fostering the perception that it was close to the center of influence, Heritage swelled in stature, much to the dismay of more established scholars at the American Enterprise Institute (AEI) and the Hoover Institution.

The idea for starting Heritage in the 1970s was hatched not when conservatives were sitting on the political sidelines, but while Richard Nixon was president and AEI was enjoying new-found prominence. Yet conservatives, though holding down the White House, still saw themselves as an embattled minority. Some of the more ardent members of Nixon's staff thought they were surrounded by hostile federal bureaucrats and a web of liberal think tanks. Even Nixon's cabinet members were relying on the RAND Corporation and Brookings, much to the chagrin of Nixon aide H. R. Haldeman, who, in May 1969, ordered a staff member to find out specifically which outside foundations and institutions were being used. In a memorandum to a colleague, he explained that "the President wants to issue an order to all White House staff people (I will have to do this verbally) as well as to Cabinet people (also have to be done verbally) that they are not to use Brookings Institution."[11]

Other staff members were unrelentingly hostile to the outside research agencies, recommending that the Internal Revenue Service (IRS) be used to pressure Brookings, the Ford Foundation, and the Institute for Policy Studies, but they were worried that they did not yet have sufficient control of the IRS to prevent leaks. "Making sensitive political inquiries at the IRS is about as safe a procedure as trusting a whore," wrote one of Haldeman's assistants. If governmental agencies could not be used to intimidate their perceived enemies, the White House could at least mount a public attack "on higher and less vulnerable ground." Nixon's most conservative speech writer, Pat Buchanan, took the lead in studying the activities of Brookings and other tax-exempt institutions, making himself the White House expert on how the liberal beast operated. The staff planned a series of broadsides for Vice President Spiro Agnew to launch "to blast the hell out of these outfits and to scare the living hell out of them." An aide to Haldeman also suggested "the low road which should not be passed by," which would link various research institutions and foundations to pro-Hanoi and anti-American activities and "arouse the wrath of the Unenlightened folks west of the Appalachians." Such material would be given to people on Capitol Hill and leaked to the press to pave the way for Agnew's "more gentlemanly attacks." Members of the White House staff were also convinced that copies of the purloined Pentagon Papers were in Brookings's possession, and a raid on the institution (anticipating Watergate by three years) was proposed as a way of really "playing the game tough."[12]

The notion of a left-wing "government in exile" haunted members of the Nixon staff, as did fears that they had not gained control of the federal bureaucracy even after four years in office. Buchanan, within days of Nixon's reelection in 1972, presented the president with a lengthy memorandum on how "to make permanent the New Majority." Perhaps the most pressing need was to create "a new 'cadre' of Republican governmental professionals who can survive this Administration and be prepared to take over future ones." As Buchanan saw it, one of the main difficulties was "credentialitis." Too few genuine conservatives were qualified by training or experience to serve in important governmental posts, and during Nixon's first term, ideological commitment had not been the first criterion of appointment; it would have to be in the second term.

An enduring Republican majority also required the building of an institute that would serve as "the repository of its political beliefs." Such an institute would serve three roles: as a "talent bank" for Republicans when in office, a "tax-exempt refuge" when out of office, and a communications center for Republican thinkers across the nation. "The AEI is not the answer," Buchanan asserted. Buchanan wanted an institution with imaginative leadership to provide "a realistic and principled alternative" to programs and policies emanating from "an essentially liberal-left bureaucracy" and their allies in places like the Brookings Institution. "We should not leave office without such an Institution in being." He saw an institute sustained by governmental contracts and corporate contributions, as well as foundation funds. If the administration kept up the pressure of its political attacks on the Ford Foundation and continued to threaten the foundation's tax-exempt status ("the Ford Foundation, like the American Left, is a paper tiger"), he saw a time when there would be "a cornucopia of Ford funds for Republican and Conservative causes."[13]

The conservative activists on Capitol Hill already had in mind an institution that was very much like the one Buchanan described. They, too, felt that the Nixon administration had been pulled away from conservative principles by the entrenched federal bureaucracy. And they were certain that AEI had been lured to the center in its quest for academic respectability. In fact, Feulner tells of once receiving a solidly researched and well-argued AEI report on the supersonic transport that reached his desk a day or two after Congress had voted not to provide funds for it. Feulner asked a friend at AEI why the report had been released too late to have an impact on the debate in Congress. His friend explained that given its tax-exempt status as a research institution, AEI was wary about influencing the vote. At that moment, Feulner claims, his ideas about the Heritage Foundation crystallized.[14] AEI had grown almost as staid and academic as Brookings, Feulner thought. And the policy debate had grown narrower and more tightly focused on executive decision making, with Democrats and mainstream Republicans engaged in a constricted dialogue. "A vacuum had developed in the public policy arena on the conservative side," explained another member of the Heritage staff. AEI's books and reports seemed increasingly academic, more and more tangential to the legislative process.

Heritage, whose organizers cut their political teeth on congressional staffs, rather than in research organizations, university departments, or executive branch agencies, set out to sharpen the political dialogue. A handful of extremely conservative congressmen and their staff had already decided that they could not press their political agenda through the formal channels of the House of Representatives or their own leadership in the Republican party. Feulner, who then served on the staff of Illinois Republican Congressman Phillip R. Crane, and his friend Paul Weyrich, who then worked for Republican Senator Gordon Allott of Colorado, concluded that there was not enough reliable or timely research to support hard-core conservative members of Congress. Thus, in 1971 and 1972, Feulner and Weyrich set about organizing a conservative House faction, modeled on a twelve-year-old liberal counterpart called the Democratic Study Group.[15]

The immediate spur to the creation of the Republican Study Committee, as the group came to be called, was President Nixon's apparent slide to the center and the willingness of the Republican leadership in the House to embrace the administration's social agenda, especially the Family Assistance Plan and the Child Development Act. "Nixon divided the Republican party in the House," explained Weyrich. His proposals "separated the real conservatives from the pragmatists."[16] Ideological conservatives, like Buchanan and Weyrich, saw how Washington tended to pull all nonideologues toward the center. The "real conservatives" on Capitol Hill banded together in a formally organized faction that tended to be independent, if not actually hostile, to the Republican party. They organized at a propitious moment. By the early 1970s, all congressmen had greater staff resources at their command. From an average of three or four in the 1950s and 1960s, House members now saw their staffs grow to fifteen or more, while senators commanded staffs of about thirty members on average and, in the case of committee chairs, upwards of seventy.[17]

The resources for policy-related activities were seldom adequate, however. Most personal staffs devoted their energies to serving their constituents and answering the mail; an overworked assistant or two handled the policy issues confronted by the average congressman. Policy development was especially difficult for the most conservative House members who did not have committee chairmanships and the staffs that go with them. Moreover, these representatives were profoundly suspicious of the experts in the Congressional Research Service and did not trust information and data supplied by executive agencies. The General Accounting Office, though often praised by members of both parties for the quality of its work, was frequently thought to release its reports too late to be of use in the legislative process.

Conservative congressmen, sensing that they might wield more power if they coordinated their research and legislative strategies, forged alliances with outside groups of activists and policy-minded academics, many of whom were alienated from their own campuses and eager to join the cause. In 1973 the conservative congressmen hired an executive director to head their Republican Study Committee and arranged to pool some of their legislative staffs. Most of the committee's work in those days was aimed at blocking legislative initiatives, but the seeds of a more ambitious undertaking had been sown.

The organizers of this conservative faction had learned, from watching Brookings, RAND, and other think tanks, that private research institutions in the United States seemed to carry greater intellectual authority than did organizations that were tied either to parties or to the government. If conservatives in Congress were to take the initiative, they would have to create their own policy proposals and try to recast the public debate.

The group responsible for forming the committee, led by Feulner and Weyrich, sought financial support for a new policy research institute. With $250,000 from Joseph Coors, the Colorado brewer and funder of conservative causes, the Heritage Foundation opened its doors in 1973. Its small staff, headed initially by Paul Weyrich, moved into a cluster of offices near Union Station. The earliest financial backers of the new enterprise included John Scaife, a Mellon heir, whose first contribution was $900,000; the Noble Foundation of Oklahoma, with financial resources based on oil and gas interests; and the John M. Olin Foundation, a longtime supporter of conservative causes.

The Heritage staff and budget grew exponentially during the 1970s. Wealthy individuals who had backed the conservative movement and conservative foundations whose grant making became much more professional contributed. But Heritage, true to its "New Right" origins, also relied on direct-mail fund-raising. Individual donations, many of them in the $25 to $50 range, have accounted for as much as 40 percent of its annual budget, a marked contrast with the more traditional policy research organizations. By 1977, when Feulner left his position as executive director of the Republican Study Committee and became president of Heritage, its annual budget exceeded $2 million. Growing at more than 30 percent in some years, its budget reached roughly $10 million by 1983 and close to $18 million by 1989. Its staff currently numbers about 135.

Heritage chose early on to serve a particular clientele, primarily members of Congress and their staffs, but it has nonetheless reshaped the broader market in which all research organizations now compete. Heritage is the salesman and promoter of ideas par excellence, issuing nearly two hundred publications each year, from short policy briefs to full-length books. Feulner judges many of his products by what he terms "the brief-case test"—analyses and recommendations should be as concise as possible, able to be read and absorbed in a limousine on the way to a meeting. Its shortest format, the Executive Memorandum, outlines an argument on a single sheet, front and back. "We specialize," says Feulner, "in the area of quick-response public policy research and in marketing the academic works for public policy consumption."[18] With an eight-member government-relations group, Heritage spends considerable time updating lists of congressional and administrative aides and arranging to deliver briefing materials to the right office at precisely the right time.

In aiming to influence public decisions, Heritage comes close to the legal boundary that separates research and education from outright lobbying. Feulner knows that the foundation is more aggressive than other tax-exempt policy research institutions, but he explains, "We are free to express our views as outspokenly as we want, but we must discuss issues or general policy." Thus, when a memorandum deals with specific legislation, it outlines both the advantages and disadvantages of a bill. But that format still leaves plenty of room to maneuver. "Many other think tanks have been overly cautious in deciding just how far they can opine," Feulner says, "and the result is that their impact has not been nearly as effective as it should be. We set out to change this."[19]

Feulner and his team have defined a product and a market. Heritage is a self-professed intellectual retailer, "a secondhand dealer of ideas," in Feulner's words, with a considerable portion of its budget (35 to 40 percent) devoted to public relations. Its most avid consumers are members of the conservative congressional staffs who must brief their bosses and supply them with legislative arguments, pro or con; the conservative appointee in an executive agency who is leery of relying on the expertise of civil service employees and may want to consult with an ideologically compatible expert; and the journalist who wants to balance an article with insights drawn from an authoritative conservative source.

The market metaphor—so fundamental a part of the Heritage Foundation's ethos—now holds sway among institutions across the political spectrum, all of which feel increasingly crowded by competition for public attention and funding. And it is a sadly appropriate metaphor in a political environment shaped by advertising, market research, and the packaging—and repackaging—of political candidates. Political ideas have become commodities to be sold, and "experts" are often those who gain the most routine access to the media.

The promotion of ideas is, often, the promotion of the spokesmen for them, elevating people to the "quote circuit," as one journalist terms it. Consequently, a number of policy research institutions now devote considerable energy to the publication of press handbooks and directories of experts. A pioneer in these systematic media ventures, Heritage has produced *The Annual Guide to Public Policy Experts,* which now lists 1,500 conservative scholars whose expertise is catalogued in 70 subfields.[20]

Marketing and the resulting symbiosis between the entrepreneurs of think tanks who promote their "goods" and a Washington press corps that seeks novelty and controversy have brought experts into the public debate—a generally healthy development. But the process has also compounded the difficulties of determining whether the claims of expertise are rooted more deeply in scholarship or in skills in handling the mass media. Moreover, the market metaphor is also intrinsically at odds with the commitment to research, common intellectual inquiry, and forthright debate. Marketing tactics, however momentarily successful, are not necessarily the ingredients of long-term influence on the policy process—or for a meaningful public dialogue. Nonetheless, as Herb Berkowitz, the foundation's director of public relations, dryly observed, in Washington "perceptions of influence are influence."[21]

People Are Policy

In the euphoria of Ronald Reagan's election, the conservative think tanks were quick to congratulate themselves on their success in marketing conservative ideas. Yet looking back on the election seven years later, Martin Anderson sought to downplay the role of such institutions in fostering the intellectual changes that preceded the Reagan "revolution." "It's a myth that Reagan had these research institutes," he remarked. "No institute is big enough to provide all the advice a candidate needs."[22] Indeed, Anderson had put together a huge advisory team for Reagan, using some 450 experts with a wide variety of backgrounds. Over the long term, in Anderson's view, Reagan's triumph had much less to do with the promotional efforts of conservative think tanks than with the growing frustrations the electorate felt about prevailing liberal policies.

The election represented the political ratification of ideas that had been germinating slowly in the intellectual world for more than thirty years. Individual writers and their books had made a gradual difference, but the conservative research institutions had been relatively late arrivals on the scene. Anderson saw conservatism as "a glacial movement that finally had political consequences," while Milton Friedman, his colleague at the Hoover Institution, described the conservative institutions more as epiphenomena of the conservative movement than as its causes. These think tanks provided a base of operations for some conservative thinkers.[23]

The movement of conservative ideas gathered force, not on the strength of institutionalized propaganda campaigns or public proselytizing by think tanks—the hard-sell marketing of ideas—but as the public's ideas about programs and policies changed. The research and public commentary of the conservative intellectuals simply echoed and explained what many people already felt.

The long-term success of the conservative think tanks lay less in their efforts to persuade and exhort the public—market metaphors notwithstanding—than in helping to shape a conservative policy elite that could claim that it was capable of governing. Indeed, in fostering a counterelite, the work of the conservative think tanks paralleled, though in a much foreshortened way, developments that had taken place over more than half a century in the older research institutions. Think tanks of the Right did not make a revolution; rather, they prepared the revolutionary cadres who ascended to power in 1980. These self-conscious revolutionaries used policy research organizations in new ways, challenging the assumptions on which Brookings, RAND, the Urban Institute, and others had operated while casting further doubt upon the long-term political contributions of experts who were trained in the social sciences.

The Heritage Foundation's success and high visibility in the 1980s can be accounted for, in part, by the stumbling mismanagement of its older rival, AEI. Although AEI sent roughly twenty of its research fellows into the administration in 1981 (thus fulfilling the role of temporary home and shelter for conservatives who were out of power in the 1970s), it was left without a clear sense of intellectual mission. Unlike Heritage, it seemed confused about the role it should play once conservatives had acceded to policymaking positions. In some respects, its work in the 1960s and 1970s, especially on deregulation and defense, had paid off by 1980. But in 1978 when William Baroody, Sr., handed over the presidency to his son, Bill, Jr., AEI lost the confident leader and fund-raiser it had for nearly a quarter century.

Baroody, Jr., had ambitious plans to construct new offices on

Pennsylvania Avenue near the White House and to endow new chairs and research programs. These plans were similar to those at Heritage. But while Feulner had put together a strong team of managers and proved himself adept at delegating and building loyal external constituencies, Baroody, Jr., ran a one-man show and soon learned that he had none of his father's gift for raising money or holding the confidence of foundations and corporate donors.

For an institution that preached fiscal responsibility to governmental managers, AEI's accounting and management systems were archaic and its long-range planning fanciful. "It was like something out of a Dickens novel," said one scholar. There was no budget; grants came in for specific projects and were siphoned off to meet general operating expenses. "I made a conscious decision to expand rapidly," said Baroody, Jr. "I thought the programs were needed and the funding would follow because we had a track record." Instead, funding declined, and the institution ran up nearly $3 million in debts.[24] By 1985, the board and staff began to learn the magnitude of AEI's financial difficulties. There was room in the budget to eliminate subsidized lunches, parking privileges, and some of the more lavish spending on public relations, but not enough to avoid trimming the staff. First, secretaries lost their jobs and then members of the research staff were fired or put on "challenge status," which was a way of asking them to raise funds for their own salaries. Baroody, Jr., lost the confidence of both the staff and the board. In June 1986, resisting to the end, he resigned.

Christopher DeMuth, a scholarly lawyer who had headed the program in deregulation at Harvard's Kennedy School of Government and served for three years at the Office of Management and Budget, took over as head of the financially troubled AEI in late 1986. The core budget was only about $7.5 million, a little more than half what it had been at its peak. More troubling was AEI's loss of its well-focused mission. Baroody Jr.'s vision had been expansive, but it was never particularly well articulated. DeMuth would later characterize it as an effort to build "a university without students," suggesting that the research program had become unfocused and that the goal of contributing to current policy debates had been neglected. But as he began to redefine the institute's agenda, retaining a core of thirty scholars, he knew that he was in for a long period of reappraisal and financial adjustment.

Baroody Jr.'s grandiose plans were in sharp contrast to the clear strategic vision of Ed Feulner. Despite the Heritage Foundation's early links to the New Right, Feulner wanted to make the foundation a tent under which all the strains of conservative thinking could be at home. Accordingly, he tempered Heritage's role in promoting a divisive right-wing social agenda that had the potential to offend libertarian allies; he successfully drew prominent neoconservatives into the Heritage camp by making clear that the foundation was strong in its support of Israel (and in doing so drew some of them out of AEI's orbit). While staying close to the "true" conservatives in the Reagan and Bush administrations, Heritage has often walked a fine line between defending the administrations and acting as a goad and sharp critic of policies when they have seemed to stray toward "pragmatic" compromise with liberals and moderates.

The foundation's policy research program reaches from urban policy to outer space. Heritage has departments for domestic policy, economic policy, and foreign policy and defense, and centers for Asian studies and international economic development. With the exception of such notables as Distinguished Fellows Jack Kemp, Richard Allen, and Edwin Meese and a few longtime members of the research staff, like Burton Y. Pines, vice president for research, and Stuart Butler, who heads the Domestic Policy Studies program, most of Heritage's "policy analysts" are energetic, graduate-student-age policy activists. Relatively few have Ph.D.s. They enlist because they are willing to lend their talents to the institution's aims. The staff tends to resemble that of a congressional office, rather than that of the more academically inclined research institutions whose expertise has been won through academic publications and perhaps a period of governmental service. As conservative political appointees left the Reagan administration, however, Heritage added a few eminent conservatives to its staff. Its academic tone was also enhanced by visiting conservative scholars who were brought to Washington for short-term appointments.

Heritage is quick to admit, however, that its purpose is advocacy, rather than academic research. The staff marshal facts and ideas for use on behalf of their cause. Burt Pines, a former correspondent for *Time* magazine and erstwhile graduate student in European history, is typically forthright in explaining what Heritage does: "We state up front what our beliefs are and admit that we are combatants in the battle of ideas. We are on one side and we make that clear. We are not just for better government and efficiency, we are for particular ideas." Pines sees his research staff as consisting of "experts," but not in the sense of those who work out of Brookings or the Urban Institute. The researchers at Heritage know the general academic literature on a given subject and are familiar with the established lines of policy debate, but, as he puts it, "the staff uses its expertise to mobilize arguments. They are advocates . . . We make it clear to them that they are not joining an academic organization but one committed to certain beliefs. We tell them that they will write papers with a format that is not for a professional peer group."[25] At Heritage, the aim is self-consciously to shape and influence the debate in line with a preconceived set of ideas or principles, rather than simply to pursue research questions in whatever direction they may lead. Burt Pines describes the Heritage staff as the shock troops or marine landing parties of conservative policymaking, compared to the staff at Hoover and AEI, who are more like heavy artillery bombarding the enemy from a distance. But although the voluble, outgoing Pines relishes the military metaphors, the market metaphor suffuses the discussions of other members of the Heritage staff.

In Washington, the marketing of ideas is often indistinguishable from the promotion of people who are capable of articulating them—individuals who, by one means or another (and think tanks are now the accepted means) can establish themselves as authorities in a given field. In the past two decades, the most important function served by the network of conservative think tanks has not been the germination of new ideas, but the creation of a "new cadre" of professionals, the group whose absence Patrick Buchanan had lamented in 1972. Not only have the dozens of conservative think tanks created a framework for disseminating ideas that exists largely outside the established infrastructure of academic journals, university presses, and commercial publishing (though commercial publishers, on the strength of Charles Murray's *Losing Ground*, George Gilder's *Wealth and Poverty*, and Allan Bloom's *Closing of the American Mind*, have increasingly recognized that conservatives constitute a literate book-buying audience), they have also designed career vehicles for conservative activists and thinkers. The opportunities to publish and write within this "alternative" infrastructure have given high visibility to some conservative policy analysts, often short-circuiting slower academic routes to prominence. Conservative think tanks were quick to encourage their staffs to write op-ed essays and to distribute the essays to newspapers (understanding, too, that news outlets beyond New York and Washington would welcome their articles). While AEI experimented for a time with its own television and radio productions, the libertarian Cato Institute has recently proved successful in promoting its affiliated scholars as regular radio commentators.

With an eye to the future of the movement, Heritage has also conscientiously nurtured a "third generation" of conservative leaders, sponsoring college interns and young policy aides who come to work in Washington's bureaucracy and providing a meeting ground for them while they are in town. By the end of the 1980s, it was sponsoring graduate-level courses as part of a "Conservative Curriculum." It has quickly become apparent that for many bright young activists, the conservative policy network can be a much quicker route to a political career and public influence than can toiling in academe. Indeed, the conservative movement's orientation toward fostering the careers of young people has set its think tanks apart from the more traditional research centers, in which training remains the prerogative of graduate schools and careers proceed along more conventional academic routes.[26]

Ultimately, the promotion of ideas also involves placing their proponents in governmental positions, where they can shape policy. The notion that "people are policy"—a phrase often heard at Heritage and echoed in government offices—led the foundation to play an active role in seeking official positions for its roster of bona fide conservatives in the 1980s. Heritage operated a "talent bank" during the first Reagan transition and is reported to have delivered 2,500 resumes to Bush's transition team. With its third-generation project and talent bank, Heritage signaled the end of its insurrectionary intellectual role—if not of the conservative political movement properly so called—and the beginning of efforts to govern. While Heritage was the most successful of the conservative think tanks in Washington during the 1980s, its long-term test will come as it tries to resist the strongest gravitational force in Washington—the relentless pull toward the center.

The Process Ethos

Ideas may have consequences, as many conservatives insist, but over the course of this century, the nation's policies have more often been a consequence of opportunity, circumstance, and compromise than of intellectual convictions working their way relentlessly through the political process. Despite the best efforts of policy promoters and idea brokers, the process is too diffuse and too open to countering influences for the outcome to be driven exclusively by ideological impulses. Hard experience often makes a greater impact on the mind than does intellectual argument; and policies, if they are to be not merely enacted but sustained over time, must reconcile competing needs and interests.

The gravitational force in Washington works inexorably to pull policy research institutions and experts toward the center. Even Heritage has tempered its voice on divisive social issues and has worked quietly with experts in other institutions on questions of trade policy and welfare reform. Ideological impulses tend to exhaust themselves in a political system that is structured to devise pragmatic means, and ideologues cannot long sustain a policy "triumph" because policies are always subject to change and review. Thus, the research institutions that have survived over the long term have had to devise strategies for finding and straddling the center.

David Abshire, an affable Tennesseean, helped found one such institution—the Center for Strategic and International Studies. CSIS has defined its role in less combative terms than has the Heritage Foundation and, over the years, has moved closer to the operating center of the foreign policy process. Abshire is an idea broker who is in a different mold from Baroody, Sr., Campbell, or Feulner. He was trained at West Point, earned a doctorate in history from Georgetown University, and learned American politics on Capitol Hill. His perspectives were not shaped by interest-group lobbying, as were Baroody's, nor by movement politics, as were Feulner's. He entered the world of policy and legislative politics upon leaving the army in the late 1950s, when he found an opportunity to work for Clement Zablocki, minority leader of the House, on a national security report. Congress, with its shifting coalitions, fluidity of ideas and opinions, and constant interplay of arguments and actions, captivated the former army officer, who was much more accustomed to formal lines of authority.[27]

William Baroody, Sr., drew the officer-scholar into AEI's orbit, and it was there that Abshire hatched the idea for a Washington-based strategic studies center, to be patterned on London's Institute for Strategic Studies. The London institute was launched by Alistair Buchan, with help from the Ford Foundation, but there was nothing like it in Washington in the early 1960s. Baroody encouraged Abshire's efforts and—along with W. Glenn Campbell, several congressmen, and former officials from the Eisenhower administration—agreed to serve on its board of directors.[28] With a budget of $120,000, raised largely from Pittsburgh's Scaife Foundation and California businessman Justin Dart, CSIS opened in 1962.

CSIS, which was affiliated with Georgetown University until the university cut the ties in 1986, was modestly envisioned as a place where strategic research and writing could be monitored, collated, discussed, and refined. The center, whose early pronouncements echoed the hard-liners' language, aimed to examine alternative strategies for dealing with communism. They spoke of the need to refurbish Western moral values and of an open society in a life-and-death struggle against its enemies.[29]

The center's uniqueness lay, not so much in its tough line, but in a conception of strategy that was at odds with the kind of strategic analysis being pursued by civilian planners at the Pentagon and adherents of systems thinking in the early 1960s. The founders of CSIS held to an older, Clausewitzian conception of strategy, going beyond the issues encompassed by high-technology weapons systems, least-cost analyses, and decisions about procurement. This conception is not surprising, since men with military experience in the army and navy, rather than the air force, were among the center's founders. Joining Abshire, who had done much of the initial organizing, was Admiral Arleigh Burke, former chief of naval operations. Questions of leadership and morale, as well as geopolitical concerns, were more important to them than to air force officers, who were concerned with nuclear strategy and weapons engineering and were familiar with the cost-accounting and systems-analysis methods of the RAND Corporation. Since the early 1960s, CSIS has grown from a university-affiliated, seven-person operation with a small budget to an independent institution with a budget of about $10 million, contributed by conservative and mainstream foundations. Along the way, it has worked hard to shed its early right-wing image.

Over the years, CSIS has attracted more historians, political scientists, and regional specialists than economists and engineers. Among its 150-member staff, the mainstays have included Richard V. Allen, Reagan's first national security adviser; historian Walter Laqueur, an expert on terrorism and intelligence; Edward Luttwak, a military historian and theorist; Robert Kupperman, a specialist in counterterrorism; and Ray Cline, former deputy director of the Central Intelligence Agency and a specialist on the Soviet Union and China. Many distinguished former senior officials, including Henry Kissinger, James Schlesinger, Zbigniew Brzezinski, and Robert McFarlane, have maintained affiliations with CSIS as "counselors" to the institution.

The work at CSIS ranges across functional fields concerning communications policy, science and technology, energy policy, and the politico-military balance; it also covers specific regions of the globe. While some of the projects result in scholarly books—and most CSIS fellows seem to wish that more and better scholarship were done under the center's auspices—the emphasis is on serving the policy process in more immediate ways. That is, CSIS sponsors working groups, policy groups, study groups, and seminars that are designed to bring together the principal Washington players in such fields as arms control, energy, terrorism, and other foreign policy subject.

The rise of CSIS parallels a number of fundamental shifts in the institutional patterns of American foreign policymaking and in the structure of public debates about foreign policy. Two phenomena stand out, shaping the role the center has chosen as a private player in the game of nations. The more assertive participation of Congress in devising foreign policy since the late 1960s—initially sparked by the Vietnam War but persisting into the 1980s in disputes over aid to the Nicaraguan contras, war powers, trade, and arms control— created a niche for the center as an intellectual resource for newly active congressmen and their staffs. Indeed, Abshire, whose familiarity with Congress landed him the post of assistant secretary of state for congressional relations under President Nixon, views Congress as CSIS's major constituency (much as does Feulner of the Heritage Foundation). But CSIS sees its utility to the process less in terms of providing ammunition for the debate about policies than in serving as a broker for discussion and accommodation.

American business, which has also become more international in its outlook since the 1960s, is more keenly interested in the policy decisions made in Washington. The concern with foreign affairs, which was primarily limited to investment houses, banks, certain mining interests, and the law firms that assisted them in the first half of the twentieth century, has spread to every economic sector. As interest expanded, CSIS has seen business not only as an audience but as a source of financial support. Briefing businessmen and consulting with firms on the global context in which they must operate has become a more important function not merely of CSIS but of think tanks like Brookings.

CSIS is, in itself, symptomatic of another shift in foreign policymaking—a gradual transformation of the elite that is engaged in international issues. Just as experts in social and economic policy rose to prominence in the decades before World War II, specialists in foreign policy who are trained in various academic fields have become more central to the making of foreign policy over the past quarter century. These specialists are a different type from those who were drawn primarily from the East Coast, educated at Ivy League schools, and served apprenticeships in law and investment banking firms. On leaving the government, they are not as likely to return to the investment houses and law firms that for generations provided the private institutional bases for aspiring public servants. Moreover, they are often driven by ideological imperatives that did not arouse practical-minded bankers or lawyers. Their careers depend upon polemical and expository skills, novel ideas, and intellectual formulations, and those traits must somehow be brought to the attention of those in power.[30]

The set of quasi-academic institutions that has sprouted in Washington—roughly sixty out of a hundred deal with matters of foreign policy and national security—is the means for many of these policy types to make their way, retaining a base in Washington, where the issues are debated and discussed, where opportunities for governmental and private consulting exist, and where political journalism is centered. As one scholar observed, "Even a mediocre institution in Washington can be more important than a first-rate institution elsewhere."[31] To serve as a marginal player in the policy game seems preferable to a forced retreat to any but the most prestigious university positions. And as university appointments proved harder to come by and academic salaries shrank in the 1970s, many who might have returned to academia stayed on in Washington, where they could be close to the policy process and not overburdened with teaching or long-term research commitments.

It is not surprising that full-time professors at Georgetown looked critically at the university's affiliated research center. Though tensions as bitter as those that rent Stanford University and the Hoover Institution never surfaced, the complaints about the "media profs" at CSIS who devoted more time to television appearances than to serious scholarship were not unfounded. The "media contacts," dutifully catalogued by the center, were indeed frequent, 4,000 to 5,000 per year in recent years. Though the ties were loose, some faculty members found the center's use of Georgetown's name in the policy arena to be troublesome, if not inappropriate, and administrators acknowledged that the two institutions were competing for funds. In 1986 an outside committee of prominent scholars, convened by the university to examine CSIS in its own version of an accreditation review, concluded that the center's work was not sufficiently academic for a university-based research institute. The university and CSIS parted in a generally amicable manner.

Unlike university scholars, the "scholar-statesmen" of CSIS, as the center styles them, have tended to operate within a loose institutional network in which talk and informal debates are more important than are scholarly research and publication. CSIS's concerns are not those of research driven by theory and discipline; it aims to put policy "in the realm of the real and the doable," says Robert Neumann, a senior adviser at CSIS who specializes in the Middle East and has served as ambassador to Afghanistan, Morocco, and Saudi Arabia. The center operates in a political culture, in which oral communication often is more valued than the written word.[32]

Researchers at CSIS speak of a "process ethos." Instead of aiming, like the Heritage Foundation, to market ideas and sharpen the lines of debate, the center favors an informal and consensual approach to policymaking. It believes that policy emerges from discussion, that ideas are honed in debate, and that there must be continuing efforts to build consensus out of shifting opinions. It is this vision of the policy process that has allowed the center to bring together people who might not otherwise focus on the same issue at the same moment. Within Washington's compartmentalized and specialized policymaking communities, CSIS like some of its counterparts—most notably Brookings's Center for Public Policy Education—offers a framework for bringing together academics, bureaucrats, legislators, leaders of interest groups, union officials, and businessmen. The various study groups at CSIS permit informal talk about issues outside the framework of congressional committees and partisan discussion groups. Indeed, the most valuable work for some Washington think tanks is less to generate novel ideas or promote policy ideas in the political marketplace than to create a space for talk and discussion outside the contested turf of bureaucratic and partisan warfare.

At times the proliferation of Washington-based research organizations, especially those that link research with advocacy, has seemed only to sharpen policy debate and to undermine the likelihood of reaching practical agreements. But the gravitational pull of the center always reasserts itself—a force created through the practical experience of politics. In time, public officials learn the limits of what they can accomplish in a relatively brief term of office. They also feel the moderating impact of their party's long-term need for reelection and further discover that they must work with the political opposition whether they like to or not.

The research organizations that have survived over the long haul have found a way not merely to occupy that middle ground but to help define it. Although the "marketplace of ideas" and the "war of ideas" are arresting metaphors, they do not portray the think tank in its most typical roles—operating discreetly to define the middle ground and providing an environment in which the knowledge of experts can be channeled to serve political ends. The sheer number of policy analysts and experts and their shared academic assumptions tend to narrow the terrain on which policies are contested. The rhetoric of commerce and warfare may excite the constituencies who provide funding for research organizations. These metaphors suggest urgency, promise direct intellectual engagement in daily political struggles, and hint at strategies for influencing decision making. But they do not explain the long-term play of ideas or the role of the expert in American politics. Indeed, they have done more to obscure than to enlighten. At a moment when the world's political systems are being transformed, and this nation seems especially to require intelligent and knowledgeable experts, as well as much better informed citizens, it is crucial to ask what we can expect of the experts and how we can employ them better.

TEN

☆

The Politics of Ideas

The Ideas Industry

If "new starts" are any indicator, the policy-ideas industry has been thriving since the 1970s. Of the approximately one hundred policy research groups now in Washington, nearly two-thirds were established after 1970.[1] And although it is impossible to tally all the newly created independent policy research institutes and university-based centers across the country, the rapid proliferation of these organizations has been obvious to many observers. Indeed, during the 1980s, the creation of new think tanks sometimes took on faddish proportions. Political candidates created them in their quest for new ideas, political partisans thought that research institutes could be incubators of winning programs, individuals with ideas to peddle set up their own tiny "institutes," and policy entrepreneurs carried the think tank model to state capitals.

Convinced that conservative ideas truly had political consequences, liberals seemed especially eager to emulate the vigorous research and advocacy-oriented centers of the Right in the early 1980s. They geared up their intellectual efforts at New York's World Policy Institute and at the Center for National Policy, the Economic Policy Institute, and the Progressive Policy Institute (among many other operations) in Washington. Meanwhile, the Right—both its traditionalist and libertarian strains—continued energetically to plant

214

the seeds for new policy operations throughout the country and around the world. And as the national policy framework changed, leaving some issues unaddressed by older institutions, activists and scholars busied themselves founding dozens of new and more specialized institutions. Indeed, specialization—or finding an exclusive market niche—was the one common trait of successful entrants into the ideas industry, including the Center on Budget and Policy Priorities, the Institute for International Economics, and the World Resources Institute. At the most fundamental level, these new entities are part of the continuing ebb and flow of organizational activity that takes place in America's nonprofit or so-called third sector. A robust pluralism and engrained habits of intellectual entrepreneurship allow new enterprises to sprout, while others wither.

Apart from the obvious impulse to imitate the success of the conservative think tanks and to focus on neglected policy issues, three other forces have shaped the recent burst of organizing activity. First, the large foundations, which had once made hefty capital gifts or committed resources to long-term research projects in a relatively small number of institutions, shifted their grant-making patterns. Pressures to give to a wider array of institutions, to hold grantees more directly accountable for their work, and to seek a more immediate effect with inflation-reduced dollars pushed them to support new organizations for more narrowly defined projects with a more immediate payoff. A number of new research centers were set up because private foundations sought novel and more flexible research arrangements. Second, universities became more entrepreneurial, creating new research centers in all fields. Like many of their colleagues in the natural and physical sciences who had tapped governmental funds earlier on, policy-oriented social scientists found expanding opportunities in the late 1960s and early 1970s to fund their applied research by means of government contracts. And then in more financially constrained times since the mid-1970s, the practice of creating research centers has allowed researchers at universities to attract funds and hire new faculty on "soft" money that does not require them to make long-term financial commitments. Third, the more ideologically charged political environment of the past twenty years energized both policy entrepreneurs and their financial backers to break away from the framework of older research institutions. Apart from their specific policy proposals, many of these new centers have challenged the authoritative status of social scientists who work in established institutions.

The tug of war between the political center and the peripheries—the centripetal force of practical action and compromise against the centrifugal pull of abstract principle—is always at work in our system. But these opposing forces intensify when the center is being redefined and its gravitational pull is correspondingly weakened. When the center ground is clearly defined, political debate can be conducted in the well-modulated tones of reasoned scientific inquiry, and the experts' authority remains generally secure when goals and directions are widely agreed on. But when the force of contradictory principles begins to exert a stronger pull against the center, it not only challenges the unexamined ground on which the old consensus rests, but calls into question the claims that experts make about their knowledge and the values undergirding their work.

In the 1970s and 1980s, a number of new research centers on both the Right and the Left tried to move the intellectual combat to the moral high ground. Some now deal explicitly with first principles. In founding the Ethics and Public Policy Center in 1976, Ernest Lefever announced his mission clearly: "to clarify and reinforce the bond between the Judeo-Christian moral tradition and domestic and foreign policy issues." Today, that moral tradition, in Lefever's view, has received its most cogent expression in neoconservatism, which he defines as nothing less than "a contemporary reaffirmation of the central Western moral consensus."[2] For Lefever, the neoconservatives have best articulated the abstract values that define the Western tradition, while operating with the most clear-headed sense of the real world, in which he judges those values to be under constant threat.

The Ethics and Public Policy Center is an aggressive moral combatant, grounding its work in "the great Western ethical imperatives": respect for individual dignity, individual freedom, justice and the rule of law, and limited government. Rather than asking what these values have meant as theoretical propositions, Lefever, with a staff of fewer than twenty and an annual budget of just over $1 million, attempts to clarify the relationship between principles and political necessity. For Lefever, a former Yale seminarian and minister in the Church of the Brethren who has held congressional staff positions and worked at Brookings, ethics is not simply a matter of stating moral ends—as most of his opponents on the Left have done—but a discipline of relating ends to means. Through conferences, seminars, and roughly ten books and short reports each year, the center has focused primarily on foreign policy and educational issues.

One of the center's most consistent objectives has been to scrutinize the policy positions and political activities of organized religious bodies like the National Council of Churches and the World Council of Churches. The center has criticized the church-led movement for corporate responsibility, as well as clerical calls for divestiture and the withdrawal of corporations from South Africa. It has taken to task peace activists and proponents of a freeze on nuclear weapons. Its publications have also criticized the U.S. Catholic Bishops for their pastoral letters on nuclear arms and the economy.

In the center's internal dialectic of principles and policy, conservative necessity is inevitably judged to win out over a pious and unrealistic liberalism. Lefever's realism means that in an evil world, one's views of freedom and justice, as well as one's faith in rational human nature, must be tempered by prudential calculation. Though the policies espoused by the center's authors are rooted in the neoconservative imperatives of national will and strength, an older conservatism is at work as well. Lefever offers a broad critique of rationalism and progress, arguing that any change must be slow and deliberate. To him, reform must be measured against creeping historical progress. Furthermore, political decisions must be tempered by a consciousness of the fragility of liberal democratic values, which he sees as threatened not only by totalitarian opponents but by naive liberals—whom he characterizes as rational idealists—who worship reason and are hopelessly optimistic about human perfectibility. "We fight back," Lefever explains. "I regard myself as in a daily struggle for truth, justice and righteousness."[3]

Other centers share Lefever's conviction that values must be brought to the fore in political debates. While Lefever's group, by and large, upholds the neoconservative strain of contemporary conservatism, the Rockford Institute in Illinois represents a more traditionalist element. With an annual budget of approximately $1 million, the institute was founded in 1976 by John Howard, former president of Rockford College, who was deeply troubled by the changes he had witnessed on American campuses in the late 1960s. Howard first conceived of his institute as a place for examining changes in college curricula and educational philosophy; but the institute has since expanded its purview, looking more broadly at the cultural sources of social and political values, especially the family and religion. Through its provocative monthly magazine, *Chronicles of Culture*, and various newsletters and reports, such as *Persuasion at Work* and its successor *The Family in America*, the institute seeks to return to first principles—those grounded in religion.

Rockford set up a New York affiliate in 1984, the Center on

Religion and Society, under the direction of Lutheran theologian Richard John Neuhaus. Neuhaus has argued that public discourse in a "naked public square," stripped clean of religious values, is dangerous and contends that a "public ethic" cannot be reestablished unless it is based on the historical religiosity of the American people. While arguing against secular liberalism, he nevertheless holds that Christian truth, if true, must be a "public truth," not authoritarian or arbitrary. He thus separates himself from those in the moral majority and others on the extreme religious right, as well as from many traditional conservatives. In fact, by the late 1980s, Neuhaus and the more conservative Illinois institute were growing less comfortable in each other's company. Neuhaus departed and the center was relocated in Illinois.[4]

From the outset, the work of the Rockford Institute was a reaction against the empiricism and neutrality toward values of the social sciences. Howard and his colleagues believed that policy choices, when framed by the reasoned analyses of social scientists, created a scientific wall that excluded values grounded in religion from public discourse. The "moral rot," as Rockford's current president Allan Carlson terms it, was longstanding, paralleling the rise of modern social science. It had already begun to set in during the first decades of the twentieth century, when the mainline Protestant churches and colleges and the social science departments of universities, he believes, adopted attitudes of "moral relativism." Echoing agrarian traditionalists like Richard Weaver and Russell Kirk, Carlson denounces the consequences of this relativism, which has fostered a critical attitude toward religious faith, norms of the community, and fixed religious principles.[5]

Rockford seeks a kind of moral restoration—a renewal of preindustrial, small-community ideals. At the core of Rockford's enterprise is the conviction that politics is rooted in cultural values. Accordingly, its concerns have been principally with the well-being of those primary value-shaping institutions—the church, the school, and the family. In its concern with family and religion, Rockford's tone is often closer to the populist social activists of the New Right—the opponents of abortion, the Equal Rights Amendment, the women's movement, homosexuality, and sex education—than to neoconservative analysts of social welfare programs. Indeed, its traditionalist stance and its eager embrace of the social issues that policy centers like Heritage and AEI have generally avoided sets it apart from—and sometimes at odds with—these Washington institutions. It has particularly opposed the assumption of the conservative movement's libertarian and free-market wing, whose *homo economicus* is the elemental unit of society and whose laissez-faire policies are corrosive of tradition.

Although Rockford's immediate impact on policies has been negligible to date, it did find a few sympathetic allies in the Reagan administration—most notably Gary Bauer, an adviser on domestic policy who produced an administration report on the family—when it criticized social security for weakening intergenerational family ties; welfare, for encouraging promiscuity and single-parent families; and tax policies that favored two-income households. Rockford proposed such reforms as raising the tax exemption for dependents and ending tax credits for child care that subsidize working mothers, rather than mothers who stay at home. It was but one of the participants in an emerging conservative coalition on family policy, which includes Paul Weyrich's Free Congress Foundation, with its *Family Protection Report*, and John Whitehead's Rutherford Institute. These groups were determined to fashion a policy agenda to restore the traditional family.

Other centers operating on the periphery of the ideas industry have also managed to turn the raw matter of conviction into finished policy products. Libertarians have been among the most energetic promoters of policy ideas since the late 1970s. Privatization has been their watchword, and others closer to the mainstream have echoed it. But the most ardent libertarians have attacked both the excesses of liberalism and the underlying assumptions of pragmatic social science. They prefer private markets not only as a means of reducing government but because they harbor fundamental doubts about the reliability of human intelligence as a tool for planning and acting in the pursuit of public ends. Beneath their imaginative and specific proposals often lies a relentless hostility to government, politics, and the organized pursuit of public purposes.

When Edward Crane, a former financial analyst and portfolio manager for Scudder, Stevens and the Alliance Capital Management companies, now president of the Cato Institute, came to Washington from California, he claims to have been stunned by a vision of thousands of federal bureaucrats in their granite office buildings actively pursuing "counterproductive" work. "Bureaucracy is a bad thing," Crane baldly states. "Government, whatever it does, is doing it because people won't do it voluntarily."[6] For Crane, devoted to the libertarian cause since his student days at the University of California at Berkeley in the mid-1960s, libertarianism is merely a return to the true principles of the American founders. Exalting Thomas Jefferson over Alexander Hamilton, Crane contends that the Virginian's wisdom lay in seeing that liberty was threatened by the natural tendency of governments to grow. Cato's elegant townhouse near the Capitol has some of the orderliness of an eighteenth-century interior, and fittingly the institute's namesake is not the Roman censor who inveighed against luxury, but a pseudonymous pair of British writers, John Trenchard and Thomas Gordon, who early in the eighteenth century issued a series of pamphlets called *Cato's Letters*, denouncing colonialism and big government.

The policy papers that issue from the libertarian think tanks go well beyond the cost-benefit analyses of the RAND Corporation or the Urban Institute, which measure programs to amend them but rarely express radical doubts about the ability of the government ever to accomplish anything; they also go beyond the Brookings Institution economists' arguments that market tests can help make government more efficient and calibrate an ever-shifting balance between the responsibilities of the public and private sectors. The libertarian's rejection of government not only elevates individual liberty and private property rights above other political values; at its core, it signals a rejection of human abilities to know or plan. It thus offers a radical critique of social science, especially the impulse to transfer the methods and aims of the physical sciences to the study of social problems.[7]

The libertarian argument is that the market not only bolsters liberty but is the best mechanism for organizing and communicating knowledge. "Markets," explains British economist Ralph Harris of the Institute of Economic Affairs, "are like a whole series of linked computers into which are fed daily information and estimates about the changing ingredients of supply and demand, and out of which pour a ceaseless feedback of signals mostly in the form of changing relative prices that guide producers and consumers in adapting to change."[8] The libertarian case against governments is that they try to act even though their knowledge is uncertain and that when they act, they distort and obstruct the market mechanisms that can remedy both economic inefficiency and intellectual uncertainty.

With seed money from the Fred C. Koch Trust (money from the Koch family's chemical company fortune still provides much of the support for the institute), Cato was founded in San Francisco in 1977. But not until it severed its close ties to California's Libertarian party and moved to Washington in 1981 did it begin to exert a significant intellectual influence on the national policy debate. Relying on only a small resident staff and a network of roughly fifty adjunct scholars, it has produced books, short policy analyses, and a journal and made good use of radio broadcasts. On the domestic side, Cato has supported proposals for replacing social security with an enlarged system of individual retirement accounts, privatizing the federal deposit and the savings and loan insurance programs, and has championed what it calls "free market environmentalism." Breaking with neoconservatives and traditionalists on foreign policy, its scholars have argued for a phased withdrawal from the North Atlantic Treaty Organization and for the European countries, Korea, and Japan to shoulder more of their own defense burden. And setting itself apart from the traditionalists on domestic social concerns, it has taken a tolerant stance on such issues as the decriminalization of drug use.

With its blend of fiscal conservatism, social tolerance, and a principled selfishness grounded in writers from Adam Smith to Ayn Rand, Cato has staked out a terrain that, in Crane's words, make it "the think tank for yuppies." It cannot be easily pinned to a fixed position on the conventional political spectrum. Indeed, Cato authors have suggested that American political ideas can best be viewed in terms of quadrants (conservative, liberal, populist, and libertarian), rather than in terms of a single right-left axis, and that the baby-boom generation may be more drawn to the libertarian quadrant than to any other.[9]

The libertarians have certainly been among the most energetic think tank entrepreneurs and the most skillful in employing intellectual marketing techniques. Cato was part of the first wave of libertarian research operations in the late 1970s (a group that included the International Center for Economic Policy Studies, since renamed the Manhattan Institute for Policy Research, and a cluster of West Coast organizations, such as the Pacific Institute and the Reason Foundation). But many more were spawned in the 1980s. These small outfits, generally relying on university-based economists of strong libertarian or "public choice" convictions to produce reports and papers on contract, have developed proposal after proposal for turning governmental functions—federal, state, and local—back to the private sector.

Los Angeles's Reason Foundation, which originally published *Reason* magazine from a small office in Santa Barbara before embarking on a larger research program, has undertaken studies that advocate privatizing the postal service, the Tennessee Valley Authority, air traffic control, and municipal firefighting.[10] In a similar vein, San Francisco's Pacific Institute has argued for market-based approaches

to the control of the quality of air and water, the management of
natural resources, and energy policy. Its classical liberal ideas have
also shaped its views on gun control, which it declares is ineffective
in reducing crime, and on the public school "monopoly," which it
calls detrimental to education.[11] There is a predictability to these
organizations' proposals, but also a real sophistication in the reliance
on economic reasoning and evidence. To these policy activists, the
government at all levels seems hopelessly inept, if not dangerous.

The libertarian think tanks have supplied a radical critique not
only of federal policies and programs, but of state and local government
activities as well. And as responsibilities for policies devolved on
the states in the 1980s, a second wave of research centers, devoted
primarily to the policies of states, was created, giving rise to a kind
of trade association of libertarian and conservative think tanks, called
the Madison Group. The new entrants in this arena include Illinois's
Heartland Institute (which has plans to establish branches in other
states), Maine's Hannibal Hamlin Institute, Pennsylvania's Commonwealth Foundation, California's Claremont Institute, and Colorado's
Independence Institute. Meanwhile, such groups as the Dallas-based
National Center for Policy Analysis, the Manhattan Institute for Policy
Research, and Florida's James Madison Institute, although they work
on local issues—rent control or crowded prisons, for example—see
as their goal the creation of policy models that are applicable
elsewhere.[12] At the state and local levels, roughly sixty research
groups, mostly with libertarian and free-market inclinations, are carrying on their battle to reduce the cost and size of government—any
government.

The libertarians' proposals, like those of the traditionalists, challenge much of the policy framework that has evolved over the past
century—from the first efforts to regulate the economy in the 1880s,
through social security and other initiatives of the New Deal, to
the social and environmental policies of the 1960s and 1970s. And
if some of these institutions' routine monthly or quarterly assessments
of press coverage are any indication, the specific critiques of policies
and programs have gotten a decent hearing in the media and thus
have widened the parameters of "respectable" opinion. Nonetheless,
both libertarians and traditionalists maintain that the way Americans
talk about policy is fundamentally flawed, if not illegitimate, and
that those who routinely hold forth on policy are deficient in what
they know. For the traditionalist, it is religious values that are too
often neglected; for libertarians, it is politics and organized interests

that too often intrude. And both will always be at odds with a policy-making process that is shaped by compromise and incremental change.

The cacophony of experts and ideologues—and a predictable perplexity about the often-obscure institutions that have magnified their voices—make it difficult for most citizens to gauge their competing claims to expertise, to identify the interests or intellectual affiliations that shape their perspectives, and to weigh their contributions to public discourse. The attentive citizen, by and large a passive witness to the disputes of the experts (as mediated by the newspaper editors who select their op-ed pieces and the journalists who interview them) now needs an expert's help to sort out the competing claims to authority.

The New Policy Elite

Some observers have lamented the disappearance of the broad-gauged public intellectual—a Lewis Mumford or a Walter Lippmann—whose vision of public affairs was synthesizing and whose predilections were familiar (and discountable). Lippmann, the quint-essential tough-minded philosopher (to borrow from William James) was an especially rare type of modern American intellectual. He combined an independent, philosophical cast of mind and probing moral sensibility with an interest in practical affairs and an empathy with the constraints under which political leaders act. He was an adviser to advisers and a counselor to presidents, from the days of Colonel E. H. House and Woodrow Wilson to those of McGeorge Bundy and Lyndon Johnson. Yet his was also a far-reaching public voice, clarifying the issues of the day for attentive citizens. As editor and columnist, his writing and public reputation suggested Olympian detachment and demonstrated a capacity to retreat into what he called his "pool of silence." He was acutely sensitive to the intellectual problems posed both by too keen an involvement in public affairs and by too passive a withdrawal. "His ivory tower was equipped with a swift-moving elevator," observed biographer Ronald Steel.[13]

By and large, the autonomous intellectual, surviving on an income from writing or on private financial means and speaking to a wide public, has given way to the academic specialist and the affiliated expert who work primarily in various governmental agencies, universities, and research centers or consult with private clients. Although public intellectuals may be in short supply, there is no dearth of public experts who are ready and willing to comment on specific issues. This new breed of policy expert represents the culmination of a hundred-year effort to bring specialized knowledge to bear on public policy. They have diversified considerably in response to the variable market for expertise. Accordingly, the policy elite today may be divided into several roughly drawn types who are distinguished by the institutions in which they work, the career paths they have followed, and the nature of the mark they seek to make on public policy. While not a rigid typology with firm boundaries—individuals typically range across several categories—the types depict the experts' various roles and the institutional settings in which they now circulate.

Foremost are the experts who have held prominent public positions in the cabinet or high-level posts as national security advisers or members of the Council of Economic Advisers. Perhaps best characterized as "scholar-statesmen," a term currently in vogue at the Center for Strategic and International Studies, they are the most famous individual members of the policy elite, accorded special deference for having weathered the practical trials of policy responsibility and for their academic expertise. Theirs is not merely the modern authority of specialized knowledge, but the ancient mystique of the counselor to kings.

A second group, whose status is based less on highly visible governmental service than on long-standing research commitments within a given area of policy, may be called "policy specialists." Scholars in this category have typically devoted more time to policy research and perhaps to teaching than to policymaking or full-time advising. Their work may have the greatest long-term impact, whether through theoretical insights that are incorporated into policy or the training of students who go on to serve in government. They can be found in university-based research centers, well-established policy institutions, and governmental research agencies.[14]

A third and typically less visible, albeit no less serious type (distinguishable more by their institutional settings than by academic training or methods), are the "policy consultants." Working usually on short-term contracts and on problems defined by a client, the consultants generate data, evaluate programs, and monitor social experiments. The majority of policy analysts at the RAND Corporation, Urban Institute, or SRI International and their colleagues in other contract-research organizations fall into this category. Their ties to the government are shaped by the specifics of their contracts, and their primary audience is the client, not the academic community or the wider public. Some consultants now also serve the business community as corporate executives increasingly seek informed assessments of international events or changes in domestic policy that may affect the private sector. Indeed, opportunities for private consulting—especially on international political and economic matters—have greatly expanded, giving rise to private, profit-making firms (Kissinger Associates is the best known) and creating opportunities for nonprofit research institutions to serve a business clientele. Both the "scholarstatesman" and the "policy specialist" sometimes play the role of policy consultant.

A fourth category that has steadily increased in number over the years is the "government expert." Government experts are not those who are appointed to high-level advisory positions but, rather, members of the bureaucracy whose academic training and expertise are made available through such operations as the Congressional Budget Office, committee staffs, Congressional Research Service, analytic units in cabinet departments, and independent agencies.

A newer type of expert that emerged in the 1970s and 1980s, sometimes disparaged as "instant experts," "media professors," or "quote doctors," may be more fairly characterized as "policy interpreters." As American journalism has moved from narrowly conceived political reporting to broader social, political, and economic analysis, it has not only sought more specialized and better educated reporters, but has come to rely more heavily on experts. Now conjoined in a symbiotic relationship with journalists and editors, this class of public experts has found opportunities on the op-ed pages of newspapers, as well as on broadcast news programs and interview shows that have burgeoned on television, including the Public Broadcasting Service, Cable News Network, and C-SPAN. Print and broadcast journalists depend on these experts to add depth to daily news coverage and the appearance of diversity and judicious balance. Indeed, the search for controversy has itself widened the parameters of debate and brought experts into the limelight whose chief claim to authority is their visibility—their availability to comment on a breaking news story or draft an op-ed essay at a moment's notice. The adjunct contributions of this type of expert to journalistic coverage have been valuable on the whole, but all too often, their claims to intellectual authority have gone unscrutinized by the journalists who rely on them.[15]

The final group within the new policy elite is best described as "policy entrepreneurs." Although they must play the role of interpreter of public policy at times and some have legitimate claims as policy specialists, they are primarily engaged in building institutions. They mobilize resources to push a particular proposal, create coalitions among diverse groups of researchers and activists, foster the careers of able and committed aspirants to membership in the policy elite, and initiate new journals or other publishing enterprises. Among them are the managers and founders of research institutions, the executives of foundations, and the publishers of policy journals.

These types are crudely drawn—and highly permeable. But they suggest the different roles that experts play in the modern policymaking process. As scholar-statesmen, they can speak with an authority that former elected officials rarely command (some ex-presidents excepted). As specialists in various fields, they formulate the broad concepts through which social problems are defined and investigated and train other specialists who may have an even more direct impact. As consultants, they monitor the programs and policies already in place and increasingly find opportunities to advise the private sector. As government experts, they collect the raw data that allows a modern bureaucracy to function and provide the day-to-day analysis needed by governmental officials. As interpreters, they speak to both policymakers and the public and set the contours for policy debate, sometimes momentarily widening its parameters, and sometimes narrowing it to practical choices. And as entrepreneurs, they direct financial resources and intellectual personnel into specific policy areas, work to broaden the policy agenda, and create new mechanisms for bringing the expert into play.

Over the long term, experts in their various roles have first defined and then reshaped the institutional structures by which their knowledge is brought to bear on policy. The enterprise of experts has grown like a coral reef built by countless busy organisms. Not only does it create its own ecological environment, harboring various delicate flora and fauna, it often changes the passages between sea and shore. Like a fantastic underwater growth, these institutions have created bridges between the public and private sectors and have filled in almost every open space in our fragmented governmental system. This growth has fed upon itself: Private research groups have prodded the government into adding specialists to executive departments, the expertise of the executive branch has compelled Congress to set up its own research units, governmental agencies have used contractual research arrangements to foster nongovernmental research centers, and universities have set up new research and training programs to respond to the shifting need for public specialists.

New venues and arrangements for the expert are continuously opening. In Eastern and Central Europe, for example, individual American economists have recently been brought in to advise on banking and financial systems, the decontrol of prices, and the transition from state-directed industries to private enterprise. Political scientists and constitutional lawyers have consulted on election laws, political parties, legal systems, and guarantees of individual rights. Further links are being forged as well. There is an all-too-obvious irony in these new advisory relationships, as experts from a nation with its own profound electoral flaws and costly breakdowns in its banking and financial system seek to lead the way for other nations. It remains an open question how Western expertise will fare in these political contexts. But the initial reliance on foreign experts can at least serve to draw attention to the staunch relationship between modern social science and the democratic culture in which it has been shaped.

Every political culture creates its own breed of expert: Daniel interpreted dreams for Nebuchadnezzar, Chinese diviners read the cracks in heated tortoise shells, and Roman augurs found meaning in the entrails of chickens or in the flights of eagles. The policy expert—whose Latin name, *expertus*, connotes a knowledge arising from practice or experience—is fundamentally a product of a given society's political practices and experience. As some nations now struggle to institute unfamiliar democratic processes and to reinvent the market system, it is not surprising that they should seek a different kind of expertise, new methods of organizing it, and (in the long term) new ways of educating an expert class. At a moment of transition, they are looking abroad for what they need and seeking to fashion indigenous institutions out of existing university and governmental research entities.

Thus, while Western economic and political experts consult in Eastern and Central Europe, it is often those countries' native writers, philosophers, and historians who play the leading role in the unfolding transformation of their societies. It is indeed an odd spectacle for Westerners who are accustomed to a public debate dominated by the argot of economists, rather than the metaphors of playwrights. But without seeking to denigrate these intellectuals' principled stands and exemplary endurance in the face of protracted repression, one must point out that their role in the emerging democratic experiments is due largely to a significant lack of experts who are better versed in the workings of market economies and democratic pluralism. While even the most tyrannical regime will have its few courageous dissidents, such systems can hardly tolerate an independent expertise in social science or produce a body of experts or organizations whose purpose is to scrutinize the operations of the government and the economy. This is not to say that the contributions of literary and cultural figures—gifted and dedicated amateurs—may not be more valuable in some ways or more necessary than those of social scientists, especially at moments of sweeping transformation of a system. But if these nations are to succeed, they will need to produce their own breed of experts—and suitable advisory institutions—as their democracies gradually evolve.

The uneasy position of experts in a nondemocratic society may be illustrated by the case of China, where economic liberalization briefly spawned a number of research institutes in which a generation of bright young economists examined the reform of prices, bankruptcy, stock markets, and private ownership. These institutions, allied with the reform-minded party leadership throughout the 1980s and participants in the short-lived "Democracy Movement" in spring 1989, were rapidly shut down in the repression that followed. Their staff researchers fled or were arrested, presumably to be remanded to the collective farms and reeducation camps that earlier had swallowed a whole generation of Chinese intellectuals during the Cultural Revolution. The old-line Party leaders have since set up their own dependent research apparatus, turning not to economists but to specialists in propaganda and doctrine. These Chinese officials, understandably, are not eager for basic economic research and the changes that may flow from it, but prefer to promote the manufacture of reassuring doctrinal treatises.[16]

A glimpse of the condition of the expert in societies that are struggling toward (or against) democracy reminds us of how deeply rooted both the social sciences and their ancillary research institutions are in our political culture. Nevertheless, the structure and organization of the expert classes can and does differ from one democratic society to another. Historically, other nations have not relied nearly as heavily on private research institutions as has the United States, a consequence, by and large, of both our more robust private philanthropic sector and wholesale skepticism of state bureaucracy. In Western Europe, on the other hand, governmental and party-affiliated research institutions are more common and reflect more ideologically partisan traditions and a greater willingness among European intellectuals to avow a party tie. Moreover, in countries with older civil service traditions and fewer political appointments, experts could be found in the bureaucracy—or in government-funded research enterprises—much earlier than they could in the American system, where nonpartisan experts typically had to be housed on the outside.

But just as American think tanks proliferated in the 1970s and 1980s, there are signs of a corresponding boom in other countries. Free market think tanks contributed to the resurgence of the Right in England, and similar ideological groups are at work on the Continent and in the Pacific basin. Business research groups modeled on the Committee for Economic Development can be found in a number of countries. Democratic-movement organizations in Latin America have founded think tanks, sometimes with the encouragement of American philanthropists or the quasi-governmental National Endowment for Democracy. In Japan, a craze for think tanks began in the 1970s, giving rise to scores of groups; many of them were spun off from research and planning units within business firms, while others were modeled on American consulting companies. In some instances, policy entrepreneurs—often American-trained graduate students from other countries—have returned home with schemes for emulating models of think tanks they had observed in the United States.

On the whole, the role and impact of think tanks in these countries are impossible to gauge from a distance. But although it is clear that experts have become vastly more important to both the operations of government and the conduct of politics, their direct influence on policy should not be overstated. That influence, though real enough, is more often diffuse than direct; it is mediated by the political process, and often the contributions of experts have less to do with policy than with administration, evaluation, and improving the data and analysis on which governments depend.

Over the years, experts have invented and refined the many tools that are necessary for running a modern political bureaucracy and monitoring a complex economy—methods of budgeting and the administration of personnel, statistical indicators of economic performance, and techniques of evaluating policies and programs. Without such techniques, there would be no social security or other large-scale governmental programs and no statistical basis for informed debate about fiscal policy or trade. Members of the policy elite and theoretically inclined social scientists have provided the insights (and continuing refinements) that undergird approaches to policy problems—theories of the business cycle, Keynesian approaches to fiscal policy, monetary theory, "public choice" theory, microeconomic methods, and theories of human capital. From time to time, they have also supplied overarching policy concepts, such as "mutually assured destruction," "first-strike capability," or "supply-side economics."

But the expert rarely contributes the flash of insight that quickly and fundamentally transforms national policy or inspires an innovative law. Instead, experts work slowly, gradually building up intellectual capital in a process one scholar characterized as "knowledge creep," an almost sedimentary increment of knowledge.[17] The serious contributions of the expert are deliberate and more likely to result in minor changes than in radical departures. On occasion, the experts' tendency toward caution frustrates political leaders, even those with legitimate claims to expertise.

Henry A. Kissinger, for one, changed his view of the role of the expert as he gained experience in the government. By the end of his governmental career, he had come to view the outside expert as largely irrelevant and the inside expert as a major hindrance to innovative policies. "Occasionally an outsider may provide perspective, almost never does he have enough knowledge to advise soundly on tactical moves," he wrote, reflecting on his early experiences as a Harvard professor and part-time adviser in Washington. "Before I served as a consultant to Kennedy, I had believed, like most academicians, that the process of decision-making was largely intellectual and that all one had to do was to walk into the President's office and convince him of the correctness of one's views. This perspective I soon realized is as dangerously immature as it is widely held."[18] Arguments that are grounded in substantive expertise are but one aspect of persuasion in the overall decision-making process and are rarely as important as political and prudential calculations.

Moreover, Kissinger, like Nixon, often appeared to distrust the advice of governmental experts, not because they were biased but because they were so often an obstacle to bold and innovative policies. Indeed, he contended that the best policy decisions are frequently made *against* the advice of experts. "Most foreign policies that history has marked highly, in whatever country, have been originated by leaders who were opposed by experts. It is, after all, the responsibility of the expert to operate the familiar and that of the leader to transcend it."[19]

Kissinger's career, like Woodrow Wilson's, is an archetypal journey for the twentieth-century expert: an ascent by raw intellectual power into the higher circles of political leadership, not merely to advise others from behind the scenes but to assume an active role, indeed a glamorous one. At the center of events, Kissinger radiated intellectual authority with a gravelly low voice, world-weary mien, and sober calm. The mystique of the modern expert lay in just this ability to project intellectual detachment while remaining immersed in the flow of political events. And just as the ancient expert communed with supernatural voices in the sacred groves, the modern expert on foreign policy was in command of information networks that brought news of the latest breaking international developments.

Yet Kissinger, like Wilson, was suspicious of the expert as a type, although he seemed to find them more to be lamented than feared. Wilson worried early in the century that experts would usurp democratic institutions, dispiriting the citizen; Kissinger seemed to find experts basically marginal, and while he hinted at tensions between the expert and the leader, he also pointed to a marked diminution of the experts' contributions once they were securely installed in government. As part of the institutional landscape, experts were no longer a source of creative ideas; instead, they merely managed the familiar, unable to transcend bureaucratic routines or to challenge well-established patterns of policymaking. Kissinger, in fact, reinforced a common complaint that expert thinking constrains innovation by merely elaborating and refining the prevailing policy frameworks.

Sometimes, however, the opposite complaint is made about the policy elite. The experts seem unable to agree, and debate becomes inconclusive. Thus, no consensus on policies can be reached. In the ideologically charged environment of the 1980s, that old complaint seems ever closer to the mark. It has become barely possible to draw the line between the politically disinterested scholar—more accurately, the scholar wrestling honestly with the biases and preconceptions that inevitably cloud any research effort—and the intellectual advocate who earnestly marshals evidence to bolster an unshakeable political position. All research begins to look like advocacy, all experts begin to look like hired guns, and all think tanks seem to use their institutional resources to advance a point of view. The experts, far from limiting debate and innovation, have created an environment in which so many arguments contend that no consensus is possible. Their never-ending controversies leave even closely attentive citizens in despair of ever coming to agreement on the most important issues.

In retrospect, it is peculiarly ironic that, at its inception, the enterprise of experts should have held out the hope of placing political debate on a scientific footing to reduce controversy and shape the terrain for understanding and agreement. Yet the ascent of the expert, at least in recent years, has had the opposite effect. As expert institutions have become part of the fabric of modern political culture, they have neither fostered public agreement nor erased our innate ambivalence about the uses of expertise in a democracy.

Expert Prospects

In 1989 the literal and figurative walls between East and West came crashing down—and with them fell the scaffolding of postwar American foreign policy. Communist parties renounced their primacy, were hounded out of power, or simply melted away. New political parties quickly coalesced, giving voice to urges long repressed within the Eastern bloc. A wave of free elections catapulted many former dissidents into the political offices formerly held by their captors. Totalitarian leaders were unseated, their crimes exposed, and in some cases brutally punished. Nationalist and ethnic sentiments were set loose, threatening the very fabric of the Soviet Union and rekindling atavistic feuds. Troop reductions reshaped the military equations in Central Europe, and the futures of both NATO and the Warsaw Pact were thrown into question. The relaxing Soviet grip on East Germany unleashed a galvanic popular movement that frightened Europe with the sudden and inevitable prospect of a unified German state. Meanwhile, the possibilities for at least a modest "peace dividend," if not a wholesale restructuring of the postwar military-industrial complex, promised to spark new debates on domestic social spending in the United States and began to recast the deadlocked politics surrounding the federal deficit.

Through it all, American editorial writers clamored about the loss of policy initiatives as events unfolded elsewhere. Some blamed George Bush, faulting his lack-luster powers of speech and inability to articulate a "vision" of America's role in the new world order. At those historic moments that called most poignantly for meaningful words—the slaughter of students in Tiananmen Square, the citizens of Berlin dancing on the wall of a newly undivided city—there was no one to articulate the sentiments of bleak despair or rising hope that so many Americans felt. Caution was the watchword of the Bush administration. Yet however emotionally unsatisfying it may have been in the face of these stirring events, the caution proved not altogether unwise. And the measured responses, when they came, were evidence that the processes of expert deliberation were at work within the executive branch of the modern presidency.

The president and his advisers did not take all the blame for what seemed the American failure to measure up to the demands of the moment. Russell Baker—bringing into focus, as the humorist so often does, the temper of the ordinary citizen—decried the "fundamental failure of the historical imagination," while going out of his way to fault precisely "our most brilliant people, those members of the secular priesthood called 'strategic thinkers.'"[20] Baker spoke for many when he mocked the policy elite for its dismal failure to predict what, in the light of subsequent events, now seems to have been inevitable.

For their part, members of the policy community readily admitted that they were scrambling to keep up. At one prominent think tank, some projects were classified as OBG—"overtaken by Gorbachev." Other research centers conceded that they simply did not have the intellectual personnel to study the changes in Eastern Europe, reminding us how long it takes to develop cadres of experts in any substantive field. Like Ptolemaic astronomers who were unable to break from the established paradigm and embrace the Copernican model, experts had built careers on their understanding of the old order and had conducted their work within a long-established framework of assumptions. Some wondered aloud how analysts of the Cold War, who had focused on the technical aspects of East-West military conflict, would fare in a new policy environment. "Can analysts trained in one era cope with another? Do they have the suppleness of mind?" asked the obviously dubious head of one university research center.[21]

Clearly, the experts had missed something in 1989—a year that promised to reverberate in history as the revolutionary years 1789 and 1848 still do. In that year, the experts were tried and found lacking. They had not foreseen the looming changes in Europe and seemed momentarily incapable of understanding the dynamics of social processes that were unfolding at top speed in every corner of the globe. In the new world that seemed to have emerged so abruptly, they had no intellectual bearings by which to reorient national policy. Meanwhile television viewers were treated to the sight (and sound) of a new set of experts pulled from their offices in the East European studies programs of various universities and thrust squinting and blinking into the glare of television studios, where they labored to supply the needed perspective in quotable sentences. Nothing better testified to the sudden and abhorrent vacuum that new experts had to fill.

The power to predict has always been the underlying source of the expert's mystique, whether the powers were Delphic oracular pronouncements or computer-based mathematical models of the future performance of a country's economy. Indeed, it is the presumed power to predict (and the mystery attending it) that has also endowed experts with the authority to prescribe. But when experts can neither foresee nor explain, as seemed the case in 1989, the shroud of their mystique is ripped away. Events unmasked the expert, as when the screen tumbles over to reveal the dreaded Wizard as a bald little wrinkle-faced man, a ventriloquist and circus performer, masquerading as Oz, the Great and Terrible. "I am a humbug," the Wizard readily confesses. But he later adds, excusing his pretensions, "How can I help being a humbug when all these people make me do things that everybody knows can't be done?"[22]

The expectations placed upon the modern expert are as high as those borne by Baum's Wizard. While modern expertise is not humbug, the experts themselves have often fostered an unrealistic sense of what they know. Consequently, as events unfolded in 1989, the experts on foreign policy had rarely been perceived as quite so feckless and impotent (enduring a crisis as difficult as economists had faced when they were baffled by "stagflation" in the 1970s). Like the Wizard exposed, however, they were still being asked to do impossible things. Experts remain so deeply embedded in the structures of policymaking in the late twentieth century that thoughtful people continue to turn to them for clarifying insights into global events.

In summer 1989, *The National Interest*, a quarterly journal of foreign affairs, published by Irving Kristol, whose advisory board includes such notables as Henry A. Kissinger, Jeane J. Kirkpatrick, Charles Krauthammer, and Midge Decter, featured an article by Francis Fukuyama, deputy director of the State Department's Policy Planning Staff. Fukuyama, a Harvard-trained specialist in Soviet affairs and a former policy analyst at the RAND Corporation, was relatively new to the State Department. And as a disciple of Allan Bloom, the Straussian political theorist, he was not altogether typical of postwar policy experts with narrowly honed technical specializations, although it has not been unusual to find Straussian-trained political theorists serving in foreign policy posts in the conservative administrations of the past decade.

Fukuyama's article proclaimed, albeit with a circumspect question mark, "The End of History?"[23] The article (written before the Beijing Spring of 1989) was a sweeping survey of the contemporary world and a briskly argued essay on the Hegelian philosophy of history.

The Politics of Ideas 235

Fukuyama, following Hegel, saw the past not as a sequence of political events, wars, or revolutions, but as the unfolding of human ideals, consciousness, and culture. It was a reassuring notion at a time when the rush of events seemed unassimilable. He suggested that history operated in the *long run* (Fukuyama himself underscored the phrase) on the plane of human consciousness. He appropriated Hegel, not because he necessarily agreed that Hegel was right about history's end—Hegel had declared history over as long ago as 1806—but because the German idealist provided him with a useful framework for exploring the weaknesses of materialistic explanations of historical change. For Fukuyama, the end of history meant the end of large-scale ideological conflict, the final resolution of the dialectical clash of ideas. With the apparent victory of liberal democratic ideals, all that would seem to follow was a mere working out of details.

Fukuyama's article found an attentive conservative audience, which reveled both in its celebration of democracy's inevitable triumph and its brisk philosophical argument. For conservatives, convinced that ideas have consequences, the article was a kind of coda to the Reagan years. And although it was decidedly not a policy brief, the attention it received was proof of the strong general appetite for a fresh philosophical outlook or a set of axioms from which specific policies might somehow be deduced. (Oddly enough, from this perspective, the Bush administration's policy of caution and passivity was arguably the most appropriate stance for an administration facing the end of history.)

The hunger for perspective and authoritative guidance also propelled the strong reaction to an article in *Daedalus*, an academic quarterly published by the American Academy of Arts and Sciences. The fact that the article was attributed to an anonymous author who signed himself "Z" only heightened the attention it received. The pseudonym self-consciously echoed George Kennan's famous 1947 article in *Foreign Affairs*, attributed to "X," which set forth a rationale for the postwar doctrine of containment, the very doctrine that events had apparently superseded.[24] Many more people seemed to be preoccupied with guessing about the article's authorship than with assessing its analysis and recommendations. But "Z" provided a tough and well-informed assessment of the Soviet Union's "terminal crisis" and the internal contradictions of Gorbachev's reforms, as well as a blueprint of a policy with specific recommendations on arms reduction and economic investments. It also counseled an ongoing sensitivity to Soviet national pride and a muting of Western triumphalism.

Viewed together, these two articles provide a convenient reminder of the philosophical fault lines that traditionally split the American policy elite into "idealists" and "pragmatists," but that have grown even sharper in the 1980s. Fukuyama and his allies see history as the dialectical clash and ultimate synthesis of ideological conflicts, with policies apparently deducible from a detached contemplation of the movement of ideas. In contrast, "Z" asks concretely whether and how the United States should help Mikhail Gorbachev.

At issue here are questions that go to the heart of what the expert class has become and how it may better serve us. What kind of knowledge will enable us to make intelligent policy choices? Is it knowledge that begins explicitly with ideals and values? Or is it knowledge of the particular, of the concrete facts and discrete circumstances in which policy choices must be made? Our large and highly specialized research enterprise seems, over the years, to have reinforced distinctions between these ways of comprehending the world, separating the "pragmatic" expert from the "principled" one and indeed fostering different and competing kinds of institutions within the universe of policy research and advocacy organizations.

At the turn of the century, pragmatic philosophers had wrestled with such epistemological questions, seeking a method of treating values as something other than abstract rules—"drugstore prescriptions" and "cookbook recipes" in John Dewey's words. The pragmatists' notion that ideas are plans of action meant that values and beliefs were really ways of interacting with the world, not timeless unattainable abstractions high above it. Truth and values amounted to something in practice; moral ends did not require unthinking obedience to lofty ideal precepts but, rather, specific methods of inquiry. The pragmatists' persistent concern for ways of linking the realm of ideas with that of action offered an approach to understanding society and politics that denigrated neither side of the equation.

But since the turn of the century, social scientists have too seldom confronted such epistemological questions and have rarely asked what is distinctive about efforts to acquire and use knowledge in a democratic society. They have too hastily and uncritically embraced metaphors from the natural sciences, and while they have propelled research in sometimes useful directions, those borrowed metaphors held out excessive hopes that social scientists could be society's doctors, industrial engineers, and experimentalists or that they could posit theories with the predictive certainty of the mathematician and physicist (one can, even now, discern the emergence of a new predictive metaphor borrowed from computer scientists who are interested in chaos theory). Inevitably, however, the social scientists *as* scientists have caused disappointment when their insights proved modest and when particular ills were not cured, systems were clumsily engineered, and events were not foreseen. Moreover, the borrowed metaphors have tended to reinforce the artificial distinction between fact and value that too often rendered the policy expert a technician of means, uncomfortable with broader questions about political ends. Indeed, by shoving values and ultimate ends to the periphery of the debate, applied social science has often held out the impossible promise of escaping from politics.

The potent modern metaphors of marketing and intellectual combat, now so much in vogue within the research enterprise (as elsewhere in society), arose out of disappointments with scientific claims of social research. Yet despite their popularity among researchers themselves, they are far more damaging to a proper understanding of the process of policymaking—and the role of experts in it—than are even the most grandiose scientific metaphors. These influential images suggest that the enterprise of experts largely involves creating and peddling innovative policy measures to citizen consumers or battling for ideas in a hostile arena in which the winner takes all. They seek persuasion of the most superficial sort, not understanding or reflection. Furthermore, the current emphasis on marketing techniques and relentless intellectual combat has little to do with either sustained research (and the steady, cumulative nature of the knowledge enterprise) or the deliberative and educational processes that best serve a democratic society and that require a structured dialogue among experts, leaders, and citizens.

Contemporary political discourse—the root of the word suggests a movement back and forth—has failed us for many (and by now familiar) reasons. Our political theater is shaped by puerile but effective campaign advertising, posturing candidates who recite well-rehearsed lines even when allegedly debating, and journalists who act less as critics than as a complicit Greek chorus in the unfolding electoral drama, wringing their hands and sending up futile prayers to the deaf gods of science and democracy. But while our political leadership and members of the press bear much of the blame for the poverty of the public debate, the policy elite must bear some of it as well, since, over the long term, their increasing specialization has helped to fragment public discourse and make it arcane and intimidating. With few exceptions, policy research institutions have thought little about broad civic education and more about advising those in the government or gaining attention from the mass media (which is not to be confused with education). Indeed, the experts who are drawn into the Washington community and whose careers are largely shaped by opportunities in it, have too often limited themselves to serving a narrow stratum of political leaders and the policy cognoscenti.

Woodrow Wilson feared the notion of a "government of experts." The powerful allure—especially strong in a democracy, with its ingrained respect for science—of a rational, efficient decision-making process would always outweigh the attractions of the messy and passionate conflict of interests envisioned by the founders of the American government. But democracy depended, in his vision, on the dedicated amateur who understood the concrete applications of a policy initiative and who could speak the common language of the ordinary citizen. "What are we for," he asked, "if we are to be scientifically taken care of by a small number of gentlemen who are the only men who understand the job?" Contemplating our present vast and complex knowledge sector, one finds it hard to resist the conclusion that much of what Wilson feared has come to pass. The expert class has interposed itself between the average citizen and the deliberations of government, often confusing and overcomplicating straightforward issues with its arcane vocabularies and giving politicians a way to duck their obligations by leaving politically difficult problems to expert commissions and study groups. It is sometimes hard to fix responsibility in such a system, and in the broader context of American political culture it is hard for the citizen to assess the often sharp disputes within the expert class. The conclusion we have drawn, as a society, appears to be that the most serious questions cannot even be posed, let alone answered, in the language of common sense.

But the underlying problem—that of linking knowledge and power in an open society—does not present itself in the convenient form of a procedural flaw to be corrected, a structural defect to be repaired, or a disease to be prescribed for and cured. It would be presumptuous and even misguided for the analyst of expert institutions to dictate changes in the complex web of think tanks, graduate programs in social science, philanthropic foundations, civic organizations, governmental research agencies, and political advisory arrangements that exist in our society. These are the principal arteries through which knowledge flows and is absorbed, like oxygen, into the bloodstream of political life. It would be misleading to suggest that the relationship of knowledge to power can be reduced to a set of structural concerns that are susceptible to improvement by institutional reform.

The relationship between knowledge and politics is one that demands constant scrutiny and reflection. It summons us to ask, again and again, what we really need to know to govern ourselves well. It demands that we test our theoretical knowledge by confronting real choices and their consequences. It requires us to use knowledge not as an intimidating bludgeon, but as a tool of education and persuasion, honestly exploring first premises and accepting the uncertainties of evidence. Above all, it compels us to admit that political wisdom is different from knowledge of the physical world and that social science can neither replace politics nor relieve us of the responsibility for making value-laden choices. Finally, it calls for a healthy egalitarian scepticism of the authority of experts.

The philosopher and expert have often been comic figures in democratic societies. Their isolation and ethereal abstraction have quite fairly been regarded as ridiculous by ordinary citizens who are confronted with practical problems; and from Socrates descending in his basket to Walter Lippmann in his elevator, experts have appeared to be detached and therefore comically unrealistic when viewed from the earthly perspective of everyday life. The truly wise man—one who may be said to have his head in the clouds and his feet on the ground at the same time—has always been a rarity. And the American attempt to bridge this gap by specialization and institutional arrangements has not produced wise democratic deliberations. While a solitary philosopher descended from the clouds on ancient Athens, today thousands of baskets come down like a flotilla of colorful hot-air balloons and empty their experts upon us. Some are more securely tethered than others—some, indeed, are quite earth bound— but their constant ups and downs suggest the true dynamic of the power-knowledge nexus. Power without knowledge is a frightful thing, while knowledge in a vacuum, untested by the practical political concerns of human life, is vain and comical. That the two must be conjoined somehow is obvious. The Wizard in the palace of authority, maintaining his mystique with smoke and mirrors, distracts us from awareness of the virtue in ourselves, while the Wizard with his basket untethered floats rudderless, higher and farther from the Emerald City, leaving the Scarecrow to rule.

Notes

Prologue

1. Jonathan Swift, *Gulliver's Travels* (1726; reprint, New York: Oxford University Press, 1974), p. 226.

2. For an interesting survey of the past three thousand years of the literature on political advising, see Herbert Goldhamer, *The Adviser* (New York: Elsevier, 1978).

3. *Think tank*, according to the *Oxford English Dictionary Supplement*, was first used at the turn of the century as British slang for the brain. The phrase, used as military jargon for a secure place to think or plan, may have been invented as early as World War I, but seems to have been more common in the American military in World War II. It was a term ordinarily used to describe military research organizations during the 1950s, entering wider usage only in the early 1960s when attention was focused on the policy intellectuals around Presidents Kennedy and Johnson. Terms such as *brain bank* or *think factory* were also used on occasion by the press in the 1960s. The proliferation of research organizations in the 1960s and 1970s propelled the term *think tank* into wider usage, both in the United States and abroad. The American expression is used in English by the Japanese and in various Germanic languages (as are literal translations, for example, the Dutch *denk tank*).

4. The national figures are based on the author's tally, drawn from *Research Centers Directory*, 9th ed. and suppl. (Detroit: Gale Research Co., 1984–85). Although the directory lists only 130 entries under the rubric "public policy," many more centers that are engaged in work on economics, the environment, transportation, and other policy fields ought to be included among the nation's institutes for research on public policy. The estimate of 100 or so nonprofit policy research organizations in Washington is my figure, which was derived from several years of looking for mention of such places in newspaper articles and research directories and browsing through the telephone book. No figures will ever be precise. Not only do institutes come and go, but it is impossible to draw precise lines around the universe of think tanks. Definitions of *policy, research*, and *institution* will always be subject to debate. One person's research institute may be another's advocacy group, and a "center" may be only a short-term or peripheral research project.

5. Abraham Lincoln, *The Collected Works*, ed. Roy Basler (New Brunswick, N.J.: Rutgers University Press, 1953), vol. 1, p. 315; and Harry S Truman, *Memoirs: Years of Trial and Hope*, vol. 2 (Garden City, N.Y.: Doubleday & Co., 1956), p. 1.

6. On Niccoló Machiavelli and executive power, see Harvey C. Mansfield, Jr., *Taming the Prince: The Ambivalence of Modern Executive Power* (New York: Free Press, 1989).

7. Francis Bacon, *Selected Writings* (New York: Modern Library, 1955), pp. 55–59 and 562–64.

8. Quoted in Henry A. Kissinger, *The White House Years* (New York: Little, Brown & Co., 1979), p. 4.

9. Quoted in Carl van Doren, *Swift* (New York: Viking Press, 1930), p. 101.

10. I have interviewed approximately 150 people from the following institutions: American Enterprise Institute, Atlantic Council, Brookings Institution, Cato Institute, Center for National Policy, Center for a New Democracy, Center for Strategic and International Studies, Center for the Study of Democratic Institutions, Committee for Economic Development, Ethics and Public Policy Center, Heritage Foundation, Hoover Institution on War, Revolution, and Peace, Hudson Institute, Independent Institute, Institute for Contemporary Studies, Institute for Educational Affairs, Institute for Policy Studies, Manhattan Institute for Policy Research, Pacific Institute, RAND Corporation, Reason Foundation, Rockford Institute, Roosevelt Center for Public Policy Studies, Russell Sage Foundation, Urban Institute, Twentieth Century Fund, and the World Policy Institute.

One / The Policy Elite

1. Quoted in John Wells Davidson, *A Crossroads of Freedom: The 1912 Campaign Speeches of Woodrow Wilson* (New Haven, Conn.: Yale University Press, 1956), p. 83.

2. Woodrow Wilson, "The Study of Administration," *Political Science Quarterly* 11 (June 1887), pp. 209–10.

3. E. M. House, *Philip Dru: Administrator* (New York: B. H. Huebsch, 1912), p. 64.

4. E. M. House, *The Intimate Papers of Colonel House*, arranged as a narrative by Charles Seymour (Boston: Houghton Mifflin Co., 1926), vol. 1, pp. 124–27.

5. Walter Lippmann, *Drift and Mastery* (New York: Mitchell Kennerly, 1914; reprint ed., Madison: University of Wisconsin Press, 1985), p. 86.

6. Martin Anderson, *Revolution* (San Diego, Calif.: Harcourt Brace Jovanovich, 1988), p. 167.

7. Richard Reeves, *The Reagan Detour* (New York: Simon & Schuster, 1985), p. 10, argued that " 'Reaganism' was at least as much the triumph of conservative intellectuals' as it was a 'spectacular personal triumph.' Working alone and in groups financed by very dedicated and very rich conservative businessmen, those thinkers of the right created a business themselves, the 'idea industry.' " Sydney Blumenthal, *The Rise of the Counter-Establishment: From Conservative Ideology to Political Power* (New York: Times Books, 1986), also wrote about Reagan's ideological appeal and the institutions of the "counter-establishment" which promoted conservative ideas.

8. Richard Hofstadter, *Anti-intellectualism in American Life* (New York: Alfred A. Knopf, 1963), pp. 147 and 149.

9. On the role of the intellectual, the most sweeping study is still Lewis A. Coser, *Men of Ideas: A Sociologist's View* (New York: Free Press, 1965). For some helpful distinctions, see H. Stuart Hughes, "Is the Intellectual Obsolete?" *Commentary* 22 (October 1956), pp. 313–19, reprinted in Hughes, *An Approach to Peace*

and Other Essays (New York: Atheneum Publishers, 1962). Essays on intellectuals and policymaking abound; two that I have found useful are Henry A. Kissinger, "The Policymaker and the Intellectual," *The Reporter* 20 (March 5, 1959), pp. 30–35; and Theodore Draper, "Intellectuals in Politics," first published in 1977 in *Encounter* and republished in Draper, *Present History: Nuclear War, Detente and Other Controversies* (New York: Random House, 1984), pp. 400–426.

10. On experts in World War I, see Robert Cuff, *The War Industries Board* (Baltimore: Johns Hopkins University Press, 1973); and Laurence Gelfand, *The Inquiry: American Preparations for Peace* (New Haven, Conn.: Yale University Press, 1963).

11. Two studies that discuss the Committee on Social Trends are Barry D. Karl, "Presidential Planning and Social Science Research: Mr. Hoover's Experts," *Perspectives in American History* 3 (1969), pp. 347–409; and Barry D. Karl, *Charles E. Merriam and the Study of Politics* (Chicago: University of Chicago Press, 1974), pp. 201–25.

12. Elliot A. Rosen, *Hoover, Roosevelt and the Brains Trust: From Depression to New Deal* (New York: Columbia University Press, 1977), presents an account of the Brains Trust that draws on Raymond Moley's perspective of the events in 1932–33 and assesses the contributions of Rexford G. Tugwell and Adolf A. Berle. The principals have also written extensively about their stints as campaign advisers.

13. On the political context of proposed cuts in funding for social science research, see the concluding essays in Martin Bulmer, ed., *Social Science Research and Government: Comparative Essays on Britain and the United States* (New York: Cambridge University Press, 1987).

14. Colin Campbell and Donald Naulls, "Social Science Training as Related to the Policy Roles of U.S. Career Officials and Appointees: The Decline of Analysis," in ibid., p. 114. The figures are preliminary ones from a 1988 survey by the National Science Foundation of U.S. scientists and engineers.

15. For a historical perspective on the authority wielded by experts, see Thomas L. Haskell, ed., *The Authority of Experts* (Bloomington: Indiana University Press, 1984), esp. Magali Sarfatti Larson, "The Production of Expertise and the Constitution of Expert Power," pp. 28–80. The role of ideas in shaping Great Society programs was the subject of Henry J. Aaron, *Politics and the Professors* (Washington, D.C.: Brookings Institution, 1978); Aaron returned to the same terrain, updating his views for the Ely Lecture at the 1988 meeting of the American Economics Association.

16. William James, *Pragmatism: A New Name for Some Old Ways of Thinking* (1907; reprint, New York: Longmans, Green & Co., 1943), p. 201.

17. Lippmann, *Drift and Mastery*, p. 151.

18. Quoted in Morton White, *Social Thought in America: The Revolt against Formalism* (Boston: Beacon Press, 1957), pp. 169–70.

19. Ronald Reagan, "Remarks by the President during the Heritage Foundation Dinner" (April 22, 1986). The text was given to the author by the Heritage Foundation public affairs office.

20. Richard Weaver, *Ideas Have Consequences* (Chicago: University of Chicago Press, 1948).

21. Reagan, "Remarks by the President."

22. Kirk O'Donnell, interview with the author, June 2, 1987.

23. Alexis de Tocqueville, *Democracy in America*, trans. Henry Reeve (New York: Colonial Press, 1900), p. 197.

Two / Laboratories for Reform

1. On the history of the American Social Science Association, see Thomas Haskell, *The Emergence of Professional Social Science: The American Social Science Association and the Nineteenth Century Crisis of Authority* (Urbana: University of Illinois Press, 1977); and the now-dated work of Luther Lee Bernard and Jessie Bernard, *Origins of American Sociology: The Social Science Movement in the United States* (New York: Thomas Y. Crowell, 1943). Early sources for the association are in American Social Science Association, *Constitution, Address, and List of Members of the American Association for the Promotion of Social Science* (Boston: Wright & Potter, 1866); the letter is quoted in Haskell, *The Emergence of Professional Social Science*, p. 10.

2. Quoted in Haskell, *The Emergence of Professional Social Science*, p. 3.

3. *Ibid.*

4. Quoted in Walter Trattner, *From Poor Law to Welfare State: A History of Social Welfare in America* (New York: Free Press, 1989), p. 91.

5. On Richard T. Ely, see Benjamin G. Rader, *The Academic Mind and Reform: The Influence of Richard T. Ely in American Life* (Lexington: University of Kentucky Press, 1966). Ely's views on the study of economics in the 1880s are in Richard T. Ely, "The Past and Present of Political Economy," *John Hopkins University Studies in Historical and Political Science* 2 (1884). Ely's comment on evolution is from his memoirs, Richard T. Ely, *Ground under Our Feet* (New York: Macmillan Co., 1938), p. 154.

6. Ibid., p. 65.

7. On the founding of the AEA, see Alfred W. Coats, "The First Two Decades of the American Economics Association, *American Economic Review* 50 (1960), pp. 555–72; and "The American Economic Association and the Economics Profession," *Journal of Economic Literature* 23 (1985), pp. 1697–1727. Ely's draft prospectus for the AEA may be found in *Ground under Our Feet*, where he summarizes his attitude toward scientific progress in the field of political economy: "We believe that political economy as a science is still in an early stage of its development. While we appreciate the work of former economists, we look, not so much to speculation as to the historical and statistical study of actual conditions of economic life for the satisfactory accomplishment of that development" (p. 140).

8. On social Darwinism and its opponents, see Thomas L. Haskell, "Introduction: What Happened in the 1890s," in Haskell, *The Emergence of Professional Social Science;* and Mary O. Furner, *Advocacy and Objectivity: A Crisis in the Professionalization of American Social Science, 1865–1905* (Lexington: University of Kentucky Press, 1975). Sumner is quoted in Richard Hofstadter, *Social Darwinism in American Thought*, rev. ed. (Boston: Beacon Press, 1955), p. 61.

9. Lester Ward, *The Psychic Factors of Civilization* (Boston: Ginn & Co., 1893), p. 261. See also, Lester Ward, *Dynamic Sociology*, 2 vol. (New York: D. Appleton & Co., 1883).

10. Quoted in Henry Steele Commager, *The American Mind* (New Haven, Conn.: Yale University Press, 1950), p. 216.

11. U.S. Bureau of the Census, *Historical Statistics of the United States, Colonial*

Times to 1870 (Washington, D.C.: U.S. Department of Commerce, 1975), part 1, pp. 382–3 and p. 388.

12. Hadley predicted that the AEA's work would be of interest to "thoughtful businessmen, newspaper men and holders of public office." See Arthur Twining Hadley, "President's Address: The Relation between Economics and Politics," *Economic Studies* 4 (1899), pp. 7–28. On the growing role of academics in government, see David M. Grossman, "Professors and Public Service, 1885–1925: A Chapter in the Professionalization of the Social Sciences" (Ph.D. diss., Washington University, St. Louis, 1973).

13. Lucy Sprague Mitchell, *Two Lives: The Story of Wesley Clair Mitchell and Myself* (New York: Simon & Schuster, 1953), p. 184.

14. See David M. Grossman, "Scholars and Statistics," in Grossman, "Professors and Public Service, 1885–1925," pp. 23–72.

15. John R. Commons, *Myself* (New York: Macmillan Co., 1934), pp. 108–9.

16. Ibid., p. 110.

17. Ibid., p. 76.

18. Ibid., p. 88.

19. Frederick T. Gates, *Chapters in My Life* (New York: Free Press, 1977), p. 186.

20. John D. Rockefeller, *Random Reminiscences of Men and Events* (Garden City, N.Y.: Doubleday & Co., 1937), p. 177. On the origins of the Rockefeller Foundation, see Raymond B. Fosdick, *The Story of the Rockefeller Foundation* (New York: Harper & Bros., 1952); and George Harr and Peter Johnson, *The Rockefeller Century* (New York: Simon & Schuster, 1988).

21. The surviving records of the Russell Sage Foundation and the letters on Margaret Sage's individual charitable contributions are held at the Rockefeller Archive Center (hereafter referred to as RAC) in Pocantico Hills, New York. A brief history of the foundation and a guide to records are available on microfiche in *The Russell Sage Foundation: Social Research and Social Action in America, 1907–47* (Frederick, Md.: UPA Academic Editions, 1988). Three staff members collaborated in a history of the foundation's first four decades: John M. Glenn, Lilian Brandt, and F. Emerson Andrews, *Russell Sage Foundation, 1907–46*, 2 vols. (New York: Russell Sage Foundation, 1947).

22. Glenn, Brandt, and Andrews, *Russell Sage Foundation, 1907–46*, vol. 1, p. 25.

23. On the beginnings of social work, see Roy Lubove, *The Professional Altruist: The Emergence of Social Work as a Career* (Cambridge, Mass.: Harvard University Press, 1965).

24. On the history of the Survey Department, see Glenn, Brandt, and Andrews, *Russell Sage Foundation, 1907–46*, vol. 1, pp. 177–96. On the Pittsburgh Survey, see Clarke A. Chambers, *Paul U. Kellogg and the Survey: Voices for Social Welfare and Social Justice* (Minneapolis: University of Minnesota Press, 1971). On the survey movement in general, see Allen R. Eaton and Shelby M. Harrison, *A Bibliography of Social Surveys* (New York: Russell Sage Foundation, 1930); and Richard B. Dusenbury, "Truth and Technique: A Study of Sociology and the Social Survey Movement, 1895–1930" (Ph.D. diss., University of Wisconsin–Madison, 1969).

25. As quoted in Glenn, Brandt, and Andrews, *Russell Sage Foundation 1907–46*, vol. 1, p. 177.

26. The comment on the Topeka Survey is quoted in ibid., vol. 1, p. 183. On the Springfield Survey, see RAC, Russell Sage Foundation, Box 33, folder 264. The minister was G. C. Dunlop, writing in the *Illinois State Register* (January 29, 1917). Vachel Lindsay talks of his *Golden Book of Springfield* and his enthusiasm for the survey in a letter to Shelby Harrison (December 20, 1920) in RAC, Russell Sage Foundation, Box 33, folder 264.

27. Edward T. Devine, "Memorandum re Russell Sage Foundation" (1906) in RAC, Russell Sage Foundation, Box 2, folder 11.

28. Quoted in Glenn, Brandt, and Andrews, *Russell Sage Foundation, 1907–46*, p. 169.

29. Letter from Mary K. Richmond to John Glenn (July 12, 1926) in RAC, Russell Sage Foundation, Box 34, folder 274.

Three / Efficiency Experts

1. Quoted in James Weinstein, *The Corporate Ideal in the Liberal State: 1900–1918* (Boston: Beacon Press, 1968), p. 93.

2. Samuel Haber, *Efficiency and Uplift: Scientific Management in the Progressive Era, 1890–1920* (Chicago: University of Chicago Press, 1964), p. ix. See also, Samuel P. Hays, *Conservation and the Gospel of Efficiency: The Progressive Conservation Movement, 1890–1920* (Cambridge, Mass.: Harvard University Press, 1959), esp. chap. 13, "The Conservation Movement and the Progressive Tradition."

3. Frederick Winslow Taylor, *The Principles of Scientific Management* (1911; reprint, New York: Harper & Bros., 1947).

4. Quoted in Jane S. Dahlberg, *The New York Bureau of Municipal Research: Pioneer in Government Administration* (New York: New York University Press, 1966), p. 4.

5. For an excellent account of the relationship between the New York Bureau and the early history of Brookings, see Donald T. Critchlow, *The Brookings Institution, 1916–52: Expertise and the Public Interest in a Democratic Society* (DeKalb: Northern Illinois University Press, 1984). The remark by Allen is from an early memorandum on plans for a municipal research bureau, quoted in ibid., p. 25. See also William H. Allen, *Efficient Democracy* (New York: Dodd, Mead & Co., 1907).

6. For a firsthand account of the reform campaigns, see Raymond Fosdick, *Chronicle of a Generation* (New York: Harper & Bros., 1958).

7. William H. Allen, "Reminiscences," quoted in Dahlberg, *The New York Bureau of Municipal Research*, p. 32.

8. Henry Bruere, *Efficiency in City Government*, quoted in Haber, *Efficiency and Uplift*, p. 112.

9. For a brief account of the Commission on Economy and Efficiency and the Budget and Accounting Act of 1921, see Frederick C. Mosher, *A Tale of Two Agencies: A Comparative Analysis of the General Accounting Office and the Office of Management and Budget* (Baton Rouge: Louisiana State University Press, 1984), pp. 19–34.

10. Letter from Charles W. Eliot to Jerome D. Greene (November 21, 1914) in Rockefeller Archive Center (hereafter referred to as RAC), Pocantico Hills, New

York, Record Group 3, Series 900, Box 18, folder 128. Other noteworthy materials on the early history of Brookings are in the collection on the Institute for Government Research (IGR), including minutes of the planning committee meetings and the "Prospectus" in the Brookings Institution Archives (hereafter referred to as BIA), Washington, D.C. Jerome D. Greene reflected on the early history of the IGR in letters to Robert Calkins (April 29, 1954) and Harold Moulton (April 5, 1952), and in 1956 Robert Calkins prepared his "Memoranda on Early History of Brookings"; all three documents are in the BIA. Greene attributed the idea for the IGR to Frederick Cleveland but said that the "initial push" came after a conversation between Greene and Charles D. Norton, who had become vice president of the National Bank of New York on leaving the Taft administration, as they stood in front of Trinity Church on Broadway. Most of the initial money was raised at a dinner meeting in New York. Many of the materials on the early history of the IGR, the Institute of Economics, and the graduate school and on the merger are in BIA, Administrative Files, Boxes 1–3.

For a brief history of IGR, see Charles A. H. Thomson, *Institute for Government Research: An Account of Research Achievements* (Washington, D.C.: Brookings Institution, 1956). Some of the same terrain is covered in Charles B. Saunders, *The Brookings Institution—A Fifty Year History* (Washington, D.C.: Brookings Institution, 1966).

The Rockefeller Foundation's abortive plans to create its own institute for social and economic research are described in documents at the RAC, Record Group 3, Series 910, Box 2, Folder 10, esp. "Institute for Social and Economic Research" (proposal), p. 2.

11. On Willoughby's career, see Critchlow, *The Brookings Institution, 1916–52*, pp. 34–36.

12. On the first years of the Bureau of the Budget, see Mosher, *A Tale of Two Agencies*, pp. 35–47.

13. For a flattering biography of Brookings, which includes much on his business career, see Herman Hagedorn, *Brookings: A Biography* (New York: Macmillan Co., 1936).

14. For a contemporary view of his war work, see William Hard, "Retarding the Allies," *The New Republic* 18, (December 29, 1917), pp. 238–40. The observations by Bernard Baruch and Chandler Anderson are quoted in Critchlow, *The Brookings Institution, 1916–52*, pp. 53–54. Hagedorn, *Brookings*, p. 261, is apologetic about Brookings's loquaciousness.

15. Hagedorn, *Brookings*, pp. 179–80 and pp. 253–54.

16. Institute of Economics, "Prospectus," (1922), in the BIA.

17. The Carnegie Corporation's statement of support is in "A Documentary History of the Institute of Economics" (January 1955) in BIA.

18. From the minutes of the meeting of the board of trustees, Institute of Economics (April 21–22, 1922), quoted in Critchlow, *The Brookings Institution, 1916–52*, p. 58.

19. Saunders, *The Brookings Institution*, p. 29.

20. "Report of Walton Hamilton to the Board of Trustees of the Brookings School" (April 30, 1926) in BIA.

21. Letter from Robert Brookings to Walton Hamilton (November 25, 1927). Brookings had already expressed his concerns about the graduate school in a letter

to Willoughby (May 18, 1926). Willoughby unloaded his complaints about the neglect of public administration in a reply (May 18, 1926). All three letters are in BIA. See also, "First Plan Presented by Drafting Committee" in BIA.

22. "Report of Walton Hamilton."

23. "First Plan Presented by Drafting Committee" in BIA.

24. The assessment is from Joseph Dorfman, "Wesley Clair Mitchell," *Dictionary of American Biography*, suppl. 4, 1946 (New York: Charles Scribner's Sons, 1974). On the War Industries Board, where Mitchell and so many other economists served, see Robert D. Cuff, *The War Industries Board* (Baltimore: Johns Hopkins University Press, 1973).

25. On Mitchell's life and career see, Lucy Sprague Mitchell, *Two Lives: The Story of Wesley Clair Mitchell and Myself* (New York: Simon & Schuster, 1953); and Arthur F. Burns, ed., *Wesley Clair Mitchell: The Economic Scientist* (New York: National Bureau of Economic Research, 1952). The quotations are from Mitchell, *Two Lives*, pp. 297 and 176.

26. Wesley C. Mitchell, "Statistics and Government," in *The Backward Art of Spending Money* (New York: McGraw-Hill Book Co., 1937), p. 42; and Lucy Sprague Mitchell, *Two Lives*, p. 187.

27. Wesley C. Mitchell, "Statistics and Government," pp. 50–51.

28. Ibid., p. 51.

29. Herbert Heaton, *A Scholar in Action: Edwin F. Gay* (Cambridge, Mass.: Harvard University Press, 1952), p. 196.

30. Nahum I. Stone quotes Rorty in telling the story of the origins of the bureau in "The Beginnings of the National Bureau of Economic Research: A Tribute to the Memory of Its Founder, Malcolm C. Rorty," which is part of "The National Bureau's First Quarter-Century," *Twenty-Fifth Annual Report* (New York: National Bureau of Economic Research, 1945) p. 6. Solomon Fabricant also recounts the early history of the bureau in "Toward a Firmer Basis of Economic Policy: The Founding of the National Bureau of Economic Research" (Cambridge, Mass.: National Bureau of Economic Research, 1984). See also, Guy Alchon, *The Invisible Hand of Planning: Capitalism, Social Science and the State in the 1920s* (Princeton, N.J.: Princeton University Press, 1985). The Commonwealth Fund archives, now held at the RAC, contain a good set of primary documents on the bureau's founding showing how Rorty's plans for the bureau changed during and after World War I. Materials from the Laura Spelman Rockefeller Memorial (LSRM) also shed light on the early years of the bureau; see, for example, "The First 3 Years of the National Bureau of Economic Research: An Informal Account of How the Bureau Works (1924) in RAC, LSRM, Series III, Box 51, folder 538.

31. "The First 3 Years of the National Bureau of Economic Research," p. 2.

32. Quoted in Lucy Sprague Mitchell, *Two Lives*, pp. 355–6. For an assessment after fifteen years' of work, see Wesley C. Mitchell, "Retrospect and Prospect, 1920–36" (New York: National Bureau of Economic Research, 1936).

33. One of the early studies is Willford I. King, Frederick Macaulay, and Wesley C. Mitchell, *Income in the United States, Its Amount and Distribution, 1909–19*, 2 vols. (New York: National Bureau of Economic Research, 1921, 1922).

34. The first part of the bureau's study, *Business Cycles: The Problem and Its Setting* (New York: National Bureau of Economic Research, 1927) discussed the contending theories of the business cycle and explained why a thorough, quantitative description of the factors that made up the business cycle must precede further

theorizing. "What is the relative importance of the factors represented as causes of fluctuations? What is the relative amplitude of the fluctuations characteristic of these factors and of the effects which they are said to produce? In what sequence do the fluctuations appear and at what intervals of time? . . . Such problems can be solved only by appeal to statistics." The bureau's study looked at historical data and attempted to understand how economic institutions had changed over time. The long view was fundamental to the search for cycles and trends, and the series of data had to be continuous, consistent, and comprehensive if the regularities of economic behavior were to be uncovered.

Mitchell and his colleagues knew that the data collections could be of use to economists who were studying other problems, as well as to policymakers and businessmen, but the expense of publishing the data on a regular basis was more than the bureau could undertake. Business annals providing historical records for seventeen countries were published in 1926 and updated periodically through 1931. But only gradually did governmental agencies begin to take over the task of publication in such volumes as the U.S. Bureau of the Census, *Historical Statistics of the United States* (1949 and thereafter) and the U.S. Department of Commerce's monthly *Business Conditions Digest.*

35. Bernard Baruch, *Baruch: My Own Story* (New York: Holt, Rinehart & Winston, 1957), p. 308.

36. On economists and economic policy in the 1920s, see Alchon, *The Invisible Hand of Planning;* William J. Barber, *From New Era to New Deal: Herbert Hoover, the Economists and American Economic Policy, 1921–33* (Cambridge, England: Cambridge University Press, 1985); and Evan Metcalf, "Secretary Hoover and the Emergence of Macroeconomic Management," *Business History Review* 49 (Spring 1975), pp. 60–80; and various works of Ellis A. Hawley, including Hawley, ed., *Herbert Hoover as Secretary of Commerce, 1921–28: Studies in New Era Thought and Practice* (Iowa City: University of Iowa Press, 1981); and Hawley, *The Great War and the Search for Modern Order, 1917–33* (New York: St. Martin's Press, 1979).

37. On the Unemployment Conference of 1921, see Carolyn Grin, "The Unemployment Conference of 1921: An Experiment in National Cooperative Planning," *Mid-America: An Historical Review* 55 (April 1973), pp. 83–107; and Metcalf, "Secretary Hoover." On Hoover's use of conferences and commissions, see Barry D. Karl, "Presidential Planning and Social Science Research: Mr. Hoover's Experts," *Perspectives in American History* 3 (1969), pp. 347–409; and Karl, *Charles E. Merriam and the Study of Politics* (Chicago: University of Chicago Press, 1974).

38. Quoted in Fabricant, "Toward a Firmer Basis of Economic Policy," p. 24.

39. Committee on Recent Economic Changes of the President's Conference on Unemployment, *Recent Economic Changes in the United States,* 2 vols. (New York: McGraw-Hill Book Co., 1929).

40. A professor at the University of North Carolina expressed his views of the opportunity: "One of Mr. Hoover's most recent private statements has been that he wants his to be a government based on facts. Even granting that he may be rushing the situation a little, this is a most important situation and we face an actual status rather than a theory. It seems to be an opportunity for unusually effective effort—an opportunity that does not come often." See letter from Howard Odum to E. E. Day (September 2, 1929) in RAC, Rockefeller Foundation, R.G. 1.1, Series 236, Box 9, folder 112.

41. On the President's Research Committee on Social Trends, see Karl, "Presi-

dential Planning and Social Science Research"; and Herbert Hoover, *The Memoirs of Herbert Hoover: The Cabinet and the Presidency, 1920–33* (New York: Macmillan Co., 1952), pp. 312–13. Documents on the early planning for the project on social trends and the Rockefeller Foundation's involvement in financing it are in RAC, R.G. 1.1, Series 200, Box 326, folder 3873; the committee's aims are set forth in "Report of the President's Committee on Social Research."

On foundations and the social sciences in the 1920s, see David M. Grossman, "American Foundations and the Support for Economic Research, 1913–29," *Minerva* 20 (Spring–Summer, 1982), pp. 59–82; and Martin Bulmer and Joan Bulmer, "Philanthropy and Social Science in the 1920s: Beardsley Ruml and the Laura Spelman Rockefeller Memorial, 1922–29," *Minerva* 19 (Autumn 1981), pp. 347–407. For a more general discussion, see Barry D. Karl and Stanley N. Katz, "The American Private Philanthropic Foundation and the Public Sphere, 1890–1930," *Minerva* 19 (Summer 1981), pp. 236–70. On the National Bureau of Economic Research and foundations, see Wesley C. Mitchell, "Retrospect and Prospect."

One of the most illuminating studies of the emergence of American social science and its role in public policymaking is Barry D. Karl's biography of Charles Merriam, *Charles E. Merriam and the Study of Politics* (Chicago: University of Chicago Press, 1974). Among Merriam's many contributions was the founding of the Social Science Research Council, whose origins are related in Karl, pp. 118–39; and in Elbridge Sibley, *Social Science Research Council: The First Fifty Years* (New York: Social Science Research Council, 1974).

Although not a policy research institution by even the most inclusive definition, the Social Science Research Council, founded in 1923, was instrumental in stimulating the support of foundations for the social sciences, spawning collaborative research projects, and maintaining a delicate balance between scientific concerns and practical applications of the social science disciplines. When Merriam first mentioned the idea of forming an overarching association of the social science disciplines, he met with considerable skepticism. His proposed research council seemed to offer unnecessary competition for scarce resources and to duplicate some of the work of the National Research Council and the American Council of Learned Societies (ACLS). Historians, seemingly content with the ACLS, and economists, some of whom had already proved adept at raising funds for their discipline, were not eager to join with Merriam and his fellow political scientists in creating another organization, especially one, as yet, without money.

Merriam persisted in the face of indifference and, at times, opposition from the better established professional associations and from individual social scientists who thought that the demands of pure science could brook no compromise with the more practical demands of philanthropists or politicians. He was able to make social and political research an appealing proposition to foundations, at a moment when they might have preferred to devote resources to the safer fields of medicine and natural science. And he was also able to maintain a connection between the intellectual work of social scientists and the realms of social and political action. In the words of Karl, *Charles Merriam*, p. 121, "Merriam accepted the technical paraphernalia of specialization, but his support of democracy as a scientific process of government and his view of the introduction of science as a nonrevolutionary extension of a democratic tradition rested on the maintenance of a continuous balance between the development of new scientific techniques, on the one hand, and the development somehow of more rapid advances in publication, on the other."

42. President's Research Committee on Social Trends, *Recent Social Trends in the United States*, 2 volumes (New York: McGraw-Hill Book Co., 1933); and Hoover, *The Memoirs of Herbert Hoover*, pp. 312–13.

43. Clippings and press summaries are in RAC, R.G. 1.1, Series 200, Box 326.

44. Adolf A. Berle, Jr., *Saturday Review*, 9 (1933), pp. 533–35.

45. As quoted in Karl, "Presidential Planning," pp. 392–93.

46. As quoted in Joseph P. Lash, *Dealers and Dreamers: A New Look at the New Deal* (New York: Doubleday, 1988), p. 86.

Four / Experts Advising

1. Quoted in Arthur M. Schlesinger, Jr., *The Coming of the New Deal* (Boston: Houghton Mifflin Co., 1959), p. 527.

2. Quoted in Raymond A. Moley, *The First New Deal* (New York: Harcourt, Brace & World, 1966), p. 356. For a historian's account of the Brains Trust that reinforces Moley's perspective on the events of 1932, see Elliot A. Rosen, *Hoover, Roosevelt and the Brains Trust: From Depression to New Deal* (New York: Columbia University Press, 1977). On Berle, see Jordan Schwarz, *Liberal: Adolf A. Berle and the Vision of an American Era* (New York: Free Press, 1987). Contemporary journalists took note of the intellectuals around Roosevelt; see, for example, Joseph Alsop and Robert Kintner, *Men Around the President* (New York: Doubleday, Doran & Co., 1939).

3. Samuel A. Rosenman, *Working with Roosevelt* (New York: Harper & Bros., 1952), pp. 56–59.

4. Rexford G. Tugwell, *Roosevelt's Revolution: The First Year A Personal Perspective* (New York: Macmillan Co., 1977), p. 4. On Tugwell's life and career, see Bernard Sternsher, *Rexford Tugwell and the New Deal* (New Brunswick, N.J.: Rutgers University Press, 1964).

5. Quoted in Moley, *The First New Deal*, p. 356.

6. Franklin D. Roosevelt, *The Public Papers. and Addresses of Franklin D. Roosevelt*, ed. Samuel I. Rosenman (New York: Random House, 1938), vol. 1, p. 646.

7. Milton Katz is quoted in Katie Loucheim, *The Making of the New Deal: The Insiders Speak* (Cambridge, Mass.: Harvard University Press, 1983), p. 121. On the transition from the New Era to the New Deal, see Albert U. Romasco, "Hoover-Roosevelt and the Great Depression: A Historiographic Inquiry into a Perennial Comparison," James Holt, "The New Deal and the American Anti-Statist Tradition," and Ellis W. Hawley, "The New Deal and Business," in *The New Deal*, ed. John Braeman, Robert H. Bremner, and David Brody (Columbus: Ohio State University Press, 1975), vol. 1, pp. 3–26, 27–49, and 50–82, respectively; Jordan Schwarz, *The Interregnum of Despair: Hoover, Congress and Depression* (Urbana: University of Illinois Press, 1970); and William J. Barber, *From New Era to New Deal: Herbert Hoover, the Economists and American Economic Policy, 1921–33* (Cambridge, England: Cambridge University Press, 1985).

8. On social scientists in government during the 1930s, see Gene M. Lyons, *The Uneasy Partnership: Social Science and the Federal Government in the Twentieth Century* (New York: Russell Sage Foundation, 1969), pp. 50–79; and Richard S. Kirkendall, *Social Scientists and Farm Politics in the Age of Roosevelt* (Columbia, Mo.: University of Missouri Press, 1966). On lawyers in the New Deal, see Jerold S. Auerbach, "Lawyers and Social Change in the Depression Decade," Braeman,

Bremner, and Brody, *The New Deal*, vol. 1. pp. 133–69; Frankfurter is quoted in ibid., p. 148.

9. U.S. Bureau of the Census, *Historical Statistics of the United States, Colonial Times to 1870* (Washington, D.C.: U.S. Department of Commerce, 1975), part 2, pp. 1102–3.

10. John Chamberlain, *American Stakes* (New York: Carrick & Evans, 1940).

11. Letter from J. H. Willits to R. Warren (August 24, 1942) in Rockefeller Archive Center (hereafter called RAC), Pocantico Hills, New York, Rockefeller Foundation, Record Group 3, Series 910, Box 3, folder 17.

12. Edmund E. Day, "Social Intelligence," Commencement Address, University of Vermont (June 15, 1931) in RAC, Rockefeller Foundation, Record Group 3, Series 910, Box 3, folder 21.

13. Letter from Russell Leffingwell to Frederick Keppel (March 14, 1932) in Carnegie Corporation Files, New York City (they have recently been moved to Columbia University).

14. John M. Glenn, Lilian Brandt, and F. Emerson Andrews, *Russell Sage Foundation, 1907–46* (New York: Russell Sage Foundation, 1947), vol. 2, pp. 515–6; and Joanna Colcord, *Cash Relief* (New York: Russell Sage Foundation, 1936).

15. Letter from Wesley Mitchell to Frederick Keppel (March 3, 1933) in Carnegie Corporation Papers, Rare Book and Manuscript Library, Columbia University.

16. "Lincoln Steffens to Frederick Howe, August 22, 1934," in *Letters of Lincoln Steffens* ed. Ella Winter and Granville Hicks (New York: Harcourt, Brace & Co., 1938), vol. 2, p. 992. On Filene's life, see Gerald W. Johnson, *Liberal's Progress: Edward A. Filene, Shopkeeper to Social Statesman* (New York: Coward-McCann, 1948); and Kim McQuaid, "An American Owenite: Edward A. Filene and the Parameters of Industrial Reform, 1890–1937," *American Journal of Economics and Sociology* 35 (January 1976), pp. 77–94. The files of the Twentieth Century Fund in New York City contain oral histories from several associates of Filene. Some of Filene's speeches are collected in E. A. Filene, *Speaking of Change* (New York: Privately Printed, 1939). On the Filene Store and welfare capitalism, see Mary LaDame, *The Filene Store* (New York: Russell Sage Foundation, 1930); and Stuart D. Brandes, *American Welfare Capitalism* (Chicago: University of Chicago Press, 1970).

17. E. A. Filene, "President's Address" (February 21, 1930) p. 3, in files of the Twentieth Century Fund.

18. Ibid., p. 4.

19. E. A. Filene, "President's Address" (March 17, 1932) in files of the Twentieth Century Fund.

20. Twentieth Century Fund, *Twentieth Century Fund Annual Report* (New York: TCF, 1933), p. 8. Studies by the fund during the 1930s included Evans Clark, *The Internal Debts of the United States* (1933); Clark, *How to Budget Health* (1933); Clark et. al., *Stock Market Control* (1934); *The Security Markets*, ed. Alfred Bernheim and Margaret Grant Schneider (1935); Margaret Grant Schneider, *More Security for Old Age* (1937); Paul Stewart and Rufus Tucker, *The National Debt and Government Credit* (1937); and Albert Hart, *Debt and Recovery, 1929–37* (1938).

21. Harold J. Laski, "Foundations, Universities and Research," *Harper's Magazine* 157 (August 1928), p. 295.

22. Robert T. Crane, "Discussion of Social Sciences Program and Suggestions for Future Development" (May and October, 1938), in RAC, Rockefeller Foundation,

Record Group 3, Series 910, Box 3, Folder 27. Jerome D. Greene, "Speech at the Dedication Exercises of the New Brookings Institution Building," in the Brookings Institution Archives, Washington, D.C., Administration—Special Observances, Box 1.

23. Quoted in Arthur M. Schlesinger, Jr., *The Crisis of the Old Order* (Boston: Houghton Mifflin Co., 1956), p. 425.

24. Quoted in Arthur M. Schlesinger, Jr., *The Coming of the New Deal* (Boston: Houghton Mifflin Co., 1959), pp. 34–35.

25. Ibid., p. 38. Adjustment had as its corollary the notion of balance. The theme of balance is elaborated in Richard H. Pells, *Radical Visions and American Dreams: Culture and Social Thought in the Depression Years* (Middletown, Conn.; Wesleyan University Press, 1973), pp. 79–80.

26. Henry A. Wallace, *New Frontiers* (New York: Reynal and Hitchcock, 1934), p. 21. Roosevelt is quoted in Schlesinger, op. cit., p. 39.

27. John Dewey in talking about a new political party during the depression addresses policy questions in "Policies for a New Party," *The New Republic* 46 (April 8, 1931), pp. 202–3.

28. On the idea of planning and its appeal in the 1930s, see Otis L. Graham, Jr., *Toward a Planned Society: From Roosevelt to Nixon* (New York: Oxford University Press, 1976), pp. 1–68. Chase is quoted in ibid., p. 14.

29. Ibid., p. 30.

30. National Resources Board, *A Plan for Planning* (Washington, D.C.: National Resources Board, 1934).

31. On the National Resources Planning Board, see Philip W. Warken, *A History of the National Resources Planning Board, 1933–43* (New York: Garland Press, 1979); and Marion Clawson, *New Deal Planning: The National Resources Planning Board* (Baltimore, Md.: Johns Hopkins University Press, 1981).

32. Graham, *Toward a Planned Society*, p. 56.

33. Alvin Hansen, *After the War—Full Employment* (Washington, D.C.: National Resources Planning Board, 1942); and National Resources Planning Board, *Security, Work and Relief Policies* (Washington, D.C.: NRPB, 1943).

34. Quoted in Richard Hofstadter, *Anti-intellectualism in American Life* (New York: Alfred A. Knopf, 1963), p. 256.

35. Sternsher, *Rexford Tugwell and the New Deal*, p. 346.

36. Documents on the plans for what became the Middletown Study are in RAC, Raymond B. Fosdick papers, esp., "History of the Small City Study," Box 2, folder 15.

37. Robert Lynd, *Knowledge for What? The Place of Social Science in American Culture* (Princeton, N.J.: Princeton University Press, 1939), p. 7.

38. Ibid., p. 146.

39. Ibid., p. 19.

40. Ibid., p. 200.

41. Ibid., p. 203.

Five / Technocratic Faiths

1. Robert E. Sherwood, *Roosevelt and Hopkins: An Intimate History* (New York: Harper & Bros., 1948), p. xiii.

2. On the federal government's support for research, see Michael D. Reagan,

Science and the Federal Patron (New York: Oxford University Press, 1969), p. 320, for the figures cited; Gene M. Lyons, *The Uneasy Partnership: Social Science and the Federal Government in the Twentieth Century* (New York: Russell Sage Foundation, 1969); A. Hunter Dupree, *Science in the Federal Government* (Cambridge, England: Cambridge University Press, 1957); and Don K. Price, *Government and Science* (New York: New York University Press, 1954).

3. On the mobilization of social scientists during the war, see Lyons, *The Uneasy Partnership*, pp. 80–123.

4. Samuelson is quoted in Robert Lekachman, *The Age of Keynes* (New York: Random House, 1966), p. 160.

5. John Kenneth Galbraith, *A Life in Our Times* (Boston: Houghton Mifflin Co., 1981), p. 163.

6. On the development of university social science after World War II, see Roger Geiger, "American Foundations and Academic Social Science," *Minerva* 26 (Autumn 1988), pp. 315–41.

7. The Twentieth Century Fund asked George Galloway of the National Planning Association to compile a directory of organizations engaged in planning. The directory first appeared in mimeograph form in 1941 and was later printed, expanded, and revised annually in 1942, 1943, and 1944 under the title *Postwar Planning in the United States: An Organization Directory* (New York: Twentieth Century Fund).

The volumes by Stuart Chase were part of a series called "When the War Ends," all published by the Twentieth Century Fund. The titles included *The Road We Are Travelling: 1914–42* (1942), *Goals for Americans: A Budget of Our Needs and Resources* (1942), *Where's the Money Coming From? Problems of Postwar Finance* (1943), *Democracy under Pressure: Special Interests versus the Public Welfare* (1945), *Tomorrow's Trade: Problems of Our Foreign Commerce* (1945), and *For This We Fought* (1946).

8. On the reception of Keynesian economics by policymakers and businessmen, see Lekachman, *The Age of Keynes*; and Robert M. Collins, *The Business Response to Keynes, 1929–64* (New York: Columbia University Press, 1982).

9. On the Business Advisory Council, see Kim McQuaid, *Big Business and Presidential Power: From FDR to Reagan* (New York: William Morrow & Co., 1982). On the history of CED, see Karl Schriftgiesser, *Business Comes of Age: The Impact of the Committee for Economic Development, 1942–60* (New York: Harper & Bros., 1960); and Schriftgiesser, *Business and Public Policy: The Role of the Committee for Economic Development, 1942–67* (Englewood Cliffs, N.J.: Prentice-Hall, 1967). In writing these books, Schriftgiesser also organized the CED's archival materials, which are on microfilm at the CED offices in New York.

10. William Benton, "Statement of the Historical Background of the Committee for Economic Development" (October 26, 1943) in CED files.

11. Beardsley Ruml, "Business Organizes to Look Ahead" (April 14, 1943) in CED files.

12. Hoffman's role in the establishment of CED is described in Alan R. Raucher, *Paul G. Hoffman: Architect of Foreign Aid* (Lexington: University of Kentucky Press, 1985). On William Benton, see Sidney Hyman, *The Lives of William Benton* (Chicago: University of Chicago Press, 1969); and in the CED files, William Benton, "Statement of the Historical Background of the Committee for Economic Development" (October 26, 1943).

In 1944 Hoffman described CED as a "temporary self-liquidating organization" (CED files, trustees meeting, September 22, 1944). From the beginning, it had been assumed that reconversion problems, by their very nature, were short-lived. It had also been necessary to depict the work of CED as temporary to win the cooperation of the U.S. Chamber of Commerce, which looked warily on the local organizing of the Field Development Division.

At the board meeting in September 1944, it was clear that Flanders, Benton, Folsom, and Hoffman had longer-term research plans in mind. Hoffman suggested that there were long-term educational goals: [We] "must bend our efforts toward developing a public understanding of essential economic facts." Folsom saw a more political role, noting that congressmen were interested in what businessmen had to say: "Businessmen are missing an opportunity to do a public service by failing to work constructively with Congress, as individuals." At a meeting in 1945, Folsom noted that Congress was playing a wider role in shaping policy, but he had noticed how inadequately staffed congressional committees were. Theodore Yntema, director of research, saw a wide-open field for research, estimating that only $500,000 per year was being spent by private institutions on policy research. For 1945, he hoped to raise a budget of $900,000, more than half of which would be for research. In early 1946, the work of the Field Development Division was terminated, and CED began to devote itself exclusively to research. Hoffman's remarks are from CED files, Paul Hoffman, "Trustees Meeting" (October 5, 1945) and "Minutes of Board Meeting" (February 12, 1946).

13. William Benton, "Statement of the Historical Background of the Committee for Economic Development" in CED files.

14. The "Economics of a Free Society" first appeared in *Fortune* (October 1944) and was republished in pamphlet form. CED issued two to four policy statements each year. Some of those issued in the 1940s included "Postwar Employment and the Settlement of Terminated War Contracts" (1943), "A Postwar Federal Tax Plan for High Employment" (1944); "International Trade, Foreign Investment: How to Make it More Effective" (1947), "Monetary and Fiscal Policy for Greater Economic Stability" (1948), and "The International Trade Organization and the Reconstruction of World Trade" (1949).

15. Herbert Stein, interview with the author, March 11, 1986.

16. On the Employment Act of 1946, see Stephen K. Bailey, *Congress Makes a Law: The Story Behind the Employment Act of 1946* (New York: Columbia University Press, 1950), which describes the legislative history of the act. The Council of Economic Advisers' first chairman tells the story of the act and the early years of the council in Edwin Nourse, *Economics in the Public Service* (New York: Harcourt, Brace & Co., 1953). On CEA from its creation to 1964, see Edward S. Flash, Jr., *Economic Advice and Presidential Leadership: The Council of Economic Advisers* (New York: Columbia University Press, 1965). For a more general interpretation of Keynesian economics and its implications for public policymaking in the United States and the United Kingdom, see Donald Winch, *Economics and Policy: A Historical Study* (New York: Walker & Co., 1969). For a broad view of economic policymaking, see Herbert Stein, *Presidential Economics: The Making of Policy from Roosevelt to Reagan and Beyond* (New York: Simon & Schuster, 1984).

17. Nourse, *Economics in the Public Service*, p. 7.

18. Ibid., p. 380.

19. Harry S Truman, *Year of Decisions* (Garden City, N.Y.: Doubleday & Co., 1955), p. 494.

20. As quoted in Flash, *Economic Advice and Presidential Leadership*, p. 25.

21. Quoted in Robert J. Donovan, *Conflict and Crisis: The Presidency of Harry S Truman, 1945–48* (New York: W. W. Norton & Co., 1977), p. 24.

22. Harry S Truman, *Years of Trial and Hope* (Garden City, N.Y.: Doubleday & Co., 1956), pp. 58–60.

23. On his early interest in the budget see Truman, *Year of Decisions.* pp. 146–7.

24. Truman, *Years of Trial and Hope,* p. 59.

25. On the RAND Corporation, from its founding to the early 1960s, see Bruce L. R. Smith, *The RAND Corporation: Case Study of a Nonprofit Advisory Corporation* (Cambridge, Mass.: Harvard University Press, 1966). Another account of RAND's founding and its role in the making of policy on national security is Fred Kaplan, *The Wizards of Armageddon* (New York: Simon & Schuster, 1983). An interesting early memoir is R. D. Specht, "RAND—A Personal View of Its History," *Journal of the Operations Research Society of America*, No. 8 (November–December, 1960), pp. 825–39. See also, *The RAND Corporation: The First Fifteen Years* (Santa Monica, Calif.: The RAND Corp., 1963).

26. The memo from General H. H. Arnold to Theodore von Karman, November 7, 1944, is reprinted in *Air Force Magazine* (August 1984), p. 71. Von Karman and his colleagues worked throughout 1945 producing a multivolume report entitled *Toward New Horizons*, which argued that there was need for a method of maintaining the "permanent interest of scientific workers in problems of the Air Forces." Passages from the report are quoted in Kaplan, *The Wizards of Armageddon*, p. 56.

27. Arnold is quoted in Kaplan, *The Wizards of Armageddon*, p. 58. Arnold moved with a sense of urgency, since he was clearly concerned about the problem of winning money from Congress after the war. "I am anxious that Air Force postwar and next war research and development programs be placed on a sound and continuing basis. In addition, I am desirous that these programs be in such form and contain such well-thought-out, long-range thinking that, in addition to guaranteeing the security of our nation and serving as a guide for the next ten- to twenty-year period, that the recommended programs can be used as a basis for adequate congressional appropriations." Memo from General H. H. Arnold to Theodore von Karman, cited in Kaplan, p. 71.

The Ford Foundation played a major role in assuring that the RAND Corporation would become an independent nonprofit organization by providing loan guarantees for the fledgling research organization. Documents on the negotiations that led to the loan and early grants are in the Ford Foundation Archives, New York.

28. RAND convened a conference of social scientists in New York in September 1947 (The proceedings were issued as RAND report, R-106 (Santa Monica, Calif.: RAND Corp., June 9, 1948). The phrase is from Warren Weaver's opening comments to the conference. It echoed throughout the sessions.

29. My account of RAND's contributions to systems analysis relies on Smith, *The RAND Corporation;* and Kaplan, *The Wizards of Armageddon,* as well as on interviews with current members of the RAND staff.

30. On the evolution of postwar strategic thinking, see Gregg Herken, *Counsels of War* (New York: Alfred A. Knopf, 1985).

31. Wohlstetter is quoted in Smith, *The RAND Corporation*, p. 200.

32. Quoted in Herken, *Counsels of War*, p. 92.

Six / Action Intellectuals

1. Quoted in James MacGregor Burns, *Leadership* (New York: Harper & Row, 1978), p. 394.

2. Porter McKeever, *Adlai Stevenson: His Life and Legacy* (New York: William Morrow & Co., 1989), pp. 315–16.

3. John Kenneth Galbraith, *A Life in Our Times: Memoirs* (Boston: Houghton Mifflin Co., 1981), pp. 355 and 357. Theodore Sorenson, with the help of Earl Latham of Amherst College, began to recruit an Academic Advisory Committee in late 1958. Among the members were Archibald Cox, Jerome Wiesner, Arthur Schlesinger, John Kenneth Galbraith, W. W. Rostow, Paul Nitze, Carl Kaysen, Paul Samuelson, Roger Hilsman, and James Tobin, all of whom served in the Kennedy administration. The group met rarely but supplied position papers and quick advice. Sorenson makes it clear that the intellectuals were a constituency to be cultivated. See Theodore C. Sorensen, *Kennedy* (New York: Harper & Row, 1965), pp. 117–18.

4. Henry R. Luce, ed., *The National Purpose* (New York: Holt, Rinehart, & Winston, 1960), p. 127.

5. Sorenson, *Kennedy*, pp. 254–56.

6. Ibid., p. 262. One of the most insightful studies of policymaking in the Kennedy White House is Roger Hilsman, *To Move A Nation: The Politics of Foreign Policy in the Administration of John F. Kennedy* (New York: Delta, 1968).

7. Ibid., p. 256.

8. Robert K. Merton, "Role of the Intellectual in Public Bureaucracy," in Merton, *Social Theory and Social Structure*, rev. ed. (New York: Free Press, 1957), p. 213.

9. On "consensus" history, see Bernard Sternsher, *Consensus, Conflict and American Historians* (Bloomington: Indiana University Press, 1975).

10. The end of ideology was first discussed by Edward Shils, "The End of Ideology," *Encounter* 5 (November 1955), pp. 52–58. See also, Daniel Bell, *The End of Ideology* (Glencoe, Ill.: Free Press, 1960).

11. Robert E. Lane, "The Decline of Politics and Ideology in a Knowledgeable Society," *American Sociological Review* 31 (1966), pp. 649–62; and Lane, "The Politics of Consensus in an Age of Affluence," *American Political Science Review* 59 (1965), pp. 874–95.

12. John F. Kennedy, "Commencement Address at Yale University," June 11, 1962, in *Public Papers of the Presidents of the United States: John F. Kennedy, 1962* (Washington, D.C.: U.S. Government Printing Office, 1963), pp. 470–75. Only a few weeks earlier, Kennedy had made similar observations in opening remarks to the White House Conference on National Economic Issues.

13. Kennedy's idealism is defined in an essay on presidential reputations by Arthur M. Schlesinger, Jr., a historian and member of the staff of the Kennedy White House: "Vicissitudes of Presidential Reputations," in Schlesinger, *The Cycles of American History* (Boston: Houghton Mifflin Co., 1986), pp. 372–418.

14. News accounts and editorials are in the following: *Washington Post*, November 20, 1960, and *Washington News*, November 17, 1960. Noting Kennedy's reliance on experts and the role of the Brookings Institution was an article "Experts on Tap," *The Economist*, December 2, 1961.

15. Laurin Henry, *Presidential Transitions* (Washington, D.C.: Brookings Institution, 1960). The memorandums on the presidential transition and correspondence with the staffs for both candidates are in "President's Files Relating to the 1960–61 Presidential Transition" in the Brookings Institution Archives, Washington, D.C.

16. In the early 1950s, the Rockefeller and Ford Foundations viewed the transition from Moulton to Calkins as an opportunity to revitalize a somnolent institution. Calkins was concerned when he accepted the job. "I was aware when I accepted the presidency of the Brookings Institution that its reputation for scholarly work of the highest order had suffered, especially among economists and political scientists, because of some of its publications, and because of the social views that were attributed to some few members of the staff." Letter from Robert Calkins to Thomas Carroll of the Ford Foundation (October 14, 1953), in the Rockefeller Archive Center, Pocantico Hills, New York, Rockefeller Foundation, Record Group 1.1, Series 200, Box 311, folder 3705.

17. For Calkins's views of Brookings's role, see an interview with him, "The Private Research Organization," *Challenge* (February 1964), pp. 18–21.

18. Ford Foundation Archives, Docket Excerpt (September 25, 1958).

19. Among the Brookings Institution's notable publications in economics in the late 1950s and early 1960s were Wilfrid Lewis, Jr., *Federal Fiscal Policy in the Postwar Recessions;* Richard Goode, *The Individual Income Tax;* John G. Gurley and Edward S. Shaw, *Money in a Theory of Finance;* Marshall Robinson, *The National Debt Ceiling;* Walter Salant and Beatrice Vaccara, *Import Liberalization and Employment;* J. M. Clark, *Competition as a Dynamic Process;* and Mark Massel, *Competition and Monopoly.* By the mid-1960s, some twenty studies of economics were being published annually.

20. The Government Studies program in the late 1950s and early 1960s produced such studies as Marver H. Bernstein, *The Job of the Federal Executive;* Charles L. Clapp, *The Congressman: His Work as He Sees It;* Franklin P. Kilpatrick, Milton C. Cummings, Jr., and M. Kent Jennings, *The Image of the Federal Service;* Paul David, Ralph Goldman, and Richard C. Bain, *The Politics of National Party Conventions;* and Harold Orlans, *Effects of Federal Programs on Higher Education.*

21. Foreign Policy Studies was the smallest of Brookings's programs and concentrated much of its research on developing countries and foreign assistance. Two of its many publications were John P. Lewis, *Quiet Crisis in India;* and Robert Asher, *Grants, Loans, and Local Currencies.*

22. On the RAND Corporation and the Kennedy administration, see Gregg Herken, *Counsels of War* (New York: Alfred A. Knopf, 1985).

23. On changes at the Defense Department, see William Kaufman, *The McNamara Strategy* (New York: Harper & Row, 1964).

24. Two classic studies of systems analysis and defense policy are Charles J. Hitch and Roland N. McKean, *The Economics of Defense in the Nuclear Age* (Cambridge, Mass.: Harvard University Press, 1960); and Alain Enthoven and C. Wayne Smith, *How Much is Enough?* (New York: Harper & Row, 1971). More critical is Ida Hoos, *Systems Analysis in Public Policy: A Critique* (Berkeley: University of California Press, 1972). The effect of analysis on defense policymaking is the subject of Peter deLeon, "The Influence of Analysis on U.S. Defense Policy," RAND Paper 7136 (Santa Monica, Calif.: The RAND Corp., August 1985).

25. *The RAND Corporation: The First Fifteen Years* (Santa Monica, Calif.: The RAND Corp., 1963), p. 14.

26. White is quoted in Fred Kaplan, *The Wizards of Armageddon* (New York: Simon & Schuster, 1983), pp. 255 and 257.

27. R. D. Specht, "RAND—A Personal View of Its History," *Journal of the Operations Research Society of America*, No. 8 (November–December, 1960), pp. 836–37.

28. Richard Goodwin, *Remembering America: A Voice from the Sixties* (Boston: Little, Brown & Co., 1988), p. 252. See also, Lyndon B. Johnson, "President's Inaugural Address," *Public Papers of the President, 1965* (Washington, D.C.: U.S. Government Printing Office, 1966), vol. 1, p. 71.

29. Goodwin, *Remembering America*, p. 284.

30. One of the general assessments of the Great Society was *The Great Society: Lessons for the Future*, ed. Eli Ginzberg and Robert Solow (New York: Basic Books, 1974), which was originally an issue of *The Public Interest*, whose pages often took specific Great Society programs to task. A more recent evaluation is *The Great Society and Its Legacy: Twenty Years of U.S. Social Policy*, ed. Marshall Kaplan and Peggy Cuciti (Durham, N.C.: Duke University Press, 1986). A favorable assessment of what the government sought to do in the 1960s is John E. Schwartz, *America's Hidden Success: A Reassessment of Twenty Years of Public Policy* (New York: W. W. Norton & Co., 1983). The argument that the government's social efforts were largely counterproductive is set out by Charles Murray, *Losing Ground: American Social Policy, 1950–80* (New York: Basic Books, 1984). The best appraisal of what social scientists contributed to the Great Society initiatives is Henry Aaron, *Politics and the Professors: The Great Society in Perspective* (Washington, D.C.: Brookings Institution, 1978). Aaron argues (p. 9) that "in many cases, the findings of social science seemed to come after, rather than before, changes in policy, which suggests that political events may influence scholars more than research influences policy."

31. Theodore H. White, "The Action Intellectuals," *Life* (June 9, 1967), pp. 43–58; the series continued on June 16, pp. 44–56, and June 23, pp. 76–78.

32. For an account of the rise and fall of planning-programming-budgeting systems, see Allen Schick, "A Death in the Bureaucracy: The Demise of Federal PPB," *Public Administration Review* 33 (March–April, pp. 146–56.

33. Johnson is quoted in Eric F. Goldman, *The Tragedy of Lyndon Johnson* (New York: Alfred A. Knopf, 1969), p. 157.

34. Ibid., p. 132.

35. Doris Kearns, *Lyndon Johnson and the American Dream* (New York: Harper & Row, 1976), p. 217.

36. Ibid., p. 132. Goldman, *The Tragedy of Lyndon Johnson*, p. 132, offers a general observation on how intellectuals influence policy: "Since the days of Theodore Roosevelt, and especially since the 1930s, intellectuals have performed brilliant services in devising and encouraging new programs. But they have done so mainly by writing seminal works and letting others do the implementing, or by functioning inside the government."

37. Jack Valenti, *A Very Human President* (New York: W. W. Norton & Co., 1975), p. 65.

Seven / At the Limits of Liberalism

1. An insightful account of the War on Poverty, which makes use of interviews and archival materials and supplements the insiders' accounts, is Nicholas Lemann,

"The Unfinished War," *Atlantic Monthly* (Part I, December, 1988 and Part II, January 1989); Heller is quoted in Part I, p. 39.

2. Daniel Patrick Moynihan, *Maximum Feasible Misunderstanding: Community Action in the War on Poverty* (New York: Free Press, 1969), pp. xii–xiii.

3. Peter Marris and Martin Rein, *Dilemmas of Social Reform: Poverty and Community Action in the United States* (New York: Atherton Press, 1969), p. 205.

4. Moynihan, *Maximum Feasible Misunderstanding*, pp. 188–89. Moynihan's conclusions about the shortcomings and uses of research during the 1960s are harsh: "We constantly underestimate difficulties, overpromise results, and avoid any evidence of incompatibility and conflict, thus repeatedly creating the conditions of failure out of a desperate desire for success. More than a weakness, in the conditions of the present time it has the potential of a fatal flaw. . . . this danger has been compounded by the increasing introduction into politics and government of ideas originating in the social sciences which promise to bring about social change through the manipulation of what might be termed the hidden processes of society" (pp. xii–xiii).

5. On the expansion of governmental research and evaluation, see Arnold J. Meltsner, *Policy Analysts in the Bureaucracy* (Berkeley: University of California Press, 1976); Laurence E. Lynn, ed., *Knowledge and Policy: The Uncertain Connection* (Washington, D.C.: National Academy of Sciences, 1978); Edward Banfield, "Policy Science as Metaphysical Madness" and the other essays in *Bureaucrats, Policy Analysts, Statesmen: Who Leads?* ed. Robert A. Goldwin (Washington, D.C.: American Enterprise Institute, 1980); *Problems in American Social Policy Research,* ed. Clark Abt (Cambridge, Mass.: Abt Books); and Peter de Leon, *Advice and Consent: The Development of the Policy Sciences* (New York: Russell Sage Foundation, 1988). The field of policy sciences is discussed in a series of articles under the general heading "Policy Analysis Explosion," in *Transaction: Social Science and Modern Society* (September–October, 1979), pp. 9–51. The expansive figure of $2 billion for social science research is from Abt, *Problems in American Social Policy Research,* p. 3.

6. Lyndon Johnson, "Government and the Critical Intelligence," an address by Lyndon B. Johnson, September 29, 1966 (Washington, D.C.: Brookings Institution, 1966), pp. 13–14.

7. Meltsner, *Policy Analysts in the Bureaucracy*, pp. 173–75. It is difficult to say precisely how many policy analysts are at work in government agencies. Meltsner concludes his search for a number saying simply, "There must be thousands of policy analysts" (p. 173).

8. Abt, *Problems in American Social Policy Research*, p. 4.

9. Henry Aaron, *Politics and the Professors: The Great Society in Perspective* (Washington, D.C.: Brookings Institution, 1978), p. 159, argues that "over the long haul R & E [research and experimentation] will be an intellectually conservative force in debates about public policy." He contends that policy analysts "can help raise the standards of admissible evidence; they can enrich and deepen understanding of complexity of problems and the unintended consequences of action."

10. The Urban Institute Archives, Washington, D.C., contain a rich set of materials on the circumstances that led to the founding of the institute. For example, a chronology and important early documents are contained in an unpublished volume: Grace Bassett, "The Urban Institute (A History of Its Organization)" (July 1969); a more recent unpublished essay by Randall Bovbjerg and Jill Shellow, members of

the institute's staff, is "A Brief History of the Urban Institute" (September 1983). An evaluation of the institute's first decade of operations was funded by the Ford Foundation; materials on the evaluation are in the archives of both the Urban Institute and the Ford Foundation; see Frederick O'R. Hayes, Anthony F. Japha, and Carl Kaysen, *The Urban Institute, 1968–78: An Evaluation of Its Performance, Prospects and Financial Problems* (1978). The Johnson speech, "America's Unfinished Business, Urban and Rural Poverty" (March 14, 1967), is in Lyndon B. Johnson, *Public Papers of the Presidents of the United States, 1967*, Book I (Washington, D.C.: U.S. Government Printing Office, 1968), pp. 331–46.

11. In preparing her history of the Urban Institute, Grace Bassett interviewed several of the principals involved, including Joseph Califano (1969). Transcripts are in the Urban Institute Archives (hereafter referred to as UIA).

12. Ibid. See also "Memorandum to the Board of Trustees from the Incorporators" (April 8, 1968), p. 6, in UIA. The Urban Institute, though modeled on the RAND Corporation, might have taken another form if Robert Wood had had his way. Wood thought that RAND was not an appropriate model: "It was a bad analogy because unlike the time when the defense studies and RAND began together, universities were already engaged, and you couldn't wish away this urban center or that center. It was bad because it missed the comparative. And it was bad because it didn't have the mix this has. It could rely essentially on one discipline— economics and cost-effective analysis. And the urban phenomenon, in my judgement, had to have a much broader base." The Urban Institute, in Wood's view, needed to be more closely linked with universities from whom it would not only benefit from multidisciplinary perspectives, but would find it easier to criticize governmental policies if the criticism came from truly independent university scholars, rather than researchers working directly under governmental contract. Grace Bassett, interview with Robert T. Wood (January 11, 1969) in UIA.

13. On the planning for the Urban Institute, the comments of Frederick Bohen are also illuminating; see Grace Bassett, interview with Frederick Bohen (December 18, 1968) in UIA. Some in the White House thought HEW funding for the Institute was inappropriate, given Gorham's connections there, and relations with HUD have been problematic under some secretaries. The Urban Institute's most difficult problem was that it was founded in the Johnson years and had to establish itself during the Nixon administration.

14. William Gorham, writing in *A Report, 1968–71* (Washington, D.C.: Urban Institute, 1972), p. 2.

15. Ibid., p. 3.

16. Kermit Gordon in *Annual Report, 1970* (Washington, D.C.: Brookings Institution, 1971).

17. The author has interviewed a number of Herman Kahn's former associates, among them Thomas Bell, William Brown, Carol Kahn, Robert Melnick, Neil Pickett, and Jimmy Wheeler.

18. Herman Kahn, *On Thermonuclear War* (Princeton, N.J.: Princeton University Press, 1960).

19. Herman Kahn, *Thinking about the Unthinkable* (New York: Horizon Press, 1962).

20. William Schneider, "Unforgettable Herman Kahn," *Reader's Digest* (July 1984), p. 82.

21. Among the books written by Hudson scholars during the 1960s were Herman

Kahn, *On Escalation, Metaphors and Scenarios* (New York: Praeger Press, 1965); Herman Kahn and Anthony J. Weiner, *The Year 2000: A Framework for Speculation about the Next Thirty-Three Years* (New York: Macmillan Co., 1967); Edmund Stillman and William Pfaff, *The Politics of Hysteria: The Source of Twentieth Century Conflict* (New York: Harper & Row, 1964); Stillman and Pfaff, *Power and Impotence: The Failure of America's Foreign Policy* (New York: Vintage Books, 1966); and Frank Armbruster et al., *Can We Win in Vietnam?* (New York: Praeger Press, 1968).

22. Herman Kahn, "Toward the Year 2000: Work in Progress," *Daedalus* 96 (Summer 1967), p. 938.

23. The various books on the future provide good summaries of Hudson's research, as well as insights into Kahn's methods and the reliance on such concepts as the "surprise-free" scenario and the Scotch verdict. See Herman Kahn, *Toward the Year 2000;* Kahn, William Brown, and Leon Martel, *The Next 200 Years* (New York: William Morrow & Co., 1976); and Kahn, *The Coming Boom: Economic, Political, and Social* (New York: Simon & Schuster, 1982).

24. David Halberstam, *The Best and the Brightest* (New York: Random House, 1972), p. 60. I spoke with Marcus Raskin and Robert Borosage about the history of the Institute for Policy Studies.

25. A sampler of books and articles by the Institute for Policy Studies was compiled on the occasion of its twentieth anniversary; see John S. Friedman, *First Harvest: The Institute for Policy Studies, 1963–83* (New York: Grove Press, 1983).

26. The attacks from the right amount to a full-scale effort to discredit IPS. IPS has been the subject of an "Institution Analysis" from the Heritage Foundation, May 1977, and of sharp attacks by Joshua Muravchik in "Think Tank of the Left," *New York Times Magazine* (April 26, 1981) and in "Communophilism and the Institute for Policy Studies, *World Affairs* (Winter 1984–85). IPS was even fictionalized in a novel: Arnaud de Borchgrave and Robert Moss *The Spike* (New York: Crown Publishers, 1980), which portrays IPS as a communist front organization.

27. Marcus Raskin, *Being and Doing* (Boston: Beacon Press, 1973), pp. xi and xviii.

28. Ibid., pp. 12, 134, and 236.

29. Ibid., p. xi.

30. Allen J. Matusow, *The Unraveling of America: A History of Liberalism in the 1960s* (New York: Harper & Row, 1984), p. 3.

Eight / The Ideological Divide

1. Theodore H. White, *The Making of the President, 1964* (New York: Atheneum Publishers, 1965) p. 88. On the political Right in postwar America, see David W. Reinhard, *The Republican Right since 1945* (Lexington: University of Kentucky Press, 1983).

2. White, *The Making of the President, 1964*, p. 208.

3. Barry Goldwater, *The Conscience of a Conservative* (Shepherdsville, Ky.: Victor Publishing, 1960).

4. The observations about Goldwater's supporters are by Paul Tellet, "National Conventions," *The National Election of 1964* ed. Milton C. Cummings (Washington, D.C.: Brookings Institution, 1966), pp. 18–19.

5. Richard Rovere, "Notes on the Establishment in America," *American Scholar* 30 (Autumn 1961), pp. 489–95, reprinted in Rovere, *The American Establishment* (New York: Harcourt, Brace & World, 1962), p. 3. Henry Fairlie, the British journalist, popularized the term in England in the mid-1950s, describing the circle of men who dominated the United Kingdom. In *The American Establishment*, p. 8, Rovere said: "The Establishment does not control everything but its influence is pervasive, and it succeeds far more often than its antagonists in fixing the major goals of American society."

6. M. Stanton Evans, *The Liberal Establishment* (New York: Devin-Adair, 1965), p. 18; and William F. Buckley, *Rumbles Right and Left* (New York: G. P. Putnam's Sons, 1963), p. 30.

7. My account of the postwar conservative revival relies heavily on the superb study by George H. Nash, *The Conservative Intellectual Movement in America: Since 1945* (New York: Basic Books, 1976). Two works by Friedrich A. Hayek are *The Road to Serfdom* and *Individualism and Economic Order* (Chicago: University of Chicago Press, 1944 and 1948, respectively).

8. Leo Strauss, *Natural Right and History* (Chicago: University of Chicago Press, 1953), p. 178.

9. Richard Weaver, *Ideas Have Consequences* (Chicago: University of Chicago Press, 1948), pp. 12, 58, and 1.

10. The book that helped many American conservatives situate themselves in an intellectual tradition was Russell Kirk, *The Conservative Mind: From Burke to Santayana* (Chicago: Regnery Press, 1953).

11. Louis Hartz, *The Liberal Tradition in America* (New York: Harcourt Brace Jovanovich, 1955). Clinton Rossiter, *Conservatism in America: The Thankless Persuasion*, 2nd ed. (New York: Alfred A. Knopf, 1964).

12. Hartz, *The Liberal Tradition in America*, p. 10.

13. Arthur M. Schlesinger, Jr., "Abstraction and Actuality," *The Nation* 164 (April 26, 1947), p. 489.

14. "Seeks Code for Management," *Business Week*, October 22, 1938, p. 22.

15. AEI has not yet organized an archive, although many boxes of materials are stored in its basement awaiting an archivist. The institution was experiencing considerable upheaval during the period I was engaged in research for this book, and the papers of William Baroody, Sr., then in the possession of his son, were not accessible. As a consequence, I had to rely on interviews, the most helpful of which, in recalling the history of AEI, were with W. Glenn Campbell, Thomas Johnson, Robert Pranger, and Herbert Stein.

16. Thomas Johnson, interview with the author, September 19, 1985.

17. A brief biography and eulogies are reprinted in *William J. Baroody* (Washington, D.C.: American Enterprise Institute, 1980).

18. The quotation is repeated in various annual reports during William Baroody's tenure at AEI. Baroody, Sr., had shrewdly realized that the support of traditionally liberal foundations might serve as a kind of imprimatur of AEI's growing intellectual respectability. He also seemed to understand that liberal foundations, such as the Ford Foundation, had been under political pressures in the late 1960s as a result of their own partisan and ideologically driven grant making and might be motivated to direct some of their resources to more conservative research institutions. Baroody's request for $5 million in general-support funds from the Ford Founda-

tion led to the foundation's review of the AEI program. The staff and the academic consultants hired by the foundation registered some surprise at the quality of the institute's work. The views of most scholars at AEI were conservative, but as one evaluator wrote, "AEI has been contributing to the discussions of important national problems with [a] clarifying and by no means superficial publications program." A staff member, noting that the board of directors, composed of some thirty business-men, met only once a year, concluded that the eleven-member academic advisory board under Paul McCracken wielded real control over the AEI program, perhaps having even greater influence than the seven-member professional staff, since much of the work was performed under contract by outside scholars. Although wary of AEI's origins as a business research group, the staff of the Ford Foundation concluded that AEI's work was generally balanced and met high academic standards.

The Ford Foundation was sufficiently impressed to make a three-year general-support grant of $300,000 in 1972. That grant was not as generous as the foundation's earlier support of Brookings, the National Bureau of Economic Research, and Re-sources for the Future, but that was a reflection of the financial constraints under which the Ford Foundation operated, more than an expression of its doubts about the potential usefulness of AEI's program. The grant, though small in terms of AEI's 1971 expenditures of $1.2 million, gave legitimacy to an institution that had depended primarily on corporations and corporate foundations, some with a decidedly conservative cast. With the Ford Foundation joining the Lilly Endowment, the Scaife Family Charitable Trust, and the William Donner Foundation, AEI could boast that its program had attained a badge of legitimacy. Years later, staff members at AEI still saw the Ford Foundation's grant as a turning point in AEI's history, an imprimatur of intellectual respectability and political balance.

The relevant documents are in the Ford Foundation Archives: No. 72–114, letter from William Baroody to Marshall Robinson, November 30, 1970; and letter from Robert Lane to Peter de Janosi, March 10, 1971. Additional details were provided by Marshall Robinson, interview with the author, June 2, 1986.

19. Robert Pranger, interview with the author, April 9, 1985.

20. On AEI's financial woes in the 1980s, see Alvin P. Sanoff, "Matters over Minds," *Regardies'* (January 1987), pp. 51–60; and John Seabrook, "Capital Gain," *Manhattan, Inc.* (March, 1987), pp. 71–79. The author's interviews with Christopher DeMuth, January 29, 1987, and Leslie Lenkowsky, March 10, 1986, also shed light on AEI's difficulties and prospects for renewal.

21. Irving Kristol, *Reflections of a Neoconservative: Looking Backward, Looking Ahead* (New York: Basic Books, 1983), p. 39.

22. Irving Kristol, "On Corporate Philanthropy," *Wall Street Journal*, March 21, 1977. Another observer has viewed the decades of the 1970s and 1980s in both the United States and the United Kingdom as "a period of unprecedented expansion of corporate political activities, whether through direct subvention of candidates, informed lobbying at the highest levels of government, or formal access to governmental decision-making processes through numerous business-dominated panels created to advise government agencies and ministries." See Michael Useem, *The Inner Circle: Large Corporations and the Rise of Business Political Activity in the United States and the United Kingdom* (New York: Oxford University Press, 1983), p. 4. See also, William Simon, *A Time for Truth* (New York: Berkley Books, 1980).

23. Kristol, *Reflections of a Neoconservative*, p. 212.

24. Simon expressed the view that conservatives were treated like "neanderthals" and wanted an organization that could locate and direct resources to sympathetic scholars. IEA's aim, as Simon put it, was to protect American values from "a self-conscious cultural establishment eager to condemn the principles, aspirations and loyalties of most Americans." Letter from William Simon to Leslie Lenkowsky on the occasion of IEA's tenth anniversary, reprinted in the *1988 Annual Report* of the Institute for Educational Affairs (Washington, D.C.: Institute for Educational Affairs, 1989).

25. Interviews with James Piereson and Leslie Lenkowsky helped me understand changes in grant-making policies in the conservative foundations.

26. Quoted in Peter H. Stone, "Conservative Brain Trust," *New York Times Magazine* (May 10, 1981).

27. The early history of the Hoover Institution is recounted in *The Library of the Hoover Institution on War, Revolution, and Peace*, ed. Peter Duignan (Stanford, Calif.: Hoover Institution Press, 1985). Over the years, the institution has published some four hundred volumes.

28. Herbert Hoover, Dedication Speech, June 20, 1941, in Hoover Institution files.

29. Hoover quoted in *Stanford Daily* (March 29, 1960).

30. Seymour Martin Lipset, interview with the author, February 6, 1986.

31. The Hoover Institution's *Annual Report—1981* celebrated Reagan's victory as a triumph for the institution. On the Hoover-Stanford controversy in 1983, see Tom Bethell, "Liberalism, Stanford-Style," *Commentary* 77 (January 1984), pp. 42–47.

Nine / The Marketplace of Ideas

1. On the meetings, see the accounts "Gorbachev's Primer on America," *Washington Post*, November 17, 1985 and "Gorbachev's Gloomy America," *New York Times*, November 15, 1985. Gorbachev's comment to O'Neill is quoted by the *Post*; the comment to Shultz is in the *Times*. Kirk O'Donnell accompanied O'Neill to Moscow and related the story in an interview with the author, June 2, 1987. Martin Anderson, interview with the author, February 6, 1986.

2. Martin Anderson, interview with the author, February 6, 1986.

3. The totals were tallied from annual reports and publications lists. It seemed appropriate to distinguish between book-length studies and either shorter reports or technical reports.

4. William Hammett, interview with the author, March 17, 1986.

5. Bruce Adams, "The Limitations of Muddling Through: Does Anyone in Washington Really Think Anymore?" *Public Administration Review* (November–December, 1979), pp. 545–52. The figure from the Obey Commission survey is cited by Adams.

6. Feulner is quoted in "Conservatives Aid Transition Plans Behind the Scenes," *New York Times*, December 5, 1980.

7. "The Heritage Report: Getting the Government Right with Reagan," *Washington Post*, November 16, 1987, summarized key points of the *Mandate for Leadership: Policy Management in a Conservative Administration* (Washington, D.C.: Heritage Foundation, 1980).

8. Quoted in *New York Times,* December 5, 1980.

9. The phrases are from Ira Allen, "What Do Conservatives Want?" UPI Wire Features, December 5, 1980, and Richard Brookhiser, *National Review* (February 6, 1981), p. 82.

10. Memorandum to Ed Feulner from Herb Berkowitz and Hugh Newton (November 12, 1980) and Public Relations Department Report (Fourth Quarter 1980) in Heritage Foundation files. Morton Kondracke, in "The Heritage Model," *The New Republic,* December 12, 1980, noted that "Heritage is astoundingly good at packaging and trumpeting conservative proposals in the media. Hardly a week goes by without some major newspaper or magazine publishing a story or an op-ed piece on a Heritage report." (p. 13)

11. Quoted in Bruce Oudes, ed., *From: The President—Richard Nixon's Secret Files* (New York: Harper & Row, 1989), p. 29.

12. Quoted in ibid., pp. 147–48.

13. Quoted in ibid., pp. 564–65.

14. Edwin Feulner, interview with the author, December 17, 1985. On other occasions, Weyrich and Feulner have said that watching Brookings's relationships with the executive branch triggered their idea for a conservative think tank.

15. On the Republican Study Committee, see Edwin Feulner, *Conservatives Stalk the House: The Republican Study Committee, 1970–82* (Ottawa, Ill.: Green Hill Publishers, 1983).

16. Quoted in ibid., p. 5.

17. Harrison W. Fox, Jr., and Susan Webb Hammond, *Congressional Staffs: The Invisible Force in American Lawmaking* (New York: Free Press, 1977); and Michael J. Malbin, *Unelected Representatives* (New York: Basic Books, 1980).

18. Edwin J. Feulner, Jr., interview with the author, December 17, 1985.

19. Ibid. See also, Feulner, "Ideas, Think Tanks and Government," speech (Summer 1985) in Heritage Foundation files.

20. Robert Huberty and Barbara D. Hohbach, eds., *The Annual Guide to Public Policy Experts, 1990* (Washington, D.C.: Heritage Foundation, 1990).

21. Herb Berkowitz, interview with the author, June 24, 1986.

22. Martin Anderson, interview with the author, February 6, 1986.

23. Milton Friedman, interview with the author, February 5, 1986.

24. The best article on AEI's financial difficulties is Alvin P. Sanoff, "Matters over Minds," *Regardies'* (January 1987), pp. 51–60. Some sense of the gap between ambitions and resources was gained in the author's interviews with William J. Baroody, Jr., on March 11, 1986, and Christopher DeMuth on January 29, 1987.

25. Burton Y. Pines, interview with the author, November 4, 1985.

26. On the new generation of conservatives and their careers in the conservative network, see Benjamin Hart, ed., *The Third Generation: Young Conservative Leaders Look to the Future* (Washington, D.C.: Heritage Foundation, 1987).

27. David M. Abshire, interview with the author, June 1, 1987. Abshire offers broad insights into the role of private research institutions in the shaping of foreign policy in "Twenty Years in the Strategic Labyrinth," *Washington Quarterly* (Winter 1982), pp. 83–105. The author's interviews with Amos Jordan, Walter Laqueur, Robert Neumann, Brad Roberts, Christa Dantzler, and John Yochelson were also helpful in understanding the role of CSIS.

28. On the eleven-member advisory board of the Center for Strategic Studies, as it was first called, were Robert Anderson, Eisenhower's secretary of the treasury; Rep. Gerald Ford (R–Mich.); Sen. Hugh Scott (R–Pa.); Sen. George Smathers (D–Fla.); Rep. Clement Zablocki (D–Wisc.); Neil McElroy, former secretary of defense; Alan Waterman, head of the National Science Foundation; two former chairmen of the Joint Chiefs of Staff; a former secretary of the navy; and a former undersecretary of the army. Its first executive board included both Glenn Campbell of the Hoover Institution and William Baroody, Sr., of AEI.

29. The tone is apparent in an early publication: David M. Abshire and Richard V. Allen, eds., *National Security: Political, Military, and Economic Strategies in the Decade Ahead* (New York: Frederick A. Praeger, 1963), pp. xii–xiii.

30. Among others who have noted the presence of the new foreign policy specialists and the way they have changed the discussion of policies are I. M. Destler, Leslie H. Gelb, and Anthony Lake, *Our Own Worst Enemy: The Unmaking of American Foreign Policy* (New York: Simon & Schuster, 1984).

31. The comment was volunteered in an interview with the author by a CSIS scholar who preferred to remain anonymous.

32. Robert Neumann, interview with the author, March 19, 1987.

Ten / The Politics of Ideas

1. My running tally of Washington research centers reached 102 by October 1989. This estimate is in line with those of Samantha L. Durst and James A. Thurber, "Studying Washington Think Tanks: In Search of Definitions and Data," paper prepared for the 1989 meeting of the American Political Science Association. A *National Journal* publication, *The Capital Source* (Washington, D.C.: *National Journal*, 1988), lists nearly 70 think tanks.

2. Lefever elaborated on his views in an interview with the author on March 10, 1986, and in a published interview, "Ernest Lefever, with no apologies," the *Washington Times*, May 30, 1984, as well as in a letter to the editor of the *Atlantic Monthly* (December 27, 1985), which he kindly shared with me. His views on morality and foreign policy during the early 1970s, when he was on the staff of Brookings are elaborated in "Moralism and U.S. Foreign Policy," *Orbis* 16 (Summer 1972), pp. 396–410.

3. Quoted in "Ernest Lefever, with no apologies."

4. Richard John Neuhaus, *The Naked Public Square: Religion and Democracy in America* (Grand Rapids, Mich.: Eerdmans Publishing Co., 1984).

5. John Howard related the origins of the Rockford Institute in an interview with the author on March 18, 1986. Allan Carlson's essays in *Persuasion at Work* and *The Family in America* define Rockford's policy agenda. See, for example, "Moral Rot in America?" *Persuasion at Work* 9 (June 1986).

6. Interviews with David Boaz and Edward H. Crane on December 18, 1985, introduced me to the work of the Cato Institute. Crane is quoted on bureaucracy in an interview with the *Washington Weekly*, September 17, 1984.

7. A useful compendium of libertarian ideas on policy is David Boaz and Edward H. Crane, eds., *Beyond the Status Quo: Policy Proposals for America* (Washington, D.C.: Cato Institute, 1985). On the limits of social science from the libertarian perspective, see James B. Ramsey, *Economic Forecasting—Models or Markets?*

(San Francisco: Cato Institute, 1980); and Murray N. Rothbard, *Individualism and the Philosophy of the Social Sciences* (San Francisco: Cato Institute, 1979).

8. Ralph Harris, "A Skeptical View of Forecasting in Britain," in Ramsey, *Economic Forecasting*, p. 86.

9. William S. Maddox and Stuart A. Lilie, *Beyond Liberal and Conservative: Reassessing the Political Spectrum* (Washington, D.C.: Cato Institute, 1985). David Boaz expressed similar views in the op-ed essay, "In '88, Who'll Win the Baby Boomers?" *New York Times*, November 7, 1985.

10. Robert Poole, who presides over the Reason Foundation, chronicled its evolution from a small magazine to a research organization in an interview with the author on January 31, 1986.

11. David Theroux, then president of the Pacific Institute and now head of the Independent Institute, offered his insights into those institutions in an interview with the author on February 5, 1986. Among the Pacific Institute's publications are Terry Anderson, ed., *Water Rights: Scarce Resource Allocation, Bureaucracy, and the Environment;* Don B. Kates, Jr., ed., *Firearms and Violence;* and Robert B. Everhart, ed., *The Public School Monopoly: A Critical Analysis of Education and the State in American Society.*

12. On the state think tanks, see W. John Moore, "Local Right Thinkers, *National Journal*, October 1, 1988, pp. 2455–59.

13. On the demise of the public intellectual and the rise of the cloistered academic, see Russell Jacoby, *The Last Intellectuals: American Culture in the Age of Academe* (New York: Basic Books, 1987). The quote by Lippmann and the observation about him are in Ronald Steel, *Walter Lippmann and the American Century* (Boston: Atlantic Monthly Press, 1980), pp. xvi.

14. Profiles of eight social scientists who might be termed "policy specialists" are in Bernard Barber, *Effective Social Science: Eight Cases in Economics, Political Science and Sociology* (New York: Russell Sage Foundation, 1987).

15. On one widely quoted think tank denizen, see, Steven Waldman, "The King of Quotes: Why the Press Is Addicted to Norman Ornstein," *The Washington Monthly* 18 (December 1986), pp. 33–40. On the growing specialization of the press corps, see Stephen Hess, "On the Rise of the Professional Specialist in Washington Journalism," Brookings General Series, Reprint 417 (Washington, D.C.: Brookings Institution, 1986).

16. "Economic Advisers Are Few in Beijing," *New York Times*, February 6, 1990.

17. On "knowledge creep," see Carol Weiss, ed., *Using Social Science in Public Policy Making* (Lexington, Mass.: D. C. Heath, 1977). A solid summary of the work on social science and policy advising is Peter deLeon, *Advice and Consent: The Development of the Policy Sciences* (New York: Russell Sage Foundation, 1988).

18. Henry A. Kissinger, *The White House Years* (New York: Little, Brown & Co., 1979), p. 39.

19. Henry A. Kissinger, *Years of Upheaval* (New York: Little, Brown & Co., 1982), p. 445.

20. Russell Baker, "Super No More," *New York Times*, February 7, 1990.

21. Robert Manoff quoted in "For Think Tanks, Lots to Rethink," *Los Angeles Times*, February 2, 1990.

22. L. Frank Baum, *The Wizard of Oz* (1900; reprint, New York: Macmillan Co., 1962), pp. 168 and 183.

23. Francis Fukuyama, "The End of History?" and "Responses to Fukuyama," *The National Interest* (Summer 1989) pp. 3–35.

24. "Z," "To the Stalin Mausoleum," *Daedalus* 119 (Winter 1990), pp. 295–344.

APPENDIX

Leading Think
Tanks

The following pages present brief accounts of the origins, finances, staff, and programs of thirty policy-research organizations. It would take several volumes to cover all the more than 1,000 American think tanks. This appendix is merely a sampler, designed to update the work of institutions treated in the narrative and to take note of others that have grown in importance during the past decade.

American Enterprise Institute for Public
Policy Research

The American Enterprise Association, founded as a business research group in 1943 and renamed the American Enterprise Institute (AEI) for Public Policy Research in 1960, has evolved into one of Washington's most prominent policy-research centers. Longtime president William Baroody, Sr., sought to build an institution that would counter the influence of the liberal intellectual establishment. He brought nationally known conservative economists into the institute's orbit in the 1950s and 1960s and built alliances with neoconservative intellectuals, such as Irving Kristol in the 1970s. Baroody proved skillful in marketing a program of conferences and seminars and built a varied publishing program. Although the organization fell on extremely hard financial times under his son and successor, it has rallied under its new president, Christopher C. DeMuth. AEI now operates with a budget of over $8 million, about half from corporations and one-third from foundations. It houses forty-seven resident scholars and research associates and embraces several dozen adjunct scholars situated elsewhere.

Still avowing its dedication "to preserving and improving the institutions of a free society," AEI describes itself as operating in "a company town where the virtues of government intervention are persistently exaggerated and the virtues of private enterprise are persistently depreciated." Its research program is organized in three broad areas: economic policy, directed by Marvin Kosters; foreign and defense policy, directed by Jeane J. Kirkpatrick; and social and political studies, directed by Michael Novak. Among the more significant contributions to the debate on economic policy in recent years have been Senior Fellow Herbert Stein's books on fiscal policy, AEI's program on the regulation of financial markets, works on health care financing, and studies of U.S. trade policy and economic competitiveness. AEI's foreign policy program, which houses former Reagan administration officials, such as Constantine Menges and Richard Perle, has recently yielded books of speeches and essays by Kirkpatrick and Novak, works on Latin America by Mark Falcoff and Joshua Muravchik, and a study of foreign aid by Nicholas Eberstadt. The scholars in AEI's Social and Political Studies group include Novak, Robert Bork, Norman Ornstein, William Schneider, and Ben Wattenberg. Their research and writing have focused on the electoral process, Congress, constitutional issues, and religious and philosophical values.

AEI publishes forty to fifty books each year and disseminates hundreds of articles and op-ed essays. Its periodicals have included *The AEI Economist, Regulation,* and *Public Opinion,* all of which were replaced in 1990 by a new bimonthly on issues of domestic and international policy. *The American Enterprise.* AEI is located at 1150 Seventeenth Street, NW, Washington, DC 20036.

Brookings Institution

The Brookings Institution is the oldest Washington-based policy center, tracing its beginnings to the Institute for Government Research, which was founded in 1916 by proponents of reform of the federal budget process and greater governmental efficiency. Named for a St. Louis businessman, Robert S. Brookings, the institution took full shape in 1927 when the Institute for Government Research merged with two other organizations in which Mr. Brookings was involved, the Institute of Economics and the Brookings Graduate School of Economics and Government. Over the years the Brookings Institution's research program has evolved in tandem with American social science and graduate education.

With an annual budget of $16 to $17 million and an endowment of roughly $100 million, the Brookings Institution is one of the most stable policy research centers. Income from endowment provides more than one-quarter of its income, sales of publications and conference fees supply nearly one-third, and private grants and gifts make up most of the remainder. With forty to fifty full-time senior members on the research staff (augmented by visiting scholars and research assistants), the institution's program is organized into three research divisions: Economic Studies, Foreign Policy Studies, and Governmental Studies. There is also an educational division, the Center for Public Policy Education, which holds conferences and seminars for governmental officials and business leaders.

The program of economic research, headed by Charles L. Schultze, has been notable over several decades for its analyses of the federal budget and studies of economic growth and productivity. The institution has recently created the Center for Economic Progress and Employment to study the problems of stagnating productivity and living standards. It has also begun to explore the interaction of the world's economies and the problems of coordinating macroeconomic policies. Brookings has devoted attention to the methods of analyzing public policies; continues to scrutinize discrete policies and programs with work in transportation, health, and education; and plans to renew an emphasis on social policy.

The Foreign Policy Studies program, headed by John Steinbruner, has focused on defense budgets, the command and control of nuclear weaponry; conventional military forces, Soviet affairs, international economic issues, and regional studies (primarily in the Middle East and Asia). In recent years, its regional work has expanded to include Africa and Latin America.

The Governmental Studies program, directed by Thomas Mann, has focused on the political institutions and processes of government. It has long been concerned with the nature of the civil service and the way in which the nation selects its political leaders, as well as with relations among the three branches of government. The program has also studied the politics of policymaking in various fields, ranging from social security to free trade. New emphases on social policy and comparative politics are now evident.

Bruce MacLaury has been president of Brookings since 1977. The Brookings Institution is located at 1775 Massachusetts Avenue, NW, Washington, DC 20036.

Carnegie Endowment for International Peace

The Carnegie Endowment for International Peace was set up in 1910 with a $10 million gift from Andrew Carnegie. Its lofty aim was to hasten the abolition of war, a goal its founders believed was within reach as they pushed for a framework of international arbitration. Early trustees, such as Elihu Root and Nicholas Murray Butler, promoted research on international law and the economic causes of war, including a 152-volume economic and social history of World War I.

Like several other research institutions founded early in the twentieth century, the Carnegie Endowment is an operating foundation, using its approximately $85 million endowment to support its own program of research and education. Since 1970 it has published the quarterly journal *Foreign Policy*. Study groups and roundtable discussions bring together current and former governmental officials to talk about U.S.–European relations, East-West relations, the proliferation of arms, U.S.–Latin American relations, U.S.–Asian relations and immigration policy. With some twenty resident and senior associates drawn from diverse professional backgrounds, including journalism, public service, and academia, the endowment's research program is as eclectic as the associates' individual interests. Among the endowment's scholars, Geoffrey Kemp is at work on the control and proliferation of arms in the Near East and south Asia; Selig Harrison is studying south and east Asia; Gillian Gunn is exploring Cuban foreign policy; David K. Shipler is examining world-wide democratization and U.S. foreign policy; and Dimitri K. Simes is studying Soviet foreign policy. The Carnegie Endowment for International Peace has offices at 2400 N Street, NW, Washington, DC 20037.

Cato Institute

Founded in 1977 by activists involved in California's Libertarian party, the Cato Institute has since moved to Washington, D.C., and built a sizable research, publishing, and media-outreach program.

Taking its name from *Cato's Letters*, a series of eighteenth-century pamphlets widely read in the American colonies, the institute characterizes its purpose as "broadening the parameters of policy debate to allow consideration of more options that are consistent with the traditional American principles of individual liberty, limited government, and peace." With a budget of about $2.5 million, it publishes approximately ten books and fifteen to twenty policy analyses each year, the thrice-yearly *Cato Journal,* a series of Cato Policy Reports, and hundreds of op-ed articles and radio commentaries. Its conferences and forums, now international in reach, are a sign of the worldwide resurgence of classical liberal ideas. Recent books have explored the theory of market failure, contributed to the literature on public choice, examined Reaganomics, offered a theoretical critique of central banks, advanced proposals for privatizing the postal service, and criticized fees for oil imports and comparable-worth proposals.

Cato's staff of twenty-five is headed by Edward H. Crane, president since its founding, and William A. Niskanen, chairman since 1985 and a former member of Ronald Reagan's Council of Economic Advisers. In its Washington office, the institute houses a handful of researchers and writers, including David Boaz, who has edited a number of Cato's publications; Peter J. Ferrara, who directs the institute's Center for Entitlement Alternatives; and Roger Pilon, who directs the Center for Constitutional Studies. Much of the institute's research and publishing is carried out by a network of fifty to sixty adjunct scholars who work at other research institutes and universities. The Cato Institute is located at 224 Second Street, SE, Washington, DC 20003.

Center on Budget and Policy Priorities

The Center on Budget and Policy Priorities was established in 1981 by Robert Greenstein, a former director of the Agriculture Department's Food and Nutrition Service, which handles the Food Stamp and child nutrition programs. The center took shape after Greenstein, with financial support from the Field Foundation, began to analyze the impact of the Reagan administration's budget cuts on food programs. With support from major foundations, it has now grown into an organization with a staff of twenty-three (twelve of whom are researchers) and a budget of $1.4 million.

The center's analytic work, still grounded in dollars and numbers, assesses programs and policies that affect low- and moderate-income households; its defense-budget project, under Gordon Adams, has grown into an autonomous research operation. Areas of particular focus include continuing research series on how state tax policies affect low-income people, the problem of affordable housing, and poverty in rural America. The center embarked on a three-year public educational project in 1989 to increase awareness and use of the earned-income credit among those who are eligible. Its offices are at 236 Massachusetts Avenue, NE, Suite 305, Washington, DC 20002.

Center for Defense Information

In operation since 1972, the Center for Defense Information (CDI), under the direction of retired Rear Admiral Gene R. La Rocque of the U.S. Navy, has analyzed defense policy and made its reports widely available to journalists and the public and, on request, to governmental officials. Often at odds with proponents of the defense buildup of the 1980s, the CDI explains that it "opposes excessive expenditures for weapons and policies that increase the danger of nuclear war. CDI believes that strong social, economic, political, and military components contribute equally to the nation's security." With the dramatic transformation of East-West relations now signaling the end of the Cold War, the CDI has argued that a defense budget of about $200 billion (roughly $100 billion less than the current spending level) would provide for an adequate national defense.

The center's staff of two dozen includes both former military officers and civilian researchers. Its principal publication is an eight-page pamphlet, *The Defense Monitor*, which has addressed the means of stopping nuclear weapons testing, criticized facilities for producing chemical and nuclear weapons, examined new military technologies, and criticized procedures for acquiring and producing weapons. The CDI also seeks to reach a wide constituency with its weekly television series, "America's Defense Monitor." The CDI is located at 1500 Massachusetts Avenue, NW, Washington, DC 20005.

Center for National Policy

The Center for National Policy (CNP) was organized in 1981 by a group of Democratic party stalwarts. Chaired by Edmund Muskie, the board includes many centrist Democrats. It characterizes itself as "progressive-pragmatist" and works to identify effective policy measures, rather than to expound on political values or to support social science research. Without a resident research staff, but drawing on such scholars as Lester Thurow, Stanley Hoffmann, and Otto Eckstein, the center has served primarily as a convening body. It sponsors off-the-record policy seminars, public symposia, and long-term studies that bring together scholars, leaders in the private sector, and public officials.

Many of its publications—generally thirty- to sixty-page pamphlets—are either essays prepared for conferences or the results of CNP's study projects. Over the years, the center has issued reports on debts in the farm sector, food and agriculture policy, health care, the country's economic competitiveness, tax policy, work and welfare, outer space, and children at risk. The CNP operates with an annual budget of about $800,000. It is located at 317 Massacusetts Avenue, NE, Washington, DC 20002.

Center for Strategic and International Studies

The Center for Strategic and International Studies (CSIS) describes its mission as "providing a strategic perspective to decision makers that is integrative in nature, international in scope, anticipatory in its timing, and bipartisan in approach." Established in 1962 and loosely affiliated with Georgetown University until the ties were severed in 1987, it has grown from a tiny research secretariat into an institution with 50 senior researchers among its 147-member staff and a complex network of adjunct scholars, senior associates, and councilors. The annual operating budget of the CSIS is roughly $10 million, the bulk of it raised from corporations (35 percent), private foundations (40 percent), and individuals (10 percent). It has built a small endowment of about $9 million, which provides less than 5 percent of its operating budget.

The center publishes *The Washington Quarterly*, a series on emerging policy issues called *Washington Papers*, monographs in a Significant Issues Series, and CSIS Panel Reports. Books by CSIS scholars are generally copublished with commercial and university presses. Publication sales and royalties account for only about 1 percent of the center's revenues. Over the years, CSIS has devoted more attention to conferences and seminars than to publishing efforts, using its convening power to bridge Washington's fragmented policy community. Although its staff includes such prolific scholars as Edward N. Luttwak, Walter Laqueur, and Georges A. Fauriol, many of its fellows have spent their careers as policy practitioners, "in and outers," advisers and consultants to policymakers. Consequently, its research agenda is shaped by a practical sensibility and a desire to engage policymakers in its various working groups, simulations of crises, conferences, and seminars.

Eleven research groups are at work at CSIS. From a strategic perspective, its program looks at what it terms "functional" matters, such as arms control and technology, international business, energy and environmental issues, international communications, and political-military issues. It also examines particular regions, with specialists focusing on Africa, east Asia, Europe, Latin America, the Middle East, and the Soviet Union. CSIS is located at 1800 K Street, NW, Suite 400, Washington, DC 20006.

Committee for Economic Development

Founded in 1942 by businessmen concerned about the transition from a war-production economy to a peacetime economy, the Committee for Economic Development (CED) continues to serve as a vehicle for business executives to meet with policy researchers and to frame approaches to some of the leading issues of the day. According to its leaders, CED "operates from the belief that the private sector should involve itself as early as possible in the development of ideas that will eventually shape public policy." Early in its history, CED focused on problems of economic growth and stability, helping the business community to accommodate itself to New Deal initiatives and the then-novel Keynesian approaches to demand management.

CED's current research interests are focused on strategies to cut the federal deficit and to encourage productive investment, to respond to the changing demographics of the job market, to reform the educational system, to rethink trade policy, and to reform the costly liability arrangements in the U.S. system. With a small staff of about two dozen and a distinguished research advisory board, CED typically commissions research papers from academic researchers, publishing them as background papers. Its two hundred trustees, working through subcommittees, meet to discuss policy problems with experts and then issue reports containing the committee's recommendations for policies. Only the trustees have a final say in its recommendations. Recent reports have dealt with the involvement of businesses in the schools, deficit reduction and tax policy, the reform of the health care system, economic development at the state level, the tort liability system, and alternative ways to resolve disputes.

CED's revenues and expenses are about $4 million per year. In 1988 some 1,300 companies contributed $3.3 million, and private foundations accounted for about $370,000. CED's offices are at 477 Madison Avenue, New York, NY 10022, and 1700 K Street, NW, Washington, DC 20006.

Economic Policy Institute

The Economic Policy Institute (EPI) was founded in 1986 by Jeffrey Faux, its president, and five other economists and policy thinkers, who still serve on its board: Lester Thurow, Ray Marshall, Robert Reich, Barry Bluestone, and Robert Kuttner. The founders thought that the national policy debate had shifted to the right and thus wanted to create an institution that could support a more activist government. They explicitly patterned the institute's program on the media-outreach and publishing strategies of the conservative organizations that had been so successful in the 1970s.

Relying on initial funding from a coalition of labor unions (the American Federation of State, County and Municipal Employees; the United Automobile, Aerospace & Agricultural Implement Workers of America; the United Steelworkers of America, the United Mine Workers of America; Service Employees International Union; and United Food and Commercial Workers International Union), EPI's budget is about $1 million, 40 percent of which is now drawn from unions and 40 percent from foundations. Its research papers, largely commissioned from scholars elsewhere, have dealt with living standards, the labor market, unions, trade policy and economic competitiveness, and the role of government in economic and social life. EPI's studies have looked skeptically at various privatization schemes, warned about the expansion of low-wage jobs in the service sector, discussed managed trade and the impact of trade deficits on jobs, and argued for more progressive tax structures. EPI is located at 1730 Rhode Island Avenue, NW, Suite 812, Washington, DC 20036.

Ethics and Public Policy Center

Ernest W. Lefever, a graduate of Yale Divinity School who had worked in the Foreign Policy Studies program at Brookings, founded the Ethics and Public Policy Center (EPPC) in 1976. Under

Lefever the center grew into an organization with a $1.2 million budget drawn from foundations, corporations, and 600 individual donors. After thirteen years as its president, he turned the leadership over to George Weigel, former president of the James Madison Foundation, in 1989. EPPC describes itself as an organization that "examines foreign and domestic issues in the light of enduring Western values."

Seminars and conferences, as well as research and publishing, in recent years have focused on religious conditions in the Soviet Union and Eastern Europe, ethics, war and peace, cultural politics, the abortion debate, human rights in the People's Republic of China, and Catholic social thought. Publishing five books in 1989, EPPC characterized its works in these words: "In reaffirming the necessary bond between basic Western values and public policy choices, the Center publishes studies that combine empirical analysis and moral reasoning." EPPC is located at 1030 Fifteenth Street, NW, Washington, DC 20005.

Heritage Foundation

Founded in 1973 by a group of conservative legislative aides, the Heritage Foundation has become the flagship of the conservative intellectual movement, with a staff of 135. Though its origins can be traced to the "New Right," it has brought together traditionalist conservatives, classical liberals, and neoconservatives in an operation with an annual budget of nearly $18 million. Its financial resources come from individual donors (43 percent), foundations (25 percent), corporations (13 percent), endowment income (13 percent), and sales of publications (6 percent).

Its international research program is organized into the Department of Foreign Policy and Defense Studies, the Institute of Hemispheric Development, and the United Nations Assessment Project, all directed by Kim Holmes. Its Asian Studies Center is headed by Roger Brooks, and its Department of Domestic Policy Studies, along with the Roe Institute for Economic Policy Studies and its Center for International Economic Growth, are headed by Stuart Butler. Research is also under way in the Congress Assessment Project and the New Majority Project. Members of the foundation's research staff produce well over 200 publications each year, ranging from one-page executive memorandums and twelve-page Backgrounders and Issues Bulletins to monographs and full-length books. The publishing program also includes a journal, *Policy Review*, with a paid circulation of over 15,000, and the *Annual Guide to Public Policy Experts*, which lists nearly 1,500 conservative experts in various substantive fields.

The foundation has been especially successful in winning attention from the mass media for its publications and policy proposals, devoting slightly over one-third of its budget to marketing; its efforts include a features syndicate and a speakers bureau. It has also devoted attention to cultivating a new generation of conservative leaders through its Third Generation program and courses in its Conservative Curriculum; the foundation brings conservative scholars to Washington in its Bradley Fellows program, while its Resource Bank maintains links with hundreds of research institutions and scholars, attempting to bring them more directly into the Washington policy process. The Heritage Foundation is located at 214 Massachusetts Avenue, NE, Washington, DC 20002.

Hoover Institution on War, Revolution, and Peace

The Hoover Institution, located on the Stanford University campus, is formally independent but within the university's framework of governance. It was established in 1919 with a gift from Herbert Hoover as the Hoover War Library—a library and archival collection of primary source materials on World War I and the postwar relief programs. It now houses some 1.6 million volumes and 4,000 archival collections on war, revolution, and social change in the twentieth century. Its collections on the Russian and Chinese revolutions are unrivaled.

Between 1960 and 1989, under the direction of W. Glenn Campbell, the institution evolved from an underfunded library with a modest publishing program to one of the nation's best known and, on occasion, controversy-ridden policy research centers. The institution has some 120 resident and visiting scholars as well as a professional library and archival staff. Hoover's most prominent research fellows have included Robert Conquest, Milton Friedman, Sidney Hook, Seymour Martin Lipset, Thomas Sowell, George Stigler, Edward Teller, and Bertram Wolfe. Its budget of about $17 million is drawn from university allocations, an endowment of over $125 million, and foundation and corporate support.

Research at Hoover proceeds in three broadly defined areas:

international studies, domestic studies, and national security affairs. The most prescriptive of the institution's policy publications are the occasional compendiums of essays, such as *The U.S. in the 1980s* (1980) and the more recent *Thinking about America: The United States in the 1990s* (1988). In the field of economics, Hoover scholars have written on tax policy and welfare and on international economics, typically taking a classical liberal view of the role of markets. The Hoover Institution has published collections of essays by such defenders of the market as Milton Friedman and Friedrich Hayek.

Much of the institution's research and publishing program is still grounded in the archival collection. Its scholars produce bibliographies, archival guides, and collections of primary source. The institution has published historical works on communist parties, communist regimes, and revolutionary activity around the world. It has published the *Yearbook on International Communist Affairs* annually since 1966. A recent series has yielded studies of the various nationalities in the Soviet Union, including books on Estonians, Georgians, Kazakhs, and Tatars.

Following Campbell's retirement as director, the Hoover Institution's leadership was in transition in 1989. It is located at Stanford University, Stanford, CA 94305.

Hudson Institute

Herman Kahn, along with colleagues from the RAND Corporation, founded the Hudson Institute in Westchester County, New York, in 1961. After Kahn's death, the institute moved to Indianapolis in 1984. Calling the institute "a lobby for the future," Kahn and his colleagues engaged in speculative studies of the future, as well as studies of defense, international politics, energy, and education. The institute now describes its viewpoint as one that "embodies skepticism about conventional wisdom, optimism about solving problems, a steadfast commitment to free institutions and individual responsibility, and a realistic view of various threats to national security."

The Hudson Institute has a senior research staff of eighteen, not all residing in Indianapolis. Contracts with the Departments of Labor, Defense, State, and Commerce, as well as the U.S. Navy, have supported recent projects; funding from foundations, especially the Lilly Endowment, helped the institute through the move and difficult intellectual transition after Kahn's death, although it has had a rapid succession of presidents in the past several years. The research program engages in research through its Center for Soviet and Central European Studies, Center for Global Food Issues, Center for Education and Employment Policy, and the National Securities Study Group; it also manages the Center for Naval Analyses in Virginia. In 1990 the institute opened a Washington-based affiliate, the American Immigration Institute, which studies and promotes all forms of legal immigration to the United States.

Among Hudson's most noteworthy current endeavors is "Project Hungary," which is designed to help that nation with its transition to a market economy. Recent books and reports have included *Workforce 2000*, a study of demographic trends, technical skills, and the future American work force; *Winning the Brain Race*, a prescription for reforming public schools; *The Information Age and Soviet Society*, a look at Soviet computer technology; *Transportation for the Next Century*, an assessment of future transportation needs; and *The Catastrophe Ahead: Aids and the Case for a New Public Policy*. Under new president Leslie Lenkowsky, the Hudson Institute operates out of the Herman Kahn Center, PO Box 26–919, Indianapolis, IN 46226.

Institute for Contemporary Studies

San Francisco's Institute for Contemporary Studies (ICS) was founded in 1972 during the last months of Ronald Reagan's term as governor of California. Among the principal organizers were Edwin Meese; Caspar Weinberger; and H. Monroe Browne, who became its first president. It was able to provide the prospective presidential candidate with research for his impending campaign. As it evolved from the early 1970s to the mid-1980s, it turned into a small publishing operation, with a staff of about a dozen, an expanding network of scholars, and a budget of roughly $1 million. It became more academic enterprise than its earliest supporters had envisioned; its books were often designed to be used in college classrooms.

In 1986, under the new chairmanship of Donald Rumsfeld and the presidency of Robert Hawkins, ICS embarked on a much-expanded effort. It now has two affiliates, the International Center for Economic Growth and the Sequoia Institute. The former is at the center of a worldwide network of institutes that are concerned with market-oriented economic policies, while the latter pursues complementary work on social and economic development in the Third World. ICS operates with a staff of about twenty-five and a budget of around $3 million.

Recent research emanating from ICS and its related institutions includes a study by Peter G. Peterson and Neil Howe of the growth of entitlement programs and their stifling effect on the economy and a book by Arch Puddington on methods of coercion in Communist regimes. ICS has also produced an overview of local governments in the United States and edited volumes on international regulations and the future of the Soviet empire. The International Center for Economic Growth has produced case studies of growth in Pakistan, India, and Bolivia; a volume on privatization and development; studies of tax reform throughout the world; and an assessment of institutional relationships between the state and market in developing countries. ICS is located at 243 Kearny Street, San Francisco, CA 94108.

Institute for International Economics

The Institute for International Economics (IIE) was founded in 1981 by C. Fred Bergsten, a former scholar at the Brookings Institution and an official of the Treasury Department in the Carter administration. Bergsten initially drew on resources from the German Marshall Fund, which committed $4 million over five years to the new enterprise, whose budget now exceeds $2 million. He assembled a team of experienced former officials and seasoned scholars, including William R. Cline, I. M. Destler, Gary Hufbauer, Stephen Marris, and John Williamson. Focusing on the problems of trade, money and finance, and debt and development, IIE has proved to be one of the most successful new research operations to emerge in the 1980s.

Recent book-length studies have examined policymaking in the United States with regard to the exchange rate, economic adjustment as the United States reduces its trade deficit, direct investments by foreign businesses in the United States, Japan in the world economy, the flight of capital and debt in the Third World. In addition to its books, IIE has published a number of briefer policy analyses and special reports. IIE is located at 11 Dupont Circle, NW, Washington, DC 20036.

Institute for Policy Studies

Marcus Raskin and Richard Barnet left governmental posts in 1963 to form the Institute for Policy Studies (IPS). They were critical of both American foreign policy and the social science research institutions that sustained those policies. Since its inception, IPS has sought to link citizens' movements and scholarship, holding to a Deweyan conviction that ideas are tested in action. Its associates have been scholar-activists and artists, filmmakers, and creative writers, including Saul Landau, John Berger, Roger Wilkins, and Barbara Ehrenreich. The work of IPS's "public scholars," as they are termed, includes writing, producing films and videotapes, and teaching in adult educational programs carried out through the Washington School. IPS is affiliated with the Transnational Institute in Amsterdam.

Recent books by IPS fellows include Barbara Ehrenreich's *Fear of Falling*, an exploration of the ambitions and anxieties of the middle class; Richard Barnet's *The Rockets' Red Glare*, which examines popular opinion and presidential war making; and Fred Halliday's *From Kabul to Managua*, which traces the shift from Cold War confrontation to negotiation. In 1989, under its new director Diana de Vegh, IPS reorganized its program into three working groups: World Economic Integration, the State of Democracy, and Post–Cold War Planning for a New Foreign Policy. IPS is located at 1601 Connecticut Avenue, NW, Washington, DC 20009.

Joint Center for Political and Economic Studies

The Joint Center for Political and Economic Studies was founded in 1970 by an emerging group of black intellectuals, politicians, and professionals who felt the need for a new research institution to deal with the issues that most affect black Americans. This new cadre of black leaders obtained financial backing from the Ford Foundation and opened their institute under the auspices of Howard University and the Metropolitan Applied Research Center, directed by Kenneth Clark. During its first two years, the center was presided over by Frank Reeves, and for the past eighteen years, its director has been Eddie N. Williams. Today, the objectives of its program of research and dissemination are still, in the center's words, "to improve the socioeconomic status of black Americans; to increase their influence in the political and public policy arenas; and to facilitate the building of coalitions across racial lines."

Early on the center sponsored training and technical assistance programs for black elected officials; it also produced a roster of black elected officials; a quadrennial *Guide to Black Politics;* reports on political techniques and management for black officials; and a magazine, *Focus,* aimed at black political leaders. In the early 1980s, without abandoning its commitment to serving elected officials, the center began to transform itself into an institution for research on public policy, one that would incorporate economic issues into its program of political research.

With a staff of approximately fifty and a budget approaching $3.5 million, the center's work includes research on economic policy, political participation, and international affairs. Recently, the center has explored ways to overcome the undercounting of minorities in the U.S. census; analyzed election results and attitudes of the electorate; and worked on urban poverty, educational achievement, and minority businesses; its international affairs program administers grants in African countries, focusing on human rights. In addition to publishing a half dozen books each year, the center has also recently produced well-regarded radio and television programs. The Joint Center for Political and Economic Studies is located at 1301 Pennsylvania Avenue, NW, Suite 400, Washington, DC 20004.

Manhattan Institute for Policy Research

Known as the International Center for Economic Policy Studies when it was founded by William Casey in 1978, the Manhattan Institute for Policy Research (as it was renamed in 1981) has provided an intellectual home for a number of prominent writers on policy issues. Over the past decade it has also created a lively Manhattan-based forum for the discussion of market-oriented policy proposals. While supporting a highly visible program of lectures and conferences, the core of its research effort lies in the Manhattan Institute Fellows program. Its authors have included George Gilder, onetime program director of the institute and author of the popular supply-side treatise, *Wealth and Poverty,* and Charles Murray, who completed *Losing Ground* under the institute's auspices. Others who have been designated institute fellows have included James Ring Adams, Roberta Karmel, Alvin Rabushka, Peter Salins, Thomas Sowell, and Walter Williams. Among the most recent institute studies are Peter Huber's *Liability* and Lawrence Lindsey's *The Growth Experiment: How the New Tax Policy Is Transforming the U.S. Economy.*

Under the presidency of William M. H. Hammett, the institute has grown from a tiny organization with a budget of under $500,000 to an operation with over $2 million in annual income. Corporations supply about one-third of its funds, foundations about two-fifths,

and individual contributors about one-quarter. Apart from the fellow-
ship program, the institute has in recent years established a Center
for New York Policy Studies, a Center for Educational Innovation,
and a Judicial Studies Program. The Manhattan Institute for Policy
Research is located at Lehrman House, 42 East Seventy-first Street,
New York, NY 10022.

Overseas Development Council

The Overseas Development Council (ODC) was established in
1969 to increase American understanding of the problems confronting
developing countries. Its program of research and public forums is
supported by some of the nation's largest foundations, corporations,
and international development banks. Focusing on both economic
and political issues that shape relations between the United States
and Third World countries, ODC describes is central objective as
helping to "establish a new agenda of development cooperation policies that take full account of both longer-term U.S. interests in the
Third World and the need to work with developing countries to
end the absolute poverty still afflicting millions of people around
the globe."

The council's analyses of policies, undertaken by staff members,
visiting fellows, and commissioned scholars, deal with international
trade and industrial policy, international finance and investment,
strategies for and assistance with development, and U.S. foreign
policy toward developing countries.

ODC's publications include the biannual *Agenda,* a series of
background briefing papers in the "Policy Focus" series, and a newly
initiated series of policy books that have recently included studies
of the environment and poverty in developing countries; the politics
of economic adjustment; the future of the International Monetary
Fund; and U.S. foreign policy and economic reform in the Soviet
Union, China, and India. ODC also convenes a variety of meetings
for policymakers and academic specialists, including the Congressional
Staff Forum on Third World issues. ODC is located at 1717 Massachusetts Avenue, NW, Washington, DC 20036.

Progressive Policy Institute

The Progressive Policy Institute was formed in 1989 under the
leadership of Will Marshall, former policy director of the Democratic
Leadership Council. Robert Shapiro, a former associate editor of

U.S. News and World Report and adviser to the presidential campaign of Michael Dukakis, is vice-president and heads the Economic Studies program. Evoking the spirit of turn-of-the-century progressivism, the institute describes itself as seeking "to adapt America's progressive tradition of individual liberty, equal opportunity and civic enterprise to the challenges of the postindustrial era." While avowing support for free markets, the institute does not shy away from governmental intervention to correct distortions in the market and to promote economic justice.

With a professional staff of seven and four others bearing the titles senior scholar, senior fellows, and fellows, the institute has outlined a broad set of research interests dealing with economic growth and equity, defense and foreign policy, social policy, politics and democratic institutions, and public health and safety. Its Center for Civic Enterprise addresses questions of democratic participation and responsibility and tries to foster the creation of new community institutions. The Progressive Policy Institute is located at 316 Pennsylvania Avenue, SE, Suite 555, Washington, DC 20003.

RAND Corporation

The Santa Monica–based RAND Corporation, formally incorporated as a nonprofit corporation in 1948, grew out of a postwar research-and-development project set up for the U.S. Air Force by the Douglas Aircraft Corporation. It is now one of the nation's largest policy research organizations, with annual revenues of $94 million. Federal contracts account for about 80 percent of its income, although RAND also receives grants from some of the nation's most prominent foundations, including Ford, MacArthur, Rockefeller, and Pew. A recent campaign has enabled it to build a modest endowment of about $42 million.

RAND is large and complex, with four major research divisions (Project Air Force, with $22.5 million in funding in 1989; National Security Research, with $28.2 million in funding in 1989; Army Research, with $21 million in funding in 1989; and Domestic Research, with $19.7 million in funding in 1989—of which $3.5 million was devoted to work at the Institute for Civil Justice). Although researchers may work on projects in various divisions, the research departments reflect a disciplinary organization; there are six departments, including behavioral sciences, economics and statistics, engineering and applied sciences, information sciences, political science, system sciences, and an office on Washington operations. There are a dozen other centers and institutes, as well as specialized research programs that cover such fields as aging, workers' health care benefits, vocational education, population research, the assessment of strategies, health care financing, civil justice, Soviet studies, the teaching profession, education and employment, U.S.-Japanese relations, and drug policy. RAND also operates a graduate school that offers a doctorate in public policy analysis. Each year RAND analysts publish over 250 research reports, notes, and professional papers on foreign and domestic issues. The RAND Corporation is located at 1700 Main Street, Santa Monica, CA 90406.

Resources for the Future

Since its founding in 1952, Resources for the Future (RFF) has used the tools of economics and other social science disciplines to examine issues of natural resources and the environment. Its origins lie in the conservation movement, the Ford Foundation's early programmatic commitment to the conservation of natural resources, and the work of President Truman's Materials Policy Commission headed by William Paley. A capital endowment from the Ford Foundation enabled the RFF to begin its work on energy in the 1950s, environmental quality in the 1960s, and world agricultural problems in the 1970s and 1980s. Over the years, RFF has developed research approaches and data that have shaped debates about natural resources and the environment.

RFF's research program is organized into four subdivisions: the Energy and Natural Resources Division, which explores energy policy, the management of renewable resources, climatic change, and outer space; the Quality of the Environment Division, which examines environmental and other health and safety regulations, valuations of natural resources, toxic-waste management, the use of pesticides, and the contamination of groundwater; the National Center for Food and Agricultural Policy, which explores the relationship between U.S. agricultural policy and the environment, the safety of food, and health; and the Center for Risk Management, which deals with health and the assessment of environmental risks, industrial accidents, the incineration of waste products, and the valuation of life-saving measures. Approximately one-half RFF's hundred-member staff are engaged in research and writing. RFF published three books in 1989, forty-odd discussion papers, policy briefs, and a quarterly periodical,

Resources. Its annual operating budget, a portion of which is drawn from its $28 million endowment, exceeds $7 million. RFF has offices at 1616 P Street, NW, Washington, DC 20036.

Rockford Institute

The Rockford Institute was founded in 1976 by John Howard, president of Rockford College, whose initial, modest objective was to examine changes in university curricula. It has expanded its scope considerably and receives national attention in the mass media as a center of traditional conservative thinking. The institute avows a commitment to certain enduring principles: religion, the family, limited government, free enterprise, morally and artistically sound literature, a strong commitment to the national interest, and a healthy distrust of universalist ideologies. Those principles define the institute's commitment to a conservatism that "strives to defend and renew those cultural mechanisms that shape responsible citizens worthy of their freedom." The commitment to particular principles has policy consequences, and Rockford speaks out on what its president, Allan Carlson, describes as "the disruptive effects of public education on family ties; the relationship of immigration policy to the degraded meaning of American citizenship; the perverse consequences of federal funding of the arts; [and] the corrupting influences of the egalitarian ideology on the social sciences and the schools."

Two centers form the core of the institute's research program—the Center on the Family in America and the Center on Religion and Society, which has recently relocated to Illinois after a dispute with its New York–based former director, Richard John Neuhaus. Rockford's periodicals include monthly newsletters from the research centers, *The Family in America* and the *Religion and Society Report; Chronicles: A Magazine of American Culture*, which attained a paid circulation of about 17,000 in 1989; and *This World: A Journal of Religion and Public Life.*

The institute has a staff of twenty-two. Its annual operating expenses are about $2.2 million, of which nearly 40 percent is for the publication of *Chronicles* and about 25 percent for the two research centers. Its income is derived from individual contributions, grants from foundations and corporations, and sales of publications (which account for nearly one-quarter of the institute's revenues). The Rockford Institute's headquarters are at 934 North Main Street, Rockford, IL 61103.

Russell Sage Foundation

The Russell Sage Foundation, established in 1907, is arguably the nation's oldest surviving policy research institution and a prototype for those that followed. Established with an initial $10 million gift from Margaret Olivia Sage, its early research and publishing concentrated on public health and sanitation, children's issues, working conditions for women, and other issues that were on the agenda of Progressive Era reformers. The foundation, staffed largely by social workers, pursued a robust program of practical research, publication, and legislative activism into the 1930s.

Since the end of World War II, the foundation has devoted itself to basic social science research, allying itself through much of the postwar era with the discipline of sociology, although economists have also helped to shape its program. With an endowment of about $90 million, it expends over $4 million each year on research, bringing twelve to fifteen scholars to its New York headquarters and supporting others at their own academic institutions. The research has sought to improve social science methods, enhance data-collecting techniques, and advance social theory. Its current program focuses on the social analysis of poverty, improving the understanding of economic behavior, and developing statistical methods for synthesizing research findings. In recent years, the foundation has published six to eight books per year. Its offices are located at 112 East Sixty-fourth Street, New York, NY 10021.

Twentieth Century Fund

The Twentieth Century Fund is an endowed operating foundation based in New York City. Founded as the Cooperative League in 1911 and renamed the Twentieth Century Fund in 1919, it is one of the oldest organizations supporting public policy research in the United States. Its founder, Edward A. Filene, made his fortune through the Boston department store that bears his family's name. Established with an initial gift of stock from the Filene Company, the Twentieth Century Fund's endowment in 1988 was valued at slightly more than $41 million. With an administrative staff of about twenty in New York, it spends nearly $3.5 million on its program.

Typically, its research projects are conducted by scholars and writers who work elsewhere but are under contract to the fund; it also organizes task forces and commissions of distinguished individuals to discuss policy issues and to advance recommendations for policies. The fund publishes six to ten books per year, two or three task force reports, and a number of shorter papers. Over the years, it has published books in virtually every area of policy, including social policy, international economics, communications policy, science, and health. Among its better known contributions are Gunnar Myrdal's *Asian Drama*, Jean Gottmann's *Megalopolis*, Fred Hirsch's *Social Limits to Growth*, and various works in the past fifty years on financial markets and social security policy. The fund is located at 41 East Seventieth Street, New York, 10021.

Urban Institute

The Urban Institute, established in 1968 at the urging of Lyndon B. Johnson and his domestic policy advisers, was conceived as a domestic RAND Corporation. Relying initially on governmental contracts from agencies, such as the Department of Housing and Urban Development and the Department of Transportation, it now has contracts and grants from some three dozen federal agencies and state governments, and its purview has ranged well beyond issues that affect the nation's cities. Since the early 1980s, a growing proportion of its work (roughly one-third in 1988–89) has been supported by grants from foundations and corporations.

Led by William Gorham since its founding, much of the Urban Institute's work over the years has been devoted to the evaluation of governmental programs and the assessment of new policy strategies. With an annual operating budget of about $13 million, its 130 staff members work in eight policy areas: health, public finance and housing, human resources, income and benefits, international activities, population studies, state policy, and changing domestic priorities. The Urban Institute Press publishes from six to twelve hardcover books per year and various research reports; the institute also issues shorter research papers and a thrice-yearly periodical, *Policy and Research Report*.

The institute has worked since its founding to improve techniques of program evaluation and measurements of productivity in the public sector. It has developed computerized models for simulating changes in governmental benefit programs, such as the Food Stamp program or welfare benefits, and to measure their likely impact on individual and family income. Among its contributions to specific policy areas, the institute has helped to design one of the nation's largest social experiments, the Experimental Housing Allowance Program, and developed a model of housing market behavior to estimate housing trends and the impact of policy changes on the housing market. Work on Medicare during the 1980s yielded a series of studies on prospective payment systems for hospitals. The institute has also evaluated work-welfare programs at the state level, studied alternative transportation strategies, explored the management of transportation systems, and analyzed changing labor markets and public employment and job training programs.

One of the most notable projects emanating from any research center during the 1980s was the institute's thirty-two-volume Changing Domestic Priorities series, which provided the most comprehensive contemporary assessment of the Reagan administration's efforts to reorient domestic policy. The institute's research agenda for the 1990s includes work on children, especially those in the underclass; the skills of the work force; and the diminishing capacity of cities to provide avenues for upward mobility. The Urban Institute's offices are at 2100 M Street, NW, Washington, DC 20037.

World Policy Institute

The World Policy Institute is a New York–based research and educational institution that focuses on international economic and security issues. Its core staff of ten works with a broader network of about one hundred policy experts; the annual budget is roughly $900,000, most of it derived from several hundred individual donors and from sales of publications. The institute, which began to emphasize public policy research only in 1982, traces its origins to a much older postwar group that promoted international law and world order by preparing curricular materials for schools and colleges.

Since 1984, its research has focused on the Security Project. The institute consistently challenges the Cold War assumptions that have undergirded American foreign policy while advancing a concept of international security grounded not in military might but in policies that will foster world economic growth. Its proposals have been summarized in a 1988 book *Post–Reagan America* and various short papers. Since 1983, its principal publishing vehicle has been the quarterly *World Policy Journal*, which has a circulation of about 10,000. The institute has commissioned opinion surveys, tested its ideas in focus groups, and presented its ideas in briefings to the press and policymakers. Its offices are at 777 United Nations Plaza, New York, NY 10017.

World Resources Institute

With a staff of more than eighty researchers, augmented by individual fellows and advisers, as well as collaborating research institutions in more than fifty countries, the World Resources Institute (WRI) helps governments and environmental and development organizations deal with environmental issues. WRI's projects focus on two concerns: the effects of the deterioration of natural resources on economic development and on alleviation of poverty and hunger in developing countries, and the emerging environmental and resource problems that threaten the economic and environmental interests of the United States and other nations.

More specific policy research projects follow from these broad concerns, including work on forests and biodiversity; economics, technology, and institutions; climate, energy, and pollution; and information on resources and the environment. The Center for International Development and Environment provides advice on policies and technical services in developing countries. WRI communicates its findings and recommendations in a variety of ways. In collaboration with UN agencies, it produces an annual collection of data on global resources and problems, *World Resources*. It has initiated a series of WRI Guides to the Environment to explain environmental problems, controversies over policies, and steps for corrective action. Recent books and reports have assessed the impact of acid rain, dealt with conserving biodiversity, explored the prospects for solar hydrogen as an energy source, examined the management of forest resources, proposed ways to curtail the buildup of greenhouse gases, and presented strategies for protecting the ozone shield.

WRI is located at 1709 New York Avenue, NW, Washington, DC 20006.

Worldwatch Institute

The Worldwatch Institute was set up in 1975 to inform policymakers about the interdependence of the world economy and the environment. It was founded by William Dietel, then president of the Rockefeller Brothers Fund, and Lester Brown, who now heads the institute and directs its research program. With a staff of about thirty, it has an annual operating budget of roughly $1.5 million.

The institute's publications include a series of policy papers on a wide range of environmental issues, *World Watch* magazine, and the highly regarded annual volume, *State of the World*, which is available in eleven languages and sells over 200,000 copies annually. *State of the World* is a compendium of statistical indicators on the world's progress (or lack of it) toward a sustainable society. Combining tables, graphs, and maps with reportage on the changing environment and arguments about how the reader can take steps to save the planet, the volume has found an audience of both policymakers and ordinary citizens. The Worldwatch Institute is located at 1776 Massachusetts Avenue, NW, Washington, DC 20036.

Bibliographic
Essay

The writing on American policy research institutions is surprisingly sparse. The two most noteworthy general books, now dated, are Paul Dickson's *Think Tanks* (New York: Atheneum, 1971) and Harold Orlans, *The Nonprofit Research Institute: Its Origins, Operation, Problems and Prospects* (New York: McGraw-Hill Book Co., 1972). Several political scientists have written about policy-planning organizations, though their work often deals more with the theoretical role of elites than with institutions: Thomas R. Dye, *Who's Running America: The Conservative Years*, 4th ed. (Englewood Cliffs, N.J.: Prentice-Hall, 1986; and Joseph G. Peschek, *Policy-Planning Organizations: Elite Agendas and America's Rightward Turn* (Philadelphia: Temple University Press, 1987). Historians, often those studying philanthropic foundations, have dealt with policy-research institutions. Barry Karl and Stanley Katz are in the process of writing a major work on foundations and public policy. Although it focuses on a single foundation, the best treatment of foundations and their role in public policymaking is Ellen Condliffe Lagemann, *The Politics of Knowledge: The Carnegie Corporation, Philanthropy, and Public Policy* (Middletown, Conn.: Wesleyan University Press, 1989). On the history of research institutions and academics as policymakers, there are two good doctoral dissertations: David W. Eakins, "The Development of Corporate Liberal Policy Research in the United States, 1885–1965" (Ph.D. diss., University of Wisconsin 1966); and David M. Grossman, "Professors and Public Service, 1885–1925: A Chapter in the Professionalization of the Social Sciences" (Ph.D. diss., Washington University, St. Louis, 1973).

On occasion, individual institutions have been the subject of chronicles by insiders or commemorative volumes. Falling into that genre are John M. Glenn, Lilian Brandt, and F. Emerson Andrews, *Russell Sage Foundation, 1907–46*, 2 vols. (New York: Russell Sage Foundation, 1947); Wesley C. Mitchell, "The National Bureau's First Quarter Century," *25th Annual Report* (New York: National Bureau of Economic Research, 1945); Adolf A. Berle, *Leaning against the Dawn, 1919–69* (New York: Twentieth Century Fund, 1969); Charles B. Saunders, Jr., *The Brookings Institution: A Fifty Year History* (Washington, D.C.: Brookings Institution, 1966); Karl Schriftgiesser, *Business Comes of Age: The Impact of the Committee for Economic*

Development, 1942–60 (New York: Harper Bros., 1960); and Schriftgiesser, *Business and Public Policy: The Role of the Committee for Economic Development, 1942–67* (New York: Committee for Economic Development, 1967).

Individual policy research institutions have rarely been studied by outsiders, although the RAND Corporation and Brookings have each been the subject of a book: Bruce L. R. Smith, *The RAND Corporation: Case Study of a Nonprofit Advisory Corporation* (Cambridge, Mass.: Harvard University Press, 1966); and Donald T. Critchlow, *The Brookings Institution, 1916–1952: Expertise and the Public Interest in a Democratic Society* (DeKalb: University of Northern Illinois Press, 1984). Three books have dealt with the rise of the conservative think tanks: Sidney Blumenthal, *The Rise of the Counter-Establishment: From Conservative Ideology to Political Power* (New York: Times Books, 1986); John S. Saloma, III, *Ominous Politics: The New Conservative Labyrinth* (New York: Hill & Wang, 1984); and Richard Reeves, *The Reagan Detour* (New York: Simon & Schuster, 1985).

Current information on think tanks is another matter. Although there is no guide to think tanks on the order of the Foundation Center's *Foundation Directory*, it is possible to learn something about many of them in the Gale Research Company's *Research Centers Directory* and its periodic supplements. The *National Journal* routinely covers the work of Washington think tanks, and its annual publication *The Capital Source* offers a list of most of those operating in the Washington area. Since most policy research organizations are in the business of disseminating books and reports, they are more than willing to send out publications lists. Many also have annual reports and newsletters.

There have been a number of studies of the uses of social science and policy research in decision making. The broadest history, now twenty years old, is Gene M. Lyons, *The Uneasy Partnership: Social Science and the Federal Government in the Twentieth Century* (New York: Russell Sage Foundation, 1969). A useful collection of essays is Martin Bulmer, ed., *Social Science Research and Government: Comparative Essays on Britain and the United States* (New York: Cambridge University Press, 1987). See also, the volume by Laurence Lynn, ed., *Knowledge and Policy: The Uncertain Connection* (Washington, D.C.: National Academy of Sciences, 1978), esp. the essay by Carol Weiss, "Improving the Linkage between Social Research and Public Policy," pp. 23–81. One book has been particularly skeptical about the uses of social science research: Charles E. Lindblom and David K. Cohen, *Usable Knowledge: Social Science and Social Problem Solving* (New Haven, Conn.: Yale University Press, 1979). Two measured assessments of the uses of policy research are Peter deLeon, *Advice and Consent: The Development of the Policy Sciences* (New York: Russell Sage Foundation, 1988), and Richard P. Nathan, *Social Science in Government: Uses and Misuses* (New York: Basic Books, 1988). While there are case studies of particular policies in the making, there are few general works on the initiation of policies. One of the most enlightening studies of how ideas make their way into political processes is Nelson W. Polsby, *Political Innovation in America: The Politics of Policy Initiation* (New Haven, Conn.: Yale University Press, 1984). Also informative is John Kingdon, *Agendas, Alternatives and Public Policies* (New York: Little, Brown & Co., 1984).

Index